*THREE
YEARS
IN
MISSISSIPPI*

INDIANA
UNIVERSITY
PRESS
Bloomington
*
London

# JAMES MEREDITH

\* \* \* \* \*

# *THREE*
# *YEARS*
# *IN*
# *MISSISSIPPI*

TO MY FATHER (1891–1965)

# Contents

*

*THREE
YEARS
IN
MISSISSIPPI*

# 1

## Return to Mississippi: August 1960

IT WAS a hot, sultry, sunshiny day—a perfect day to return to my home state of Mississippi. I had left this land—God's country claimed by the white Mississippian as his "heaven on earth"—in August 1950, spent one year at a Florida high school, and served nine years in the United States Air Force. I am a soldier at heart, and I suppose I always will be. If there is anything that I ever wanted to be, I guess it would have been a general. But let's begin our drive into Mississippi.

### Buy Gasoline in Memphis

Highway 51 is a code word for the millions of Negroes who have driven north to south and south to north for the past twenty-five years. This was the route taken by us—my wife and six-months-old son and me—into Mississippi. We were completing the last leg of the long drive from California, where we had landed after a three-year tour of duty in Japan at Tachikawa Air Force Base. I had traveled this road many times and knew practically every hill and curve, or at least I thought I did. It had long been my practice to fill up the gas tank in Memphis, so I would not have to face the "peckerwoods" at a station in Mississippi. One tank of gas would take you to Kosciusko or Jackson where you could go to a Negro-operated station. This time it was more pressing than ever to get gas because I had my wife and son with me, and God only knew what I would do if an incident occurred while I was with my family. I pulled into a station that I had used for quite a few years on this route, because they did not have segregated toilets for "White Ladies," "White Men," and "Colored." Thinking that the practice would be the same as before, I didn't go through the customary ritual used when a Negro pulls into a gas station in the South and is not sure about the discrimination practices. Since some of the white folks there are a little more human, or just plain smarter, than the crackers and rednecks, they mark their facilities for whites as just "Ladies" and "Men" and put the Negro toilet in the back where you cannot see it. The Negro will ask the attendant, "Do you have a bathroom?" (although he is looking right at the big signs that read "Ladies" and "Men"). If the attendant says, "Yes, right there," then the Negro says, "Fill it up, and check everything." If the answer is, "Yeah, go round the back," then the Negro drives away and looks for another station. I pulled up, spoke to the man, and told him to "fill it up." Then my wife left to go to the bathroom. When she reached the toilet, the sign read "White Ladies ONLY." Upon asking the attendant about the restrooms, we were told that the "Colored" was in the back. By this time the tank was already full and it was useless to tell him to stop pumping the gas. We went around to the back and found one cubbyhole for all Negroes to use—men and women and children. It was filthy, nasty, and stinking. The toilet wouldn't flush and there was no toilet paper or water to wash one's hands. It has always been said that Memphis was the northern capital of Mississippi. Now I was convinced that it was true. This was the much talked-about progress that I had been making since the 1954 Supreme Court decision that said "separate but equal" was no longer the law of the land, but left the new law of the land to the discretion of the White Supremacists.

### Welcome to Mississippi

The first thing that you see when you head south on old U.S. 51 from Memphis and Shelby County, Tennessee—the home of the Cotton Queens and the famous, or infamous, "Crump political machine" and the place where the Negro blues originated—is a big flashy sign: WELCOME TO MISSISSIPPI. This sign arouses mixed emotions in the thousands of Negroes who pass it. For many it is a joke; for others it recalls the days gone by, their work in the cotton fields in Mississippi, their migration to the North, their jobs in the war-plants during the forties and in the factories of today.

For me, it is indeed a sign of frustration. Always, without fail, regardless of the number of times I enter Mississippi, it creates within me feelings that are felt at no other time. There is the feeling of joy. Joy because I have once again lived to enter the land of my fathers, the land of my birth, the only land in which I feel at home. It also inspires a feeling of hope because where there is life there is also a hope, a chance. At the same time, there is a feeling of sadness. Sadness because I am immediately aware of the special subhuman role that I must play, because I am a Negro, or die. Sadness because it is the home of the greatest number of Negroes outside of Africa, yet my people suffer from want of everything in a rich land of plenty, and, most of all, they must endure the inconvenience of indignity.

Then, there is the feeling of love. Love of the land. To me, Mississippi is the most beautiful country in the world, during all seasons. In the spring, all is green and fresh, the air is clean and sweet, and everything is healthy. As a boy I knew that any running stream of water was fit to drink. I feel love because I have always felt that Mississippi belonged to me and one must love what is his.

In the summer there is maturity. The grass begins to level off and seed. A feeling of repose overcomes you. You have the urge to pull alongside the road and take a cowpath up into the bushes and lie down under a big tree. The effect of the heat shows everywhere. Blackberries begin to ripen; muscadine vines begin to hang from the burden of a good crop; and a black snake is likely to cross the road at any moment. Since the crops are nearly all laid by, the whole state takes on a relaxed and idle atmosphere. Summer is also the most suitable season for a lynching.

The fall of the year is perhaps the most colorful. Nature begins to fade away. The grass dries up and draws closer to the earth. Trees and bushes start to color and a slow deterioration asserts itself. All remaining fruits and nuts come to full maturity. A great feeling of urgency is generated by such abundance. You feel that time is squeezing you and harvest you must. The temptation to gather the falling nuts—acorns, hickory nuts, scaly barks, pecans, chincky berries, and all kinds in abundance—pulls you to them.

Finally, the "Welcome to Mississippi" sign reminds me of winter in my home state. Winter is my favorite season for looking at the land. Everything, except for the cedar trees and a few other evergreens, is bare. You can see for miles.

Shortly after passing the sign, I have often stopped by the side of the road and just looked at the land. The most dominant thought was, "if only I had my fair share in the running and managing of the state of Mississippi, what a wonderful land this could be." And I always ended the meditation with an assurance to myself, from myself, that I would have that share in my land or die trying to get it.

### Mississippi Country Towns

As you drive along U.S. 51 from Memphis into Mississippi, you are immediately aware of the many towns and communities—incorporated and unincorporated. The most troublesome aspect of the drive is the slow speed limit, often as low as 20 mph on what appears to be a completely open road. Of course, it is well known to the traveler, especially to the Negro, that there is likely to be a deputy sheriff or a town constable behind every house or thicket. For many a law enforcement officer in Mississippi traffic violations are a source of revenue second only to his profit from bootleg whiskey.

However, for one with an eye for discovering the road of the future through a look into the past, these towns are bursting with hints toward understanding Mississippi. Let's just take their locations: Hernando, Coldwater, Senatobia, Como, Sardis, Batesville, Pope, Oakland, Tillatoba, Grenada, Duck Hill, Winona, Vaiden, West, Durant, McAdams, Kosciusko—all are approximately ten miles apart. Mississippi, although today the most southern state, was the last area settled in the Old South. Most Mississippi farms were not established as self-sufficient units and provisions had to be obtained from the country store, which was located so that the farmer could walk to the store, buy his weekly provisions, and return home on the same day. This distance happened to be about five miles. The towns grew around the stores, and this development led to an important aspect of the Negro-white relationship in Mississippi. Provision day became a social day and the daddy of the "Satiday Night," which is still observed by Mississippians at home and away in spirit, if not in practice. On the large plantations and self-sufficient farms, the Negroes and whites were separated physically and the two groups came in contact with one another only under well-defined circumstances. At first, however, there were no clear rules in the towns: there was one store, one street, one bench, etc. Since this was the only place where the masses of Negroes came into direct contact with the masses of whites, a substitute for the organized placement and separation of the plantation had to be found for the town. Segregation in public and private establishments and facilities was the outcome. Segregation led to many of the evil practices that became a part of southern life.

The town was also the chief place of contact between the poor white men and the Negro women. The rich or well-to-do whites had more convenient means by which to satisfy their desires for a black woman. The white woman has long been considered the main object of conflict between the whites and the Negroes. I can assure you that the greatest point of friction between the races has not been the white woman; rather, it has been and still is the colored woman.

*The Last Nineteen Miles*

The last nineteen miles to Kosciusko has always been a drive that appeared to me ten times as far as it really is, probably because the trip from Durant is the same trip in my mind as it was when I was a boy. Durant is the place where everyone in the surrounding area catches the train going north. I suppose by now every Negro in Attala County above the age of seven has been to Durant to catch the Illinois Central north or, better still, "The City of New Orleans" to Chicago. In addition, Durant is where the Negroes had to go to get a legal bottle of beer. Everyone knows that Mississippi is the only dry state in the Union, but my home county went even further and forbade the sale of beer. It was six of one and a half dozen of the other for the Negro in Attala County. If he stayed in the county and took a drink of "white-lightning" or "moonshine," he was arrested for buying illegal alcohol. If he bought whiskey in Durant, which was just across the county line, he was stopped by the Attala County police as soon as he crossed the river and arrested for having "whiskey on his breath." The only advantage in going to Durant was that he could have a good time in the two or three big joints there.

At Durant we turned left off U.S. 51 onto Mississippi Highway 12 at the sign that reads—Kosciusko 19 miles. When we came to the multi-track Illinois Central Railroad line, the highway was blocked by the train just arriving from the North. We went into the train station to freshen up, get a bottle of soda pop, and see if anyone we knew had got off the train. Someone is always either going or coming that you know. The unboarding of a train in Durant is something like the docking of a large ship. There is an atmosphere of excitement, gladness, and sorrow. Whenever a Negro comes home from the North—"home" because a Negro returning to Mississippi, even though he may have been away for forty years, always thinks of himself as coming home, and the one leaving is never going home, but is always going to Chicago, St. Louis, or Detroit—the major reunion is at the station because the whole family usually meets the passenger there. The station at Durant seems to belong to the Negro since you seldom see a white passenger.

The train pulled out after unloading in Durant, and we were off to my home town. We crossed the long, frighteningly narrow bridge that spans the Big Black River and the surrounding lowlands, which are flooded as often as not. We passed the familiar farms, houses, clay hills, and newly planted tree farms, which had sprung up on the vacant land once worked by the very people whom we had seen at the station coming from and going to the North. In my county alone more than 10,000 Negroes had migrated North during the past ten years.

We drove for ten miles and passed through the only community along the nineteen-mile stretch—unincorporated McAdams. It is the same as most of the others we had passed, except for one peculiar trait that I have never understood. I have never heard of a motorist being arrested in McAdams, not even a Negro. The speed limit is reduced only to 45 mph. I guess the man for whom the community was named must have owned everything, been the chief official, and his sons must have been his deputies, and they all must have been too busy or too rich to bother with the passersby.

From McAdams we went over four large hills and around three curves, including the big curve, which many Kosciuskans have failed to make after a trip to a "Satiday Night" in Durant. On the left, just before you get to the radio tower, is a motel, the final landmark, because around the next curve is Kosciusko, Mississippi, my home town.

### A Drive through Kosciusko

*The Square.* Every time, without fail, when I return home after being away, I go first to the town square and drive around it at least once, and often more times, before taking "Beale Street" home. Kosciusko's town square is typical of town squares in Mississippi county seats. The courthouse is in the center with the major stores and offices surrounding it. With its population of 6,000, Kosciusko is one of the major towns in Mississippi. On the square, there are two banks, two or three large supermarkets, a couple of dime stores, about three drugstores, several ladies' and men's shops, some cafes and restaurants for whites only, a movie house for whites only, and a number of doctors', lawyers', and other professional offices. People always loiter around the square and gossip, trade, and socialize. Of course, the big day is Saturday when every place is crowded with the country folks. Just one trip around the square on any day, however, and fifteen minutes later everyone in town knows you are home. The fact that I was driving a big blue air-conditioned Cadillac and wearing a suit and tie when the temperature was 98° and the sun was burning down did not lessen the local interest. In addition, I had a Japanese license plate on my car. Any out-of-state tag arouses the curiosity of the people of Kosciusko, because the town is not located on a major highway and the strangers are few, but a northern license plate provokes their anger—that is, of the whites. In this instance, however, I think it was just plain confusing to see an out-of-country license.

*The Police Station.* Located in the most strategic spot on the square is the police station, the most important place in town for the Negro. It is at the southeast corner of the square overlooking the entrance to South Natchez Street, the Negro street of Kosciusko, and better known as "Beale Street." No one can enter this street without being seen by a policeman. I always drive very slowly past the police station in order to make sure that all the policemen get a chance to take a good look at me. This may seem strange, but it is perhaps the main reason why I was seldom trailed or bothered by the police during my many visits home while I was in the Air Force. It is a fact that within a very short time after one arrives in town practically everyone knows it, including the police, and if there is anything that a Mississippi cop hates, it is for someone to know something about a Negro that he doesn't know first. By giving the police the first look, the Negro relieves them of the necessity of finding the "nigger" and "getting the goods on him." When a Mississippi policeman has to suffer the embarrassment of looking for a "nigger," he is likely to make the trip worth his while. I always took great care not to give a "peckerwood" a chance to put his hands on me. No white man in Mississippi had ever put his hands on me, and God alone knows what would have happened had the event occurred.

*Beale Street.* A Negro hasn't been to town if he hasn't been to Beale Street. Actually it is just one long block extending from the southeastern corner of the square to Wesley Chapel Methodist Church, the biggest Negro church in town. About ninety per cent of the buildings on the street are owned by white landlords and rented to the Negroes. The first store is a strange combination of general store and cafe—probably the only one of its kind remaining in Mississippi. It sells everything from pencils to overalls and from groceries to farming tools, but from a very limited stock, however. The most amazing thing about this establishment is the selling of hamburgers. All day on Saturdays a Negro cook stands in the middle of the store at a grill with a counter on two sides and cooks nothing but hamburgers. They are sold from the same grill, prepared by the same Negro cook, to the Negroes for ten cents and to the whites for fifteen cents. Naturally they are served over separate counters.

*Bell's Cafe.* The first Negro-operated business is a small cafe, about twenty-five feet by fifty feet, but it is the largest eating and socializing place for Negroes in Kosciusko. This is the cafe of the Attala County elite. I would venture to say that not one of the Negroes who patronizes the general store has ever set foot in Bell's Cafe, although it is only three doors away. It is operated by a family —the manager is the wife and the chief employees are all related—that moved to Kosciusko from a rural community about twenty-five miles away. There are at least eight or nine children, all of whom were educated through college from the profits from this small cafe. There had been very little social life for me in Kosciusko, but whatever public socializing that I did as a boy was done here. To the best of my recollection, I don't remember ever buying even a hamburger at any other cafe on Beale Street. This was the place where you went with a quarter on Saturday and sat all day long. In the course of the day you were certain to see everyone in town and, in addition, anyone in the county who was visiting back home from the North. There is a jukebox and the latest records, but you would never find the soul blues or the lowdown boogie-woogie. You had to go to the lower end of Beale Street to find this type of music.

*Funeral Home.* Across the street is one of the three funeral homes on the block. The funeral business, or I should say, the Negro funeral business, is the only enterprise in which the Negro has a monopoly. With few, if any, exceptions, the most prosperous Negro in any town in Mississippi is the funeral director. Consequently, he is always an important man in the community. This particular funeral home is located on the first floor of the old Negro Masonic Temple. I understand that the lodge had been very active during the twenties and thirties, and I have heard it said that two or three of the "big"

Negroes in town had worked successfully to disband the lodge, because some of the white folks didn't think Negroes should have meetings and gatherings. The owner-operator of the funeral home is always in his office, unless he is out picking up a dead body, collecting insurance, or occasionally making an emergency call. Three or four part-time helpers are always around to aid the funeral director, and on Saturday a girl helps with the insurance collections from the people living in the county. In front of the building are two or three benches, or Coca-Cola bottle cases, for loiterers to sit on and talk and "lollygag," as they call it.

*Murray's Cleaning Shop.* A couple of doors down from the funeral home is the only Negro-owned and operated dry cleaning business in town. It is a one-man business with the man's wife as the chief assistant. With almost no formal schooling, the owner had started on a wish after the war, and with a strong will, hard work, and good "horse sense," he is now a prosperous businessman. Besides his cleaning shop, he owns a development of rental houses, a number of other profitable interests, and a beautiful new brick home for himself on the outskirts of town. He also owns the new office located next door to his shop. The sign above the office window reads, "Dr. So-and-So—Dentist." He had built this office three or four years ago in the hope of attracting a Negro doctor or dentist to the town. So far, there has been none. A Negro dentist in the Delta about a hundred miles away had promised to visit Kosciusko once every two weeks, but he had only come twice in three years. The owner will not rent the space for any other purpose. This is an excellent example of the feeling that Mississippi Negroes have for one another. The day will come, and I hope soon, when his long-felt wish for a doctor will be fulfilled.

*The Barber Shop.* The barbering profession, as the barbers like to call it, has been well established and respected for a long time in Mississippi. The barber is in the Negro middle-income group, even though haircuts are still fifty cents in some of the best barber shops. The barber shop is a sort of sanctuary for the Negro in Mississippi. The local police use all the other Negro establishments to make their presence felt, as a regular and unannounced practice; this tactic is one of the chief weapons used to enforce the doctrines and conditions of "White Supremacy" in the South. But they stay out of the barber shops for one reason or another. As a result, the conversation in the shops is the most relaxed and least guarded of any you are likely to hear in public places.

There are four or five barber shops on the block, but I have always gone to the same shop and the same barber since I started getting barber shop haircuts. We were money-poor, and my father had a pair of Sears, Roebuck clippers with which he used to give us "clean head" haircuts when we were children. The barber is a distant cousin who started a shop when he came home after the war. His barber shop is, I believe, the only establishment on Beale Street that has not made any significant physical changes during the past several years. There are four chairs but only two are operated daily; the others go into full swing on Saturday when the country people come to town. There is also a shoeshine parlor in the shop, although it is not likely to be in operation except on Saturdays. In the back is a beauty shop operated by the owner's wife. I did not know this until 1960, and it made me realize how hard it is to know what is going on in the Negro world in Mississippi. Out of curiosity I had asked the barber what was in the back and he said, "My wife's beauty shop," as if I should have known. He went on to say that his wife had been there for at least fifteen years. Evidently the women used a side or back entrance, because in the fifteen-odd years that I had frequented his shop, not only had I not known that the beauty shop was in the rear, but I had never even seen his wife.

*The Pool Hall.* At the lower end of Beale Street, where a decent woman would not be caught slowing her walking pace, is the pool hall—a Negro-owned and operated business. The building belongs to a Negro contractor and the business and concession stands are owned by a young bricklayer as a part-time venture. Boys and young men congregate around in the usual pool-hall fashion. They play the games, talk loudly, brag about their skill with the "stick" (pool-hall stick), boast about their conquests of women, and play a little "nine ball" (a game on which they bet small sums) every now and then. Kosciusko's Beale Street is not typical of Negro drags in most Mississippi towns, since there is very little open vice. Several of the regulars who hang around the pool hall are known police informers and stooges who have, as far as I know, done nothing else.

The operator of the hamburger stand in the pool hall is one of my cousins. He is best known for whipping Negroes who get colored women for white men, and he has been run out of Mississippi dozens of times for this "crime." In the late fifties he was beaten by a mob of whites, left for dead, and had to remain in the hospital for over a year. This happened in another town about thirty-five miles away when he worked as a porter for the Illinois Central Railroad. His conflict with these "peckerwoods" began when a Negro approached him at the station, I suppose because he was a porter, and asked if he knew where to get some women. When my cousin found out that he wanted the Negro women for white men, he whipped the Negro pimp. The pimp told the white men, who then proceeded to put the "nigger in his place."

*Dean's Cafe.* Down on the "low end of Beale," there are two or three honkytonk cafes. Dean's Cafe is directly across the street from the pool hall. Even at the age of twenty-seven, when I returned to Mississippi after nine years in the Air Force, I had never been inside. I could not positively identify more than two or three people whom I had seen going in or coming out. It will be difficult, if not impossible, for anyone not growing up in Mississippi to understand the deep separation that exists, not only by race but also by class structure within the races. The side aspects of a society segregated by force are tremendously important and very essential to the social system. Although the oppressed group may never accept the permanency of their oppressed status, the fact that they choose temporarily to accept this position rather than to chance death acknowledges that at the least they recognize the dominance of their oppressors and for the bare minimum of just being alive the oppressed must accept the major tenets of their oppressors' doctrines.

*The Only Residence.* While it may seem odd that the only dwelling on Beale Street is occupied by whites, it is not unusual in Mississippi. The big two-story house sits back off the street twenty or twenty-five feet, and, of course, the doors to all the businesses open onto the sidewalk. It is located next to the pool-hall building and is the last structure on the street. I am not sure that I can explain my relationship to this house, but an empathic insight is absolutely essential to understand most of what I have to say about Mississippi and the Negro, the white and myself. I remember nothing about this house. Although I passed it on my way to school at least two times a day, five days a week for eleven years, and the church I attended was directly across the street, I could in good faith swear that I had never seen anyone in or around this house. It would be difficult for me to determine whether I saw and didn't see or whether I never saw at all what was before my eyes.

It is interesting to me to look back over what I have written about my home town and to note that I have said almost nothing about the white part of town. Except in a general way, I find that I know very little about that part of Kosciusko. Frankly, I never saw any of it that was not an absolute necessity for living. I can very easily recall the names of every business and businessman in town that have been there for more than twenty years, because I have heard their names mentioned so often, but I could tell you practically nothing about their business, and I couldn't identify more than two of the men by sight. I can think immediately of several well-known places, such as Vic's Cafe, Bell's Grocery, and the movie house, and realize that in all the thousands of times that I passed these places, I never once looked at them and saw them. Separation dominated my childhood completely.

*Wesley Chapel.* At the end of Beale Street is a three-way junction and on the opposite side of this junction is located the largest Negro church in town, the Wesley Memorial Chapel. It belongs to the Methodist Episcopal division of the Methodist churches and is the only Negro church still in the white conference. To know that this is the largest church in town tells quite a lot about Kosciusko. Mississippi is overwhelmingly Baptist and the largest church in most towns is Baptist. I would imagine that perhaps three fourths of the leading Negroes in Kosciusko are members of Wesley Memorial. This is the church in which I was baptized when I was twelve years old and where I received my religious training. The Negro city-style Methodist Church has a very rigid method of conducting its services. There are no physical outbursts from the congregation like those so prevalent among the Baptists. No one gets "happy" and shouts, and an odd "Amen" is considered very much out of place. The singing is very formal and not lively and free as in the Baptist churches. That this type of religious influence is dominant in Kosciusko is of great importance to the basic character of its Negroes.

*The Schoolhouse.* Driving along the pavement—it was paved because whites lived on the right-hand side of the street—for about two blocks and then turning left, one approaches the heart of the Negro community. This road is unpaved. In Mississippi the practice is to pave the roads in the white areas and leave them unpaved in the Negro areas. This was the same road that as a boy I had walked thousands of times going the four miles each way back and forth to school. Perhaps the major difference between then and now in the road and houses and surroundings was in me. For three quarters of a mile we drove the distance of a very long hill and another half of a hill to the schoolhouse. Just before you get to the school is the Second Baptist Church. Most of the other leading Negroes in Kosciusko belong to this church. It is a very "high-class" Baptist Church, for the services are toned down and are conducted more like the

Methodist. "Second Baptist," what's in this name? You never hear of a white Second Baptist Church. The First Baptist Church in most Mississippi towns is known to be the white church. If you recall the basic premise of "White Supremacy," you will see why many Negro communities have a Second Baptist Church and no white community ever has a "second" church.

Across the street from the church is Kosciusko's Negro school with grades running from first through twelfth. Next to the Negro church, the Negro school ranks as the most important established institution. Often the Negro high school principal is the number-one Negro in a Mississippi community. In the South education has almost become a religion since the days of Booker T. Washington. The Mississippi Negro will almost concede anything and sacrifice everything to get an education. Like everyone else, the school along with the home and family had the greatest impact on my early life. When I left this school in 1950 I had never been able to use a toilet because there was none, and I had never had a teacher with a college degree. This is no reflection on the teachers or on their dedication, however. They taught what they knew in the winter for thirty or forty dollars a month, saved most of it, and went away in the summer to learn something to teach the next winter, that is, if they found a school in the state to attend.

We had now come to the last minutes of our long journey from the airstrip in Japan to the dirt roads of my home in Mississippi. In one sense I was not really returning home at this moment, rather, I was returning to a house in Kosciusko where my folks were now living. When I made that last turn off East South Street onto the yet unnamed street of my father's house, the cloud of dust trailing the wheels of my car caused me to face the hard, cold fact that the price of freedom for myself and my people is indeed high.

### Return Home

*The New House.* I wondered what the new house would be like. I was deeply involved in this venture and my future was indirectly, if not directly, affected by it. Early in 1960, as I was finishing the last months of my military career, I received the second letter ever written me by my father in his own handwriting. As fate would have it both letters were written at a time of family tragedy. The letters are filed in my permanent records under the label, "Important Accomplishments." This one-page letter, only eight lines long, stated in effect, "I am dying and I want to build a house in town for your mama before I die." My family home was a small eighty-four-acre farm four miles from town. My mother worked in the school cafeteria, my youngest brother was graduating from high school that spring, and my youngest sister walked to school alone, since there was no "colored" school bus. In order to pay for the new house, my father was going to sell his farm, and he wanted to give me first chance to buy it. But more than that, he wanted me to buy it.

Since this was the first piece of land ever owned by a member of my family, there was really nothing to consider. Certainly if God provided air to breathe, as far as I was concerned no white man would ever buy that piece of land. For a long time my wife and I had been saving for our return to Mississippi, and I immediately bought our old home place. In spite of the fact that every lending institution in Kosciusko was willing to lend my father the money to build the house, he was dead set on paying for everything; he did not want to leave his family under any possible threat from the whites. This was the kind of protective shielding that my family and I had been receiving all our lives from my father.

The last three houses on the street were new, but it was not difficult to determine which one belonged to Moses "Cap" Meredith. Even though my family had moved in only two weeks before, there was a freshly cut lawn with transplanted flowers and bushes. The street was dirt, like all Negro streets, but a concrete drive led up to the open carport. And there was the old "gallery swing," newly painted white, in the front yard. The dying man had not died. I guess it was the will to advance that had kept him alive.

*The Old Farm.* As I pulled into the driveway of this new house, I noticed a shellacked cedar post holding up the carport roof; I was certain that it was one of the old cedars which grew in the cow pasture behind the barn at our farm. I could not help but think of the old home place, now legally mine, but which would always remain, as long as he lived, my father's house. I could vividly remember all the other thousands of times that I had returned home. Instead of turning right off Highway 12, I would have turned left on the Old Natchez Trace Road, the oldest and most famous road in Mississippi, and possibly in the Deep South. I know every inch of this road. For the first half mile the houses are mostly small "shot-gun" houses (a long narrow one-unit affair shaped like a railroad boxcar, with two partitions dividing it into three rooms with a small kitchen in the middle). You can almost always assume that a "shot-gun" house belongs to a white landlord, because a Negro would never build, and very seldom buy, one. The few big frame houses scattered about usually belong to Negro schoolteachers.

Just past the "shot-guns" is the only brick house on the road. It belongs to the owner of the Negro dry cleaning shop. Across the road, a short distance away, is the house of the high school principal, probably the biggest house in town owned by a Negro. Across from the principal's house is another row of "shot-gun" houses and at the end of this row is the Kosciusko city limits sign. A little farther on, at the top of the hill, is a vacant one-room store—the only business that had existed between my old home and town. It ceased operation when the lady operator died. It is at the corner of the only Negro-owned farm on the main road. The old house on this farm sits an unusually long distance back from the road. For many years it was customary for Negroes not to build their homes on the main road in rural areas; even if they owned the land, they had to build their homes on the side roads. My father had often expressed his displeasure with this practice to me when I was a boy. At the corner of this farm is the Negro graveyard.

Across the road from the cemetery is Shine's house. Shine was a well-known dealer in bootleg whiskey; I don't know if his name derives from his trade in moonshine or from the common custom of calling Negroes "Shine." Down from his house is the only white house, and I don't mean the color of the house, between my old farm home and town. All the other houses are occupied, if not owned, by Negroes. The fact that only one white-occupied house was between my old home and town was very important to me as a child, because it made possible an environment in which I never had to come into direct contact with whites and therefore was never forced to conduct myself in a consciously inferior manner.

Up the hill from the white house is the main barn of the richest man and by far the largest landowner in the county. He owned every acre on the left side of the road all the way to my old home and ninety-nine per cent on the right side. He was in every type of operation: timber, cattle, and farming of all sorts, except cotton, which was most unusual in Mississippi. All his farm help were paid by the day and not on the traditional sharecrop basis. The workers always knew that they would have at least some money at settlement time. He held his workers in a position that was hardly better than the sharecroppers, however. All of them had to call him "Cap'n Sam." He often amused himself by hitting his "niggers" with the heavy walking cane he always carried or by throwing nickels and pennies into the air and watching the Negroes fight over them. Beyond the big barn there are few dwellings, since the land is kept cleared for farming or for cattle.

Finally we come to the "mailbox." In rural Mississippi it is often possible to know the economic, social, and racial circumstances of the owner of a particular mailbox. Ours was middle size. I remember the many steps into the bigger box era. During the latter part of World War II our last mailbox status change was the result of an allotment check from a brother in the Army, money sent home from a brother and two sisters working in war plants in Detroit, and the biggest cotton harvest on record for our farm and the highest price ever paid for cotton. I recall that a trip to Jackson was made to buy the new mailbox. By that time there was an addition—a nameplate, "Moses Meredith, Route 2, Box 10." My father retained his box number, although there were hundreds of new numbers between our farm and town by 1960.

At the mailbox you turn off the main road and drive three quarters of a mile of narrow, winding road to the house. You go through a swamp-like hollow, where the undergrowth is thick and tall, known as "hant hollow" to us (ten children). My oldest brother swears that hants dwell in it. For years a big sweet gum tree (two trees grown together) stood in the middle of the road. I can remember that I used to tease one of my older sisters by splitting the tree (when two or more persons are walking together and they do not pass the tree on the same side). She believed to the end that it was bad luck to split a tree. My father's first wife, the mother of my older brothers and sisters, had died when the youngest half-sister was still a baby. Their mother had been extremely superstitious, while my mother was not superstitious at all.

I come from the hill section of Mississippi. For nearly a half mile the last stretch of the road runs up a long hill. About two hundred yards up the next hill in the southeast corner of our eighty-four-acre farm is located the old house—the place where I was born. This is the end of the road. Anytime someone came down this road, you knew he was coming to Cap Meredith's house. This farm was called "my own place" by some of the descendants of the scattered children of African origin mixed with European and American Indian blood, identified by the ethnic name of Negro, incorporating within its meaning a past condition of slavery, and by the acquired name of "Meredith." My father was the first member of his family ever to own a piece of land. In his house I learned the true meaning of life. Here I learned that death was to be preferred to indignity.

The greatest intangible that the house had to offer was pride. The second was order. If these are taken away, only poverty is left. At the time my family moved into the new house in town—years after the atomic bomb, in the era of jet airplanes and rockets orbiting the earth—my old family home had no toilet, no bath, no running water, and the wind still blew freely through the unblocked cracks in the walls of half the rooms. The beds which had been acquired during the days when my father was a sharecropper, some forty-odd years earlier, were still in use. But there was pride and there was order.

My father kept his boundary line fences always in good repair. Although the neighboring landowners, all white, wanted to go together on the boundary fences to split the cost and work, my father insisted on pulling his fences back two feet from the actual line and maintaining them on his own. He did not want a white man ever to have an excuse to invade his privacy. If anyone was a king in his own domain, it was Cap. It was as if our eighty-four acres constituted a sovereign state and we neither recognized nor had any diplomatic relations with our neighboring states. The house of a white family was within one hundred yards of the back side of our place, and yet I never saw it. Because of his desire to shield us, my father forbade us even to go to that area of our farm. Some Negro families lived on the white man's farm and their children were our best friends. Since we were not allowed to visit them, they had to come over to our side of the fence to play with us.

When I left Mississippi in 1950 I had never seen the inside of a white person's house, chiefly because a Negro had to enter by the back door. I was taught to believe that the most dishonorable thing that a Meredith could do was to work in a white woman's kitchen and take care of a white man's child. I know that I would starve to death rather than do either. I am sure that the Negroes with the greatest sense of pride come from the farms, because working in the fields never carried the disgraceful connotations that working in the white folks' kitchens did.

Perhaps I should approach the old home place from another point of view: the estimate of our peers. To the average Mississippi Negro we were indeed well off. We had a very big house with eleven rooms, and for as long as I can remember there was paint of some quality on the outside. There was some kind of furniture in every room; the living room, main bedroom, and guest room were always presentable, so that my folks were never embarrassed by their home —as most Negroes have been from time to time. I can recall listening to the first Joe Louis championship fight over the radio at home, and I cannot remember a single day that my father did not listen to the evening news. We had a radio when few whites and very few Negroes had one in Mississippi. I have sopped bread and molasses for breakfast, dinner, and supper for many weeks at a time, but never did I go without food. Windowpanes were usually in the windows and the screens were sufficient to keep away most of the mosquitoes. While I have been conscious of our home's shortcomings when it is compared with the typical white American's, at the same time I have been aware of our fortunate circumstances compared with the average Mississippi Negro. As I remembered my old home, I was certain that I was returning to Mississippi by choice.

*Why I Returned*

To understand the events that occurred during my three years in Mississippi, one must always remember that I returned to my home state to fight a war. I had spent every year of my adult life and the three years before my twenty-first birthday in the Armed Forces; in other words, I grew up in the military. During all those years I was conscious of my purpose in being a soldier—to secure my country and its principles against any enemy. It also must be remembered that I served as a soldier and not as a Negro soldier, although I was always aware of my personal heritage. A soldier must at all times be ready, without hesitation or question, to die for his country and his cause.

That the Negro American was to become legally and officially free and equal was no longer a question in my mind. I was sure that it would become a reality. Whether or not the Negro would become actually and effectively free and equal was not so certain, and it was for this I was prepared to fight. What most Negroes and their organizations were fighting for—the principle of equality, the idea that "I am not inferior to you"—was to me a foregone conclusion.

An important factor that one must understand is the condition of ending the war. Different wars have different goals: defending and repelling, attacking and conquering, forcing an enemy to negotiate a settlement, and, as in the case of the Allies of World War II, demanding unconditional surrender. My objective in this war was total victory: victory over discrimination, oppression, the unequal application of the law, and, most of all, over "White Supremacy" and all of its manifestations.

*The Divine Responsibility.* Everything that I have done, I did because I had to. A very long time ago some force greater than myself placed before me my life's role, the mission that I was to accomplish. How my divine responsibility was to be carried out was left to me. Obviously I was returning to Mississippi to work at the task of fulfilling my mission. By now a definite procedure and method had been worked out. A decision-making and action-creating machinery had been devised, and it was only with the machinery that I had to concern myself. I think of this machinery as something like a computer, into which one programs all the different data, and the result is the best possible answer that the available facts are capable of producing.

My most stabilizing belief is that I have never made a mistake in my life, because I never make arbitrary or predetermined decisions. Every decision made and every action taken is always an impersonal result of the processing of every available bit of data. Many things that I find it necessary for me to do in order to accomplish my divine mission are against my personal liking and taste.

*A Part of the Master Plan.* The most important thing that one must remember is the word "Negro." I am a Negro, and I am directly affected by all that is inherent in the word. For the record, I believe that the term clearly identifies a particular and exclusive group of people and is in no way derogatory.

Ever since I was fifteen years old I have been self-consciously aware that I am a Negro. Of course, I had known that I belonged to a group that was distinctly different from at least one other group, but until I was fifteen I did not know that my group was supposed to be the inferior one. Since then I have felt a personal responsibility to change the status of my group. There is no way for one Negro to change his basic status without first changing that of all Negroes. I have long recognized the folly of advocating a change simply because it is right, because it is humane, because it is Christian, because it is in the Constitution, or for any other non-practical reason. I am aware of another important fact: if I were a white man, I would not give up my favored position unless there was an extremely good reason. The greatest hope for a major change in the basic status of the Negro is to convince the American whites that it is in their best interests. It is my firm conviction that the solution must result in the material improvement of both groups concerned—the oppressors as well as the oppressed.

I had returned to Mississippi because I had developed a master plan to replace what I considered the Negroes' worst enemy: the principles and doctrines of "White Supremacy." I have no desire to destroy the customs and systems of the South; instead, I intend to build a better system and to replace the old unsuitable customs with more desirable ones. The first step in the master plan was to return to Mississippi.

## The First Quarter at Jackson State College
### September-December 1960

FOR several years my wife and I had saved and planned for the future. All the arrangements had been made before we left Japan for us to enter as full-time students at Jackson State College in September. I had considered most of the Negro schools in the country and many of the predominantly white ones before making a final decision. Since my purpose was to fight the state of Mississippi, I felt the most appropriate arena was on its own ground in a state-supported institution. Also important to me, the school had recently been reorganized to include a liberal education curriculum. (Liberal education is a vague alternative to liberal arts, which is considered undesirable for Negroes by many white Mississippians.) A degree course in history and political science had been added and was being offered for the first time in a state-supported Negro school in Mississippi. Had I graduated from Jackson State College—I entered as an advanced junior—I would have been among the first graduates in this course from the school. Finally, Jackson was a city and my wife and child would not have to suffer the indignity of being Negroes in a small Mississippi town or rural community.

*Jackson State College*

The well-kept grounds and buildings impress the visitor. It is a typical example of the extraordinarily good use that the Mississippi Negro makes of what little he has. The buildings, although few and inadequate, are all spotlessly white. They must paint them every year, or wash the ones for which there is no paint. The grass is always freshly cut and the flowers and shrubbery are well cared for. The school is located in the middle of the most densely populated Negro community in Jackson. Because the campus is small, it is hard to tell where the college ends and the community begins. It is not located in the main Negro business district, however, and most of the businesses in the area are service establishments for the college community.

Across the street from the campus, as a result of the thoughtfulness of the city fathers, with a keen eye to the future, the city of Jackson had built a large auditorium for Negroes, probably the only one of its kind in the world. Also close by are a branch of the Jackson City Public Library, a swimming pool, a children's recreation center, and a park for Negroes. Would this scheme to deprive the Negro of his rightful use of public facilities work?

What the University of Mississippi is to the white society of Mississippi, Jackson State College is all this and more to the Negro society of the state. The entire social apparatus of the upper- and middle-class Negroes radiates out of Jackson, with the college at the center. This is also true of the athletic and financial organizations throughout the state. Even the religious life of the Negroes finds its roots in the college.

*The Students.* With few exceptions, every student is a Mississippian. He usually comes from the upper lower class or the lower middle class, depending on which standard one uses. (All Americans like to consider themselves middle class.) He very rarely, if ever, belongs to the Negro privileged group. The chances are at least 10 to 1 that the student will be studying to become a teacher. On the Mississippi Negro's road from poverty to middle-class status, becoming a teacher is a very real step forward. The average student makes an immediate transition during the period from graduation in May to the beginning of the split session in July (many schools begin classes in July and stop in September until the cotton is picked) with his first teaching contract. Although Mississippi Negro teachers are the lowest-paid teachers in the United States ($2,960 is the beginning salary), the graduate is instantly earning twice the amount or more of his family's total income prior to his appointment.

I have a friend, Billy Curtis, who is a typical student. He is from Silver Creek, Mississippi, in Jeff Davis County, named for Jefferson Davis, the first and only President of the Southern Confederate

States. Negroes outnumber whites there 2 or 3 to 1 and probably no Negro has ever voted in the county. Billy is an individual of the highest quality, his demeanor is above reproach, his integrity beyond question, and his pride, if it were tangible, could be divided into enough pieces to satisfy the needs of all the people on the North American continent and still have a surplus. But Billy is poor. Although the tuition per quarter is only fifty-five dollars and he had worked all summer and saved for school, he had had to borrow part of the money to enroll for the first term.

He told me about his struggle for a place in the sun. To pay for his keep Billy was the trash and garbage collector for the girls' dormitories. Because of the college's puritanical rules, he had to perform this chore between four and five in the morning, supposedly before the girls were awakened from their dreams. He admitted that this task of collecting trash from inside the dormitories, even at such an ungodly hour, had its moments of excitement. All of the girls were not asleep; occasionally, some of them would tease him about his lowly task in a flirting sort of way, and usually they would not be wearing their Sunday-go-to-meeting attire. To Curtis, however, this job was as low as one could stoop; he often told me of the mental agony that one must endure in order to advance in a Mississippi setting and still retain one's personal dignity. But Billy Curtis will make it. He may some day be the governor of Mississippi.

*The Faculty and Staff.* In general, I would say that the faculty and staff were as dedicated, honest, and well-balanced as any Negro in Mississippi. But they were under-educated, under-paid, and usually over-worked. The greatest pain an oppressed people must bear is the knowledge of its oppression. Certainly the educated group must be more aware of the conditions of its existence. Of course, there were also the disillusioned, the rejects, the frustrated, and the queers. Every college campus has these types, but I believe that the Negro colleges in Mississippi have a larger percentage.

There were the rejects from the North and the Old South, who feel themselves superior to the Mississippi Negro. Some of them would not dare speak to a student on the campus, lest he might begin to feel that he was as good as his teacher. There were the queers, who use personal conferences, campus sidewalks, and even open classrooms to proposition the handsome boys. Probably most numerous, and certainly most vicious, were the faculty and staff girl chasers. Every advantage in the book was taken of the girls. Some instructors even carried the seduction to the point of making the passing of a course and even graduation itself dependent on the condition that the girl go to bed with them. I must emphasize the fact again that the majority of the faculty and staff had the highest type of personal character, and efforts were being made to rid the school of the undesirable elements whenever possible.

*The Negro Golf Course*

If ever there was a time of action in Mississippi, it was during the three years after I returned. The mounting pressures brought changes that had only been talked about for decades. Recreational facilities of any kind had seldom been considered for the Jackson Negroes. Yet within three months after my arrival, a golf course had been built for them. Ten years earlier when I left Mississippi a Negro had better not be caught talking about playing the white man's most jealously reserved game.

The building of this golf course was a sight to see. The entire ground-working machinery of the city of Jackson, plus perhaps some other, was now all concentrated in an unsettled area of North Jackson, located in the heart of "Shady Oaks," a new middle-class Negro residential area. Mississippi whites, Negroes, and I imagine a few "outsiders" were working on the project. A new paved road ran right through the middle of the golf course. Perhaps this was done to make it easy for all who cared to come and "see for yourself" what we are doing for "our Negroes." Even a viaduct had been built for the railroad tracks so no one would have to wait for the train at the crossing. A new mobile temporary clubhouse had been provided and the grand opening date had been set. A golf course had been built for Negroes in Mississippi, because it had been suspected that some Negroes might attempt to play at one of Jackson's lily-white golf courses.

*James Allen, Jr.* The most significant thing about the golf course for me was that it led to my meeting James Allen, Jr. The first time I went out to look at the new course it was still under construction and it had not officially been opened for play. Standing near the clubhouse, I overheard two or three fellows talking about the pros and cons of the new Negro course. Three of us had clubs in our cars and talked ourselves into playing a few holes. One of these was James Allen, Jr., a tall, slender youth of twenty-two who had just completed a tour of duty in Korea, winding up his three-year voluntary enlistment in the Army. Most sensitive to the racial segregation and discrimination in his home state, he was a restless and apprehensive young man. His most striking characteristic is his persistence in sticking with the thing that interests him, in spite of his restlessness. On this particular day his interest was to beat me at golf. Even though I had played much longer and was obviously a more consistent golfer, Allen with his wild swinging and wide field of play (his first drive sliced across three fairways) often beat me, and was totally disgusted with himself each time he failed to win.

James Allen, Jr., as he liked to be called, could be counted on. Our future relationship well proved this to me. He was the only person who witnessed my first act of war against the system of "White Supremacy" in Mississippi, and he was a part of every other important campaign. And he was present on the last day to witness the awarding of my battle citation (my degree from the University of Mississippi). If I were the general that I would like to have been, certainly James Allen, Jr., would be my chief officer.

*Mayor Allen Thompson.* Thompson loved to boast of his achievements during his many years as mayor of Mississippi's only city. While he was mayor, Jackson had grown from a small country town into a large and, by Mississippi standards, a prosperous metropolitan area. It was also during his tenure that Jackson had its most trying years since the Civil War. Although the new Negro golf course was far from complete, the pressure of the Negro's struggle for equality would not allow Allen Thompson to wait any longer to announce that "we are taking care of our Negroes" in Jackson. The ceremony had been well planned and well publicized.

The first ball was to be hit by Pete Brown, ex-caddie at one of the bigger white courses in town and now manager and pro at the Negro club. Pete teed up and missed the first drive I have ever seen him bogey. He was very conscious that the Negro community was regarding the Negro golf course idea with some suspicion. This knowledge, plus the excitement of the event, I suppose, was too much for him. Of course, the mayor gave Pete another new ball. This time he hit his normal drive, about three hundred and fifty yards or more, straight down the middle.

Pete is a perfect example of how segregation and discrimination can deny the Negro an opportunity to develop his potential. Up to this time he had been a helper at a white course for a few dollars a week, although his ability made him a professional golfer by any standard. Pete Brown may very well become the first Negro golfer to win all the Big Golf tournaments. Only a year or so after this ceremony in Jackson, he was on the road as a full-time professional, playing with Arnold Palmer, Jack Nicklaus, and all the others. After three years as a professional, he is one of the top Negro money winners, and the only Negro ever to win a PGA tournament. And he is still in his twenties.

This was Allen Thompson's show and he was in fine form, and I must acknowledge that he is a real politician. He made a whooping gesture at Pete Brown's second drive and went into his act. I can't recall if his stage was the number 5 tee, or the number 7 green, or if it was a makeshift one. I do remember that it was very close to the temporary clubhouse. The ceremony began as usual with a prayer. One of the mayor's "fine Negro citizens" had been tapped to do the honors. I kept an eye on Allen Thompson, and he definitely did not bow his head. Of course, it was just a Negro preacher praying. However, I am sure that the preacher did not believe some of the tributes he paid to the "fine white citizens," the progressive city of Jackson, and its illustrious and fair-minded mayor. Certainly the preacher couldn't have expected God to believe all this.

Almost before the long ordeal was over, Allen Thompson broke in with "Preacher, that sure was a fine prayer," and looking at the audience which was quite large, "Wasn't that a fine prayer? Well, look who's here, there's ole So-and-so. Why, ole So-and-so knew me when I was a boy," and old So-and-so acted his part, scratching his head with a finger. The one-finger scratch is an undeniable scratch. Often the more sensitive Negroes scratch with all the fingers, and later when their friends question them about the head-scratching business, they can argue that they were just rubbing their hair. This head-scratching could have been a coincidence, but I rather think it was part of the program. It is a typical trick to generate a feeling of contact with a Negro audience.

The mayor then told us about the fine progress that the Jackson Negroes were making—"paved street," "good jobs," "no racial disturbances." "Just look at this golf course. Isn't it grand?" I almost believed him myself. I almost forgot the difficulty that I had had a couple of days before finding a spot of grass in the fairway and that half of the greens still had not been sodded. Some courses play winter rules in summer when the fairways are not in the best of condition, that is, you are allowed to move the ball with the club not more than six inches in order to find grass. But at this course there was a special rule that permitted you to find grass wherever you could.

The mayor finally climbed down from his stage and started to shake hands with every person present. He was a man always ready with a word and a grin. At last he approached James Allen, Jr., and me where we were standing near the clubhouse. He shook Allen's hand and came toward me with his hand outstretched and a wide smile on his face. I just looked at him. He held his hand out for a moment and the grin seemed to freeze, with his mouth half open. Allen Thompson was not a man to give up easily and I was not going to spoil his program. He continued on to the next man. The Negroes were somewhat reserved and all eyes were on the mayor. Suddenly, everyone just disappeared—perhaps out of fear, maybe out of frustration, or it may even have been out of anger.

James Allen, Jr., has asked me hundreds of times why I refused to shake the mayor's hand. I do not know if I have ever given him a suitable answer. Apparently not, for he continues to ask. The best reason I can give is that I did not want to betray the mayor by allowing him to assume that this was the way to handle the racial problem in Jackson. Allen Thompson was probably not over fifty years old, and at the time of his birth "White Supremacy" had long been in force and well established in Mississippi. The chance of birth had dictated his position just as it had dictated mine. Faith in a cause had made me an aggressor in this war, and his faith had made him a defender in the struggle. From his point of view, Allen Thompson may have felt himself the blessed achiever and a generous distributor of human justice. He must have thought that he had done his duty and fulfilled his obligation to the Negro community of Jackson, consequently, they too must all be satisfied. He could go away with a relieved mind, confident that all was well. Even if the occasion seemed to call for it, I could not allow my actions to contribute to the mayor's easy assumption that his way was the right solution.

### After Class

I had attended several colleges and universities as a part-time student during my nine years of military service. If I were to be absolutely honest about my immediate objective prior to my marriage, I would have to concede that my desire to find out what was happening after class was a little greater than my diligence to absorb what was going on inside the classroom. Jackson State College has its share of after-class activities, and I believe that what one learns outside the classroom is equally as important, perhaps even more so, than what is absorbed inside. This is especially true in Mississippi where a Negro teacher of social science, who has never been allowed to vote, is the enthusiastic propagator of the virtues of the American democratic system, or in a white school where the intoxicated lecturer assures the students of the merits of the state's prohibition laws. In Mississippi the hard, cold facts of reality can be the best and most effective teacher of all.

At Jackson State College one first notices the girls. Girls, girls, girls, and more girls. They outnumber the boys about 3 to 1, and the ratio in the city is even higher. The system of segregation and discrimination has caused this imbalance. The Negro male simply is forced out of the state. By the time he is eighteen, the boy has gone by one route or another—the military, big city, work project, or just wandering. The girls have no place to go. There can be little argument that the Negro women of Mississippi are among the world's most beautiful. What else can be expected from a production machinery consisting of pure fresh air, hard work, plenty to eat, and rape. Rape of Negro girls and women by white men.

As a Mississippian, I was acutely aware of the inherent dangers of a surplus of women to a man possessing two eyes, two arms, and two legs. I had long pondered the prospects of evading the temptation of the lonely, healthy, adventurous women at the college and in the city of Jackson. I had even discussed this matter with my chaplain and sought his suggestions before I was discharged from the Air Force and returned to Mississippi. Certainly I had many of the material things bound to provoke temptation—two cars and pocket change perhaps the most desirable attractions. What does a man do in a situation like this? Only one solution appeared satisfactory to me: I must be genuinely concerned with their problems and make their right to ample and suitable companionship a major goal in my war against "White Supremacy."

The future of the girl in a Mississippi Negro college is precarious. Her chances of meeting and marrying her mate are probably no greater than 1 in 5. She can look to a variety of alternatives, all unsuitable, whether real or imagined. She can either marry someone with less education and less earning capacity or try to find some stray somewhere in her category, an extremely chancy business. This situation results in a great strain on the Negro society and is particularly felt by the Negro male. The husbands in the "married down" (when the wife has more education) class are a disenchanted group, forever self-conscious of the fact that they are considered inferior to their wives. The husbands who do meet the specified qualification—college education or a high-earning capacity—are subject to open assault by the unmarried women.

I remember one young man whom I will call Henry Lee. At the age of twenty-three he was beginning his third year as a teacher in one of the Negro schools in Jackson, his home town. Along with many of his childhood friends, he had entered college after completing high school. One of his new classmates was an out-of-town country girl. She was as pretty as a Japanese doll and immediately stole Henry's heart from his old sweethearts. During their sophomore year, they married and he continued in college with his old classmates, while his wife dropped out to start a family. When I met Henry, he was a very mixed-up and frustrated man. A couple of his old girlfriends, who had graduated from college and found themselves without husbands, had refused to concede victory to the little country girl, whom they suspected of using unfair tactics in her conquest. They unhesitatingly suggested that the first premature baby might not have been so at all. Even after four years of marriage he was still pursued as fair game and was caught between the devil and the deep blue sea. He loved his wife and was loyal to her. On the other hand, he understood the problems and frustrations of his former classmates and could not find a justification for casting them out totally to the miseries of their dilemma.

*The College Inn.* The College Inn traditionally has a kind of semi-official status with the college. Although the location, which is just off campus, has changed each time the college has expanded and the management or ownership has changed countless times, there has always been a "College Inn" at Jackson State College. When I entered the college, it was located on Lynch Street, the main street, directly across from the college dining hall. (Lynch Street did not derive its name from the obvious "Lynch" but was named in honor of Congressman John Lynch, who served several terms both in the state legislature and in the U.S. Congress, the only Negro ever to serve as Speaker of the House.) The most innocent girls could boast of a visit to the College Inn at one time or another during their stay at Jackson State College.

The College Inn is mainly a place of daytime congregation. After the close of the school day and on weekends it is practically deserted. Total volume of sales—of cheap sandwiches and knickknacks, light meals, soft drinks, and beer—was the key aspect of its business. It can legally sell beer, but the college has forbidden the students to drink beer there. I do not think sales were hurt by the prohibition;

it just made buying the beer more exciting, and it tasted better. The latest records are always on the jukebox. The College Inn is one of the few places left in Jackson where one can still play a record for a nickel.

At the back of the inn is a permanent "temporary" partition. Behind it are found the more interesting aspects of the College Inn. There is a special course known as "College Innology" among the students, and the backroom is the main classroom. There is dancing, often of a very sensuous variety, and illegal card playing (which the management forbids because it receives no profit from it). Many of the strategies of the war against "White Supremacy" were discussed in this backroom.

*The Tea Room.* I am sure that there must be some who have attended Jackson State College who did not get to the Tea Room, and I am also sure that none would admit it. If Mississippi has any club that could count itself a Negro society club, it would be the Tea Room. The name is misleading. It is a big sprawling white house that sits far enough back from the road on all sides to allow space for a driveway with full-car-length parking on both sides of the gravel-covered yard. The grass which would normally be there is conspicuously missing. I have never noticed a sign to attract business at the Tea Room, but this is typical of the illegally operated Mississippi clubs. No sign is needed, however, because, even though it is some seven miles out of town in the Lynch Street Subdivision Number 2, whenever any four Negroes in Mississippi get together, at least one of them knows where the Tea Room is located.

There has undoubtedly never been a cup of tea either made or consumed in the Tea Room. Furthermore, Mississippians may occasionally drink iced tea but they do not drink hot tea. At the Tea Room you buy only the best Bourbon and Scotch whiskies. The Negro with "class" in Mississippi just simply must drink Scotch. Mississippi is a dry state and the sale of whiskey is illegal. The most important aspect about the Tea Room is that it is safe; its bootleg tax has traditionally been paid to the right man. To my knowledge, the Tea Room is one of the only two completely safe Negro spots in the whole state. I have never seen or heard of a police officer going into the Tea Room. And one need never fear the state patrolmen who park in large numbers along U.S. Highway 80 in the vicinity of the Tea Room every weekend and often during the week.

It is not a meeting place. One either goes with his party to the Tea Room or makes definite arrangements prior to meeting his guests there. One quickly feels the air of intrusion if he walks in and takes a seat at the table even of someone he knows. There is no dance floor and no band, just a jukebox. The greatest offering of the Tea Room is "class"—and a dependable supply of the best liquor.

*Stevens Rose Room.* If Jackson has a Negro middle class, Stevens Rose Room would qualify as its general social meeting place. One can also count on seeing the big-shot Negroes, including the big preachers, at some function or other at Stevens during the course of a year. Since the average income of the Negro family in Mississippi (4½ members) was only $1,162 in 1960, the great majority of Negroes are eliminated from the Rose Room Set by their paychecks.

The Rose Room is the largest Negro nightclub in Mississippi. It has traditionally drawn a large and consistent crowd which enables it to channel the proper amount of money along the path of corruption. The highest-paid government official in the United States is the Mississippi bootleg tax collector. Hinds County is definitely his biggest source of revenue.

Ironically, the payoff man who collected from the Negro operators of illegal establishments—mainly gambling and drinking—for the county and state vice lords and government officials is a Negro who is well known and accepted among the Negroes of Jackson. He is very rich, a leading deacon, and the biggest financial contributor to his church, which happens to be one of the biggest, if not the biggest, church in the city of Jackson and the state of Mississippi. He almost lost his position once because of his wife. She is a very attractive "high yellow," and one of the state's leading white citizens, having an uncontrollable lust for pretty Negro women and a particular liking for the wife of his chief money man, took his liberty as a "white man" and shared the Negro's wife. Being jealous, as he should have been, the deacon lost his head one night and followed his wife in her pretty new Cadillac to her rendezvous with her admirer. He ended up at one of those well-known Jackson roadside motels ("white only," naturally) and for this foolish act he almost lost his life, as well as his position. But this was Mississippi and he lost neither.

*The Elks Rest.* I shall view this establishment of the Order of Elks only from the standpoint of its general public function relative to Mississippi society. As a nonmember, I never really felt completely at home in this fraternal order. Yet when one passes the "members only" sign at the entrance, he is secluded from all that is outside. Technically I was always a guest of some member of the club. Fortunately I could, as most others, enter on my own identity. The

Mississippi Elks is definitely Negro middle class in nature and structure. Since all Americans, except the admittedly poor and the exclusively rich, consider themselves in the middle class, all who were welcomed at the Elks could feel themselves at ease among their peers, even if the mutual feeling ended the moment they emerged from behind the "members only" sign. Everyone was equal inside the Elks Rest: the salesman, the barber, the cook, the doctor, the lawyer, the schoolteacher, and the college professor.

*Across the River.* "Across the river" is a term that has great symbolic meaning to the students at Jackson State College, although few actually make many trips across the Pearl River into the adjoining county of Rankin. Who has not heard the name of Rankin in America? Rankin and Bilbo were in the U.S. Congress together. Rankin stayed longer and for this reason he certainly must have done more harm. Hinds County is vile and corrupt, but it cannot begin to compete with Rankin County. Going across the river for a student is almost synonymous to "getting into something." The joints are usually too rough for the students and their visits are limited to the daylight hours. Gambling, drinking, prostitution, and slot machines are all out in the open. There are cheap motels available and practically every cafe, beer joint, or old house has cheap rooms to rent for "short-time" pleasure.

*Mr. P's.* In my search for truth and knowledge, I felt it my duty to regularly visit every segment of my society. Except for the study and observation of the enemy—"White Supremacy" and its perpetuators—I spent more time and energy studying my people than anything else. Without question, the great majority of Mississippi Negroes belong to the lowest economic class. A joint called "Mr. P's" provided me with one of the best laboratories for studying this particular group of my people. I consider this place typical of the most dominant type of entertainment available to the majority of Mississippi Negroes. It would perhaps be untypical only in that it is a little bigger than most places of its kind and consequently offers a little more than most.

I can remember one night: it could have been any of four nights—Friday, Saturday, Sunday or Wednesday (the last is half-price night). However, Saturday night is usually best. This Saturday I got there around 1:30 A.M., the best time to arrive because the band (two guitars and one drummer with a two-piece drum contraption) was just hitting its pace after the first intermission. The cooks and nursemaids who have to work in the white woman's kitchen and take care of the white man's baby are out on the town by this time. The white folks know that "Cookie" will leave the food on the table and the baby crying in the crib if the boss "ain't home" by 1:00 A.M. on Saturday night. By 1:30 everybody has got high and fallen in the groove.

When I drove up, I was lucky and found a parking place, because someone was just backing out from a spot near the door. I pulled in and parked between two cars. A girl was sitting on the front end of one of the cars with her legs crossed high and her dress halfway up her thigh. She was holding onto the shirt of her boyfriend standing in front of the car and raising a heap of hell about some other woman. When I reached the door, it was blocked by too many people trying to get in. The heat and odor both hit me as I slid inside the door.

The band was playing one of its favorite songs, "Shake Your Money Maker." This was a sure satisfier for this crowd. It had a fast sensuous beat and was loud and moving. Sometimes the band would play it for thirty minutes or longer without stopping, and the crowd would continue to beg for more when it was over. "Shake your money maker, shake your money maker" was repeated over and over throughout the song, basically an instrumental number. The band leader, Elmo, loved to hear the crowd beg, and the audience knew that he had to be treated with tender care, because the least thing might upset him and he would refuse to play a note. But he was good at his trade. The kind of music that he played has not yet been documented by writing or recording. It is known by many names—gut-bucket, down in the alley, back in the woods—but to me it is folk music of the highest order. It tells the story of the Negro—the history of slavery, segregation, discrimination, prejudice, poverty, and hope. I have learned more about the Negro from listening to and digesting this music than from any other source. Finally they stopped playing "Shake Your Money Maker." I now had a chance to edge my way up toward the front.

There was no dance floor as such; the dance floor was everywhere—in the aisles, between the tables, on the tables, or anywhere you could find a little space. It was the usual crowd. The dress ranges all the way from expensive furs and hundred-dollar dresses to loud, weary colors and maid uniforms. The men will wear anything from seventy-dollar shoes and three-hundred-dollar suits to four-colored shirts and purple trousers to musty, sweaty, sawmilling overalls that they have worked in all week. The talk was loud, bad, and nasty. The women are just as free and foul-mouthed as the men. These are the Negro masses at play.

I finally made it to the front and here I heard a piece of logic from a young boy that opened my eyes to a broader world. A couple in front of the bar where I was standing began to dance the next number. Before the dance was over they had a tight circle around them, a rare occurrence for this place, because here everyone is usually his own star. On any night you would see a show that could be seen in very few places: shake dancing, belly rolling, stunt cutting, trick dancing, and the sexiest kind of sexy dances.

Evidently this couple had just returned from their first trip North, and they had to show that they were now "hip." The girl wore a fur dress, apparently made from some cheap imitation fur, and the boy had on a tight-fitting shirt that was a solid color in back and two loud colors in front. The design was identical on both sides, but one side was turned upside down, and the big buttons were covered with the same color as the back. He had on a loud-colored tight-fitting pair of pants and wore a pair of pointed-toe imitation alligator shoes. He was really "cutting a rug," jumping all over the place, and executing some very difficult and tricky steps.

But the "fur-dress" girl was stealing the show. She was a beautiful woman: young, lively, fair-skinned, and "built up from the ground," with nice feet, trim ankles, shapely legs, wide hips, a neat, small waist, bust just right (on the big side), a cute face, and beautiful hair. The dress was loosely fitted and cut low around the top. The first look gave the impression that she wore nothing under the dress. She could dance and she let her "hair down" because of all the attention she was getting. She went through a belly process that would have put "Little Egypt" to shame. Most exciting of all was the way that fur dress could work its way up over her hips and just as it looked as if all her pretty thighs would be revealed, she would push her dress down again and start the heart-taxing process all over. This was all done to the beat of the "Whistling Song." The drummer was called the whistling man because of this song that he had "dreamed up," as he once told me, and carried around in his head.

When it was over, you could hear derogatory comments from the onlookers. They were accusing the team of showing off and of thinking they were somebody because they had been up North. It always gets under the skin of the Mississippi Negro when one comes back "putting on." A slender, mild-mannered boy of fifteen or sixteen, who in spite of his age was his own man, turned to me and remarked in his untrained English, "Oh, they jest trying to have a little pleasure." I cannot now remember his features, but his words and the manner in which he spoke them have lingered in my mind. From that day to this I have made it a practice to try to get the facts before I judge.

About this time Elmo started another one of his most popular numbers, "Dust My Broom." He had really gotten "his spirits on" and turned the picking over to his second guitarist, a quiet-looking young man. He was as good as the old pro himself. Elmo now dealt only with the mike, "I say raise your window, baby, I say raise your window, baby, and let me ease out real slow, I hear somebody knocking; it may be your husband, I don't know." At two o'clock in the morning on a Saturday night in Mississippi, after the people have worked hard all week long, listened to their white boss man raise hell all day, every day, and to their wives or husbands half the night, this is the kind of music and singing that the poor Negroes want to hear.

While everyone continued to "dust their broom," I made my way through the crowd to the hall that led into the back half of the building. This backroom was divided into three sections. Actually it was not meant to be divided, but the crowds were usually so big that the spectators had to be blocked off from the participants by a series of two by fours. Except for the slot machines in the main section, all the gambling took place at a huge dice table and two very large card tables. The dice game, I suppose, was run in the usual way, but I am sure the interest and "carrying on" at the table are unmatched anywhere. One would have to want to play very much in order to push through that crowd to get close enough to place a bet, and he probably would never see so much money on one table even in Las Vegas.

The big-shot gambling houses may have their poker and blackjack games, but for the masses in Mississippi the card game is strictly "skin." I had never seen a game of "skin" played until I returned to my home state. After nine years in the Air Force, including a tour in Nevada, I thought I had seen every gambling game in the book; and maybe I had at that, because I doubt very seriously that "skin" rules are laid down in Hoyle. It is a very simple game, if you can remember fifty-two cards and the way they fall twenty different times to seven different players. In "skin" you don't bet that you will win, but rather that everyone else is going to lose. Each player gets one card down, except the dealer who gets his card up. On the basis of the card he holds, the player is free to bet everybody else as much as he chooses that cards matching all the other players' cards will come off the stack before one matches his. This is when the money really changes hands. Some of the professional gamblers win and lose in the hundreds or even thousands in a matter of a few hours.

After nodding a greeting to several of my fellow Mississippians in the gambling room, I went back to the front. Just as I had taken up a new position at the bar, the "law" and his deputies walked in. You knew they were the law, because they were white and at this hour of the morning no other white men would come into a Negro joint. They carry big five-battery flashlights and, more important, guns. They walked toward the front and no one became excited. The band did not stop playing; the bartender acted as if he had not seen them. The waiters continued to carry the illegal whiskey and setups on their trays which they held high above their shoulders. One of the lawmen finally got the attention of the bartender and whispered something to him. One of the deputies sent word to the band to play a special tune.

After the special dedication was over, I saw one of the character- istic incidents of Mississippi life enacted. Indiscriminately the law pointed to four or five Negroes. These were the victims for that night. While the waiters served bottle after bottle of illegal whiskey and no one made an effort to remove the bottles from the tables, the law was arresting victims for drinking whiskey. They chose one man for having a bottle of illegal whiskey in his pocket; I guess they thought he had bought the bottle at some other place. They took their victims out to two waiting cars and went on their way. This arbitrary method of arrest is one of the main devices of the system of "White Supremacy." As a method of oppression it is far more effective than an arrest for specific crimes; it keeps all the Negroes in a state of fear, because one can become a victim for not committing a crime as readily as for committing one.

## Sunday

Sunday is the Lord's day in Mississippi for the great majority of the Negroes. Not only is the church a place of worship but it is also the center of all organized life in their society. The church is the nearest thing that the Negro has that he can call his own. Certainly it is impossible for any student in a Negro school in Mississippi not to be affected in some way by the Negro church. Jackson State College had been a Baptist school before the state took over its management in 1940. The outdated puritanical codes of behavior were continued and had changed little in twenty years. The restrictions that are imposed on the student body, particularly the women students, are almost unbelievable. This situation tended to make Sunday all the more important for whatever reason—religious or social. It was the only day that the girls could make a move without a strict accounting for their actions. Of course, it was assumed that there was no other place that one could go between the hours of 9:00 A.M. and 1:00 P.M. on Sunday.

The importance of these puritanical codes cannot be overemphasized. Conforming to them is almost a required prerequisite to getting an education and of becoming a part of the power structure. In the rural areas, which is most of Mississippi, where everybody is poor and there are few physical differences in the general appearance of the Negroes, one's class is determined by his moral character. It is not uncommon for members of the same family to be looked upon as belonging to separate classes and for a son or daughter to be later separated by class lines from his parents. This social pressure forces the college student to conduct his life in such a manner that his letter of recommendation for a job in Mississippi can at least carry the required statement affirming his belief in the "Christian Way."

*High-Class Baptist Church.* In every major town there is at least one high-class, or city style, Baptist Church. Traditionally the Methodist Church is the town church and the established Negro leaders are usually Methodists. This rare order of high-Baptist meets the needs of the country-style Baptists who have attained positions of prominence but are unwilling to break their ties with their denomination. The high-Baptist differs from the regular Baptist Church in practically every way, except in the basic structural organization. All Baptist churches are entities in themselves; there is no formal hierarchical structure. Otherwise, the conduct of the services, the preaching style of the minister, and the reaction of the audience are entirely different.

There is no shouting, clapping, jumping, impromptu singing, or coming out of the pulpit and bounding around through the congregation by the high-Baptist preacher. The same effects are usually accomplished by emotional expressions: tone and pitch, satire, and the "fussing" aspects of the style of delivery used by the well-trained ministers, who often hold academic doctors' degrees.

And there is little, if any, verbal audience reaction—no soul-stirring singing, no amens, absolutely no "shouting" or "getting happy." Money is collected in envelopes or by pledges and there is no marching around the table. Money raising is the job of the preacher and not of the deacons. Overdressing and stiffness, especially on the part of the women, are more apparent than in the town Methodist churches, because there is still an uneasy self-consciousness among these high-Baptists as to their status in the class structure.

*The Methodist Church.* The average student is a Baptist by church membership at home, but he probably attends the Methodist Church while he is in college. If he just has to hear some of that good "old-time" singing and praying and preaching, he will tune his radio to one of the Sunday morning broadcasts, but he is not likely to venture into one of "those" churches. The Methodist Church belongs to the Negro middle class in Mississippi: doctors, dentists, teachers, businessmen, barbers, and the better-off farmers. The Methodists are a hierarchical group, with bishops and elders, and so forth. If one aspires to class and status, and most, if not all, of the students do, one can always be sure that he is on solid footing if he follows the path of the Methodist Church. Certainly the Methodist Church is the most puritanical and morals-conscious of all the denominations in Mississippi.

*The Baptist Churches.* "Must Je-sus bear t-h-e cross a-lone and all the w-o-r-ld go fr-ee? N-o! T-he-re's a cross f-o-r ev'-ry-o-n-e and the-re's a cross f-o-r me." The church members pick up the tune in a hum as the leader gets down on one knee, looks up toward the heavens, and begins his long, emotional prayer. There is no introduction or instruction to the congregation, because everyone knows his part and his place very well. The preacher is still back in his study putting the last touches on his text or maybe he has not even yet arrived at the church; but the service has begun. It is known without announcement who is going to offer the first prayer, because the church is essentially built around a small group of lay leaders. Since the preacher is a once-a-month and revival-week man, the deacons and elder sisters of the church carry on the active religious functions. Each regular Baptist preacher has at least four churches that are his pastorates.

"This morning, our heavenly Father, we bow our humble heads in prayer, thanking you for watching over us for the seven long days and nights of the last week. We know you are watching over us, heavenly Father, because we heard your voice in our trying hours. We felt you wipe the sweat from our fevered brow and we felt your loving arm around us when we were in pain. Lord, we know you protect us when we are in trouble. Lord, Lord, Lord, you know we are your humble children. . . . Oh Lord, now when we come to the end of our journey and we face that great getting-up morning, let us enter into your kingdom, we pray in Jesus' name, Amen." Throughout the prayer the whole congregation is totally involved; there are moans, shouts, amens, and "calling on the Lord's name." Then the chorus will rise and sing. There is nothing like a good Baptist chorus made up of five- to seventy-five year olds. "I ain't goin' let nobody turn me round. I'm gonna keep on a-walkin', keep on a-talkin', goin' up to the promised land."

In the middle of one of the soul-stirring songs the preacher walks in and takes his seat. This event, always timed precisely by the most successful preachers, stirs a sensation in the congregation that is felt by all, and the sister singing the lead in the song strikes her best form at this point. After a few more songs and a couple more prayers, the preacher takes his text, which is certain to deal with one of the bigger names in the Bible, or a well-known event or Bible story. Most of the preachers are illiterate or semi-illiterate and the sermons are preached from memory. Thumbing through the Bible is strictly a ceremonial act, even for the literate preachers. Furthermore, a preacher is not judged by his message but by his performance. The preacher snorts, yells, shouts, begs and pleads, howls, jumps around, and no matter how cold it may be, he had better work up a good sweat; if he reaches his climax and a sister has not gotten "happy," he will probably have to start looking for a new church. The height of a Baptist preacher's glory is for so many sisters to get "happy" that the ushers can't hold them all down.

Why have I emphasized the importance of the Baptist Church? In the United States, and particularly in Mississippi, the great majority of Negroes wrap their troubles up in the Baptist-style package and send it to the Lord. Even the ones who denounce this type of religious activity partake of this soul-cleansing more than one would imagine. Why this is so I do not claim to know, perhaps no one knows but God. On the other hand, I know many reasons why the Baptist Church dominates Negro life. The Negro church is the soul of the Negro people. The Negro Baptist Church, and those churches styled after it, is the possession of each individual member of that particular church. It is his only reality of Freedom.

Why don't the Negro Baptist churches unite? Why doesn't the preacher have one large church, instead of looking for four small ones? The Negro's basic social and human need for personal and private freedom and self-assertion has cried out for a place of expression more loudly than his need for public freedom and recognition. Who pays the Negro any attention under ordinary circumstances? He has to accept degradation in every form just to work for the white man and, make no mistake, a white boss is no more unsympathetic than a Negro who has risen to the position of boss under the vicious system of "White Supremacy." If a poor Negro is sick, so what? So are many others. Who cares about him personally or about his individual rights? He is a nobody in his job. Even when he goes home at night his wife may not be of any comfort to him because she too has slaved all day in somebody's kitchen or over somebody's hoe; his children are brokenhearted because he can offer them only a beginning to life and little else. But when he goes to church—his church, when he prays to God—his God, when he testifies to the true faith, he is "somebody." Everybody gives him the floor, he does not have to be self-conscious of his dress, ashamed of his speech; he does not even have to worry too much about saying something that will cause the walls of oppression to close in on him. He is somebody at this moment. He is free. He has individuality; he is not just another Negro. He is his own somebody. Anyone who thinks that he is going to give up this chance of being identifiable to himself is foolish.

*Other Negro Churches.* Another important category of churches with a wide following among the Mississippi Negro masses is the "Spiritualistic Church." I have never been able to make a clear distinction between them and the regular Baptists, except for the two or three forms of worship which they practice that the Baptists frown upon, such as dancing in church, the playing of musical instruments, and the position of women in the church organization. One notable group in the mainstream of Negro religious life which is found in most states, but not in Mississippi, is the prophet-type church—those of Father Divine, Daddy Grace, and Prophet Jones, for example. The Islamic faith is practically unknown in Mississippi.

## The Presidential Election of 1960

The presidential election, which took place within three months after I returned to begin my war, played a dominant role in my strategy. To me, it is a tragic coincidence that John F. Kennedy's years as President correspond almost identically with my three years in Mississippi.

The most significant aspect about the election was to be found in the parties and not in the candidates, although as individuals they were very important. Because of the growing pressure against the principles of racial superiority, both at home and in the former colonial empires in Asia and Africa, the United States, for the first time since Reconstruction, was forced to deal with the question of "White Supremacy." This problem had been a major one since World War II, but not until 1960 did it reach the point where the whole political machinery of the nation was involved. Both major parties had strong civil rights planks in their party platforms. Of course, it was generally believed that the Democratic Party had promised the most to the second-class citizens. Certainly there could be no doubt that Candidate Kennedy was more forthright in his acknowledged commitment to work for the equality of Negro citizens.

*My Debate with Gardner.* The mandate for change was having its effect on the traditional cautiousness of the administration and faculty of Jackson State College. To the surprise of almost everyone, the administration had publicly committed itself to the principle that all citizens should have the vote, including Negro college professors in Mississippi. The president of the school had urged all his faculty and staff to register, although most did not accept the challenge. To my astonishment, in his welcoming address to the students for the new term, he had even suggested that they form a political club. There was also a voter registration drive by the Student Government Association—the most militant ever elected in the history of the school—with the backing of a substantial number of the instructors.

Out of this activity came the idea of a debate on the civil rights planks of the parties. All the students were willing to debate on the Republican side; no one at Jackson State College was willing to exalt the virtues of the Democratic Party. This is not surprising when one remembers that all the Mississippi senators and congressmen were members of this party, and that until 1960 the Democratic Party had done nothing to indicate to the Mississippi Negro that it was not indeed the party of Senator Eastland. It was during the Eisenhower–Republican Administration that many of the things that the Negro most cherished had become a reality—the 1954 Supreme Court decision, the 1957 use of troops in Arkansas, and the 1959 integration of the University of Georgia.

Beverly (Doc) Gardner, a senior history and political science major, past president of the Student Government Association, and a philosophy classmate of mine, was the standard bearer for the campus Republican group. Since he had found no one who was willing to speak for the Democrats, he asked me if I would. I suppose my first few weeks on campus had placed me in another camp as far as the Gardner faction was concerned. I had not been conscious at the time of how much friction I was managing to create. I had already frustrated three power takeovers of leading student positions by a traditional clique made up of the members of one fraternity and a sister sorority, by simply demanding that proper parliamentary procedures be used in nominating and electing officers, instead of what I used to call the Baptist Church method, which goes something like this:

*First speaker:* Mr. Chairman, I nominate Willie Tucker as president of the money spending committee for all student activities.
*Second speaker:* Mr. Chairman, I move that the nominations be closed.
*Third speaker:* I second the motion.
*Chairman:* It has been moved and "properly" seconded that the nominations be closed with the nomination of Willie Tucker. . . . Question ready to vote. All in favor say aye. . . . Opposed, no. Motion carried. Since Willie Tucker is the sole candidate in nomination he is unanimously elected president of the money spending committee. Meeting adjourned.

The debate was marked by careful planning and wide publicity. I am sure that there were more high administration officials and faculty members present at this affair than at any other similar event during my ten terms at the school. Because I was the only student willing to speak for the Democrats, the original plan for two opposing teams was replaced by a debate between Gardner and me, with a three-man panel to ask us questions after the debate. Enthusiasm was so high that the audience was permitted to pose a few questions.

The day after the debate a model election for President was held on campus. It was perhaps more hotly contested than the real election in Mississippi, because a power struggle just as important to the future of the state was in the balance. I had one powerful group as allies, if only because I represented a convenient point of leverage to them. The new president of the Student Government Association was a junior history and political science major. It is interesting to note that although the history and political science curriculum was just beginning its fourth year, and its students numbered less than twenty, they had taken over the leadership of the student body. Walter Williams, the new president, was a militant orator in direct contrast to the moderate Gardner, who still seemed to overshadow him on campus. Williams was determined not to stand in anyone's shadow, especially Gardner's. He suspected that if the Gardner group controlled the counting of the ballots the Republicans would win, and he therefore insisted that the Student Government Association be responsible for making sure that the ballots were cast and counted properly.

On election day I remember one lady professor who stood out front as the students went into the hall to cast their ballots and urged her students to vote Republican and not to "embarrass" her by permitting a Democratic victory. When the final vote tally came in from the more than seven hundred voting students (over half of the student body), the Democratic candidate had won by a mere thirteen-vote margin. But Walter Williams had won.

Perhaps I had not won anything, but I now had the right to speak on certain matters among my fellow students, and this right is respected in my home state. I was now required to be active in the social science extracurricular activities. And as a result I acquired the experience in organization and coordination which I was called upon to use so often in the future. I helped to form a number of new campus organizations. One of the most important was the first debating society in a state-supported Mississippi Negro college. This Debaters Club actually became the nucleus around which most of my activities were centered during my three years in Mississippi.

*Nixon in Mississippi.* Although Senator Kennedy had been considered an underdog throughout the election, the suddent decision of Vice President Nixon to come to Jackson on September 24 was a clear indication that his group was scrambling for votes, even including those of the "White Supremacists" in Mississippi. This was the first occasion in a long time that either a Vice President or a candidate for President had come to Mississippi. The state showed its true hospitality. Politics was "white folks' business," and the Negroes thoroughly acknowledged this principle on Nixon's day there.

I went out to the airport to see the show. It was the largest crowd that I had ever seen at the airport. Nixon emerged from his plane and made a short airport address. I could not hear one word. I am not at all certain of the reason; whether it was because of inadequate sound equipment or an intentional malfunctioning. His long caravan headed for the governor's mansion where a platform had been set up on the lawn. By the time I arrived, the crowd, even larger than the one at the airport, was already there as well as their speaker. After a short ceremony, the Vice President took the stand and for the first few minutes said what amounted to exactly nothing. His curiosity-dominated audience was hardly any more clear in its responses, which almost amounted to none. His advisers managed to whisper in the candidate's ear. Mr. Nixon now spoke on the subjects of "Mississippi Beauty Queens" (Mississippi had just had two successful candidates for Miss America in a row) and the Mississippi football team (the "Ole Miss Rebels" was a top team in the country), and this time he drew large ovations and wild cheers from the crowd. He had learned, probably too late—because unpledged electors won and cast the state's electoral votes for South Carolina's Senator Strom Thurmond—that in Mississippi if one aspires to political office the least acceptable subject for a campaign speech is politics. Although his ill-advised trip to Mississippi did not help Nixon, he can be credited with giving the Republican movement in that state a tremendous boost.

*Democratic Campaign Promises.* The campaign stirred up energy that had lain dormant among the Negroes for over sixty years. The Negro began to talk openly about rights and privileges and about social, educational, economic, and political problems to a degree unequaled in the memory of any living Mississippian.

I remember an incident that occurred in early September at a joint called "Charlie Boy's." One Saturday night I had gone there with some of my new golfing partners. The place was full and "the good times were rolling," until I started a conversation about Negroes' voting in Mississippi. At the table where I was sitting were some nine or ten persons. Not only did they leave my table but in no time the whole place was nearly deserted. One of the golfing partners felt it his duty to warn me of the danger of such talk, "Man, you don't know which one of these niggers is a white man's nigger. They'll go back and tell everything you said. You have to be careful who you talk like that to around here." Two months later this same individual was shouting from street corners that the Negro was going to vote in Mississippi, and the fact that a policeman was within hearing distance made no difference to him in stating his position.

This radical change in attitude and opinion confirmed my belief that the old adage about the great length of time required to effect the necessary changes in the status quo is invalid. Just as suddenly as we went to bed one night afraid to talk and woke up the next morning unafraid and talking, we will go to bed one night soon in Mississippi politically insignificant and wake up the next morning politically powerful. The change cannot be gradual, it must essentially be quick and drastic.

## Civil Rights Groups and the College

The civil rights groups had been trying to form campus organizations among the students, but their efforts were never completely successful during my three years in Mississippi. Because his successor was still unknown off campus, Gardner, the former student body president, was the logical person for outsiders to contact regarding civil rights matters. When he received an invitation to attend a CORE meeting in New Orleans, he was undecided whether or not to accept. He came to me to discuss the invitation and was surprised that I had never heard of the organization. He was further amazed at my basic ignorance of the NAACP. To me, its only significance could be found in the name of Thurgood Marshall and the 1954 Supreme Court decision. In the military these organizations were completely eclipsed by the Armed Forces Integration Program and simply did not have relevance to the average G.I.

Gardner decided to go to the CORE meeting "quietly." He expressed great admiration and respect for Medgar Evers, the NAACP field secretary, whom he had come to know during the years Mr. Evers had unsuccessfully attempted to organize a campus chapter. At the same time, however, it seemed that he had not been too impressed by the NAACP. When he returned from New Orleans, he arranged my first meeting with Medgar Evers.

## The Shaping of My Thinking

The first two months that I spent at Jackson State College were very important in the development of my ideas. It is hard to adapt raw ideas, hopes, and aspirations to the realities of life and circumstances. For eight or ten years I had studied the prospects of breaking the system of "White Supremacy" and had devised plans to accomplish this mission. After leaving Mississippi at the age of sixteen, I had not spent more than two weeks at a time there until I returned in August 1960. Consequently, I could not know the full meaning of the life of a Negro in Mississippi.

My philosophy course during the first quarter in particular helped me to focus my thinking and gave me an opportunity to write out my thoughts and goals. I recall two papers that I wrote for this class that first term. The main purpose in recounting this is to indicate how ideas are shaped into usable form. I have reread the first paper many times and frankly I don't know exactly what I wanted to say. I believe that my uncertainty and frustration were due to the cultural shock that I experienced as a result of leaving the relatively integrated military life and returning to totally segregated Mississippi.

The philosophy instructor came to class the very first day and gave us an assignment to write a paper on "What I Believe." The conclusion of my paper expressed my uncertainty:

I hope by the end of this study I will have confirmed, disproved, or replaced some of my beliefs. But I must add that I am going to be hard to convince that anyone knows the exact philosophy that I should believe. Evidently no one knows the right approach for me and my people to use in our struggle, because to this time no one has led us from our miserable position.

Two months later the last required paper was entitled "My Philosophy of Life," and the summary of my thoughts on political action was as follows:

Why are men afraid to speak in a society whose very existence is based on freedom of expression? Why are men afraid to meet when the law says that freedom of assembly is an undeniable right? Why do men call good bad and right wrong, when they know its true nature? Is this freedom? My answer is NO.

Negroes in Mississippi talk about their constitutional rights. . . . They complain that the law failed to dispense justice in a lynching case. The fact is that every facility of the law did operate to the purpose for which it was established: To protect the white man and to provide conditions under which he could control everything around him, including the black man. This white man took the facilities at his disposal and made them work for his benefit. He intends to preserve all that he has in his favor and to add more, if possible.

We have just had an election. Negroes keep talking about what President Kennedy is going to do for the Negro. No one seems to care what Barnett has already done to the Negro. We talk about the new administration that is going to give us more voting privileges. The state of Mississippi has just put into its laws new restrictions on voting. Unless WE do something ourselves nothing of value will be done.

Three days after the paper was completed I wrote a letter to the students and faculty at Jackson State College, suggesting the organization of a debating group on campus. And three weeks later the Jackson State Debaters Club had been organized and its temporary officers selected.

# 3

*

## The Application to the University of Mississippi
### January-May 1961

B Y THE time I was in high school whenever anyone asked me what I wanted to be or what I wanted to do, I would reply: "I want to be a man, run for governor of the state of Mississippi, and get a degree from the University of Mississippi, in reverse order." I would then explain that by "to be a man" I meant in contrast to being a Negro man or a colored man. The stress in "run for governor" should be placed on "run." I never wanted to be elected, I simply wanted to run and get the vote of every Negro in Mississippi. With this unity the Negro could name the governor. To "get a degree from the University of Mississippi" was a necessary prerequisite to the other two ambitions. This three-point schedule served many purposes. It gave me a psychological sense of continuity. And it gave the more cautious Negro an opportunity to express himself on the race issue. He could treat it as a joke, and could then jokingly speak his sober mind.

### The Decision to Apply

By January 1961 the group of intellectuals at Jackson State College of which I was a part were ready to assert themselves. The first quarter was over and we were well into the second term. The hard core of the group, the "In Group" (ten or twelve of my closest associates), had the highest academic record on the campus. They were disciplined schemers of the highest caliber who were capable of delivering by hand subversive pamphlets (only by Mississippi standards) to the six colleges, including two white, nine high schools in five different cities, the Citizens Council office, the sheriff's office, Jackson police headquarters, the homes of several racist leaders and their lackeys, the state capitol building, and the governor's mansion, all within a half hour and not one was ever caught. My closest call came when I was stopped by a red light after making a run to the governor's mansion or the state capitol, I don't remember which, and we were being pursued by a security guard. We overran the light and outran the police. There is little reason for me to doubt that this group kept me thinking of definite action. I imagine that at some time in the month preceding the decision to apply every possible course of action had been explored by the group. I can still hear one of the members (Ruby McGee) asking, "But J., what can we do?" or "What are we going to do?" or "Well, when are we going to do something?"

*The Election of President Kennedy.* I was firmly convinced that only a power struggle between the state and the federal government could make it possible for me or anyone else to successfully go through the necessary procedures to gain admission to the University of Mississippi. I was also sure that only the recognition of the authority of the federal government would insure a successful completion of a course of study once admitted to the university. The election of President Kennedy provided the proper atmosphere for the development of such a situation. The strongest point in our favor was the civil rights platform which Kennedy had insisted upon at the Democratic convention. Since the election was one of the closest in the history of the United States and the Negro vote had been widely reported as being the decisive factor, the new Democratic administration was on the spot and would be forced to act if put under pressure. The Negro was determined to get his rights of citizenship, while the Republicans were sure to shout hypocrisy if the Democrats did not live up to their promises.

An important consideration for the new administration would be the Mississippi political situation. Elected to office the year before the national election, Governor Barnett had taken an unprecedentedly firm stand for the perpetuation of the system of "White Supremacy." In addition, the so-called unpledged (Democratic) electors had won in 1960, and Mississippi was the only state that did not cast a single vote for either of the major party candidates. It had not been a landslide victory for the Barnett forces, however; the loyal Democrats, led by former Governor James P. Coleman, had cast a respectable number of votes for President Kennedy. Certainly it was logical to count on the loyal Democrats, with luck and help, to recapture the state in the next election. This split in the Democratic ranks made it difficult for the die-hard "White Supremacists" to develop unquestioned solidarity on the race question. A substantial segment of the white population would be amenable to a conciliatory position.

*The Pressure for Action.* The new spirit that had swept Mississippi in the three months or so before the end of January cannot be overrated. The fact that I could hear talk and whispers and even loud voices among the multitude of the Negroes was significant. Voter registration groups that had been dormant since the shotgun slaying of Reverend Lee in 1955 again raised their voices—although a bit weakly. Children talked about "Freedom" on the streets and in the classrooms. Even the country preachers and the conservative schoolteachers would put in a word if they could find a way to camouflage it.

## My Reservations

There had been an element of uncertainty about the course to be followed in the pursuit of my destiny. The great decision was whether to choose an academic or an economic road, and I had always leaned toward the latter. Education and training could only be aids in the accomplishment of my mission. It was my belief that anything I could do with an education I could basically do without it. Furthermore, the master plan called for the establishment of a solid economic base as a necessary preparation for the all-out offensive against the evils of human inequality. Although my savings had been reduced considerably when I bought my old home place less than a year before, the idea of starting a business enterprise was still very much alive.

The decision to apply for admission to the university was based primarily on tactical considerations. But if only academic versus economic factors are considered, I would have to conclude that the decision was an economic one. When I investigated all areas of business possibilities, I learned that there were limitations inherent in the system of "White Supremacy" that would always keep the Negro from going beyond a certain arbitrary level in the economic structure that paralleled the system. Before I could engage in business at the level that I desired, the system would have to be broken. Within the limits allotted to the Negro I had no bounds save my own personal capacity, and theoretically I was convinced that a capable and aggressive Negro could rise to the top—as far as a Negro could go —in a very short period of time.

An experience that I had during the few weeks preceding my decision to apply greatly affected my thinking. A district manager for one of the leading oil companies in Jackson had heard about my interest in business and was anxious to talk to me about a gas station in one of the all-Negro areas in which his leading rival had a new thriving station. The meeting was arranged.

He was a top business executive and he knew how to be courteous in the business manner. I am sure that he would serve the company just as effectively dealing with Negroes in New York as in Mississippi and his personal attitude toward Negroes could have been favorably compared with that of whites anywhere in the United States. He enthusiastically introduced himself as "Mr. So-and-so" and in an extremely cordial manner began to talk. After a few minutes he asked, "What is your name?" (He already knew.) I told him Meredith. A minute or two later he asked, "Now, what did you say your name was?" I started to say Meredith, but he cut in to say no, he meant my first name. He still remained friendly and unruffled as I told him my initials. Actually I have no given name and it was only after the Mississippi crisis that I became widely known as James, but initials are also awkward for a white man to use when referring to a Negro in Mississippi; therefore our negotiations were doomed to failure.

This experience only emphasized the inherent checks imposed upon the Negro businessman under the system of "White Supremacy." An insurance company in Mississippi, in order to protect itself, must necessarily charge the Negro more for the same coverage because in the event of a claim, even when adjusted fairly under the laws of the system, they would essentially favor the white party to the claim. If, for instance, the delivery van of a Negro business hit two pedestrians, one white and one Negro, and broke each one's little finger, under the rules of "White Supremacy," it would mean awarding one thousand dollars to the white and one hundred dollars to the Negro. I considered it unfair and unacceptable for a Negro to have to attempt to engage in business under these conditions.

*The Application*

President John F. Kennedy was inaugurated on January 20, 1961. The next day I sent my first letter to the University of Mississippi:

REGISTRAR
UNIVERSITY OF MISSISSIPPI
UNIVERSITY, MISSISSIPPI

Dear Sir,
Please send me an application for admission to your school. Also, I would like to have a copy of your catalog and any other information that might be helpful to me.
Thank you.

Sincerely,<br>J H MEREDITH

The Registrar sent the application forms on January 26, 1961:

Dear Mr. Meredith:
We are very pleased to know of your interest in becoming a member of our student body. The enclosed forms and instructions will enable you to file a formal application for admission. A copy of our General Information Bulletin, mailed separately, will provide you with detailed information.
Should you desire additional information or if we can be of further help to you in making your enrollment plans, please let us know.

Sincerely yours,<br>Robert B. Ellis<br>Registrar

I wrote to the three universities (University of Maryland, Washburn University, and the University of Kansas) that I had previously attended to send my transcripts to the University of Mississippi. I explained to them the necessity of sending the records immediately: "I plan to enroll for the second semester beginning 6 February 1961 at the University of Mississippi and will need my transcript forwarded as soon as possible."

In the case of Jackson State College, which was controlled by the same college board as the University of Mississippi, I was more cautious because I knew there was a chance of foul play. I sent my letter to the college by registered mail and said nothing about plans to enroll at the university.

29 January 1961

REGISTRAR
JACKSON STATE COLLEGE
JACKSON, MISSISSIPPI

Dear Sir:

Please forward a copy of my transcript of work completed at your school to the Office of the Registrar, University of Mississippi, University, Mississippi. Please forward as soon as possible and notify me when this has been accomplished.

Thank you.

Sincerely,

J H MEREDITH

*Letter to the Legal Defense Fund.* On January 29, 1961, after I had received the application forms from the University of Mississippi, I went to see Medgar Evers, who was the first person, outside of the In Group, to learn of my intentions to enroll. He suggested that I write to Thurgood Marshall, the director of the NAACP Legal Defense Fund. Mr. Evers was keenly aware of a restriction that forbade him to become directly involved in any relationship between a client and the Legal Defense Fund because of some tax law regarding the nature of the NAACP. The Fund was tax exempt, but the NAACP was not. The NAACP, of which Mr. Evers was a national staff member, as well as field secretary for Mississippi, had its own legal staff. However, he very wisely elected to steer me to the more experienced Legal Defense Fund. He later told me that he had come under heavy fire from his superiors for bypassing them in this instance. But he knew what he was doing. I sent the following letter to Mr. Marshall:

January 29th, 1961

Mr. Thurgood Marshall
Legal Defense and Educational Fund
10 COLUMBUS CIRCLE
NEW YORK, NEW YORK

Dear Sir:

I am submitting an application for admission to the University of Mississippi. I am seeking entrance for the second semester which begins the 6th of February, 1961. I anticipate encountering some type of difficulty with the various agencies here in the state which are against my gaining entrance in the school. I discussed this matter with Mr. Evers, the Mississippi Field Secretary for the NAACP, and he suggested that I contact you and request legal assistance from your organization in the event it is needed for I am not financially able to fight a legal battle against the state of Mississippi. I hope your decision on this request will be favorable. Below is a brief history of my background which might help you in reaching a decision.

I am a native Mississippian. All of my elementary and secondary education was received in this state, except my last year of high school, which was completed in Florida. I spent nine years in the United States Air Force (1951-60), all of which were honorable. I have always been a "conscientious objector" to my "oppressed status" as long as I can remember. My long-cherished ambition has been to break the monopoly on rights and privileges held by the whites of the state of Mississippi.

My academic qualifications, I believe, are adequate. While in the Air Force, I successfully completed courses at four different schools conducting night classes. As an example, I completed 34 semester hours of work with the University of Maryland's Overseas Program. Of the twelve courses completed I made three A's and nine B's. I am presently enrolled at Jackson State College, here in Jackson. I have completed one quarter of work and I am now enrolled in a second quarter at Jackson. For the work completed, I received one A, three B's, and one C.

Finally, I am making this move in what I consider the interest of and for the benefit of: (1) my country, (2) my race, (3) my family, and (4) myself. I am familiar with the probable difficulties involved in such a move as I am undertaking and I am fully prepared to pursue it all the way to a degree from the University of Mississippi.

Sincerely yours,

J H MEREDITH

Evers was aware that in general I was not very impressed with the ability of the NAACP to deal with the Mississippi situation. Not one of my fellow students had ever actually worked with the NAACP during the three years that I was in Mississippi. It was not that we distrusted the intentions of the NAACP leaders or their personal ability or integrity—there is no American for whom I have greater respect than Medgar Evers, it was simply that we were never able to see how the organization could command the needed following among Mississippians to seriously attack the system of "White Supremacy."

In a few days I had a message from Marshall. He wanted further information. When I went to see Evers, he thought we should call Marshall but not from his office. That evening I went to Evers' home and he placed the call. He stayed on the phone in his kitchen, and I went into one of the bedrooms to use the extension. My conversation was very brief. Marshall wanted some documents to prove that I was legitimate. I said that I had included everything in my letter to him over "my signature," all courses completed and grades received, military records, including two honorable discharges and five good conduct medals. The voice on the other end indicated that he might still question the truth of my letter, and I simply hung up the telephone and left the room. I had never allowed anyone to question my integrity in any way, and as far as I was concerned the case was closed. Other alternatives would have to be pursued. Evers tried in vain to get me to talk to Marshall again.

I must give sole credit to Medgar Evers, his expert knowledge of human nature and his ability to deal with people, for the case moving beyond this point. He was aware of the great apprehensions that I, as well as the In Group, had. We had discussed this matter at great length. The request that Marshall was making for documents was, of course, in keeping with good legal practices, but at the time it seemed only to confirm our suspicions. Finally, after much consideration I agreed to tell Mr. Evers where to write to secure the needed documents, which he did and forwarded them to Mr. Marshall. Later in the year we expressed much concern over the speculation that Marshall was to be appointed to a federal judgeship, and we explored the possibility that some deal could have been made between the new Democratic administration and the NAACP. We could not understand this unprecedented possibility, and we felt that the best brains were needed in the field of battle.

Now the process of trying to gain admission to the University of Mississippi began. The application was officially filed on January 31, 1961. The following letter accompanied the application:

OFFICE OF THE REGISTRAR
THE UNIVERSITY OF MISSISSIPPI
DIVISION OF STUDENT PERSONNEL
UNIVERSITY, MISSISSIPPI

Dear Mr. Robert B. Ellis:

I am very pleased with your letter that accompanied the application forms you recently sent to me. I sincerely hope that your attitude toward me as a potential member of your student body reflects the attitude of the school, and that it will not change upon learning that I am not a white applicant.

I am an American—Mississippi—Negro citizen. With all of the presently occurring events regarding changes in our old educational system taking place in our country in this new age, I feel certain that this application does not come as a surprise to you. I certainly hope that this matter will be handled in a manner that will be complimentary to the University and the state of Mississippi. Of course, I am the one that will, no doubt, suffer the greatest consequences of this event, therefore, I am very hopeful that the complications will be as few as possible.

I will not be able to furnish you with the names of six University Alumni because I am a Negro and all graduates of the school are white. Further, I do not know any graduate personally. However, as a substitute for this requirement, I am submitting certificates regarding my moral character from Negro citizens of my state. Except for this requirement, my application is complete. All colleges previously attended have been contacted and my transcripts should already be in your office or on the way. I am requesting that immediate action be taken on my application and that I be notified of its status, as registration begins on February 6, 1961, and I am hoping to enroll at this time.

Thank you very much.

Very hopefully yours,<br>
JAMES H MEREDITH<br>
Applicant

Four days later I received this telegram:

Western Union Telegram                    Dated: Feb 4, 1961, 2:05 PM
J H MEREDITH
FOR YOUR INFORMATION AND GUIDANCE IT HAS BEEN FOUND NECESSARY TO DISCONTINUE CONSIDERATION OF ALL APPLICATIONS FOR ADMISSION OR REGISTRATION FOR THE SECOND SEMESTER WHICH WERE RECEIVED AFTER JANUARY 25 1961. YOUR APPLICATION WAS RECEIVED SUBSEQUENT TO SUCH DATE AND THUS WE MUST ADVISE YOU NOT TO APPEAR FOR REGISTRATION.

ROBERT B ELLIS REGISTRAR

Meanwhile, no attempt was made to hold up my transcript at Jackson State College:

February 6, 1961

Dear Mr. Ellis:

The transcript for James H. Meredith is forwarded to your office at his request. This transcript shows courses he is pursuing for the Winter Quarter.

Very truly yours,<br>
Lionel B. Fraser<br>
Acting Registrar

cc: Mr. James H. Meredith

Two days after I filed my application for admission to the university I attended a social science senior lecture on the Negroes' rights at Tougaloo College. My history professor at Jackson State College introduced me to William Higgs, the speaker, and arranged for a short private talk with him after his lecture.

*The Letter to the Justice Department.* William Higgs had recently returned to Mississippi after graduating from Harvard Law School and had become very active in the civil rights movement in the state. He had filed the case against the Mississippi Sovereignty Commission for giving money to the white Citizens Council.

He had obtained an office in the Barnett (Governor Barnett's) Building, located across the street from the governor's mansion in the main downtown area of Jackson. It was not enough for Bill Higgs, who had become the chief gadfly to the white Citizens Council and the segregationists in Mississippi, just to have an office in the Barnett Building, he had also hired a Negro secretary. Higgs had asked me to come to his office. The day that I visited him was the first day that his Negro secretary had come to work. Although there were some difficulties when she arrived, I don't believe they were very serious at first. By the time I came in the afternoon, however, the affair was over and the Negro secretary was gone for good.

Higgs told me that he had been in communication with the Assistant Attorney General of the United States, Burke Marshall. Marshall knew that I was coming to his office and was expecting us to call him. Higgs placed the call, and the two of us talked to the Assistant Attorney General for some time. The only thing that I particularly recall about this conversation was that Marshall indicated that he and the Civil Rights Division were very interested in my efforts to gain admission to the University of Mississippi and were willing to offer me any and all assistance that they could.

The next day Higgs told me that the Justice Department wanted to know more about me and my plans. He would not identify the person or persons and asked me simply to address a letter to the Justice Department and give it to him to send on. One week after the application was filed this letter was sent:

February 7, 1961

TO: The United States Justice Department

It is with much regret that I present this information to you concerning myself. Whenever I attempt to reason legically about this matter, it grieves me deeply to realize that an individual, especially an American, the citizen of a free democratic nation, has to clamor with such procedures in order to try to gain just a small amount of his civil and human rights, and even after suffering the embarrassments and personal humiliation of these procedures, there still seems little hope of success. To be in an oppressed situation is not in itself very difficult, but to be in it and realize its unfairness, and then to have one's conscience compel him to try to correct the situation is indeed agonizing and often miserable.

Before going further, I want to state my immediate situation. I have applied for admission to the University of Mississippi. I have not been accepted and I have not been rejected. Delaying tactics are presently being used by the state. This is the important fact and the reason I am writing (one major reason) to you. Other Negro citizens have attempted to exercise their rights of citizenship in the past, but during the period of delay, that is, between the time the action is initiated and the would-be-time of attainment of the goal, the agencies of the state have eliminated the individual concerned. I do not have any desire to be eliminated.

Why do I feel that you will or should be concerned about me? I have no great desire to protect my hide, but I do hope to see the day when the million Negroes that live in the state of Mississippi will have no cause to fear as they fear today. High-ranking officials of this state, including the Lieutenant Governor during the absence of the Governor on his South American trip, have made public statements saying that the law enforcement agencies of this state will not be used to enforce laws as proclaimed by the federal courts. I have no reason to believe that they will protect citizens that seek to bring about such decisions; in fact, I believe that if they are used at all it will be to intimidate such citizens.

America is a great nation. It has led the world in freedom for a long time. I feel that we can and we must continue to lead in this respect. However, I believe that a greater use should be made of the Negro potential. In my state, this is impossible under the present setup. All of the professions (except teaching and preaching), nearly all of the technical fields or trades, and the Commissioned Officers rolls are not open to a Negro born in Mississippi. Instead of the restrictions being lifted, they are now more rigorously enforced. I feel that this is not in the best interest of our country and certainly not in the best interest of the Negro people.

At the present time much is being said by the radio and press about a Negro wanting to go to the University of Mississippi. Much is being made of prior attempts by Negroes to go to "all white" Mississippi schools. They elaborate on the fate of these individuals; for instance, the last one to try is now serving a seven-year prison term on trumped-up charges subsequent to his attempt to go to the school. If this is to be the fate of any individual who seeks to exercise his rights of citizenship, then I certainly believe that this is an undesirable situation.

My background: I was born on a small farm in Attala County, Mississippi, the seventh of thirteen children. I walked to school, over four miles each way, every day for eleven years. Throughout these years, the white school bus passed us each morning. There was no Negro school bus. I never had a teacher during grade and high school with a college degree. But I was fortunate, because I was able to go to school. Each day I passed by one of the largest farms in the county, and there I saw boys my own age and younger working in the fields who to this day cannot even read road signs. I have never known how I could help solve this situation, but I have always felt that I must do my best.

During my last year of high school, which was spent in Florida, I entered an essay contest sponsored by the American Legion, and I was a winner along with two white girls. The title of the essay was "Why I Am Proud To Be An American." My theme was that I was not proud because I was born with as many or more of the desirable things of life as the next man, but because in my country an individual has the opportunity to grow and develop according to his ability and ingenuity and because he is not restricted from progress solely on the basis of race. Basically, I still believe in this possibility.

I served nine years in the United States Air Force. All of this time was spent in the so-called "integrated" service; because of this experience I feel that there is no logical reason to justify denying a law-abiding citizen the rights of full citizenship solely on the basis of race.

What do I want from you? I think that the power and influence of the federal government should be used where necessary to insure compliance with the laws as interpreted by the proper authority. I feel that the federal government can do more in this area if it chooses and I feel that it should choose to do so. In view of the above information I simply ask that the federal agencies use the power and prestige of their positions to insure the full rights of citizenship for our people.

Sincerely,
JAMES H MEREDITH

*The Legal Defense Fund.* On the same day Thurgood Marshall replied to my letter of January 29:

Dear Mr. Meredith:

This will acknowledge your letter of January 29th and also confirm our telephone conversation yesterday. If you will send us immediately the transcripts of your record plus the latest catalog of the University of Mississippi, we will be in a better position of considering your case.

I think it should go without saying that we are vitally interested in what you propose.

Sincerely,
Thurgood Marshall
Director-Counsel

My answer to Marshall's letter was sent the day I received his letter:

February 10, 1961

Dear Mr. Marshall:

Reference to your letter dated February 7, 1961. My school records and the latest catalog of the University of Mississippi have been forwarded to you under separate cover. For your additional information, I am sending you a copy of all correspondence between the school and myself.

I hope this matter can be solved satisfactorily without too much difficulty; however, I can never let myself forget that we are facing a bitter enemy.

Thank you.

Sincerely,

J H MEREDITH

The next letter I received from the NAACP Legal Defense and Educational Fund was from Mrs. Constance Baker Motley, who had been assigned to the case. Her assignment is the best possible thing that could have happened. I do not believe that anyone else could have survived two and a half years of Mississippi courts.

February 16, 1961

Dear Mr. Meredith:

This replies to your letter of February 10 to Mr. Thurgood Marshall which has been referred to me for consideration and reply. We have received the catalog of the University of Mississippi and your college records which you forwarded under separate cover. We have also received the following correspondence between you and the University of Mississippi: a letter to the registrar requesting an application; letter from Robert B. Ellis, Registrar, dated January 26, 1961 to you; letter dated January 31, 1961 from you to the registrar; telegram dated February 4, 1961 to you from the registrar. We have also received a copy of the formal certificate which you apparently had signed by five responsible citizens of Mississippi. If you have copies of these certificates in full, I wish you would forward copies of same to me.

It appears to me that it is too late to secure your admission for the second semester of the 1960-61 term, since the last day a student could register is the 17th of February 1961. I am, therefore, suggesting that you look forward to enrolling in the September 1961-62 school year. In this connection it seems to me that you should write a letter to the registrar asking him to consider your application for admission to the University of Mississippi a continuing application for admission at the earliest possible time, indicating that you are interested in enrolling in the summer term which apparently begins sometime in June and in the September 1961 term.

I assume from your letter to the registrar of January 31, 1961 that you have already forwarded copies of your transcript to the University. If you have a copy of your application, will you please forward it to me? You should also check with the registrar, in writing, as to whether all of your college credits have been received by him from the various schools which you have attended since you are a transfer student and the catalog requires that the University be advised of all the schools which you have attended. You should make sure that each of these transcripts contains a certificate of honorable dismissal and eligibility for immediate readmission.

As soon as you have heard from the registrar regarding the possibility of your being admitted in the summer term or the September term, I wish you would send me, immediately, a copy of the registrar's letter or, better still, send me the original and keep a copy for your own files. Also, I would like to suggest that you not send any [extraneous] communications, as, you undoubtedly know, it will have to be introduced in the trial of your case if a lawsuit becomes necessary.

As Mr. Marshall has already advised you in his letter to you of February 7, we are very much interested in your proposed admission to the University of Mississippi and we will be happy to give you whatever legal assistance appears to be necessary.

> Sincerely yours,
> Constance Baker Motley
> Assistant Counsel

*The Correspondence Continues.* The letter writing continued after the last day of registration had passed for the semester for which I had sought to enroll.

February 20, 1961

Dear Mr. Robert B. Ellis,

Reference your telegram dated February 4, 1961. I am very disappointed because it was found necessary to discontinue consideration of applications for admission or registration for the second semester prior to the receipt of my application. In view of this fact, I am requesting that you consider my application for admission to your school a continuing application for admission during the summer session beginning June 8, 1961.

Have you received all of the information necessary to make my application for admission a complete one? Did you receive transcripts from the University of Kansas, Washburn University, The University of Maryland, and Jackson State College, complete with a certificate of honorable dismissal or a certificate of good standing?

I am requesting that immediate action be taken on my application and that I be notified of its status. Again, I would like to express my gratitude for the respectable and humane manner in which you are handling this matter and I am hopeful that this procedure will continue.

Thank you very much.

Sincerely yours,
J H MEREDITH
Applicant

February 21, 1961

Dear Mr. Meredith:

Since we were unable to accept your application for admission, I am returning your money order in the amount of $10 which was submitted as a room deposit.

Sincerely yours,
Robert B. Ellis
Registrar

23 February 1961

Dear Mr. Ellis:

Reference your letter of February 21, 1961. I am returning to you the money order in the amount of $10.00 for a room deposit since I have requested that my application be considered for acceptance during the summer session.

Sincerely yours,
J H MEREDITH
Applicant

March 7, 1961

Dear Mrs. Motley:

In reference to your letter of February 16, 1961, your recommended action of requesting that my application be considered a continuing one was taken immediately, as you will note by the attached copy of my letter to the registrar. You requested that I wait for an answer from the registrar and forward it to you, as I suspected there has been no answer. I know that they received my letter because I have the "return receipt" dated February 21, 1961. Please advise me as to what my next move should be. I am anxious to register on June 8th for the first summer session.

I do not have a copy of the application I sent to the University on January 31, 1961. A friend secured an additional application form for me; however, it is not an identical form, but the information required is basically the same. I am forwarding this copy to you.

I do not have additional copies of the signed "moral character" certificates. I did not attempt to get the signatures for you because of two reasons. First, I have been thoroughly warned not to appear in my home town, lest I be arrested for some cause, and so far I have not tested the validity of this warning. Second, the Negroes of Mississippi are fearful (not particularly of this move), and even though I explained fully to each of the individuals what I planned to do and the possible consequences to them for signing the certificates, I hesitate at this time to ask them to sign additional copies unless it is absolutely necessary.

Thank you.

Sincerely yours,<br>
J H MEREDITH

March 14, 1961

Dear Mr. Meredith:

Thank you for your letter of March 7, 1961, enclosing copy of your letter of February 20 to the registrar of the University of Mississippi.

I think you should write a follow-up letter, for the record, requesting substantially the same as you requested in your letter of February 20, i.e., you should request: one, that your application be considered as a continuing one for the summer session and the fall session 1961; two, that you be advised whether all of your transcripts from the various universities which you have attended have been received by the registrar, complete with a certificate of honorable dismissal or a certificate of good standing; three, whether there remains any further prerequisites to admission which you have not yet completed.

We are presently studying the possibilities of bringing legal action in your case. Please keep us advised of all correspondence which you receive or send to the University.

Sincerely yours,<br>
Constance Baker Motley<br>
Assistant Counsel

18 March 1961

Dear Mr. Ellis:

Reference my letter of February 20, 1961, which was received by your office on February 21st, 1961, to date I have not received an answer.

I am requesting that my application be considered as a continuing one for the Summer Session and the Fall Session, 1961; also, please advise me as to whether all of my transcripts from the schools listed on my application have been received, complete with a certificate of honorable dismissal or a certification of good standing; further, advise me whether there remains any further prerequisites to admission which I have not yet completed.

Please acknowledge this letter.

Thank you.

Sincerely yours,<br>
J H MEREDITH<br>
Applicant

20 March 1961

Dear Mrs. Motley:

I was very glad to receive your letter of 14 March 1961. As you can see by the attached letter, I immediately initiated the action suggested by you. I am very pleased to know that you are studying the possibilities of bringing legal action in this case. I certainly hope that the prospects are favorable. Of course, I realize that you are legal experts and that your interest in our problems are probably as great as our own, but on the other hand, prior to my initiating this action, I had some very definite ideas as to the best method of winning this fight. The central theme of these ideas is expediency. I will certainly keep you advised of all developments here; however, I am not expecting the University to answer my correspondence.

Sincerely yours,
J H MEREDITH

The Legal Defense and Educational Fund had taken my case seriously by this time and my reservations about them were fast disappearing. On March 24 I received the following letter:

Dear Mr. Meredith:

Thank you for your letter of March 20. I have just made a study of the bulletin of the University of Mississippi for 1960 which you sent me. The matters contained therein which I think are relevant to your admission to the University are set forth in the enclosed Memorandum. I wish you would study each one of these to see whether you have fully complied with each.

I want you to note, specifically, the requirements on page 82 regarding the recommendations from responsible citizens. You sent me a copy of a certificate which you said you had signed by five responsible citizens and sent to the registrar with your application. I would like to call your attention to the fact that the requirement is that the citizens recommend your admission to the University in addition to certifying to your good character. The form which you sent me indicated that five citizens have certified to your good moral character, but have not recommended your admission to the University. This is an admission requirement which you should take care of immediately.

I should also like to call your attention to page 83 regarding transcripts of credit in the case of transfer students. These official transcripts must "certify honorable dismissal *and* eligibility for immediate readmission." You should take care of this matter immediately and make sure that all of the schools which sent transcripts placed on their transcripts these *two* requirements.

You should also note on page 83 that the registrar, under the direction of the Committee on Admissions, will provide you, as a transfer student, "with an evaluation of the credits acceptable at the University." I think you should write the registrar immediately requesting him to send you this evaluation.

On page 83 it is also pointed out that the Dean of the College or the school to which you are admitted will inform you of the extent to which your credits will apply toward the degree sought. You should also note on page 84 that you can get certain credits for your armed forces service.

I would like to call your attention to page 90 describing "Benefits for Veterans." I would like you to advise me if it is possible for you to transfer to the University of Mississippi and still get G.I. benefits. I think you should check into this matter.

I should like to call your attention to page 100 regarding residences for married students. I note from your papers that you are married and if you intend to apply for an apartment you will have to do so in advance.

Finally, I would like to call your attention to pages 121, 122, and 123 regarding requirements for registration as a resident student at the University. As you know, nonresident students are charged extra fees. It seems to me that the requirement is that you must be in residence for twelve months immediately prior to your registration in the University if you intend to qualify as a resident student or you must have resided in Mississippi for twelve months after you reach the age of twenty-one. Please let me know your status with regard to these requirements. What address did you use as your home (domicile) when you were in the armed forces? This would be relevant.

On page 122 it says the following:

"Requirement of Twelve Months of Residence. No student may be admitted to the University as a resident of Mississippi unless his legal residence, as defined, has been in the State of Mississippi for a continuous period of at least twelve months immediately preceding his admission."

If you gave your Mississippi address as your residence in the army, then it seems to me that under the requirements on page 122 defining "Legal Residence of an Adult" you would qualify.

Please write me soon regarding these matters and study the other matters which I have listed on the enclosed Memorandum.

Sincerely yours,
Constance Baker Motley
Assistant Counsel

P.S. If you do not have a copy of a catalog, please send for another one. It may be that they have a later issue.

26 March 1961

Dear Mrs. Motley:

I received your letter of March 24, 1961. I had to burn a little "midnight oil," but I hope that the reward will be to furnish you with satisfactory answers to your questions.

From the same five Negro citizens that signed the original certificates of good moral character, I obtained letters attesting to my good moral character and recommending that I be admitted to the University. I am enclosing a signed copy of each for your information.

I wrote to each of the schools concerned, regarding my transcripts. (See attached letter.) As you will note by my letter to the registrar, I asked him to send me a copy of my evaluation of credits.

I sent along with my application for admission an application for housing in the men's dormitory, including the required $10.00 deposit. I do not plan to take my family on campus to live during the summer. Whether I take my family on campus to live at a later date will depend on future developments. I checked with the Veterans Administration regarding my G.I. benefits and I can change schools and still get my benefits.

I don't believe that there is any doubt that I am a legal resident of the state of Mississippi. I have not resided in any other state for a year or more, at any time in my life, except for the time I spent in service. I used both Michigan and Mississippi addresses while in service (see attached DD Form 214, items 23 & 33). However, these addresses are for military purposes only, and in no way establish or affect legal residence. Further, I am a registered voter in this state and eligible to vote in all elections.

Thank you.

Sincerely yours,<br>J H MEREDITH

Enclosures:
1. Ltr to registrar
2. Ltrs fr citizens
3. Ltrs to schools
4. DD Form 214


One of the letters of recommendation:

Kosciusko, Mississippi<br>March 26, 1961

REGISTRAR
THE UNIVERSITY OF MISSISSIPPI
UNIVERSITY, MISSISSIPPI

Dear Sir:

I have known J.H. (James Howard) Meredith for at least two years. I certify that he is of good moral character and recommend that he be admitted to the University of Mississippi.

Sincerely yours,<br>HENRY NEWELL

Letters to schools attended (Jackson State College, Washburn University, University of Kansas, and University of Maryland):

March 26, 1961

Dear Sir:

Reference my letter of January 29, 1961, requesting you to forward a copy of my transcript to the University of Mississippi. It is essential that this transcript contain a certificate of "good standing and eligibility for immediate readmission." Please check your records to be sure that such a certificate was included on my transcript sent to the University of Mississippi.

Please advise me as soon as possible.

Sincerely yours,

J H MEREDITH

March 26, 1961

Dear Mr. Ellis:

Reference my application for admission to the University of Mississippi, dated January 31, 1961, my letter of January 31, 1961, my letter of February 20, 1961, and my letter of March 18, 1961.

Please note the Bulletin of the University of Mississippi, General Catalog Issue 1960, page 83, which states that "the Registrar, under the direction of the Committee on Admissions, will provide each transfer student with an evaluation of the credits acceptable to the University." Please send me a copy of my evaluation immediately.

Also, on page 83, it states that "the dean of the college or the school to which the student is admitted will inform the student the extent to which his credits will apply toward the degree sought." If it is appropriate at this time, I would like to be informed on this matter.

Note also, on page 82, under "Admission Requirements," reference my letter of January 31, 1961, which contained as enclosures, five certificates attesting to my good moral character, but did not recommend me for admission to the University of Mississippi. Attached herewith is an additional letter from each of these five persons, certifying my good moral character and recommending me for admissing to the University.

Again I would like to take this occasion to express my sincere hopefulness that my application will be processed in the normal manner and that I be informed of its approval or disapproval. However, realizing that I am not a usual applicant to the University of Mississippi, and that some timely items might need to be considered, I certainly hope that the entire matter will be handled in a manner complimentary to the University of Mississippi.

Thank you and I hope to hear from you soon.

Sincerely  yours,
J H MEREDITH
Applicant

Enclosures:
1. Ltr fr Rev. S.L. Brown
2. Ltr fr Mr. L.L. Keaton
3. Ltr fr Mr. Milton Burt
4. Ltr fr Mr. Henry Newell
5. Ltr fr Mr. Lannie Meredith
    P.S. Send me a 1961 catalog.

April 11, 1961

Dear Mr. Meredith:

Thank you for your letter of March 26th. I assume that you have not heard from the registrar of the University of Mississippi, but I am wondering whether you have received replies from the registrars of the University of Maryland, Jackson State College, the University of Kansas and Washburn University in reply to your letter to each of them dated March 26, 1961.

It is absolutely essential that you comply with all of the requirements with which it is possible for you to comply regarding your admission prior to bringing suit, otherwise, the case could be dismissed on the ground that you have failed to comply with the requirements. I realize that you cannot comply with requirements regarding certification from alumni and you have already so advised the registrar. We have already won a case in Georgia regarding the alumni certificate point. But as to the requirements regarding transcripts and letters from citizens, these requirements must be strictly complied with. This is the reason for my pressing you with regard to these matters. I see that you have gotten proper certification from 5 citizens certifying to your good moral character and recommending your admission to the University. Therefore, the only thing about which I am not sure at this time is whether your transcripts were sent and contained the required information. Please write me immediately regarding this point.

I notice by the Bulletin of the University of Mississippi for 1960, on the inside of the cover, that the catalog is issued nine times a year as follows: 1 in October, 3 in February, 4 in March, and 1 in April. I would like you to write for or secure and mail to me a copy of the April 1961 issue of the Bulletin, as I would need the names of the present members of the Board of Trustees.

If you have heard from the four registrars with regard to your transcripts and they are now in proper order, and if you have not heard from the registrar of the University of Mississippi, you should send a letter to the Dean of the College of Liberal Arts of the University. I have drafted a letter which I am enclosing herewith which you should send to the Dean over your signature.

I will come down to Jackson to discuss the case with you on April 29. By that time you should have heard from the Dean.

Sincerely yours,
Constance Baker Motley
Assistant Counsel

April 12, 1961

Dr. Arthur Beverly Lewis
Dean, COLLEGE OF LIBERAL ARTS
UNIVERSITY OF MISSISSIPPI
OXFORD, MISSISSIPPI

Dear Dr. Lewis:

In January 1961, I obtained an application for admission to the University of Mississippi from Mr. Robert B. Ellis, Registrar of the University and mailed same to him on January 31, 1961.

After my application was received by the Registrar, I received from him a telegram on February 4, 1961, advising me that applications for admission or registration for the Second Semester received after January 25, 1961, were not being considered.

On February 20, 1961, I wrote to Mr. Ellis and advised him that I would like my application to be considered a continuing application for the Summer Session beginning June 8, 1961.

I did not receive a reply from Mr. Ellis and, therefore, on March 18, 1961, I wrote him once again requesting that my application be considered a continuing one for the Summer Session and for the Fall Session of 1961. I have not received a reply to my March 18th letter.

On March 26, 1961, I wrote Mr. Ellis again regarding my application. Again I have not received a reply from Mr. Ellis.

When I forwarded my application to Mr. Ellis on January 31, 1961, I stated in a letter to him and in my application that I am a Negro citizen of Mississippi. Because of my failure to hear from Mr. Ellis since his telegram to me of February 4, 1961, I have concluded that Mr. Ellis has failed to act upon my application solely because of my race and color, especially since I have attempted to comply with all of the admission requirements and have not been advised of any deficiencies with respect to same.

I am, therefore, requesting you to review my case with the Registrar and advise me what admission requirements, if any, I have failed to meet, and to give me some assurance that my race and color are not the basis for my failure to gain admission to the University.

Sincerely  yours,

J H MEREDITH

April 15, 1961

Dear Mrs. Motley:

I received your letter of April 11th. I have not heard from the University of Mississippi. I did receive answers from all of the other schools regarding the good-standing certificate (enclosed) except the University of Maryland, I am writing them again today regarding this matter. However, I did receive notification from the University of Maryland (enclosed) that my transcript had been forwarded to the University of Mississippi, but nothing was said about the certificate in question.

The latest copy of the Bulletin that I was able to secure is the February issue. I have written for the latest issue myself, and I have friends trying to get it for me. I will send it to you, if I can get a copy. In the meantime, I am sending this copy under a separate cover.

I sent the letter to the Dean of the College of Liberal Arts, even though I had not received an answer from my last letter to the University of Maryland. Since they had notified me that the transcript had been sent to the University of Mississippi, plus the fact that the copy sent to Jackson State College earlier, of which you have a copy, did include this statement, I felt that it would be reasonably safe to send the letter to the Dean. Of course, I know that there are no grounds for the University of Maryland to issue a certificate other than one of good standing.

Everyone is looking forward to seeing you in Jackson.

Sincerely,

J H MEREDITH

Enclosures:
1. Card fr U. of Maryland
2. Ltr from Jackson College
3. Ltr fr Univ. of Kansas
4. Ltr fr Washburn Univ.

P.S. It is amazing and perplexing to note that at age 27 Gagarin makes a trip into outer space, while at the same age I am seeking an opportunity to get a public education to which I have been theoretically entitled for nearly a hundred years. Well, at least, by the grace of the [police] dogs, Mississippi got on the map one week before man conquered outer space. [This refers to the first use of dogs against civil rights demonstrators in Jackson, Mississippi, in April 1961; old men, women, and children were bitten by the dogs and clubbed and kicked by the Mississippi police.]

18 April 1961

Dear Mr. Meredith:

Thank you for your letter of April 15, with the enclosures from the several universities. You were correct in sending the letter to the Dean since, as you indicated, you had already had knowledge of the fact that the University of Maryland sent your transcript in proper form.

I will discuss the details of your case with you when I see you in Jackson on the 29th.

Sincerely yours,
Constance Baker Motley
Assistant Counsel

At long last the University of Mississippi wrote its first letter to me since it discovered that I was a Negro (and returned my room deposit).

May 9, 1961

Dear Sir:

I have seen your letter of April 12, 1961, to Dr. Arthur Beverly Lewis, Dean of the College of Liberal Arts. Of course, your application has been received and will receive proper attention.

In connection with your inquiry as to receipt of transcripts of credits from the colleges listed in your application, I have received the transcripts each of which shows a certificate of honorable dismissal or certification of good standing.

As to your request for an evaluation of your offered credits, I believe I should advise you at this preliminary stage that my evaluation of your credits indicates that under the standards of the University of Mississippi the maximum credit which could be allowed is forty-eight (48) semester hours if your application for admission as a transfer student should be approved. By your transcripts you offer a total of ninety (90) semester hours credit.

My evaluation of your credits is not in any way a determination or decision as to whether your application for admission will be approved or disapproved or of its sufficiency.

In view of the foregoing, please advise if you desire your application to be treated as a pending application.

Yours truly,
Robert B. Ellis

May 10, 1961

Dear Mrs. Motley:

The enclosed letter from the University of Mississippi can tell you more than I. The evaluation as indicated is acceptable. Of course, I desire to have my application processed.

I hope that this will give us the proper grounds to seek entrance for the summer session. As you can see, I am not getting credit for the work being done at my present school.

Please advise as to the next step.

Sincerely yours,
J H MEREDITH

May 11, 1961

Dear Mr. Meredith:

Thank you for your letter of May 10 and the letter of May 9 from the Registrar of the University of Mississippi. I am sending you herewith a copy of that letter for your files and I am keeping the original.

In accordance with Mr. Ellis' letter, I think you should advise him immediately that you desire your application to be treated as a pending application for admission to the Summer Term, 1961 or the Fall Term, 1961 and *ask him again to advise you if there is anything further that you should do in order to complete your application.*

Sincerely yours,
Constance Baker Motley
Assistant Counsel

May 15, 1961

Mr. Robert B. Ellis
REGISTRAR

Dear Sir:

I received your letter of May 9, 1961, and I am indeed pleased to know that my application will receive proper attention.

In answer to your question as to whether I desire to have my application treated as a pending application, it is my desire that my application be treated as a pending application for admission to the Summer Session, beginning with the First Term, June 1961; and please advise me if there is anything further that I should do in order to complete my application.

Also, you stated in your letter that your evaluation of my credits was not in any way a determination or decision as to whether my application for admission will be approved or disapproved or of its sufficiency. Of course, at this point, it is imperative that I be positively informed with respect to approval, disapproval, and/or sufficiency of my application, because I am married and will have to make appropriate arrangements for my family in any event. Therefore, I will be pleased to know the status of my application at the earliest possible date.

It certainly would be a grand accomplishment if we could devise a system of education whereby all capable and desirous prospective recipients could receive the desired training without having to suffer the consequences of undesirable concomitant elements.

Thank you.

Yours truly,<br>J H MEREDITH

Enclosure: Letter of Application to the Director of Men's Housing.

May 15, 1961

DIRECTOR OF MEN'S HOUSING
THE UNIVERSITY OF MISSISSIPPI
UNIVERSITY, MISSISSIPPI

Dear Sir:

Please regard this letter as an application for occupancy of one of the University apartments appropriate for my family size. I have a wife and one child—age one (1). I have already on file with your office an application for housing in one of the Men's residence halls. If I am admitted to the University, and it is at a time prior to the availability of an apartment, I would desire dormitory accommodations until an apartment becomes available.

Enclosed is a money order for $25.00 as a security deposit.

Thank you.

Yours truly,<br>J H MEREDITH

May 18, 1961

Dear Mr. Meredith:

Have you received a reply from the registrar to your latest letter advising that you would like your application to be considered as a pending application for the summer term, 1961? If you have not received a reply from him, I suggest that you write him again asking him to please advise you when applications for the summer term will be acted upon as you would like to make plans for attending the institution this summer. As soon as you have heard from the registrar, please let me know.

The registrar's letter to you of May 9th clearly indicates that you are qualified for admission and I see no reason why you should not be admitted this summer.

If you do not hear from the registrar, I suggest that you present yourself for registration on Thursday, June 8, as indicated by the latest catalog, copy of which you sent me.

Sincerely yours,<br>Constance Baker Motley<br>Assistant Counsel

May 21, 1961

Dear Mrs. Motley:

I received your letters of May 11th and May 18th. I complied with the first on May 15th (see enclosed copy). I have prepared an answer or rather a letter to the registrar, however, I will wait until Monday to mail it so that it may be sent by certified mail. (See enclosed copy.)

I have not heard from the registrar; of course, I will let you know as soon as I do. I agree with your suggestion to appear for registration on June 8th, but I will no doubt hear from you again before then.

Thank you.

Yours truly,
J H MEREDITH

May 21, 1961

Mr. Robert B. Ellis
REGISTRAR

Dear Sir:

You wrote me on May 9, 1961, requesting that I inform you whether I still wanted my application considered as pending for admission. I indicated in my reply that I did wish admittance for the First Summer Session, beginning June 8, 1961. To date, I have not received an answer. I assumed by the nature of your request that my application was entirely complete and that I have met all of the pre-registration requirements of the school, and that I am otherwise qualified, and now all I need is a "statement of admission" from you.

Please advise me on this matter, so that I can make plans for attending the University this summer.

If you have already sent such instructions to me, please excuse this letter.

Thank you.

Yours truly,
J H MEREDITH
Applicant

May 23, 1961

Dear Mr. Meredith:

I have your letter of May 21, 1961 and the enclosed copy of the letters of May 15 and May 21 to the registrar and the enclosed copy of the letter of May 15 to the Director of Men's Housing.

Did you write to Wayne University in Detroit asking for a letter indicating your honorable withdrawal from that University? If so, will you please send me all of the return receipts which you have for certified mail to the registrar and the Dean of the College of Liberal Arts. We will need each of these items if it becomes necessary for us to file suit to secure your admission to the summer term, so please forward these immediately.

Sincerely yours,
Constance Baker Motley
Assistant Counsel

P.S. Please call me collect at the number above or at my home, when you hear from the registrar, as the mail takes about two days and every minute now will count.

May 26, 1961

Dear Mrs. Motley:

I am going to Florida today for one week to try to get a little relaxation. However, my wife will contact you immediately if I hear from the registrar, and get in touch with me if necessary.

I am sending the return receipts as requested and other material as shown.

Thank you. I am almost late for my final examination.

Sincerely yours,
J H MEREDITH

May 25, 1961

Dear Mr. Meredith:

I regret to inform you, in answer to your recent letter, that your application for admission must be denied.

The University cannot recognize the transfer of credits from the institution which you are now attending since it is not a member of the Southern Association of Colleges and Secondary Schools. Our policy permits the transfer of credits only from member institutions of regional associations. Furthermore, students may not be accepted by the University from those institutions whose programs are not recognized.

As I am sure you realize, your application does not meet other requirements for admission. Your letters of recommendation are not sufficient for either a resident or a nonresident applicant. I see no need for mentioning any other deficiencies.

Your application file has been closed, and I am enclosing with this letter your money orders for $10.00 and $25.00 which you submitted to me earlier.

Sincerely yours,
Robert B. Ellis
Registrar

# 4

## Strategy to Survive: January-May 1961

HOW to engage in this war without becoming a casualty was of prime importance once the decision had been made to invade the enemy's most sacred and revered stronghold. Some precedents had occurred in recent Mississippi history, while James P. Coleman was governor. Clennon King (a teacher at the Negro Alcorn A. & M. College in Mississippi, who attempted to enroll at the University of Mississippi) had been hustled off the university campus in 1958 and taken to a mental institution and later driven from the state. Clyde Kennard (who tried to gain admission to Mississippi Southern University at Hattiesburg) had been taken from his interview with the president of that university in 1959 to a cell in a Mississippi jail, and then to the penitentiary where he would remain until shortly before his death.

In view of these facts of life in Mississippi, what would be the successful strategy to survive the ordeal? For a long time I had been impressed by a certain maxim which says, "The wise man learns by the mistakes of others, the average man learns by his own, and the fool never learns." King and Kennard must be witnesses to the fact that life is too uncertain in Mississippi for us to risk learning by our own mistakes.

The most obvious similarity in the fate of the Negroes who had challenged Mississippi's system had been their willingness to collaborate with the enemy. There is always that element of trust in the "good faith" of one or of a few of the men who make up the backbone of the system. I would not question the individual integrity per se of, say, the president of Mississippi Southern, but it would make no difference whether he was trustworthy or not, because under the system of "White Supremacy" it is not the individual that counts, only the system. The system always prevails.

Not once during the three years that I was in Mississippi did I have discourse with the enemy without the public as a witness. This included meeting with their "niggers" as well. There were many third- and fourth-person overtures contained in a rumor form. "I heard that Professor So-and-so told Reverend So-and-so that he heard that So-and-so had been told by the Citizens Council or the Sovereignty Commission to tell Meredith such-and-such." One fact that I prize highly, and it confirms my faith in the basic trustworthiness of all my people, is that no Negro ever approached me to make any deals for the "white folks." However, I must admit that I deliberately made myself unapproachable by anyone white or black.

The primary tactics that I chose to use were (1) to act secretly and quickly and (2) to capitalize on public concern and public opinion. The objective was to make myself more valuable alive than dead. This was the strategy that I followed during the entire period.

### Maneuvers to Stay Alive

Contrary to what people might think, the one year that I spent at the University of Mississippi was not nearly as dangerous for me personally as the two years in Mississippi before I was able to gain admission to the school. What people saw on television—the mobs, the violence, the intolerance, the hate, and the indignities that the Negro was the victim of—had gone on for years and years in the same or in a more vile form. The only difference was that the rest of the world was seeing it for the first time. The traditional practice in Mississippi has been to eliminate potential troublemakers before they get a chance to cause trouble. Far more Negroes have been lynched for having a bad or wrong attitude (by Mississippi "White Supremacy" standards) than for committing a particular crime. Whenever a Negro questioned the status quo in Mississippi he just simply disappeared. Knowing this about my home state, I naturally was concerned for my life.

There was much debate about this question of my safety among the people close to me. The majority, which included Medgar Evers, maintained that an armed guard should be posted at my house and that I should never go anywhere alone. They insisted that I always travel with at least two cars and that the one without me should be armed.

I rejected these precautions from the beginning for several reasons. I was of the opinion that the proceedings would be long, and the security measures would only tend to suggest to the opposition that they were obligated to take care of me. I knew that these security measures would only last for a while, because the people keeping watch would soon tire of the extra burden and drop the guard just when it would really be needed. And I was convinced that one should never waste his energy where there is no "clear and present danger." Furthermore, I knew that the very best possible protection against my particular enemy was the enemy himself.

My greatest concern was for the safety of my family and parents. The problem was how to draw attention to myself and keep the focus always on me, and thereby lessen the probability of an assault on my family and parents.

## The Scare Tactics

Fear is the natural reaction to violence and the threat of violence. Although the Negro community was constantly in a state of siege by the white community, the ultimate enforcement of the principles of "White Supremacy" among the Negroes was done indirectly by the whites. The direct aspects were carried out by the Negro community itself. The less frequent manifestations, such as a lynching, served mostly as symbolic acts to impress the Negro community. Usually when the white community wanted someone or something in the Negro community, it simply said, produce whatever it is we want or you will suffer. Although violence is a very definite part of Mississippi life, it is resorted to only occasionally. Some communities go for generations using only the threat of violence, and there has been no need for direct action. In fact, most whites are incapable of committing violence except under certain ritualistic conditions.

*Kosciusko.* The initial reaction to my application to the university was in Kosciusko and followed the time-tested formula for weeding out the attackers of the system. The first step was for the police to go around the Negro neighborhood, asking questions about me and my family. As a rule, this act has been enough to trigger off panic in the Negro community. One of the more intensified methods was to go to the homes of several of my parents' neighbors, often within sight of my parents' home, and pretend to look for them. The idea was to let the social pressure from the community and the neighborhood force the nonconformer to conform. The last resort of the white community, before taking direct action, is to call upon "its Negro leaders" to use their personal influence to bring about conformity.

I was well aware of these tactics and had previously briefed my parents, although they already knew even better than I what was to come. The last resort was to be the burden of the high school principal. It must have been a terribly painful experience for him. He was a member of the church in which I had been baptized, and every Sunday morning he and my mother went to the same church. The "powers-that-be" called on him to give my family what amounted to an ultimatum. The principal went to the home of my parents. The ultimatum was for my parents to tell me to withdraw or face the understood consequences. He suggested that my fate would be death if I continued, and my mother's answer was, "If someone has to die, who is my child more than anyone else's child to die?" The principal left in sorrow.

There was no rest in my father's house that night. About three o'clock in the morning, I heard my doorbell ring. I opened the door and it was not the Ku Klux Klan or the white Citizens Council making a night call. The system had worked to the extent that my ailing father had my sixteen-year-old sister drive to Jackson to pass the news on to me. There they stood: a frustrated and excited father, a bewildered and determined mother, and a nonchalant sister. Many thoughts ran through my mind. Had they been run away from their home? What did this unexpected visit mean?

They came in and my father would not even pull off his hat. He did not intend to linger; he only wanted me to know what was going on. Although he was obviously excited, my father spoke slowly and unemotionally. He told me what had taken place during the last couple of days and asked me to be careful and not to worry about them. He wanted me "to do whatever you think is right" at any cost. My mother was just plain mad at those "scary niggers" in Kosciusko, and my sister appeared ready to take them all on by herself—the white folks and their "niggers." In less than five minutes my father was ready to go, and I knew him well enough that if he was ready to go he was going. Before he left, he cautioned against using the telephone because he was sure that his phone had been tapped. He warned me against what would happen to me if I went to Kosciusko, and he didn't want me to come there.

*Jackson.* The Jackson tactics were different from those used in Kosciusko only in their application and instrumentation. Just one month before I applied for admission to the university, I had moved into what is known as the "Maple Street Project." Actually it was not a housing project at all, instead it was a number of apartment buildings owned by a private corporation. My small two-bedroom apartment, quite adequate and comfortable, was located on the second floor at one end of the building. There was another apartment building on the east, the railroad tracks on the west, a busy through street on the south, and a play area on the north.

It is interesting to observe the effects of separation in Mississippi. The railroad tracks were the dividing line between the white neighborhood and the Negro residential area. The street was called Maple Street on the Negro side, but the name immediately changed to Longino when you crossed the last rail to the white side. (The railroad tracks were, of course, on the Negro side of the dividing line.)

The technique used in Jackson was to set the traditional apparatus in motion so that the Negro community would expel the nonconforming elements from its midst. Ruffians were used instead of the police, however. (They were probably law officials, but they were not in uniform or in a police car.) By the time the stories reached me they had gone through the passing-the-word stage and were highly exaggerated.

I had met the neighbor who first gave me the warning in the Jackson State College recreation hall, where we were strong rivals in the daily card games. After graduating from college, he had taught in a rural school for some time. He had given up teaching to become a redcap in the Illinois Central Railroad depot, not only because he could make more money there but because he could then live in Jackson, his home town. Under one pretext or another he had managed to spend most of the afternoon in my presence, and finally he indicated that he had something extremely important to tell me.

His story was that he had heard that some men had been asking a number of people in the neighborhood which apartment I lived in. Of course, no Negro knew where another lived when suspicious-looking white men were trying to find him. Two days later, he said that he had seen a late-model Cadillac circling around the neighborhood and parking in different places. The next day the same car was parked near his house when he came home around 4:30 in the afternoon. His wife, an elementary school teacher, had been very upset when a white man came to their house shortly after she returned home from school and inquired about my whereabouts.

My friend stated that it was his duty to go see the man. As he approached the big Cadillac, one of the men got out. He described him as a great-big-mean-looking cracker in his middle forties, who stood over six feet tall and weighed two hundred pounds or more. He had a big potbelly, and a big Army .45 was stuck under his belt. The redcap told the man that his wife had said that he was at his house. The cracker said, "Yeah, you that nigger trying to go to Ole Miss?" He said, "No." "Where do that nigger live?" "I don't know." "Well, you tell that nigger we are going to kill him." He then got into the Cadillac and drove off.

Apparently he did not return. His job was finished. He had put fear and apprehension into my neighborhood, and the rest would take care of itself. But the system is breaking down; the Negro community is changing. This technique, however, is still a powerful force in Mississippi.

It is not surprising that the other Negroes did not warn me of the danger, because the whole community was involved in my card-playing friend's action. It had chosen him to deliver the message and he had. When I checked the story in the neighborhood, I learned that there undoubtedly had been a rather rough-looking white man, who drove a late-model Cadillac, asking about me, and he had been seen on at least two different days. Even one of my closest neighbors and friends confirmed the story several months later. I also learned that a systematic watch had been organized by my neighbors to keep my apartment under constant surveillance. Even a car-parking pattern had been designed to hamper would-be vigilantes.

### Provoking the Attention of the Police

One aspect of being subjected to police surveillance in Mississippi is often overlooked. Mississippi cops are very jealous of their prerogatives, and once they have been assigned to do the job of "taking care of a nigger," their prey then becomes their prized possession and they are duty bound to make sure that he does not fall into the hands of others. Police surveillance can serve both as harassment and as protection. Since harassment is a part of the Negroes' way of life in Mississippi, it was not a really significant consideration but the protection aspect was.

To understand its importance, one must remember that it was Mississippi that protected me from January 1961 until September 1962 when the federal government finally entered the case. It must also be remembered that Mississippi needed a "live body" to prove its point, just as much as the federal government and the NAACP did. By 1960 Mississippi was fully prepared for a showdown on the question of integration. The state government had decided to draw the line and retreat not one inch more, and strange as it may seem, the best minds in Mississippi were absolutely convinced that they could win their case before the full judgment of the people, the courts, and the government of the United States. How else could Barnett have become so famous, how else could Johnson have been elected governor of the state, how else could Bill Simmons (Citizens Council) have gained such stature?

Aware of the zeal with which Mississippi cops look after their Negro assignments, I endeavored to make sure that they were kept on my trail. Mississippi society is very legalistic and no injustice is committed against a Negro without some semblance of an excuse (the excuse can be real or imaginary). Where there is no excuse Mississippi creates one, as in the Mississippi Southern University–Clyde Kennard case. I always made it my object to stay near the borderline of the law. I would sometimes look mean or suspicious at the law officers on patrol, or drive too slow (never too fast) if they were behind me on the streets.

My most effective play with the law, and I have all along believed that this saved me from being set up or framed by the police, was that I carried an out-of-county license plate (Attala County in Hinds County) on one of my cars. Technically, I was violating the law, but according to practice I was not, since the law that required the licensing of automobiles in the county of dominant use was not usually enforced in the case of students. I was stopped by the police numerous times for this offense, and each time the charges were dropped. In the process I became fully acquainted with the police headquarters and the sheriff's office, and even the county tax assessor came into the picture for a long conference.

It ended late one night when I was awakened by the continuous ringing of my telephone. I had been summoned to appear in court the following morning. Apparently there had been a meeting of the head men, and one had been appointed to pass the decision on to me. I answered the phone with some apprehension, because only a very few people knew my telephone number and they would not be calling at this hour of the night. The voice of the caller was that of a Mississippi white man who wanted to know if I were James Meredith. I hesitated, what was this? Was it the night that had been expected? My wife was there beside me and my son was in the other bedroom. I told the man that I was James Meredith. He said he was "Mr. So-and-so" and was calling me about the car tag case that was to come up in court tomorrow.

"We looked into this matter further and you just forget about it."

"What about court in the morning?" I asked.

"You just forget it."

"Will I need to go or call to let the people downtown know?"

"No, we have already taken care of that; you can tear up that summons; you just forget it."

Apparently he was right. I did not go to court; I was not stopped again by the Jackson city police; and I never heard any more about the car tag question.

### The All-Night Session

Reports came to me from my intelligence sources at the state capitol that an all-night strategy session was held two or three days after my application had been received by the university. I understand that there were bitter differences among the whites as to the "proper" way to handle this matter. And in spite of the fact that I had been sent the telegram of rejection on February 4, state troopers were still called out to guard the University of Mississippi against an invasion by me.

### Interview with the Press

By now I suppose it was inevitable that I would come more directly into the public picture, since the "Integration of the University of Mississippi case" had already taken the number one place in the state news.

My first interview with the press will perhaps remain one of my most memorable. A few days after I had been rejected for admission I was visited late one evening by a mild-mannered, southern-looking white man. He identified himself as being with the United Press–

International News Service, and asked to talk to me. I invited him to come in and have a seat. Perhaps there was a great deal of caution in my actions and attitude. It was quite apparent to me that the newsman also exercised an extremely high degree of caution. He said that he had information that I was the unknown party who had filed an application to enter the university. Both the university and the state had been going through the pretense that they were keeping my identity a secret. I was well aware that everyone who was involved in the matter knew exactly who I was and where I was.

We talked about the application, and I confirmed that I had applied. We then discussed at some length why I was making an effort to gain admission to the University of Mississippi. The reasons that I gave were that it was the best school in the state and for the future of my son. I queried him as to how he knew my identity and whereabouts, and at that time he answered that "important sources or high officials" had given him the information.

Later, he called to ask some more questions that he said would help clarify some of the things he didn't fully understand. I was extremely careful not to give any information on the phone because of the possibility of misquotes. I recall particularly that he did not tell me, while at my house, who had told him who I was and how to find me. But once he was back in his office and on the other end of the telephone, he told me that he had gotten his information from high officials of the white Citizens Council. I never did fully understand why he gave me this information, in the particular way that he did.

## My Relations with the Negro Community

*Teachers and Administrators.* By the time I had filed the application to the university, I had become more or less settled in my courses at Jackson State College. I had no intention of stopping my education there while attempting to gain admission to the university, and the relationships that I enjoyed with my instructors were important to me as a morale factor. Tacitly, and often openly, there was great support and even much enthusiasm, particularly among those whom I knew well.

It became apparent to me, however, that something was going on in the administration. I never knew what it was, however. I am sure that various attempts were made by the Mississippi power structure to pressure the administration into taking some type of action against me that would have prejudiced my case in one way or another.

There was no direct communication from any members of the administration, but the facts would clearly indicate that all attempts to pressure these Negro administrators were rebuffed. This has always given me a great feeling of pride.

*The Students.* I had a hard battle to win approval of my endeavor from my fellow Mississippi Negroes. One can hardly imagine the extent of the opposition. On March 20 I sent a letter to the Negro college students in Mississippi:

Dear Fellow Students:

I am now involved in a struggle to gain admission to the University of Mississippi. I am coming to you at this time as college students seeking what I will call "a vote of confidence."

I am cognizant of the fact that many of my colleagues are opposed to this move, and I acknowledge the right of anyone to be against anything that they have investigated thoroughly and concluded logically that it is not the proper action. However, my purpose is not to discover the ones who are against, but to see who is for. (Of course, if someone wants to voice his opposition, it will certainly be acknowledged and appreciated.)

I do not seek to enter the University of Mississippi simply to add Mississippi to the list of "mixers." I am concerned with the whole problem of social, economic, and political advancement of the Negro in Mississippi. Then, the question is: whether this action, as opposed to whatever other choice or choices of action, is appropriate at this time. My answer is yes. If after careful study your answer also is yes, I am asking you to give me your vote of confidence by signing your name to the following list.

Thank you.

> Sincerely yours,
> J H MEREDITH
> Student
> Jackson State College

Although one hundred and twenty-eight students indicated their approval at Jackson State College alone, which I thought was quite good, I still knew that I had a big job ahead of me to convince the others and win their support. On March 24 I prepared a statement and sent it to the Negro students and other Negro groups in the state:

WHY I PLAN TO GO TO THE UNIVERSITY OF MISSISSIPPI

I wish to explain why I plan to go to the University of Mississippi because I want the people of our society to know my reasons, since I believe that there are many false conceptions about them among the Negroes of Mississippi.

*First, there are my constitutional rights.* It has been duly decided that no citizen of the United States can be denied the privilege of getting an education because of his race. The fact that no Negro has ever attended the school in question indicates to me that this right to an education has not been acknowledged.

My birthplace dictates to me the school of my choice. I think here of President Kennedy's statement, "If Africa is not for the Africans, then who is it for." I sincerely believe that Mississippi education is for the citizens of Mississippi; therefore, the only question is whether or not the Negro of Mississippi is a citizen. If he is not a citizen, then he is not entitled to this education; if he is a citizen, then he is entitled to this education.

*The Negro has his own educational facilities!* My only answer to this statement is that there is a limit to the number of teachers that can be utilized in the state and a greater limit to the number of preachers needed, in addition to the fact that not every young Negro seeking to gain a position of leadership desires to be a teacher or a preacher. Furthermore, I feel that it is a great injustice to force all our Negro male college graduates to serve as privates in the armed forces, without giving them the privilege of obtaining a commission through the ROTC program as can the white graduates of Mississippi schools and all other students in the U. S. This situation is not only detrimental to the individuals concerned, but to our country as a whole, because of the need to place the most capable persons in positions of leadership and work.

*Problems.* The greatest problem we face today, as I see it, is to stop the trend of our young Negroes toward an attitude of hopelessness. This is a demoralizing trend and will prove detrimental both to Mississippi and the nation if it is not stopped. It will truly be hard for others to conceive of the fears and inferior feelings that prevail among our people. Our young people, to the detriment of themselves, the state, the nation, and the world, are willing to give up what is theirs by right and nature for what they consider to be the only alternative they have.

I have read widely and have traveled a good deal, and I am firmly convinced that the American nation is truly the greatest among nations. From reports and from personal observation I feel that during the past three or so years the peoples of the world have begun to question our greatness because of our inability to solve the problem of unequal treatment of our citizens. The Negro is not by any means the only example of this unequal treatment, but I think that it is true that we are the greatest example. And Mississippi ranks first in the unequal treatment of its Negro citizens. I believe this is true, not because Mississippi has the worst group of people by natural endowment, but because the state has now, and has always had, the greatest number of Negroes in proportion to the number of whites. For this reason, the whites have been able to excite the hates and fears of the masses in order to hamper our progress. If the United States is to maintain its position of leadership, then it must solve its problem of unequal treatment of its citizens. And Mississippi must start progressing toward this end.

*Why do I feel that I am the one individual to take direct action?* I do not. I have no choice in the matter. I have seen very clearly all the faults in the society in which I live, and I am powerless to restrain myself from seeking to correct conditions that need to change for the benefit of all. Probably my greatest single reason to act is my son. He is only one year old, and yet I have already spent countless sleepless nights, trying to answer this question of my conscience, "When he grows up and sees all of the injustices and learns the illogical justifications upon which they are built, he will ask me, 'What have you done to correct these conditions?' What will I give as an answer?" I do not think that "Shut up, boy" will be an appropriate one.

*Fears of the so-called Negro leadership.* "I'm goin' to lose my job." They might have closed schools in Prince Edward County, Virginia, where only a handful of students were involved, but Mississippi schools will never be closed. Of all the unreasonable acts I hold against the powers-that-be in Mississippi, committing the inhumane act of closing the schools and denying hundreds of thousands of children the right to secure an education is one thing that I am positive that no respectable citizen of this state would even seriously consider. If the schools of Mississippi are not closed, then Negro teachers will be teaching Negro students here long after all of us are gone.

*White position.* Most white people to whom I have talked, and I have talked to all with whom I have had the opportunity—from the man who installed my telephone to banking officials, agree that Mississippi carries segregation to unreasonable limits.

Most of my contact with white Mississippians was during my service in the armed forces. I did not meet any white Mississippian in the Air Force with whom I could not work to complete our assigned task together. One of my greatest inspirations came from an Air Force colonel, who was born and raised in Mississippi and told me that he was a personal friend of the then governor. When I sought my last promotion in service, I had to meet a board of three colonels. Normally the questions asked an applicant are about his job and military procedures, but I was asked about the race question. They wanted to know how I felt about Mississippi and Mississippians, what my parents thought, and what other Negroes thought. When they had finished and I started out, the colonel from Mississippi, who was president of the board, called me back to tell me that, when he had checked my record, he had noticed that I was a Negro from Mississippi and he had persuaded the board to interrogate me in this unusual manner. He made this statement, "We are with you, but the degree of success attained in this new move to unify the potentials of our country will depend on you." "You" I interpreted to mean the Negro.

I have also talked with many white students in Mississippi. None of them seems to want or expect any radical changes, but all agree that certain changes will have to be made before there can be any progress in the state.

*Am I afraid?* This is somehow the most asked question. Before answering it, we must answer the question, "Afraid of what?" Am I afraid of failing to attain the goal of reducing the unequal treatment of our people? Yes. No one has ever gone into outer space and returned alive. [This was written shortly before the Russians sent their first cosmonaut into space.] When the day comes that we make our first attempt, I suspect that there will be many doubts as to its success. No Negro has gone to a school in Mississippi heretofore proclaimed for whites only, and for this reason I realize that I too might fail. Am I afraid of something happening to me? Or to my family or to my friends? By any logical interpretation, to my knowledge I seek to commit no crime, to break no law, or to infringe upon the rights of anyone; therefore, if this is the case, and something is to happen to me, then surely something has already happened to me.

Finally, I plan to enter the University of Mississippi for the good of my people, my country, my state, my family, and myself.

J H MEREDITH

*The In Group.* The student group of intellectuals with whom I had been associated at the college were very much involved in this question of my going to the University of Mississippi. This was a tactical move and, in view of the overall objectives of our group, it was just one question among many to us.

An incident which will shed more light on the nature of this group occurred when the state of Mississippi sent a superpatriot to speak to the students at Jackson State College. The state had hired this ultra-anti-Communist and forced him upon us. I imagine all the schools, certainly all the Negro schools, must cooperate when "the man" recommends a certain speaker. It becomes simply a matter of making arrangements for the speech.

The dean of students was the victim, because he was chosen to host the superpatriot during his stay at the college. The president of the college, a very shrewd man, always somehow managed to stay away from these affairs. The speaker was accompanied by one of the famous (or infamous) Negro editors in the state. It was generally believed that this Negro's paper was being financed by the white Citizens Council. As a matter of fact, he had acknowledged that the council was making certain contributions to his paper.

The meeting was to be held in the science lecture theater. There was always a crowd at these meetings. The dormitory matrons would order all students out of the dormitories; since they could not all slip off the campus, naturally, they would have to go to the affair.

The In Group had done a thorough research job on this speaker. How they obtained all the material I have no idea. They had copies of his previous speeches and every conceivable bit of information regarding his other activities. The members of the group scattered themselves throughout the audience and obtained the most strategic seats.

The superpatriot made his speech without interruptions. He called former President Eisenhower "pink" and asserted that President Kennedy was the best and most willing helpmate that the Communist movement ever had. He maintained that Communists were behind all Negro movements and protests in America; he listed every Negro leader or outstanding personality as being in one way or another a willing or unwilling dupe of the Communists. He told about a plot that had been uncovered to overthrow the white government of Mississippi and install a black dictatorship.

During the question-and-answer period after the speech, the students, not so much discussing the speech they had just heard, asked about his previous speeches instead. He was completely inconsistent and attempted to answer the questions with qualifications; they would then recall a speech, give the date and place, and point out that he had said just the opposite. Without going to the trouble of chasing him and his Negro friend from the building and from the campus, as there were those prepared and willing to do, they simply made his visit ineffective by showing up the fallacies and inconsistencies of his position.

### Freedom Riders: May 1961

The Freedom Riders, after being attacked by bus burners and gaining worldwide attention in Alabama, were the main news story in the civil rights movement in May 1961. When they left Alabama, they came to Mississippi. Had they come two months earlier, they would have ridden into the state, used all the facilities that they wanted to test, and ridden out again. This was the way Mississippi had planned to "handle" them. What caused the change?

*Tougaloo's Library Sit-In.* Even though the Mississippi college students were affected by the momentum built up by the sit-ins and stand-ins occurring around the country, there were many reasons why they were hampered in their desire to act. They were very small in numbers; the largest student body—only 1,200 or 1,300— was at Jackson State College. The students were getting their education at a very great sacrifice on the part of their families and themselves. Over ninety per cent of them were receiving some form of financial aid, and most of them did part- or full-time work. Finally, the average student entering college in Mississippi had a reading ability below the seventh grade level; consequently, he had to devote most of his free time in studies to make up for what he had missed in grade and high school. He simply did not have the time to scheme and plot and plan.

Nevertheless, the Tougaloo College NAACP chapter wanted to do something. I feel sure, however, that the impulse to act came from Medgar Evers. Never giving up hope of organizing a chapter among the students at Jackson State College, he had invited some of us to attend a meeting in his office, at which the Tougaloo students were to discuss a probable course of action. I would guess there were fifteen or twenty people at this meeting, and the majority were Tougaloo students whom I did not know. At this time there was no definite plan, but there was a good deal of talking, especially by the advisers of the Tougaloo College chapter and the Jackson City Youth chapter. I had seen both of these men, one the chaplain at Tougaloo and the other the dean of Campbell College, but I did not know them. When I was called on to speak, I followed my philosophy of "tell the truth or say nothing." Not impressed by the talks given by the two advisers, my urgent advice to the group was to find new counselors as a first step in the right direction.

For the next few days everything was quiet. Then on March 27, 1961 the news came that some students from Tougaloo had been arrested at the Jackson City Library. This could have easily passed into history as a typical example of Mississippi's handling of would-be violators of its way of life, if it had not been for a more fundamental development that took place in the heretofore "safe" environs of Jackson State College.

*The Demonstration.* About four o'clock in the afternoon of March 27 the word began to pass that there would be a sympathy demonstration at 7:30 that evening for the Tougaloo students still in jail. The word was well circulated and everyone knew of it, including the administration. The timing of the demonstration was significant. It had been argued that the best time was around four or five o'clock, since classes were over at four and the students usually loitered in great numbers around the campus in the springtime before supper. In addition to this, over half the students lived in the city and they could take part in the demonstration before they went home. We reasoned, however, that the best time to stage a spontaneous demonstration, such as was needed in Mississippi at that time, was between dusk and dark. Darkness would provide a protective covering for the participants; to begin at any other time would have been tantamount to failure.

When I arrived on campus at 7:30 a small group had begun to form around the garden pool in front of the new library. Milling about the campus were unusually large numbers of curious want-to-would-be'ers, many of whom were to become full-fledged participants. By eight o'clock the crowd had grown to around five hundred. The football and basketball coaches were ordering all "their" boys back to the dormitories, and the other students were supposed to follow their example. It didn't work this time, although it had always worked before. Perhaps it was felt that a new day was at hand. Maybe it was because the students were deeply aroused by the growing civil rights movement. There was another factor, however, which I believe caused the change in student reaction. Some three months earlier a secret organization known as M.I.A.S.—Mississippi Improvement Association of Students—had been formed. Without this group I do not believe the Mississippi movements that were to capture the center of public attention for years thereafter would ever have gotten off the ground. And certainly not at this time.

M.I.A.S. was a completely secret organization in its councils of leadership; yet it was open to all in general membership and in public action. Only one man knew all the oath-taking members. Five oath members were required for a forum and all decisions were absolutely binding. Discussion and debate were open and unlimited in council. An oath member was free to choose not to participate in council, but once he chose to participate he was bound by the decision of the council and to carry out his assigned role. Loyalty was irrevocable. It was literally impossible for an oath member to betray the organization or any of its members. Only security such as this would encourage a Negro in Mississippi to venture into the forbidden realm of "White Supremacy."

This organization had gained the allegiance of most students in high school and college, from Alcorn to Greenville, at the same time that the Mississippi State Sovereignty Commission was trying to trace its operations, and the dean of students at Jackson State College had almost lost his composure trying to run it down. Many students had been threatened with expulsion for participating in the group, but they obviously knew no more about it than anyone else.

What had M.I.A.S. done during the three months before the demonstration? First, it had established a set of goals on which all could easily agree. Second, and most important, it had operated in a conscious atmosphere of secrecy and intrigue. Every action was done as if it were forbidden, although all its acts were completely desirable and absolutely legitimate. This aspect of secrecy was of tremendous importance in the closed and intolerant society of Mississippi. Anything that can be done openly, even if it is supposed to be against the status quo, is not worth paying attention to. Short supply was another major tactic. M.I.A.S. would never put out more than one hundred and fifty copies of a piece of propaganda for each one thousand readers. It was imperative that communication should be by hand or mouth in a private and personal way. In this way you found out whom you could trust. The object was to make it the greatest joy to get one's hands on a copy of M.I.A.S. literature. The greatest crime was not to finish with it as soon as possible and pass it on to a friend. Another method used by M.I.A.S. was to get into the classrooms after the janitor had cleaned and washed the blackboards and write, "M.I.A.S. vs bias, who are you for?"

M.I.A.S. took control of the Jackson State College demonstration at about 8:30 and sustained the activities for two days. With a definite plan of action and a fairly good knowledge of crowd and group action, its leaders—fifteen highly disciplined oath members— set up a communications system among the crowd which now numbered around seven or eight hundred. Word was passed to tighten up the group in order to give it cohesion. The students marched around the pool and sang songs. The coaches and deans panicked after they failed to disperse them, and the president of the college hastened out to restore order. At this stage the group had no visible signs of leadership. A visible leader would simply have been a candidate for expulsion from school. M.I.A.S. wanted no one expelled.

The president approached the campus in his usual confident way, perhaps in haste, but not in panic. When he came everyone was told to turn their backs and bow their heads in prayer. Emmett Burns, a senior who had probably never been involved in anything more exciting than stealing a peach pie from his mother's icebox, was tapped to lead a common prayer. How could he refuse to pray? President Reddix stood next to Emmett and just stared for awhile, but he did not bow his head in prayer. The praying moved the spirit in Burns, because he just kept on. Reddix told him to break it up and go home, but Emmett continued to pray. Finally, the president lost his composure. Burns disappeared in the crowd and a girl in the middle of the group was tapped to continue the praying. There was no way for Reddix to get to her, and his campus police could not get through, even if they had wanted to. Reddix at this point was just snatching students at random and shoving them toward a policeman or dean with orders to expel them.

The highlight of the episode involved the president's alleged slapping of a girl. I did not see him slap or hit the girl, but I did see him with his hands on her and I saw the girl later getting up from the ground. I believe the official verdict was that he had shoved her or brushed up against her and she had stepped into a hole beside the pavement and fell. Whatever the truth of this matter is the consequences were still the same. The headlines in the morning paper were that the president of Jackson State College had slapped a coed during the demonstration. Certainly I do not believe that Reddix is a man who would deliberately slap a girl.

Nevertheless, this incident introduced another factor into the demonstration, because it reminded the students of their many long-standing grievances against the administration. These ran all the way from forced prostitution to unorthodox regulations concerning girls and boys.

When the president was convinced that he was only making matters worse, he left. Word was later spread that the police and their "nigger dogs" were coming. The campus police were very anxious to restore order before the city police came, and M.I.A.S. was eager to cooperate with them on this point, although, as a matter of principle, the best possible thing would have been to provoke the city police to attack the students on the grounds of the college campus.

Word was passed, however, and the students literally melted away in a matter of minutes. When the police and their dogs arrived, the campus police told them there was no trouble.

M.I.A.S. leaders immediately held a strategy meeting. It was past midnight when the decisions were reached. Ironically, it had almost been forgotten that the demonstration was to have been in support of the jailed Tougaloo students. Since Barnett had threatened to close the school, if order was not restored in a very short time, now the goal was to force the state of Mississippi to commit some indefensible act that would cause the people to act. The decision was to boycott all classes on the following day, to continue the demonstration, and to demand that no students be expelled or otherwise punished for taking part in the demonstration.

The word was sent around that everyone would "fall-out" in the early morning, before breakfast, in the school colors for the girls and dark pants and white shirts for the fellows. Many of the girls were up all night washing and ironing their blue and white clothing. By 5:30 the whole campus was awake. Everyone was keyed up for action.

Walter Williams, the student body president, had relatives and friends in the administration; he was even a distant cousin of the president. He came to the dining hall from a meeting with the president and other officials of the college. I don't know what they had talked about, but at least he was willing to stand in the limelight and to suffer the consequences; however, he did not know what to do. Word came to him from time to time from the administration, and he broadcast it.

M.I.A.S. took control of the situation and established order. After breakfast the students assembled in front of the dining hall and marched to the basketball gymnasium. En route they had to pass the athletic barracks. The athletes had been restricted to their dorms, as had all students, but they were the only ones to obey the order not to take part in the demonstration. The football and basketball players, instead of hiding their faces in shame, stood in the windows and threw rocks and bottles at the brave little girls desiring only decency and respect.

When the students reached the gym, the doors were locked. The weather was somewhat chilly and it was sprinkling rain, but the demonstrators did not seem to notice. They formed a tight group and were told to lock arms while they sang different songs. The mood and temperament of the crowd was controlled by the type of songs that were sung. By now the city police with their dogs had again arrived on campus and had set up an encircling blockade around the students. They did not come closer than a hundred yards to the group, however. For some unknown reason, after a few hours, the police got in their cars with their dogs and left the campus.

Later the dean of the college, the second highest official on campus and perhaps the official who aroused the least animosity among the students, came to the gym and asked the demonstrators to form a committee to talk to the administration. The result was that they succeeded in turning the students' attention away from the administration, the agent of "White Supremacy" and much more strategic at this crucial stage of the struggle, and to refocus it on the Tougaloo students, who were still in jail. If they would back down from their demands on the college, the administration assured the students that it would be blind to any action that they took off campus.

M.I.A.S. was absolutely opposed to any demonstration off campus; any goal could be accomplished just as effectively with a demonstration on campus and going into the streets would be playing into the greedy and willing hands of the Mississippi police. This would be the same as taking an antelope out of a lion-infested jungle and throwing it into a cage of hungry lions. By three o'clock in the afternoon M.I.A.S. had had a brief meeting and decided to withdraw from the demonstration. It really wouldn't have mattered because M.I.A.S. had lost effective control anyway.

*The March to City Jail.* The officers of the Student Government Association spent the afternoon choosing a group to march on the city jail. Their plan called for limiting the number of marchers to fifty. At four o'clock at a brief mass rally all students except for the few selected for the march were asked to stay on campus. The marchers were instructed to walk single file down each side of the street, so they could not be stopped by the police for blocking traffic or other pedestrians.

By the time the demonstrators were a block away from the campus the number must have grown to at least two hundred. When they reached Pearl Street, two blocks away, police were coming from every direction and had begun to set up blockades. They ordered the students to turn around, but they were not given a chance to obey before the dogs were set on them. The police shot tear gas at the marchers and began beating both girls and men. They meant to convince everyone that they intended to end demonstrations for all time; student marchers, observers, and people at home, all were to get the message. It was an experience that no one involved in will ever forget. The story was printed in newspapers around the world; Mississippi was now a place to watch in the Negro's struggle. Even Premier Khrushchev of Russia sent a telegram to the mayor of Jackson protesting the treatment of the Negroes. And most important of all, it set the stage for the Freedom Riders, who were to come two months later.

*The Freedom Riders.* What would Mississippi do with the Freedom Riders? When their bus arrived at the Mississippi state line with a badly battered group of crusaders, along with the Alabama National Guard and a battalion of newsmen from all over the world, they were met by a no less motley group of Mississippi patrolmen, National Guardsmen, and sheriffs and their deputies. The showdown was to come at Jackson.

The radio was giving a blow-by-blow account of the activities and I knew the minute the bus was in town. I drove to downtown Jackson to watch. The bus station area had been cleared and behind the police lines were hordes of Mississippi whites. I judged most of them to have been local persons and not many were prepared to participate in any real action. These were Mississippi "soft whites." The main street going past the bus terminal was open to traffic, and I drove by about five minutes after the Freedom Riders' bus had stopped. They were already putting the Freedom Riders into the waiting police vans. The state had decided to arrest them and shift the focus of the civil rights movement to Mississippi.

The war cry went out from the Freedom Riders "to fill the jails." A grand idea perhaps, but for some other place. In Mississippi it was not only improbable, it was impossible to fill the jails.

### How To Reach the Goal

The ultimate goal that my friends and I sought was always to break the system of "White Supremacy" in Mississippi and the South and not to accomplish any specific individual end, such as integrating a school, which was in itself a relatively unimportant matter.

*Petition of Grievances.* Various plans were considered as ways to win human dignity and equality of opportunity for the Negro in Mississippi. The legitimate petition is perhaps the most appropriate, certainly the most peaceful, way of asserting one's grievances against a government. There are two vital requisites to the effectiveness of the petition. First, the aggrieved must be able to assemble to draft their grievances into a petition. Second, the government concerned must be willing to accept the petition and be ready to take steps to correct the wrongs. Neither condition existed in Mississippi.

*Mass Resistance.* A form of protest that all governments must give attention to is mass resistance. However, one must be careful to note the distinction between "giving a group attention" and "giving a group what it wants or needs." In order for a movement to be effective, a large majority of the group desiring change must participate. No large or vital segment of the group can be either opposed to the mass resistance program or neutral to it. Otherwise, the government can defeat the movement by appeasing the nonparticipating elements of the aggrieved group.

Only a well-organized movement can ever be successful, because the demonstrative aspects can never last long enough to do anything more than to signify that the grievances are real and that the group is aware of them. Effective organization constitutes the threat that can force the government to change its policies. The existence of a genuinely organized group that can back up the threat is the real power. No organization among the Negroes in America has ever been truly effective, because the opposition has clearly seen that the threats made by so-called Negro leaders would fall apart if their bluff were called. There must be the concentrated action of Negroes solidly behind a truly representative leadership and not a handful of people who travel about the country telling everyone they speak for the Negroes.

What are the potential forces in Mississippi, or in the United States, that could make a mass resistance movement effective? So far the forces are not there, but the raw material is. Human beings are the basic element, and with human beings all things are possible.

Perhaps the most logical, certainly the most likely, group to organize for such a purpose is the students and their teachers. This group is the vanguard of the active public life of any modern society. It is from the students that the majority of those who formulate the rules and orders of society come. The student is being trained to operate the machinery of civilization.

A minority student group must be very closely, often secretly, organized to perform acts that would result in changing the society in which it lives. It would also have to be a highly disciplined group. The needs of a minority student group are quite different from those of a majority student group. A loosely organized majority student group would still be effective, because it would have the dominant sympathies of society on its side. It would be necessary for a Negro student group to organize into highly disciplined groups, perhaps in units of ten students, blocks of ten units (one hundred students), and squares of ten blocks (one thousand students). Each unit would have one head, each block would have one captain chosen from among the unit heads, and each square would have a commander chosen from among the block captains. The students would include both high school and college students. It must always be remembered that no student movement can ever be totally successful without the cooperation of the teachers.

The next group to fit into a mass resistance movement is the working group. Labor unions, if they exist, are the natural allies of any meaningful protest. However, the nonexistence of any powerful labor union, as in Mississippi, does not preclude the participation of the worker. Nor does the lack of a labor union mean that the worker cannot be organized. Working-class groups can be effective against any government, if they are well organized and all major elements of their groups participate. When these two groups—students and teachers, and workers—are not coordinated together, or there is not a full participation by important segments of each group, any movement is doomed to failure.

The work strike alone—that is, apart from the public demonstration of the strikers—could bring the government to its knees. Just think what would happen if the Negro maids stayed home for one week in Mississippi. The whole economy would break down: The white wives would have to stay home, the banks would be forced to fold up, the government offices would be unable to conduct business, car notes and house mortgage notes could not be paid, and the white schools would have to close. On the other hand, if the Negro maids just spent two dollars more for food the weekend before, the only change in the Negro community would be that the maids would have a week of rest, probably for the first time in years.

Another alternative is a tie-up or breakdown of communication arteries. The wheels of civilization turn on the axles of communication. Any breakdown would slow the processes of society to the ineffective stage. Actually it would be a relatively simple task to stop communication; the human elements that grease the machine could simply withdraw their human oil for a period of time. Certainly in the case of Mississippi Negroes it would be a justifiable tie-up, since this particular group does not benefit from the fruits of the system because of a selfish denial of their rights.

*Guerrilla Warfare and Vigilante Organization.* It is a well-established fact that Mississippi maintains its "way of life" by violence and force of arms and by the full use of the coercive powers of the state. It is not so well known that the present Democratic organization control of the state was begun not by the democratic process of free election, but by force of arms.

I doubt whether anyone would be able to convince me of the logic of my not taking necessary steps to insure the protection of the lives and property of myself and my family. As I understand the American ideal of justice, the final responsibility for law and order rests with the individual citizen when the higher levels of local, state, and national government fail to protect him.

*Community Improvement Associations.* The surest way to render the Negro unstoppable is to saturate him with pride. If any human being is sufficiently imbued with pride, nothing short of death will hold him in an inferior position. This pride is not to be associated with equality, rights, freedoms, or dignity. One can possess all these things and still not have pride. Yet one cannot possess pride and accept a permanent denial of freedom and dignity.

Why is pride so necessary? It will not be enough for the Negro to become free and equal as a citizen of the United States. Some of the most free-and-equal peoples have done the least to advance civilization. As I see it, there are two equally important factors involved in the rise or fall of human civilization: the creation of the products of civilization and their distribution. The most obvious problem facing the Negro in America today is the question of the distribution of what our civilization has produced. This is not necessarily the greatest problem confronting civilization as a whole, however. It may well be that the greatest problem facing the majority of black people in the world today is not distribution but production.

Pride can lead the Negro to become one of the world's greatest producers. I not only want the right to participate in an established government, but I have the desire to fashion a better government; not only the right to buy an automobile, but the desire to build a better kind of transport; not only the right to become an astronaut, but the desire to build a superior spacecraft; not only the right to be an employee in a nuclear plant, but the desire to build a better and more effective bomb. The Negro will be able to fill this needed role of producer and builder only if he has imbued himself with unadulterated pride by the time the doors of the world are open to him.

One way the Negro can develop this pride is through the organization of community improvement associations in all the lands inhabited by Negroes. These associations will give the Negro the chance to help himself through cooperation and unity. The end result will be pride in himself, in his family, in his neighborhood, in his community, and in the Negro race.

The association must be composed of the elements of each individual community, and it must serve a general community purpose and function. It must not be a protest group and negative in its objectives. The stress must always be on positive goals, such as paved streets, better street lighting, and better garbage collection. It must encourage such projects as better homemaking, improved diet, better sanitation practices in the home, lawn improvement, more wholesome social programs for the community, cooperative regulation of juvenile activities, and the introduction of arts and theater activity. Every Negro community in the United States should have a community improvement association.

## The Potential Power of Mississippi Negroes

I believe in the human element. The very existence of the human being makes everything possible. Just as the Negro suffers, he may be exalted. Just as he is disdained, he can have unassailable dignity. I believe that within twenty years Mississippi will be the Negro show place. Mississippi will not, Mississippi cannot, change gradually. The change mut be sudden and abrupt. The Mississippi white will accept a new situation, but he cannot accept a process of change. In Mississippi the change must happen because of the action of a unified Negro movement or it will not happen at all.

When the time is right, the Negro will go to bed one night weak and will wake up the next morning strong. What Senator Bilbo of Mississippi predicted for labor unions will happen to the Negro. It is reported that he told a labor representative, "If you show me where you can produce votes, I'll be the damnedest champion of labor you've ever seen."

The federal government is filing hundreds of lawsuits, the Civil Rights Commission is having all kinds of meetings and filing all kinds of reports, making all kinds of recommendations, some of them utterly ridiculous, and civil rights organizations and student groups are holding voting classes, registration campaigns, and whatever else they can think of. And the Negro vote still stands at six per cent of the eligible voters after ten years of this nonsense. Why?

Because of the poll tax, literacy test, moral test, and intimidations.

But the main reason is that the Mississippi Negro is no fool. He does not want this type of change. We have always had a privileged Negro voting class of between six and ten thousand in Mississippi. One must not think that this group could not easily be increased to forty or fifty thousand in a matter of months or weeks. All the Negro principals, preachers, undertakers, and well-to-do farmers need do is to talk to the big men in the county or city and it would be done. But the majority of the Negroes in Mississippi do not want this—neither the privileged Negroes nor the great mass of Negroes. It is the Negro who is keeping these piecemeal operations and token-improvement projects from being successful. It would not make any difference in Mississippi, and everybody knows it—black and white, educated and ignorant, whether ten or fifty thousand Negroes are registered to vote. They would be wasting their time voting under these circumstances. There are a half million or more Negroes eligible to vote and unless sixty per cent of that number—300,000 or more—are voting, they may as well stay home. The Negro in Mississippi knows what he wants and he will be ready to MOVE to get it when his chances are right.

*Meeting the Time Schedule*

My friends and I had spent many hours every day discussing and analyzing the problems before us. The most immediate question during the spring of 1961 was the need for speedy and expedient action. In my case, we explored ways of getting the Legal Defense Fun to meet our rapidly changing timetable.

The NAACP Legal Defense and Educational Fund wanted to go through the routine procedures, such as appealing to the various boards and committees connected with the college and university system in Mississippi. Time alone would have defeated us had we followed this course. We felt that it was essential to go into the lower courts and get some adverse decisions against us in order to keep the Mississippi vigilantes from taking matters into their own hands.

# 5

## *

## The Trial: June 1961-June 1962

ACCORDING to the American ideal of justice before the law no undue delay should accompany its application. How then does one explain the federal courts' acceptance of the long delays when a Negro seeks his rights as a citizen of the United States? The judiciary, in this instance, is attempting to play a role that goes far beyond the simple question of justice before the law. In the case of the Negro, the federal court is attempting to play the political role of policy maker effecting a basic social change.

There is no question of right or wrong in the denial of the Negro's rights. The judges could all have determined on the basis of history that I was being denied admission to the University of Mississippi because I was a Negro. The long trial was not only to render justice to me, the individual citizen, but also to effect a change in public opinion by giving the people bits and pieces of the doctrines of the new order. In this case, the Negro should not be held in his static social position by denial of certain education and training.

The Brown case (the 1954 U.S. Supreme Court decision outlawing the separate but equal doctrine) began this process of educating the public to respect the right of a Negro to a general education in America. This method worked in the Brown case in Kansas and reasonably well in other border states, and it can work to a lesser extent in the heavily Negro-populated areas of the North and West, but it has not worked well and cannot in the Deep South. The sanction of law can insure the acceptance of a social change only where

**104**

there is a wide spectrum of opinion on the question. This was true in the border states and the North and West. On the other hand, where there is an almost unanimous counter agreement on the issue by the dominant forces in the society, judicial sanction is of little or no value even when the judiciary is respected. And the federal court is not always respected in its civil rights decisions in certain areas of the country.

*The Lawsuit*

*The Night of May 30, 1961.* The University of Mississippi formally denied my application for admission on May 25, 1961. Mrs. Motley at first wanted to appeal to higher college and university board officials, which I opposed because of the time factor. She then made plans to file the lawsuit. It was May 30, Memorial Day (and my mother's birthday), when Mrs. Motley arrived in Jackson. She had been highly regarded in Mississippi since 1949, when she argued a case for equal pay for Negro teachers against the state. I had met her once before and been greatly impressed. I was not apprehensive over the fact that my chief lawyer was a woman, since it was Mrs. Motley.

The first thing was to find a place to meet in Mississippi. Tension was high. The Freedom Riders incident, which had gained worldwide attention, had occurred only two weeks before. Mrs. Motley had a friend whom she had met in New York. But New York is not Mississippi, especially for a Negro schoolteacher, and when Mrs. Motley showed up to spend the night, the friendship must have undergone quite a strain. She lived in a new fashionable Negro neighborhood, on the same street where Medgar Evers lived, and we had to slip in under cover of darkness for our lawyer-and-client meeting.

There was a major crisis at this point. In order to file a lawsuit in a Mississippi court you had to have a Mississippi lawyer, and no lawyer seemed willing to take on the state at this time. Jack Young, a Negro lawyer in Jackson, had been asked but he declined the case. Although R. Jess Brown was not their first choice, he did take the case. For this I will always pay him due honor.

I had to sign all the necessary papers in the petition, which then had to be notarized. Finding a trustworthy notary public in Mississippi for a secret operation such as this—the plan was to catch Judge S.C. Mize in the morning session of his Meridian Court completely by surprise—was no easy task. Finally, they found the right person to notarize the papers. She lived across the street from the house where Mrs. Motley was staying; she came in, performed her task quickly, and left immediately.

The lawyers then asked me to leave for a few moments so they could discuss some matters. Of course, it was not very difficult to decide what the consideration was since I was wearing my most widely known outfit—a khaki suit, black leather cap, black shoes and socks, had a full-grown, full-faced Abraham Lincoln beard, and carried my favorite bamboo cane. No one had even hinted that they had noticed, but this was now the problem of the hour: how to get me to shave.

After they talked, I went back into the room and was apprised of their feeling that I should shave in order to project the "proper image" of the Negro. I understood and appreciated their position but made no promises. I explained the great value of these objects as tests and symbols, but I don't believe they understood my reasoning. Mrs. Motley is a sharp lawyer and left the decision to me, but I am sure that she felt certain that I would shave. I did.

*Filing the Lawsuit.* The big day was at hand. Many Negroes had tried to gain admittance to the so-called white colleges and universities in Mississippi. Some had been imprisoned, others had been committed to mental institutions, many had been run out of the state, and some like Medgar Evers had found other ways to fight the system of "White Supremacy," but none had ever sought redress in the courts.

The first problem was to get the right car for the trip. Brown's Chevrolet did not have a back seat; Medgar Evers' car was too well known; and Mrs. Motley said her legs were too long for my Volkswagen, while my Cadillac just would not have been appropriate. Jack Young's Pontiac was eventually chosen. The thing I remember most about his car was that on the window, by which I sat, "KKK," the initials of the Ku Klux Klan, had been freshly carved. We set out: Mrs. Motley, Brown, Evers, and myself. Meridian was ninety miles away.

About halfway there we stopped at a little town called Pelahatchie to place a call to Judge Mize and get an appointment. To us, it was a mean-looking town and tension was apparent. After a good bit of confusion and fumbling, we left without getting the call through.

We drove straight to the federal court, located in a downtown building with parking meters all around. We decided not to park at a meter because we might have to wait in the court for some time before being granted a hearing before the judge, and no one wished to deal with the Meridian police—not even for a parking ticket. We found a place to park and walked about two blocks to the court building. There was a long flight of steps leading up to the entrance. We must have looked strange and conspicuous going up to the proper floor of Judge Mize's courtroom, where we encountered a guard or a clerk who took the message into the judge's office. In a very short time we were led into the courtroom and given seats. I believe there was some case being heard dealing with large-scale embezzlement. I know it was a hotly contested case and tempers were running high. Finally Judge Mize interrupted this case to hear Mrs. Motley's plea. The case was now in the hands of the federal court—the Mississippi federal court.

The press evidently had been tipped off and were on hand. One local newsman seemed pleased to be the one to break the story. He wanted some pictures and caught a shot of the three of us—Mrs. Motley, Brown, and myself—about halfway down the long flight of steps in front of the court building. This picture was in the next issue of the *Meridian Star*, the first time that my picture was on the front page of a newspaper. The editorial accompanying it was very revealing of the Mississippi white's mind.

### NEVER SAY DIE

James H. Meredith, Kosciusko Negro, has filed suit in federal court to enter the University of Mississippi for the summer session.

Fortunately, his case can't be heard until June 12 in Biloxi. This gives grounds for hope that he won't really become a serious problem, at least until the second semester of summer school in late July.

The Negro filed suit on behalf of himself and "all others similarly situated."

Some people will say that even if Meredith wins the suit only a few Negroes will apply for admission.

Some misguided people ask what difference it makes if only a few Negroes go to a white school.

The difference is that the first Negro is only the opening wedge for a flood in time to come.

Integrationists, according to their own statements, will never be satisfied with "token integration."

Massive integration will mean future intermarriage.

Intermarriage in the South, where we are so evenly divided white and colored, means the end of both races as such, and the emergence of a tribe of mongrels.

The term "moderate" is a complete misnomer. There are only three kinds of people—segregationists, integrationists, and those who want to supinely submit to the integrationists.

If you value your racial heritage, if you have even the smallest regard for the future of this South of ours—you will be for segregation one hundred percent.

We must lock shields. We must fight for our race and for the South to the last bitter ditch. We must never lose heart.

We can triumph—we will triumph—we must triumph.

After the filing of the lawsuit, Mississippi was to me basically the same. White folks still ran everything and I was still a Negro. My usual routine of studies at Jackson State College went on, along with schemes and intrigues, football games and golf games, night life in the Negro world of Mississippi, and my all-night-long sessions watching my people at play in the low-class juke joints and gambling dens. This routine was interrupted many times by days and weeks in the courtroom. In general, I don't know whether I had any particular thoughts about it or not. If I did, I guess it was contempt for a world that forced me to use my short life for such a nonproductive purpose. Yet I went on because I had everything to gain, including life itself. All I had to lose was my life.

## The Deposition: June 8, 1961

A rule in federal law gives the accused party the right to ask the accuser practically any question that he wants to. This is called taking the deposition. At least the state had to pay my way to the court. The place was again Meridian, where Judge Mize was still sitting. The Judge would not be present at the session, but he would be available in case of a breakdown between the two parties, which was more than likely. For me this was a chance to get an idea of what the whole thing was going to be like, since I had never been in a court case before.

Mississippi had placed its case in the hands of its number one anti-civil rights strategist, Assistant Attorney General Dugas Shands, who was a thoroughbred Mississippian, a topnotch lawyer, and one of the best that I have seen at the bar. He had a deformed hand and a complete command of the English (Mississippi version) language. His chief assistant was Assistant Attorney General Ed Cates, a top-rated lawyer and the man to watch when it came to special assignments.

The deposition started and in ten minutes I knew that I could out-maneuver Shands any day of the week for any length of time. With all his finesse, his pattern was crystal clear. It is what I always refer to as the "Nigger Treatment," the most common and basic system used in dealing with Negroes in the Mississippi courts. The tactic is to provoke the Negro, to frighten him, and then to break him down and cross him up. The aim is to imply that the Negro is dishonest, immoral, a thief by nature, and generally unworthy of being considered fully human.

Shands was a master at the "Nigger Treatment" tactic. Over the years it must have proven infallibly successful for him. He had an unswerving faith in it, and I was destined to lead him down many roads of no return. There was no time while Shands asked questions that I did not feel confident that I had a definite advantage of him in the courtroom. There is a saying among white folks that they know their Negroes. I had spent fifteen years systematically studying white folks, especially southern ones, and I had little doubt that I knew more about every white man than he knew himself, certainly insofar as his relationship to the Negro is concerned.

The following excerpts from the deposition are examples of the pattern followed by Shands and the state of Mississippi.

DEPOSITION OF JAMES HOWARD MEREDITH*

Taken by Defendants
Meridian, Mississippi
June 8, 1961

Q. James, are you James H. Meredith?
A. That is right.
Q. Speak loud enough, James, so they can hear you. What was your answer?
A. That is right, sir.
Q. James, do you understand what your function as a witness is in this lawsuit, as a party plaintiff?
A. Yes, sir.
Q. James, when did you first see this complaint? Do you know what a complaint is?
A. Let's see. The day before it was filed.

* 19475. United States District Court, Southern District of Mississippi, Jackson Division, Civil Action No. 3130: JAMES HOWARD MEREDITH, on behalf of himself and others similarly situated, PLAINTIFF, v. CHARLES DICKSON FAIR, President of the Board of Trustees of State Institutions of Higher Learning of the State of Mississippi, Louisville, Mississippi, ET AL, DEFENDANTS.

Q. Who prepared it?

A. Mrs. Motley.

Q. Where was it prepared?

A. I don't know.

Q. Where did you meet her?

A. In Jackson, Mississippi.

Q. Did you call her or did she call you?

A. I called her.

Q. Who told you to call her?

A. Well, I don't know if anyone told me. I checked with Mr. Evers—he is the Field Secretary—to find out how to contact Mrs. Motley and he informed me and I called her.

Q. He is Medgar Evers, Field Secretary of what?

A. NAACP.

Q. What have they got to do with this lawsuit?

A. Nothing.

Q. Nothing? Are they furnishing you your lawyers?

A. No, sir.

Q. They are furnishing the money for this lawsuit, aren't they?

COUNSEL MOTLEY: We are going to object to your going into the question of financing of the litigation on the ground that it is not material or relevant to the issue of this lawsuit. The issue in this lawsuit is whether the University denied him admission solely because of his race and color. How he manages to finance the lawsuit is not relevant to that issue and we are instructing him not to answer as to how the suit is being financed.

Q. Have you spent any money on this lawsuit yourself?

COUNSEL MOTLEY: It is the same thing, Mr. Shands. I think maybe if you are going into this line of questioning we had better go down to the Judge and get a ruling on it. We are objecting to questions which have to do with the financing of the lawsuit on the ground it has nothing to do with the issue in this case.

Q. What property have you got, James?

. . . . . . . . . . . . . . . . . . . . . . . . .

Q. When you first saw this complaint, when was that?

A. It was on the day before it was filed.

Q. Where did you sign it?

COUNSEL MOTLEY: Doesn't the paper say it was signed before a Notary and give the name? He doesn't have to go into that. This is not relevant. The best evidence is what it says on that paper. If you want to bring the Notary to see whether he, in fact, signed it before him, I think you can do that. You can subpoena that Notary to find out whether that paper was signed in Jackson.

Q. Did you sign it in a hotel room?

(*No answer.*)

Q. Did you sign it at the office of the NAACP in Jackson?

(*No answer.*)

Q. Did you sign it at the Notary's house?

(*No answer.*)

COUNSEL SHANDS: I think we better suspend at this point and take these matters before the Court.

COUNSEL MOTLEY: All right.

Someone went for the Judge. The questioning continued until he arrived.

Q. How long have you been intending to file this paper?

A. For a number of years.

Q. The only reason you came to Jackson College was to try to get in Mississippi and lay a basis for trying to get into the University of Mississippi, isn't that true?

A. Mississippi is my home. I didn't come for a visit, I came to stay.

Q. You had been in touch with the NAACP before you came to Mississippi, had you not?

A. No, sir.

Q. You had not? You applied at Jackson College, didn't you?

A. Right, sir.

Q. Why didn't you apply to the University of Mississippi then?

A. I didn't think it was the appropriate time.

Q. I want to know what you mean by appropriate time.

A. I didn't think that I knew enough about what I wanted to do to try to do it at that time.

Q. Now, James, let's talk a little bit about you—when were you married?

Shands then asked a whole series of irrelevant questions: "Who married you?" "Where did you get your license?" "Where was your wife living then?" "Do you have credit cards?" "Do you pay cash for everything you buy?"

Q. Where is your wife from?

A. What do you mean?

COUNSEL MOTLEY: We object to that. Where his wife is from has no relevance to the issue in this case and is not material. We instruct the witness not to answer. His wife doesn't have anything to do with this lawsuit.

Q. Where did you first go when you got out of the army?

A. I went to California to visit my brother. Well, I visited relatives and friends in California, but mainly I visited my brother.

Q. When did you leave there?

A. I don't remember the date.

Q. Let's think some, James, I want you to remember this very carefully. As you are testifying under oath, I want to give you time to think. When did you leave there to come back?

. . . . . . . . . . . . . . . . . . . . .

Q. Did you come in your Volkswagen or your Cadillac?

A. My Cadillac.

Q. Are you working for the NAACP now?

A. No.

Q. Are they paying a part of your expenses?

A. No.

COUNSEL MOTLEY: We object to this general business.

Q. Have you been on any military base since you were discharged?

A. Brookley Air Force Base in Mobile, Alabama.

Q. What were you doing there?

A. Visiting a friend.

Q. Visiting a friend; who was that friend?

COUNSEL MOTLEY: We object to this.

COUNSEL SHANDS: This is testing his recollection.

COUNSEL MOTLEY: No, you can't test his recollection by asking him irrelevant questions. His friend at some military base has nothing to do with this lawsuit and the issue in it, and we object and instruct him not to answer these irrelevant questions.

Q. Did you get anything or bring anything away with you from the base?

A. No, sir.

Q. Do you own a typewriter?

A. Yes, sir.

Q. Where did you get it?

COUNSEL MOTLEY: We object to that on the ground it is not relevant and we instruct him not to answer.

Q. You won't answer where you got your typewriter? Is that the typewriter you used to type these recommendations on?

A. Yes, sir.

Q. Where did you get the paper you typed it on?

COUNSEL MOTLEY: We object to that on the ground it is not relevant.


At this point the Honorable S.C. Mize, U.S. District Judge, Southern District of Mississippi, came into the room where the deposition was being taken.


JUDGE MIZE: I understand you sent for me?

COUNSEL SHANDS: We were to come to the Court.

JUDGE MIZE: I thought the reporter had machinery set up, and it might be better for me to come here.

COUNSEL SHANDS: We have several questions and it has previously been agreed that if there were questions and objections made to them and the witness, upon counsel's advice, refused to answer the questions, that we would present them to Your Honor. So Your Honor is here by virtue of the agreement of the parties, to pass upon these objections. The reporter, I assume, would read the questions?

JUDGE MIZE: Yes, let him read the questions and the objections.

COUNSEL SHANDS: Would the Court prefer that counsel for the parties make a preliminary statement to the Court, for the benefit of our views as to why the questions are proper or improper?

JUDGE MIZE: Let me hear the questions first.

The reporter off-the-record read from his notes.

JUDGE MIZE: One question having been read back to the Court for adjudication in substance was a question by the Assistant Attorney General as to whether or not the NAACP was assisting him in financing the cost of the litigation in this particular suit, to which counsel for the plaintiff raised an objection. Mrs. Motley, do you desire to be heard further on that?

Mrs. Motley argued her case.

JUDGE MIZE: I overrule the objection and will require him to answer, without stating at this time the point upon which I can very easily see that it is relevant. Of course, when it comes down to a trial on the merits of the case, very probably it would not be relevant—I am not so sure about that—it depends on what develops throughout the trial, but there is one question in the case that it would be relevant upon. So I am going to overrule your objection and require the question to be answered.

Mrs. Motley argued that such questions would subject me to undue exposure.

JUDGE MIZE: I don't know—undue exposure of him, if it should happen to be morally degrading, it would have something to do with it. Of course, if he is a citizen of Mississippi and of good reputation, and so forth, it would be irrelevant, but in determining whether or not he is a citizen of Mississippi, the ownership of property, where he was born, where he has been and his background, and so forth, are very material in determining a close question as to whether a man is a citizen of a certain state or not. So on that issue, I would hold that this is competent for this hearing and would require those questions to be answered.

Mrs. Motley was also overruled on the extent and degree of cross-examination.

JUDGE MIZE: I disagree with you on it as to the question of cross-examination where he alleges he is a citizen and, of course, his moral character must be established as a good moral citizen. Of course, his answers may absolutely clarify everything. If he is a man of good moral character, then the answers to these questions are not going to hurt him and I will exclude them for consideration certainly on the merits, upon motion, unless they are shown either on the record or at some future proceeding in the record, why they would be excluded on motion at the time. So I think this is a case wherein a wide cross-examination is allowed and after the answers are in, I will permit you to move to strike and give you ample opportunity to be heard fully on it.

Just as you say, if you object to every question, and so forth, you would be here or in Biloxi for a week, because I am leaving in the morning and will be in Biloxi, of course, for the next two weeks. However, if you let the examination go on, I will give you full opportunity to make your motion to strike. By what I am saying now, I don't want you to waive a single right and when you think you want to make an objection, you go ahead and make it and I will hear you on it. But I am giving this short dissertation of what my general thoughts are on the question of objections at this time. I don't want anybody to waive any right or fail to object when they desire.

The Judge left and the questioning by Shands continued.

Q. James, back to your statement that you didn't think that last July, 1960, was the appropriate time to file this suit to try to get in Ole Miss, who told you it wasn't appropriate?

A. I made that decision myself.

Q. You believe in the NAACP, don't you?

A. I agree with most of the tenets upon which they are founded.

Q. You have been a member of the youth organization of the NAACP, haven't you, at Jackson College?

A. I have never been a member of the youth organization.

Q. When did you join the M.I.A.S. [Mississippi Improvement Association of Students]?

A. What do you mean when did I join? I didn't join.

Q. You didn't join? You have been going to their meetings, haven't you?

A. I imagine that all of the students have been.

Q. You believe every student of Jackson College is a member?
A. Yes, sir.
Q. You have been to their meetings?
A. I don't know if they have had any meetings.
Q. Haven't you worked with their Board, which issues some pamphlets, with the group that is writing pamphlets?
A. Yes.
Q. Furthermore, do you believe in what they stand for?
A. What I know about them, I do.

Shands had been given a free hand by Judge Mize to use his "Nigger Treatment" tactics. He took full advantage by asking a wide range of questions. He jumped from one subject to another without any pattern. The object, of course, was to confuse me.

Q. Where did you go after you were discharged?
A. First, I went to Edwards Air Force Base in California.
Q. Where did you go from there?
. . . . . . . . . . . . . . . . . . . . . . . .
Q. Did you leave those bases with anything you didn't have when you went there?
A. I don't know what you mean.
Q. Did you acquire anything there, did you get anything there?
A. You mean did I buy anything from the PX or steal anything?
. . . . . . . . . . . . . . . . . . . . . . . .
Q. Did you pay for your mother's and father's new house which they built?
A. What do you mean "did I pay for it"?
Q. Did you pay it in cash?
. . . . . . . . . . . . . . . . . . . . . . . .
Q. Did you have a bank account then?
. . . . . . . . . . . . . . . . . . . . . . . .
Q. Now, back to this typewriter, where did you get that typewriter?
A. I purchased that typewriter when I was stationed in Omaha, Nebraska. I wouldn't remember the exact date, I am not sure of the place.
Q. With the government?
A. That is right.
Q. As to the signing of this complaint, who was present at that time?
A. Myself, the two counsels, and a Notary Public.
Q. In the Notary's home? How do you spell Notary Public?
A. N-o-t-a-r-y  P-u-b-l-i-c.
Q. Back to the letters of recommendation, you say you wrote them on your typewriter?

A. That is right, sir.

Q. Where did you get the paper that they were written on?

A. My personal paper.

Q. You bought it, tell me where you bought it?

A. I don't know.

Q. Did I ask you where you got that typewriter? I believe you said you bought it.

A. That is correct.

Q. Do you still have it?

A. Yes, sir.

Q. Would you equip yourself with the serial number?

A. Yes, sir.

Q. Do you recall where you bought it?

A. Yes, sir.

Q. What kind of machine is it?

A. Smith-Corona.

Q. Did you buy it new or secondhand?

A. New.

Q. James, I want to talk about these letters that you got signed up there. It has been some little while since I asked you about what it was you told Keaton when you were there on January 29, 1960. Did you tell him what your plans were then—to try to enter Ole Miss?

A. Yes, sir.

Q. When you went to see Keaton, what did you tell him as to why you wanted this certificate? What did you tell him you wanted that certificate for?

A. I told him that I was considering gaining admission, trying to gain admission to the University of Mississippi, and I needed a moral and character rating from responsible citizens and asked him to give me one.

Q. What did he say to you, if anything?

A. I don't recall anything outstanding that he said.

Q. Did he sign it without any argument or comment or did you have to argue with him?

A. He signed it on his own initiative.

Q. What did he ask you, James?

A. I don't recall particularly, but I recall he did sign it.

Q. I want you to think about that a moment, James, and see if you want to amplify your answer.

Q. By the way, where did he sign it, where were you and he?

. . . . . . . . . . . . . . . . . . . . . . . .

Q. Were you driving your Cadillac or your Volkswagen?

. . . . . . . . . . . . . . . . . . . . . . . .

Q. James, just tell me why you wrote the certificates instead of asking them to write you a certificate of good moral character.

A. I wanted to save them the trouble; I knew they probably didn't have a typewriter and the convenience and I did.

Q. In your first certificate as to your good moral character, you made no mention in the certificate of any recommendation on their part that you should be admitted to the University of Mississippi, did you?

A. No, sir.

Q. Who told you those certificates were not what they ought to be?

A. I knew that. There were some items we left out and I indicated that in my first letter to the Registrar.

Q. You said "we" left out, who else, who is the other part of that?

A. I always refer to myself as "we" generally in my speech, I have been told about that several times.

Q. Who told you to say "we"?

A. No one. I say I have been told that I always say that as a figure of speech, when I am speaking of myself I say "we," rather than I. I meant I.

Q. Let me suggest where you got that. You got that from writing pieces for newspapers and for pamphlets, didn't you, because that is the language that a columnist always uses, isn't that where you got it?

A. I don't have any experience in writing columns for newspapers.

Q. But you have had experience in writing pamphlets?

A. I don't have what I would consider experience in writing pamphlets.

Q. You reminded me of something else: How long were you a clerk-typist?

A. Nine years.

Q. Were you told the importance of keeping copies of documents?

A. Yes, sir.

Q. That was pretty well drilled into you, wasn't it, James, as it is every serviceman in your position?

A. Yes, sir, it is good business.

Q. James, let me see that jacket you have got right there that you have to keep those papers in, that thing right there—that jacket.

A. Oh, this here?

Q. Yes. Where did you get that?

A. I wouldn't particularly recall. These were used by the Army years ago; they don't use them any more.

Q. How long ago were they used?

A. I don't know; I was never in the Army.

Q. Do you say on this record that they do not now use them?

A. The Air Force doesn't use them any more, sir.

Q. Do you have bank accounts now?

A. Yes, sir.

Q. Have you received any money from the NAACP since you started talking with them about this lawsuit?

A. I have not.

Q. Have you received any money from any member of the NAACP in Mississippi?

A. I have not.

Q. What about the Jackson Chapter of the NAACP?

A. I have not.

Q. Or from any chapter of the NAACP in Mississippi?

A. I have not received money from anyone.

Q. Have you gotten a promise from any of them?

A. I have not.

Q. Have you gotten any money from any organization, M.I.A.S., or any organization in connection with this suit?

A. I have not.

Q. What is the source of your income now?

A. I am on the G.I. Bill.

Q. And that is all the money you have?

A. What do you mean "that is all the money I have"?

Q. Who is your tenant up there on your sharecrop farm?

A. I don't know his name at this time.

Q. You don't mean you have a tenant and don't know his name?

A. My father has told me his name, but I forget names very easily. My father is taking care of my business while I am in school.

*A Place For Us To Eat.* Of course, it was no new thing in Mississippi for Negroes to be discriminated against in eating places, but to face this reality, after a confrontation with the all-privileged, legally superior white folks on a theoretically equal basis, assuming that Negroes are on an equal footing with their foes before a federal court in a civil rights case, was the height of indignity. To add to this affront, it was suggested by the assistant attorney general that we only take a twenty-minute lunch break, so that we could get on with the deposition because the state attorneys wanted to get back to Jackson early. This amount of time would be sufficient for them, because there were several restaurants within a five minutes' walk of the building.

Mrs. Motley casually asked where there was a nice place to eat. One of the helpful Mississippi lawyers quickly named four or five familiar-sounding names. I don't know whether he was deliberately being insulting or just unconsciously assumed that we would not mind going to the back door like the other Negroes and take our sandwiches in a bag. In Mississippi it was customary for most white restaurants to sell food to Negroes through a back door. The lunch break was extended to forty minutes, so that we could search the town for the "colored" cafe. We found it, and Mrs. Motley is still talking about those greasy chops that she was served.

*The First Hearing in Biloxi*

The first hearing was set for June 12, 1961, in Biloxi. We had arranged to stay at the cottage of a Jackson funeral director in a little place called Waveland, thirty-five or forty miles down the coast from Biloxi. It was a Methodist Church resort and the only place on the Mississippi Gulf Coast where Negroes could use the beach. The cottage was privately owned, but we ate our meals in the resort dining hall. There were four of us: Mrs. Motley and Derrick Bell from the NAACP Legal Defense Fund and Brown, the Mississippi lawyer, and myself.

*R. Jess Brown's Suit.* The first excitement came when we started to unload our baggage from the car. Jess Brown had brought along a bright red suit, which he handled with obvious care. Mrs. Motley blushed for a few moments and could not hold her peace any longer. "You are not going to wear that suit into the courtroom, are you, Jess?" she asked. Brown was naturally offended, and I thought for a while we would break up before we got started. Brown has an instinctive taste for fancy clothes, but you would have noticed him whatever he was wearing, because he is not a typical-looking Negro with his ruddy complexion and long red hair. R. Jess Brown is a fine gentleman in every respect. We managed to overcome this crisis quickly.

*The Pre-drill.* After we had finished our dinner, which was quite good—I particularly remember that three African students from Alcorn College were working in the dining hall during the summer, a rather unusual phenomenon in Mississippi—we went back to the cabin by the sea for a pre-drill of the court sessions that were to start the following morning. I never cared for acting or pretending, and this made the run-through a bit difficult for Mrs. Motley. She kept saying, "Now, Meredith, you've got to speak out so the judge can hear you when you get on the witness stand."

*Ellis on the Stand.* We arrived at the Biloxi courtroom early. They were expecting us and the clerk made sure that we were properly taken care of. I remember a fellow who came up and introduced himself as a lawyer from the Justice Department; he was there to observe the proceedings. The press was well represented and sat in the jury box and in the lawyers' observation section.

After the preliminary procedures, during which each side asks the judge to throw the other side out on one basis or another, the hearing began. The first witness called to the stand was Robert H. Ellis, the Registrar of the University of Mississippi. According to his testimony, he didn't know anything and, most of all, he had no idea whether or not a James Meredith existed. The strategy was to get me on the stand quickly, a possibility which Mrs. Motley honestly dreaded, but it was only a matter of minutes before I was summoned to take the oath. It was months before I was given my first break from the witness stand. Shands had won the first round. He had his "Nigger," and all he had to do now was to apply the "Treatment."

*Meredith Takes the Stand.* My first act on the stand was to read all of the correspondence which had been exchanged between the University of Mississippi and myself. Judge Mize seemed surprised to find that I could read. When I had finished reading the letters, which took up fifty-six pages of transcript, Mrs. Motley asked a series of questions.

Q. Where were you born?
A. Kosciusko, Mississippi, Attala County.
Q. Are your parents living now in Kosciusko?
A. Yes, ma'am.
Q. How long have they lived there?
A. All of my life, and I believe all of their lives, in the general community or area.
Q. Were your parents born in Mississippi?
A. Yes, ma'am.
Q. Where did you attend elementary school?
A. In Kosciusko, Mississippi, Attala County Training School.
Q. Is that a public school?
A. Yes, ma'am.
Q. Where did you attend high school?
A. The first three years was in Kosciusko at the same school, Attala County Training School. The last year was in St. Petersburg, Florida, Gibbs High School.
Q. Did you graduate from Gibbs High School?
A. Yes, ma'am. I graduated in June, 1951.
Q. How did you happen to go to high school in St. Petersburg your last year?
A. I wanted to go to a better school, and my parents also wanted me to go to a better school.
Q. Have any other members of your family attended that Gibbs High School in St. Petersburg, or are you the only one?
A. Yes, ma'am, my baby brother just graduated on June 8th from that same school. He spent his first three years at Attala Training School and the last year there at Gibbs High, the same school I attended.

Q. Did you have any other brothers and sisters to attend school outside the state of Mississippi?

A. Yes, ma'am, my brother Everett attended his last year of high school in Detroit, Michigan.

Q. By the way, how many brothers and sisters do you have?

A. Ten living. There were thirteen children born to my father.

Q. How many of your brothers and sisters are high school graduates?

BY MR. SHANDS: We think that is going too far, how many of his brothers and sisters—

BY THE COURT: Yes, sustain the objection.

Q. What did you do after you graduated from high school?

A. I went back to my home in Kosciusko, Mississippi, and stayed a while. Then I went to Detroit, Michigan, to visit my older brothers and sisters there.

Q. How long did you stay in Detroit?

A. A few weeks, maybe a month, and shortly, in July, I enlisted in the United States Air Force.

Q. Did you enlist in the Air Force or were you drafted, or what?

A. I volunteered.

Q. How long a period did you enlist for?

A. Four-year period.

Q. Did you receive any medals or accommodation awards?

A. Yes, ma'am, I received the good conduct medal and the National Defense Service medal, I'm sure of. I might have received one or two others, I'm not positive.

BY MR. SHANDS: We object to speculation and guess.

BY THE COURT: Yes, exclude that.

Q. Did you ever have any disciplinary action taken against you?

A. No, ma'am.

Q. What type of discharge did you receive?

A. Honorable.

Q. Now, Mr. Meredith, during the time that you were in the service, did you take any courses, educational courses?

A. Yes, ma'am. Generally I can say and specifically that all during my service almost all the time I was engaged in some educational activity.

Q. Are you a registered voter, Mr. Meredith?

A. Yes, ma'am, state of Mississippi.

Q. When did you register to vote?

A. February, 1961.

Q. Where?

A. I registered at the Hinds County courthouse.

Q. Is that in Jackson?

A. Yes, ma'am.

At this point Shands started his cross-examination.

Q. James, let's start at the back of your testimony. You are registered in Hinds County?

A. That's right.

Q. How many elections—You haven't voted in any elections?

A. I have not voted in my life.

Q. Why haven't you voted?

. . . . . . . . . . . . . . . . . . . . . . . . . . .

Q. You were living in Jackson, a resident of Jackson, Hinds County, Mississippi, on February 2, 1960?

A. I was in the service at that time.

Q. I asked you if you were living in and a resident of Hinds County, Mississippi, on February 2, 1960?

A. No, sir, but I'll say this: When I went to register to vote there wasn't any question that I was asked, and he called me a nigger in the first place, and he did all the talking, and then he filled out the form and—

BY MR. SHANDS: We object to all that and move to exclude it.

BY THE COURT: Overrule the motion.

Q. All right. Go ahead then.

A. I just told him I had been in the service, he told me to fill out the paper and then he told me to go out and tell all the niggers they can register and vote in this county; all they got to do is pass the test. And I didn't have much to say.

Q. Who was that?

A. This was the clerk.

Q. Let's get back to the question I asked you. Were you living and residing in Jackson, Mississippi, on February 2, 1960?

A. No, sir.

Q. Did anybody tell you what you had to do in order to qualify to register?

A. Yes, sir, and I told him that I had been in the service. I told him that I had never lived in Hinds County. I told him I had always lived in Attala County.

Q. I didn't ask you that. At the time you took that oath you knew it was untrue?

A. I explained to him my situation. I explained it to him thoroughly, that I was a permanent citizen of Attala County. I explained I had never lived in Hinds County prior to coming to school there. That is when he went on to tell me about anybody could register to vote in his county, and I didn't have much to say in that clerk's office when I registered to vote.

Q. All right. Now, when you attended Wayne University where were you living?

A. With my sister in Detroit.

Q. What address did you give?

A. 2303 Pasadena.

Q. Why didn't you give Route 2, Kosciusko, Mississippi?

A. Because I wasn't residing at Route 2, going to Wayne University. I was staying at 2303 Pasadena.

Q. You were not residing in Attala County at that time?

A. Yes, sir, and that was 1955.

Q. Have you tried to leave the impression in this Court that you had been a resident of Attala County for the entire period of time prior?

A. Yes, sir, that was established—

Q. It was established?

A.—while I was in service.

Q. Tell me how you established that?

A. Because I was under 21 at the time I went in the service.

Q. Who told you that the residence of a minor was that of his father?

A. My legal officer on my base.

Q. That is what I'm getting at. Now then, where was your residence when you went into the Army on your second hitch? You got to be 21 just before you went in for your second hitch.

A. As far as I know, it was Mississippi.

Q. I'm not asking as far as you know. I asked you where it was.

A. I was staying at 2303 Pasadena, attending Wayne University.

Q. I'm asking you where was your residence on the date you went into service beginning your second hitch?

A. Kosciusko.

BY MRS. MOTLEY: We object to that. We think that where the plaintiff's residence is is a conclusion of law to be determined by the Court. He can ask where he was residing, but he can't ask where his residence was. That is a legal conclusion.

BY THE COURT: Overrule the objection. It can be a mixed question of law in fact so I will let him answer.

Q. Now James, do you consider you have had a good Army record?

A. Excellent.

Q. You are proud of your record?

A. Yes, sir.

Q. You think your papers show that you had a good record?

A. Yes, sir.

Q. Would you have any objection to authorizing the defendants in this case to examine your Army record and papers in the hands of the Government? You have any? You probably don't. You don't have any?

A. No, sir. However, if I have the authority to give that right, I'm not giving that right, but I have no objection. I have records myself.

Q. Why won't you give that right if you have no objection to it?

A. Because I don't want to set—if I'm successful in getting into the

University of Mississippi, I don't want to set a bad precedent to Negroes where they have to go through a special procedure to get there; that is, by showing all of these things I don't believe is required from a normal applicant.

Q. James, you have nothing to hide in this matter, do you?

A. No, sir. I was just fixing to answer.

BY MRS. MOTLEY: We object to that question; also to that kind of tone of examination as if this man is hiding something. There is an attempt, I think, to entrap the man into saying something he does not intend to say. He said three times he would not authorize the state to have his record, he has no objection, but he would not authorize it unless it is required by the rules of the University.

BY THE COURT: I will overrule the objection on this theory: I want him to have a full opportunity. He has answered, I think, fairly clear; however, there is a rule of law that if a person has something in his possession and over which he has control and he declines to authorize that, then an unfavorable inference can be drawn if it was examined it would be unfavorable. So I think it competent in cross-examination to question him fully, and I overrule the objection.

Q. Upon reflection, James, do you still stick to that?

A. I will say that you have my permission to examine all my military records.

Q. Very good, in the event it should become necessary, by some government regulation, that you sign some document to evidence that, will you sign that if the government regulations require that?

A. I will. However, I don't go along with it.

Q. James, do you have any information one way or the other as to whether, if you were admitted to the University of Mississippi and if you were given no more credit for the hours given, submitted, than the letter from Mr. Ellis stated, that was written to you, do you know whether or not that would affect your G.I. Bill of Rights period of educational advantages under the government money?

A. No, sir, I do not.

Q. Have you made any investigation of that?

A. I checked with the Veterans Administration on changing schools. They said I could change schools.

Q. But if it was to affect it under the circumstances that I told you, do you still want to change schools and go to Ole Miss if it causes you lose some of your G.I. Bill of Rights?

A. Yes, sir.

Q. You still do? Even though you are going to lose money that you would otherwise be entitled to?

A. Yes, sir. I want to get a good education.

Q. Now, James, what is it that you are asking for by this suit? Is it that you want equal treatment upon admission to the University of

Mississippi? Do you want to be treated just like you think someone would be treated if they are a white applicant? Is that what you want in this lawsuit? Or do you want special treatment?

A. I want the same treatment of my application, normal.

Q. You want to comply with the same requirements that would be required of a white applicant? Is that correct? Or do you want special treatment?

A. I certainly don't want any special treatment. However, I realize there are some things that will be different in my situation.

Q. My question, James, was do you want to comply with the same requirements that are required of white applicants? Equal treatment? Is that what you want?

A. Yes, sir, those that are fair.

Q. Those that are fair. Now, suppose you would think some are not fair—

BY MRS. MOTLEY: I think this is arguing with the witness. . . . He is only entitled to the same rights that white persons have in this state, and this is an argument with the witness as to what he thinks the law to be, or something to that effect. The Court will rule on what rights he is entitled to, and it is settled he is entitled only to the same rights the other persons have. This is an argument with the witness about what he thinks the law to be.

. . . . . . . . . . . . . . . . . . . . . . .

Q. James, I hand you what appears to be the original complaint that you filed in this suit and ask you to look at the date of your so-called affirmation to the oath on the last page. What is the date of that?

A. 31 May 1961.

Q. Anywhere in that complaint do you say that your permanent home, or that your domicile, or that you were a citizen of Attala County, Mississippi?

A. Not as I know of. I don't particularly recall.

Q. And you don't remember now whether on February 2, 1961, which was two or three days after you sent an application to the University of Mississippi, whether you said that you had been a resident of Hinds County since September 12, 1960?

A. I did not say so.

Q. You didn't say so. James, I want you to reconsider that answer, because I do not want to take advantage of you in any way. I want you to reconsider it, and after reconsideration tell me whether you did or did not, according to your best recollection, make oath on February 2, 1961, that since September 12, 1960, you had been a resident of Hinds County, Mississippi?

A. Would you clarify what you mean by residence, please?

Q. Your domicile. Do you know what domicile means? You have read the catalog of Ole Miss, haven't you?

A. I don't know what you mean when you say residence. I am a student. I was a student in January, 1961, and I am going to school in Jackson, Mississippi. I do not live in Attala County and drive here every day. I stay in Jackson and go to school here.

Q. James, how far have you gotten along in Jackson College out there?

A. You mean the grade?

Q. What is your present standing out there, what grade—freshman, sophomore, junior, senior, what?

A. Senior.

Q. And you don't know what residence means?

A. Not in the way you are saying it. It has more than one meaning.

Q. You stated that you had participated in the preparation of pamphlets which were put out and circulated among the students by M.I.A.S.?

A. Yes, sir.

Q. That is true. Now, what does M.I.A.S. stand for?

A. I think it's "Mississippi Improvement Association of Students."

Q. James, what is the purpose of M.I.A.S.? You worked with them in preparing pamphlets. What was that outfit trying to do?

A. Well, I don't know for sure, but I thought it was just as the title says, "improvement."

Q. How many pamphlets did you help prepare, or is that something you can't remember? I can understand how maybe you wouldn't remember that.

A. One or two.

Q. James, who else sat in with you and helped prepare these pamphlets, how many of you were there?

A. Exactly what do you mean by "prepare"?

Q. Well, what's your definition of "prepare"? You said you helped write them or prepare them.

A. To write them.

Q. Who sat in with you on that, how many?

A. I don't remember the number—two or three.

Q. Who were they?

A. I'd rather not answer that unless it is absolutely necessary. I don't know all of them. I know some of them.

Q. Tell me why it is that you think you would rather not tell who it was. There is nothing in your mind wrong in these pamphlets, is there?

MRS. MOTLEY: We object to this on the ground that this is a state institution, these students are in a state school and this sort of information is now sought from the plaintiff and could be used against these students to expel them from the institution, or some such thing, and we object on the ground it is not relevant or material to the issues in the case for him to know who the students were. If this were an independent college, it would be a different thing. This is a state college and the suit is against the state and they are seeking this information, and we think they are not entitled to get it on that ground. It's common knowledge that people who do these kinds of things in Mississippi, write these sorts of pamphlets, are visited with all kinds of economic reprisal, harassment from the white Citizens Council and similar things from those who oppose Negro activities of this kind, and we object on the ground it is not relevant or material to the issues in this case.

MR. SHANDS: We take very sharp issue with and deny such statements as made by counsel of economic reprisal and white Citizens Councils and that sort of thing.

MRS. MOTLEY: What's the relevancy?

MR. SHANDS: I want to show who he is, what he does, what and how it should be brought about.

MRS. MOTLEY: And the document speaks for itself and you could put that in evidence and it will show what he stands for, and to expose other students to expulsion—

THE COURT: Let me see the documents.

MR. SHANDS: I can't understand why if there is nothing wrong with it—

MRS. MOTLEY: We know exactly what is going to happen to those students.

THE COURT: One at a time, now. Have you finished your argument, Mr. Shands?

MR. SHANDS: I can't understand if there is nothing so awful about them why so much objection is made to it.

THE COURT: Very well, Mrs. Motley.

MRS. MOTLEY: The documents speak for themselves, and as I said before, this is a special kind of situation, it is not the ordinary and usual case. Those students are enrolled in a state institution. The state policy is to oppose and object to Negroes who agitate for reforms along the lines of Negro rights, such as advocated in that pamphlet. What is going to happen to those students, we already know because it's happened in Alabama and other states where Negroes participated in this sort of thing, they have been expelled. The Fifth Circuit decided last Friday a case involving that. So I'm not making things up. There has been a case like that.

MR. PATTERSON (*Attorney General for the State of Mississippi intervened*): Counsel has made a good propaganda speech but cannot verify one iota of the charges against the state of Mississippi about expulsion of Negro students in state institutions.

MRS. MOTLEY: No, but this plaintiff has had his insurance cancelled—

THE COURT: (*interrupting*): Very well, I believe I've heard enough argument from both sides. On one theory of the law it would be competent, to show who his associates are, but the extent to which it would go would be that he and some others prepared these two documents, and I doubt if it would throw any light on his credibility, so I sustain the objection.

Shands went on with his questioning.

Q. James, do you know Aaron E. Henry?
A. Aaron E. Henry?
Q. Yes.
A. Are you talking about the President of the Mississippi NAACP?
Q. Yes.
A. I don't know him personally. I know who you are talking about.
Q. Did you ever talk with him about your lawsuit?
A. Never talked with him, period.

Shands moved on to the certificates of recommendation. The university required that the recommendations come from graduates of the university. I did not attempt to get their recommendations because all graduates of the school were white.

Q. Do you know every alumnus of the University of Mississippi personally?
A. No, sir.
Q. How do you know whether they are or aren't members of the Caucasian race?
A. I have read it.
Q. Oh, that is the point. You are saying what you have read, not what you know?
A. That's right, sir.
Q. Now, how in the world did you assume all of that, James? Are you sensitive on the subject of race?
A. Very much so.
Q. Oh, you are? How long have you been so sensitive on the subject of race?
A. All my recollecting life.
Q. All your life since childhood, isn't that right?
A. That is right.
Q. You have had nervous trouble, haven't you?
A. Nervous trouble?
Q. Yes.
A. Oh, I don't know. The Air Force doctor didn't think so.
Q. Did you ever think so?
A. I thought so, possibly. And sometimes when these racial incidents

would come up throughout the years, at the peak of them, I would become a little tense in the stomach.

Q. You really had a complex about that thing?

A. I had an interest.

Q. It would excite you?

A. I was interested in it. I was very concerned.

Q. Wouldn't it cause you to be highly nervous and excitable and wouldn't you lose your temper over race matters?

A. I don't recall ever losing my temper or becoming nervous and excited.

Q. James, you have even been under psychiatric care, haven't you?

A. No, sir.

Q. Psychiatric. Do you know you had a psychiatric report in your Army record?

A. Yes, I was quite aware of that, an examination. It was that examination that formed the conclusion for this answer.

Q. Have you ever read that psychiatric report?

A. No, sir. They don't let us see it.

Q. I think you have a surprise. If you never did see the report, how could the report have changed your mind?

A. The doctor's report to me changed my mind.

Q. You don't reckon he'd write one thing and tell you something else, do you?

A. I don't know what doctors would do.

Q. Read that thing. (*Hands document to witness.*)

A. (*reading*): "This is a 26 year old Negro SSgt who complains of tension, nervousness, and occasional nervous stomach. Patient is extremely concerned with the 'racial problem' and his symptoms are intensified whenever there is a heightened tempo in the racial problems in the U.S. and Africa. Patient feels he has a strong need to fight and defy authority and this he does in usually a passive, procrastinating way. At times he starts a crusade to get existing rules and regulations changed. He loses his temper at times over minor incidents both at home and elsewhere. No evidence of a thinking disorder. Diagnosis: Passive aggressive reaction, chronic, moderate. Recommendations: No treatment recommended."

Q. Does that square up with—Would you also read the last line, Recommendations?

A. "Patient declined any medication." Now I explained that. He wanted to give me some tablets to relieve my nerves. I told him I didn't want them, I would rather just go on.

Q. What is the provisional diagnosis made? Read it.

A. "Provisional Diagnosis: R.O. Obsessive compulsive neurosis."

Q. Now, James, did I understand you to say that the problem of yours had been going on for many years?

A. You mean, ever so often getting tension?

Q. Yes, sure, a bit disturbed by racial problems?

A. That's correct.

Q. That's right. And is that what you had reference to in one of your letters when you said in one of your letters to the University of Mississippi that you were an unusual student?

A. No, sir. I meant Negro, when I said unusual.

*The Courtroom Scene.* At the first hearing in Biloxi there were only three or four Negro spectators in the courtroom. I don't know whether it was a lack of interest or because of fear that the local Negroes did not attend the trial. One of the Negroes in the room was my youngest brother, who had just graduated from the same high school from which I had graduated nine years earlier—Gibbs High in St. Petersburg, Florida. He had come to spend a brief visit with our parents in Mississippi before going into the Air Force. I remember his expressing to me his satisfaction in seeing how quickly Judge Mize straightened up and leaned back in his chair in amazement when I started reading the first letter, as if it were a great surprise, if not a real shock, to discover that a Negro could read. My brother's presence gave me a great feeling of strength. To me, he was a living testimony of what I was fighting for.

*The Court Moves to Jackson*

After bouts in the towns of Meridian and Biloxi, Judge Mize saw the logic of moving the court permanently to Mississippi's only city —Jackson. This was extremely important to the Negro side, because it was a real burden to find lodging and eating accommodations in the small Mississippi towns. Although they would have tried, frankly I do not see how Mrs. Motley and her assistants could have endured sixteen months in Mississippi, if the court had not moved to Jackson. I am sure the move was not made for the convenience of us Negroes, however. Jackson was the state capital, and the State Attorney General and all of his top assistants were involved in the case full time, while their other duties were piling up. It would greatly facilitate the legal machinery of the state of Mississippi to move the court to Jackson.

I feel sure that our side benefited more by the move to Jackson. Jackson State College was located there, and I could continue my studies without interruption. In spite of all the weeks I spent in the courtroom, I never missed a class. In addition, my family, friends, and cohorts were in Jackson. It is hard to say how much effect the presence of only a few Negroes in the courtrooms outside of Jackson had on me, but there can be no doubt that the fact that every session in Jackson was jammed with Negroes was a great source of inspiration and strength to me. I never walked into the courtroom when Negroes were not already there waiting, often an hour or more before the court was scheduled to begin. Sometimes the courtroom would be filled a half hour before the court was in session. Because of this demonstration of their feelings, there is virtually no limit to the extent that I would be willing to trust the Mississippi Negro. They ranged from the Negro conservative to the restless Jackson-corner-gang boys; from the spirited Baptist preachers to the silent sisters; from college students to elementary school students, and every day all day long, those Negroes had to look at a mural on the federal courtroom wall depicting the "Mississippi Way of Life."

*The Mural.* This picture must be on affront to God himself. It shows the segregated society in all its glory. On the right were, of course, the white folks of culture, dressed neatly in their clothes of class, engaged in the conduct of the affairs of civilization, and climaxed by a scene of solemn worship. In the middle were the operators of the system of white dominance, the foreman, boss, and overseer, with the emphasis on the white tally keeper writing down the pounds as the Negroes placed the cotton sacks on the weighing scales. On the left were us. We were strung out in the vast cotton fields with heads bent down and hands reaching out for another cotton boll. We were emphasized in the most vivid form singing and dancing or generally depicted as loafing and idling our time away. I do not know whether I had been fully aware of just how bad my relative position was before I saw the system so explicitly laid out in this federal courtroom. Basically the picture was more real than false, if one takes Mississippi as it is without making a value judgment.

*A Newspaper Article:* "A Smart Cooky." A few days after the court moved to Jackson an article appeared in my home-town newspaper, the Kosciusko *Star-Herald*, August 24, 1961:

Faithful reader David Wasson calls our attention to an interesting item in The Summit Sun by Editor Mary Cain relating her informal coverage of the federal court hearing on the case of James Meredith. No comment here, for Mrs. Cain has said it all in her usual straight-forward manner.

"Instead of holding our regular meeting last week, directors of the Paul Revere Ladies gathered at the federal district court in Jackson for the hearing on the case of James Meredith, the 28-year-old Negro Army veteran who is trying to enter Ole Miss, thus breaking down the bars of segregation in our institutions of higher learning.

"After sitting there, listening to the incredible story drawn from him by Assistant Attorney General Dugas Shands, I came to the conclusion that he doesn't need to enter any college if his story is true: he can get a job anywhere as executive director of almost anything he wishes. In essence, he told the court that he gets $160 a month from his Korean G.I. Bill, and he has no donations or gifts from anyone, but on this slender sum he has:

"Supported a wife and a child;

"Bought a Volkswagen and a Cadillac;

"Bought an 84-acre farm in Attala County on which he owes nothing;

"Attended summer school for two sessions in Jackson, at a cost of $70 or $35 per session;

"Paid $40 per month in Jackson for rent, while in school.

"All of which adds up to one of three things: His wife is a woman of means who is 'keeping' him; he's a genius; or finally, he's a plain old garden variety of liar. And I incline to the last-named hazard.

"The whole business moved too slowly for me and was insufferable. I wouldn't have been in Mr. Shands' place. When the high-brown gal who is Meredith's attorney challenged Mr. Shands' pronunciation of the word 'Negro'—as 'Nigar'—which is the way most of us pronounce it— Judge Sidney Mize, who was presiding, told Mr. Shands to 'indulge her' in her desire that it be pronounced 'knee-grow'. (That reminds me that it's reached the place in bars, they tell me, where one no longer asks for a 'jigger' of whiskey: the word is 'jeegrow'.')

"In Mr. Shands' place, I think I'd have told Judge Mize, 'Now, Judge, are we here for lessons in English, or to find out what this man really is? You know most of us say "Nigra", and many of us say "nigger".'

"They bent over backward to be polite to her.

"Not only is this 'Nigra' a smart cooky in a financial sense, he's also smart—as far too many Negroes are—at establishing residence in several states. He says he is a native of Kosciusko, Attala County, but he has lived in Gary, Ind., Detroit, Mich., somewhere in Florida and the Lord knows where else. Mississippi has been keeping birth certificates, I understand, since 1911. If he was born in Kosciusko, the birth records ought to show it. And if he was born out of wedlock and has no record of birth, the burden of proof should be on him, not the state. And we have no obligations to educate non-residents, black OR white.

"I see from Sunday's papers that when Judge Mize postponed a continuation of the hearing until Tuesday, the Motley woman (that really IS her name!) charged that the state is deliberately stalling and that Meredith is entitled to a 'speedy hearing without delays.'

"Thank Heaven, Judge Mize overcame his politeness sufficiently to remind her that 'the court itself must determine when cases will be heard.'

"(Mr. Shands was scheduled to represent the state Monday in a civil rights voting case filed by the U.S. Government.)

"The courtroom was a demonstration of 'segregation within integration.' One row of Negroes sat in one section, and there were four or five rows of Negroes near the back in the other section. (Only a handful were real Negroes—the rest were, like the Motley woman and her aides, high-browns.) The courtroom was filled with white citizens who look with distaste upon the reprehensible effort of these Negroes to break down barriers constitutionally established. Above their heads a mural revealed the role of the Negro as cotton pickers and I could not help wondering what thoughts ran through the minds of the Negroes and high-browns who faced it.

"It takes a strong stomach to be able to stand federal court today— Mine's very weak."

Mary Cain is a well-known Mississippi woman. She has run for governor on several occasions. She is one of the state's most outspoken segregationists.

## Judge Mize's Ruling: February 3, 1962

After many, many more days of court proceedings and one year from the time I had originally requested admission, on February 3, 1962, Judge Mize issued his ruling:

Plaintiff, James Howard Meredith, is a member of the Negro race and a citizen of Mississippi. He filed this suit against the members of the Board of Trustees of State Institutions, the Chancellor of the University of Mississippi, the Dean of the College of Liberal Arts, and the Registrar of the University. He alleged that he sought admission to the University of Mississippi as a resident, under-graduate, transfer student to that Institution and that he was denied admission solely because of his race. The complaint was answered by the Defendants, denying that he was refused admission solely because of his race.

The only question now posed for decision is whether or not the Plaintiff was denied admission to the University of Mississippi solely because of his race or color and only a question of fact appears for determination. The evidence overwhelmingly showed that the Plaintiff was not denied admission because of his race. The Plaintiff, during this hearing on the merits, called as adverse witnesses nearly every member of the Board of Trustees, who testified unequivocally and definitely that at no time had the question of the race of a party ever been discussed at a meeting of the Board of Trustees or at any other place and that so far as the members of the Board of Trustees was concerned all policies and regulations were adopted and followed without regard to race, creed or color, and that at no time was the application of James Meredith, the Plaintiff, ever discussed by any members of the Board of Trustees. The Registrar, who also had testified on the motion for preliminary injunction, again testified to the effect that the question of the race of the Plaintiff was not discussed or considered in any way whatsoever when his application for admission to the University was being considered. All of the other officials of the University testified to substantially the same thing. One member of the Board of Trustees was not used, in addition to a few members who were not called because of ill health.

The effect of this additional testimony heard during the trial on the final merits strengthens the former finding of the Court that the Plaintiff was not denied admission because of his race, rather than weakens it.

The proof shows on this trial, and I find as a fact, that there is no custom or policy now, nor was there any at the time Plaintiff's application was rejected, which excluded qualified Negroes from entering the University. The proof shows, and I find as a fact, that the University is not a racially segregated institution.

Inasmuch as Plaintiff has failed to meet the burden of showing by a preponderance of the evidence that he was denied admission to the University of Mississippi solely because of his race, the complaint must be dismissed. The Plaintiff undertook to bring the action as a class, acting under Rule 23 (a)(3) of the Federal Rules of Civil Procedure, but since Plaintiff failed to maintain this action in his own behalf, he cannot maintain it as a Class Action.

This is the 3rd day of February, 1962.

## A Temporary Injunction Denied: February 12, 1962

The decision of Judge Mize was immediately appealed to the U.S. Fifth Circuit Court of Appeals. We requested that the decision of Judge Mize be overruled and that a temporary injunction be issued so I could begin school in February 1962. In a split decision, the temporary injunction was denied. The majority opinion was written by Judge John Minor Wisdom:

This case was tried below and argued here in the eerie atmosphere of never-never land. Counsel for appellees argue that there is no state policy of maintaining segregated institutions of higher learning and that the court can take no judicial notice of this plain fact known to everyone. The appellees' chief counsel insists, for example, that appellant's counsel should have examined the genealogical records of all the students and alumni of the University and should have offered these records in evidence in order to prove the University's alleged policy of restricting admission to white students.

We take judicial notice that the state of Mississippi maintains a policy of segregation in its schools and colleges.

We hold that the University's requirement that each candidate for admission furnish alumni certificates is a denial of equal protection of the laws in its application to Negro candidates. It is a heavy burden on qualified Negro students, because of their race. It is no burden on qualified white students.

The fact that there are no Negro alumni of the University of Mississippi, the manifest unlikelihood of there being more than a handful of alumni, if any, who would recommend a Negro for the University, the traditional social barriers making it unlikely, if not impossible, for a Negro to approach alumni with a request for such a recommendation, the possibility of reprisals if alumni should recommend a Negro for admission, are barriers only to qualified Negro applicants. It is significant that the University of Mississippi adopted the requirement of alumni certificates a few months after Brown v. Board of Education was decided.

A full trial on the merits is needed in order to clarify the muddy record now before us. Within proper legal bounds, the plaintiff should be afforded a fair, unfettered, and unharassed opportunity to prove his case. A man should be able to find an education by taking the broad highway. He should not have to take by-roads through the woods and follow winding trails through sharp thickets, in constant tension because of pitfalls and traps, and, after years of effort, perhaps attain the threshold of his goal when he is past caring about it.

Accordingly, the order of the district court denying appellant's motion for a preliminary injunction is affirmed. The motion of the appellant that this Court order the district court to enter a preliminary injunction in time to secure the appellant's admission to the February 6 term is denied. It is suggested that the district judge proceed promptly with a full trial on the merits and that judgment be rendered promptly, especially in view of the fact that a new term of the University of Mississippi begins February 6, 1962. The Court's mandate will be issued forthwith.

A dissenting opinion was written by Chief Judge Elbert Parr Tuttle:

I respectfully dissent. I think the record already submitted, without the benefit of the record in the trial on the merits, calls for our granting the injunction pending appeal.

If Meredith continues as a student at Jackson State College, which he must do in order to continue to be entitled to his G.I. educational benefits for himself and his family, he will graduate in June of this year and he cannot thereafter enter the University of Mississippi as a candidate for a bachelor's degree. I do not believe that he should be required to leave college at the beginning of his final term to prevent his appeal from becoming moot. Unless he is admitted to the University by February 15, just three days hence, he cannot transfer until the next term. Therefore, if he is denied the injunction and does not quit school for a term (to keep from graduating), he will be forever denied the right to enter his state university as a candidate for an undergraduate degree, which right I think this Court may well ultimately decide he is entitled to.

I do not think this Court ought to concern itself with any possible damage to the appellant by granting his motion for injunction. He does not need for us to help him decide whether he really wants what he is here fighting so hard to get.

I therefore respectfully dissent.

## The Return from New Orleans

On our trip to New Orleans to appeal to the U.S. Fifth Circuit Court of Appeals, we had driven down in Bill's car at his suggestion. Two whites—Bill Higgs and Charlie Butts—and two Negroes—R. Jess Brown and myself—had made the trip together. I wasn't taken with the idea at all.

When the court session was over, we were all quite tired and very hungry. Naturally we would have to stick together—one for all and all for one. But where would we eat? There was only one slim chance. The Interstate Commerce Commission had ruled that all interstate bus passengers must be served at the lunch counters in bus stations. We headed for the bus terminal and sat on stools in the lunchroom. The waitress started with Bill, took his order and then Charlie's order; Brown was next, but she just looked at him curiously; I guess she was trying to figure out if he were a foreigner or something. She walked away and brought Bill and Charlie their coffee and their orders. Brown got impatient and asked if we could get some service. The waitress then came over to me and said, "Boy, you got a ticket?" I asked what she had said, and she answered, "I said, let me see your ticket." By now Bill got into the act and confessed that he had no ticket and that we were together. The waitress made it clear that they (the whites) didn't need a ticket, but that Brown and I would have to show her our tickets before we could be served. Of course, we all left—one for all and all for one—still hungry, however.

We drove out of town but by the time we reached the outskirts, hunger had changed our minds. Bill suggested a grand compromise. He proposed that we stop at a white restaurant and he would go inside, buy sandwiches for all of us, and bring them to us to eat in the car. This was totally unsatisfactory to me, and I suggested that we stop at a Negro cafe and I would go inside, get sandwiches for everybody, and bring them out to eat in the car. We finally agreed to stop at a grocery store and buy some knickknacks. Most grocery stores in Louisiana permitted Negroes and whites to buy from the same counter.

This crisis foreshadowed others which would occur on this trip back to Jackson. Twenty-five or thirty miles out of New Orleans, we drove into what turned out to be the worst winter conditions in Louisiana and Mississippi since the turn of the century. It started to sleet and snow. Soon the roads were completely iced over. We were in northeastern Louisiana, the most desolate and hate-ridden part of the state; therefore, we kept driving.

Suddenly the car was out of control and over in a ditch. Although it was only about 8:00 P.M., it was cold enough to freeze one to death in three to four hours. We had to get out of there and we all knew it. Two whites and two Negroes in one car and, ironically, the two Negroes had on suits and ties and the two whites did not. For thirty minutes or more we three pushed and shoved the car, while Bill kept spinning the tires in the mud, and it never moved an inch. It seemed hopeless. Finally, we decided to change drivers and I got under the wheel. I don't know which part of the change was decisive—Bill was almost twice my size—he stood over six feet and weighed over two hundred pounds; he didn't look very athletic but he must have been strong as an ox. I had had years of experience in driving in mud and getting out of ditches and gullies. There definitely is a trick to this type of driving. Bill got on the side of the car and practically lifted the whole side of the car up, and in short order we were back on the highway.

Slowly and cautiously, but finally, we reached Franklinton, Louisiana, which has a widely known reputation as a "real mean" town. Suddenly we four realized that our lot was just as precarious in this town as it had been in the ditch by the side of the highway. We all agreed that to try to continue our trip would be suicide, however. We had to spend the night here.

We drove around and looked at the town for a while, and for no reason other than not having one, we stopped at a gasoline station. Bill knew a "liberal" white minister in town whom he called, but the minister could only wish us luck; he didn't even have a suggestion. The situation was becoming more alarming. Bill and Brown kept putting their heads together and whispering. I knew that this wasn't going to do in this town. I weighed the situation carefully, trying to decide who was the man that called the shots. There was an unusually large number of people in the station—several Negroes but more whites. A nickel-matching game was going on in the grease-rack section; whites and Negroes together were thumping nickels in the air and "calling it" before they hit the concrete. I told Bill and Brown that they had better stop whispering, because the crowd was getting suspicious. Bill, following the idealism of "one for all and all for one," suggested that Brown and I get down low in the car; he and Charlie would go to the motel that we had passed coming into town and each get a room; then Jess and I would slip in and we would share the two rooms. By now the gambling game had broken up and all the Negroes had disappeared, except the ones working the gas pumps. The cash register man was looking suspiciously at us. News of the Meredith case appeal in New Orleans had been on the radio every hour, and he may have recognized us.

I walked over to the cash register man and told him that the weather conditions had stranded us and wondered if he knew where we could find a place to stay for the night. Brown and Bill were visibly shaken by my approaching the man, but you have to know the people you are dealing with. The man instantly, or instinctively, called the name of Ole Rev. So-and-so, he usually "put folks up" for the night. "Yeah, let me see, no, he ain't got no phone no more." I looked out and saw one Negro carefully observing everything but acting as if he didn't see or hear or care. Then I asked the man if "anybody" around here knew where the preacher lived. "Yeah, Leroy knows where he lives and I was just about to let him go, so I'll let him show you."

Sure enough, Leroy got in his old '53 Ford and led us to the Reverend's house. Coincidentally, just as we approached the house about six sets of car lights appeared in back of us and almost caused a panic, because Bill knew for sure it was a mob following us. We had agreed that I would go in and talk to the preacher, but before I got to the steps the whole crew was on my heels. However, the other cars slowly drove on past. We went in and Leroy announced us to the woman of the house. She told us that her husband—a Holiness preacher—was out of town holding a revival meeting and she could not take us in his absence. However, she made a phone call and then called me into another room to tell me that the Baptist preacher could take in Jess and me but not the white men. I assured her that I would handle that matter.

We left for the other preacher's house, and on the way I informed the group that we were splitting up—period. I didn't want to debate the idealistic aspects of the situation. When we got to the preacher's house, we gave his address and phone number to Bill and Charlie with the understanding that Leroy would lead them back to the motel. They got rooms in the all-white motel with no trouble.

Then we had another crisis. Jess wanted to conceal our identity from our host; I felt that we were obligated to tell him who we were and I proceeded to do so. When I started to tell him, the Reverend finished the story and said that he had recognized me "right off." We had a very pleasant stay. He told us about his recent encounters with the forces of "White Supremacy," as a result of his voters' registration activities.

The situation was improving. Jess had been able to reach his wife by phone and she had agreed to get in touch with my wife. The next morning we had a good breakfast, and the preacher took us in his car to the motel where Bill and Charlie were. We loaded up and headed toward Mississippi.

Just outside of town we noticed the temperature gauge was registering very hot. The radiator was frozen tight and about five miles farther on the car stopped completely. Bill went to a nearby farmhouse to use the phone, but no one was at home. Fate was with us again for about this time an empty wrecker happened along going toward the town. It was so unbelievable that we almost let him pass without flagging him down. He towed us back into town to the garage, and in a couple of hours we were out on the road again.

The roads were very bad, and we had to get out and push the car up almost every hill. It took us at least five or six hours to travel the fifty-odd miles to McComb, Mississippi. Once in McComb we decided to abandon the automobile. Charlie stayed behind with the car and Bill, Brown, and I caught a train to Jackson.

## The Question of Graduation

While the state of Mississippi had been stalling in the courts, life and work had continued at Jackson State College. The time had now come to look beyond Jackson, because I had completed all the requirements for a degree by December 1961. I was now thinking of furthering my education. The Woodrow Wilson National Fellowship Foundation was just beginning to make it possible for Mississippi Negro college students to apply for their fellowships. I was nominated by my department for a preliminary evaluation. For this purpose I submitted the following letter to the Jackson State College representative:

October 31, 1961

### MY ASPIRATIONS AND PHILOSOPHY OF LIFE

It is my solemn desire to devote my time and energy to the accomplishment of my assigned task. My job, as assigned by some power greater than myself, is clear and definite. First, it is to aid mankind in every possible way to attain the highest level of human existence. Second, on a national level, I am committed to the task of bringing the actual state of affairs into line with the high ideals of our country in regard to the idea of the "equality" of mankind. Finally, on the state and local level, it is my task to foster and to aid appropriate programs designed to raise the Negro populace from its present inferior position.

To aid in this mission, I am presently pursuing a course of formal study. The primary purpose of this study is to equip myself with the tools of communication in order that I may effectively convey ideas to others. Another purpose of this endeavor is to become acquainted with as many facts as possible that might aid in the accomplishment of my assigned task. As an undergraduate, I am concentrating on History, Government, and Political Science. After completion of this work, it is my desire to study law and, if appropriate, to do further study in Government.

Further, as a measure of security, in the event that it becomes expedient for me to leave my beloved home state of Mississippi, I hope to be qualified to serve in a foreign nation as a representative of my country.

The principles that I follow in the conduct of my activities are simple and few. Of course, here I will deal with those principles most directly concerned with the accomplishment of my life work. First, I believe in hard work. I believe that the accomplishments of an individual depend to a very large extent upon how, and with what degree of efficiency and effectiveness, one uses his time and energy.

Second, I believe that the responsibility for improving culture rests with the enlightened (those individuals who are able to gain an insight into the nature of things—not to be confused with education, the learning of facts, or the gaining of information). I believe that the failure of a society to obtain a desired goal is due to the inability of the enlightened to efficiently and effectively lead the masses, and not due to the ignorance of the masses.

Third, I believe that the colored peoples of the world are destined to play an ever-increasing role in determining the course of human history. I base this belief upon the two following assumptions. That the colored peoples of the world are becoming enlightened in great numbers for the first time in modern history. And that the energy of the white man is waning. I believe that this is due mostly to the growing obsolescence of his basic principles and to the increasing number of persons of that race who are unwilling to perform certain necessary tasks of a progressing culture, such as raw exploration and certain demanding military duties.

Further, I feel that the American Negro, providing he avails himself of the opportunity, is in a position to play an important part in this new development. I believe that this is so because we are one of the largest groups of Negroes (blacks) with a common heritage. We are also citizens of the richest nation of the world, which is, in addition, the leader of the Western or democratic world. We are among the best-trained and educated Negroes of the world (not to be confused with enlightenment, because I do not believe that the American Negroes are the most enlightened among the Negroes of the world). Therefore, I feel that if a unifying medium is ever discovered, the American Negro will contribute significantly to the molding of our future civilization.

I was selected as one of the two students from the social science area at Jackson State College to submit applications to the Regional Chairman of the Woodrow Wilson National Fellowship Foundation for a fellowship during the 1962-63 school year.

The question of whether I should accept my degree from Jackson State College became increasingly more pressing. Of course, it would probably make me ineligible for admission to the University of Mississippi as an undergraduate, thereby making the pending case moot, even if we won. But the best use of my time was involved: How much should one give up to prove a point? Many interested groups asked me not to graduate, including the NAACP Legal Defense Fund, the Justice Department, and the Federal Appeals Court, which had suggested in its opinion that I procrastinate.

By the spring of 1962 my graduation was long past due and I could no longer keep my name off the list of graduates. My diploma was ordered, along with the yellow tassel to indicate that I was graduating with honors. The only way that I could prevent myself from receiving my degree was to decline to pay the $4.50 fee, a final requirement for graduation. It is a great disappointment to see your classmates leave you behind; the graduating class of May 1962 was the second that I would have to watch as a nonparticipant. Another crucial factor was that I was living primarily on my past savings, and, above all, I could never allow my family to suffer from a lack of the necessities of life. It was a difficult decision to make.

Meanwhile, I had been accepted for admission to Howard University Law School and had been admitted to the Atlanta University Graduate School with a scholarship to study political science. Atlanta's director of admissions was probably decisive in making it possible for me to continue my efforts. He had assured me that I would be permitted to enroll at Atlanta at any time that I felt it no longer feasible to try to enter the University of Mississippi. Without this assurance, I would probably have chosen to get my degree from Jackson State College and go on to graduate study. I was quite aware that Negroes recognize only "Success" and "Titles." The Negro has no place for a loser, no matter what the circumstances may be. I will never knowingly buck a rising tide without an alternative.

I continued to enroll each succeeding term at Jackson State College, however; I studied practically every subject offered—from Dairy Farming to Negro History.

# 6

## The Courts Decide: June-September 1962

FINALLY, on June 25, 1962, my twenty-ninth birthday, the U.S. Fifth Circuit Court of Appeals ruled that I should be admitted to the University of Mississippi. The three-judge court (composed of two circuit judges and one district judge) was split on this decision. Judges John R. Brown and John Minor Wisdom ruled in my favor and Judge Dozier A. DeVane dissented. Judge Wisdom wrote the majority opinion.

### The Decision: June 25, 1962

The Meredith matter is before us again. This time the appeal is from a final judgment after a trial on the merits. The judgment denies James H. Meredith, a Mississippi Negro in search of an education, an injunction to secure his admission to the University of Mississippi. We reverse with directions that the injunction issue.

A full review of the record leads the Court inescapably to the conclusion that from the moment the defendants discovered Meredith was a Negro they engaged in a carefully calculated campaign of delay, harassment, and masterly inactivity. It was a defense designed to discourage and to defeat by evasive tactics which would have been a credit to Quintus Fabius Maximus.

After the trial on the merits, the district judge found "as a fact, that the University is not a racially segregated institution." He found that the state had no policy of segregation. He did find that segregation was the custom *before* Brown v. Board of Education . . . was decided in May

1954. But, he held, "there is no custom or policy now, nor was there any at the time of the plaintiff's application, which excluded Negroes from entering the University." This about-face in policy, news of which may startle some people in Mississippi, could have been accomplished only by telepathic communication among the University's administrators, the Board of Trustees of State Institutions of Higher Learning. As the trial judge pointed out in his opinion, "nearly every member of the Board of Trustees, testified unequivocally and definitely that at no time had the question of race of a party ever been discussed at a meeting of the Board of Trustees or at any other place and that so far as the Board of Trustees was concerned, all policies and regulations were adopted and followed without regard to race, creed or color."

In our previous opinion in this case, . . . on the appeal from a denial of the preliminary injunction, it seemed to us that "what everybody knows the court must know." We took "judicial notice that the state of Mississippi maintains a policy of segregation in its schools and colleges." (We find nothing now in this case reaching the dignity of proof to make us think we were wrong to take judicial notice of Mississippi's policy of segregation.) Nevertheless, on that appeal, giving the University the benefit of the doubt, it seemed to us that a trial on the merits would be in the interest of justice: for reasons not attributable to the endeavors or competency of counsel, it was impossible to determine from the record whether there were valid, non-discriminatory grounds for the University's refusing Meredith's admission.

The district judge found no reason in the trial on the merits to change his earlier findings of fact and conclusions of law. He held that the evidence "shows clearly that there was no denial of admission because of his race and color." In reaching this conclusion the trial judge adopted the findings of fact in his earlier opinion on the motion for a preliminary injunction. It is necessary therefore to review the case from the beginning. Such whole-case review has the advantage of enabling the Court to consider the various contentions in context and to determine whether the pieces fit together to make a pattern of unlawful discrimination.

I

James H. Meredith was born in 1933 near Kosciusko, in Attala County, one of the rural counties in Mississippi. After graduating from high school in 1950 he volunteered for service in the United States Air Force. When his hitch was over he reenlisted. In the Air Force he rose to the rank of staff sergeant. He was discharged in the summer of 1960. He was never in trouble with civilian or military authorities. Meredith received an honorable discharge and the Good Conduct Medal.

Meredith got his education the hard way. Sometime in 1953 he decided to improve himself. He turned first to "Fundamentals of Speech" and "Composition and Literature," extension courses of the University of Kansas. In 1954 he enrolled in a course in "Government of the United States" at Washburn University in Topeka. He received the grade of "C" in each of these subjects. From 1954 to 1960 he took advantage of college level courses of the United States Armed Forces Institute, for which Jackson State College credited him with fifty-seven quarter hours credit. Meredith's most fruitful years, educationally, were the two years he spent in Japan just before leaving the service. He attended the Far East Division of the University of Maryland. He tackled difficult courses such as "Russian," and he carried a heavy schedule. In 1958-1959 he had 5 "B's"; in 1959-1960 he had 3 "B's" and 3 "A's". The University of Maryland credited him with thirty-four semester hours for twelve courses.

Promptly after returning home, Meredith registered at Jackson State College, a "Negro" college in Hinds County, Mississippi. He moved to Jackson with his wife and child. At Jackson State his grades were almost all "A's" and "B's". In January 1961 he applied for admission to the University of Mississippi. When asked on the witness stand why he wished to transfer, he said Jackson State was "substandard."

These facts raise a doubt as to the defendants' good faith in asserting that Meredith was not in good faith in applying for admission to the University of Mississippi. That Meredith's transfer would mean the loss of credits and possibly the loss of some G.I. Benefits, that he was in his late twenties, that he might find the University of Mississippi considerably more difficult than Jackson State College, demonstrate his perseverance and fit in with the character of a man who is having a hard time getting a college education but is willing to pay the price exacted of a Negro for admission to the University of Mississippi.

II

The defendants' Fabian policy of planned discouragement and discrimination by delay is evident from the correspondence between Meredith and the University.

Sometime in January 1961 Meredith wrote the Registrar for application forms. He received a prompt reply thanking him for his interest and enclosing the forms. January 31 he wrote the Registrar, enclosing the executed forms. In this letter Meredith expressly informed the University that he was a Negro. This was not a gesture of defiance—the forms require a photograph and an indication of race—but a predicate for pointing out that although he could not furnish the names of alumni who reside in his county and have known him for at least two years, he was submitting certificates regarding his moral character from Negro citizens who had known him in the county of his birthplace. As is apparent from the letter, Meredith was "hopeful that the complications [would] be as few as possible." We read this letter as showing no chip on the shoulder and no evidence of such abnormal concern as to support the defendants' contention that from the start Meredith's letters indicate he was "belligerent," a "trouble-maker," and had psychological problems. We think it not unreasonable for a Negro to have some concern over his reception on the "Ole Miss" campus.

February 4, 1961, two days before registration began for the second semester, the Registrar telegraphed Meredith:

"For your information and guidance it has been found necessary to discontinue consideration of all applications for admission or registration for the second semester which were received after January 25, 1961. Your application was received subsequent to such date and thus we must advise you not to appear for registration."

In his holding on the preliminary injunction, the trial judge found as a fact that this first refusal of admissions was a proper refusal because of "overcrowded conditions." In February 1961, however, there were only 2500 to 2600 male students on the campus. As of September 1961, as the Director of Student Personnel testified, there were about 3000 male students on the campus.

February 20 Meredith wrote the Registrar requesting that his application be treated as a continuing application for admission during the summer session. He called attention to his transcripts having been forwarded from the Universities he attended. He concluded, "Again, I would like to express my gratitude for the respectable and humane manner in which you are handling this matter and I am very hopeful that this procedure will continue." The next day his room deposit of ten dollars was returned.

February 23 Meredith returned the ten dollars, explaining that he had requested his application be considered for the summer session. After waiting a month for an answer Meredith wrote the Registrar again. This time he requested that his application be considered as a continuing one for the summer session and for the fall session. He inquired whether his transcripts had been received and whether there were "any further prerequisites to admission." After waiting eight days for an answer, and apparently thoroughly alarmed by eloquent silence from the University, Meredith again wrote the Registrar. It is the letter of a man of perseverance, but a man of patience and politeness. He asked the Registrar to please let him have the University's evaluation of his credits acceptable to the University "if it [were] appropriate at [that] time." He enclosed five certificates certifying to his good moral character and recommending him for admission to the University; the earlier letters were silent on the subject of recommending him. He said that he "realize[d] that [he was] not a usual applicant to the University of Mississippi, and that some timely items might need to be considered."

Another month went by. Still no answer. April 12 Meredith wrote the Dean of the College of Liberal Arts at the University. In laconic style, barren of comment, Meredith told of his application and his unanswered letters. He concluded:

"When I forwarded my application to Mr. Ellis on January 31, 1961, I stated in a letter to him and in my application that I am a Negro citizen of Mississippi. Because of my failure to hear from Mr. Ellis since his telegram to me of February 4, 1961, I have concluded that Mr. Ellis has failed to act upon my application solely because of my race and color, especially since I have attempted to comply with all of the admission requirements and have not been advised of any deficiencies with respect to same.

"I am, therefore, requesting you to review my case with the Registrar and advise me what admission requirements, if any, I have failed to meet, and to give me some assurance that my race and color are not the basis for my failure to gain admission to the University."

The Dean did not reply to this letter. Belatedly, May 9, the Registrar replied, advising Meredith that "the maximum credit which could be allowed is forty-eight semester hours [for the 90 hours submitted] if your application for admission as a transfer student should be approved." The letter asked Meredith to "please advise if you desire your application to be treated as a pending application."

Meredith took this as a good omen. May 15 he wrote that he wished to attend the first term of the session starting in June, and that it was imperative he be informed with respect to his admission because he would have to make arrangements for his family. He enclosed a letter to the Director of Men's Housing, applying for an apartment appropriate for his family size—a wife and small child. Not having received an answer by May 21, Meredith wrote again. He said that since the Registrar had asked if his application should be considered as pending, he had "assumed by the nature of [the] request that [his] application was entirely complete and that [he had] met all of the pre-registration requirements."

The axe fell May 25, 1961. On that date the Registrar closed his correspondence file on the application and returned the money Meredith had deposited. He gave the following reasons for returning admission:

"The University cannot recognize the transfer of credits from the institution which you are now attending since it is not a member of the Southern Association of Colleges and Secondary Schools. Our policy permits the transfer of credits only from member institutions of regional associations. Furthermore, students may not be accepted by the University from those institutions whose programs are not recognized. As I am sure you realize, your application does not meet other requirements for admission. Your letters of recommendation are not sufficient for either a resident or a nonresident applicant. I see no need for mentioning any other deficiencies."

We pause in narrating the facts to observe that the explanation is inadequate on its face. (1) It ignores the credits from Washburn, Kansas, and Maryland. (2) The "programs" from those institutions are of course "recognized" by Mississippi. As for Jackson State, its program was established and is supervised by the identical Board of Trustees supervising the program at the University of Mississippi. (3) The letters of recommendation refer to the requirement of alumni certificates, a patently discriminatory device.

Up to this point the University had successfully avoided decisive action on the 1961 Fall term. And, because of the lateness of hour, the University was in a favorable position to resist the expected assaults on the summer sessions.

III

May 31, 1961, Meredith filed a complaint in the United States District Court for the Southern District of Mississippi. The defendants were the Board of Trustees of the State Institutions of Higher Learning, the Chancellor of the University of Mississippi, the Dean of the College of Liberal Arts, and the Registrar of the University. The Governor of Mississippi appoints the Board with the consent of the state senate. The Board, a constitutional body, is vested with the management and control of all Mississippi's colleges and universities, including the Negro colleges.

The complaint is filed as a class action. It alleges that the defendants are pursuing a state policy, state practice, state custom, and state usage of maintaining and operating separate state institutions of higher learning for the white and Negro citizens of Mississippi; that under this policy Meredith was denied admission to the University solely because of race and color. At the first hearing the plaintiff was denied permission to introduce evidence relating to other colleges and universities in Mississippi. (In view of the theory of the complaint that segregation was a state policy being carried out by the Board charged with administering all of the state's institutions of higher learning, this ruling was clearly erroneous.) The evidence, therefore, relates only to the University.

At the time the complaint was filed counsel for Meredith sought a restraining order; the summer term was about to begin. The trial judge denied the order.

The case was set for a hearing on the plaintiff's motion for a preliminary injunction, June 12, 1961. This was four days *after* commencement of the summer session. About 3:30 p.m. on the afternoon of the hearing the trial judge stopped the trial and continued the case on the ground that because of his crowded docket he had set aside only one day to hear the case. The case was continued until July 10, 1961, at which time, according to the court, the entire case would be heard since, in the interim, the answer would be filed, the issues "definitely framed and we can begin the case and finish it." In practice, in almost all cases, a hearing on a motion for a preliminary injunction is held before an answer is filed.

The case was not heard on July 10 because of a scheduled three-judge court case which required the presence of the trial judge below and involved counsel for both parties. Meredith's counsel therefore filed, June 29, another motion for a preliminary injunction, since the second summer term would commence July 17. The motion was fixed for a hearing on July 11. On July 10 the chief counsel for the defendants, Assistant Attorney General Shands, was ill. His illness caused the case to be continued to August 10, 1961. By that time any possibility of attending the second summer session had gone winging.

June 9 and 30, 1961, and again July 27, July 28, and August 4, 1961 Meredith's counsel sought to take the Registrar's deposition. The efforts were singularly unsuccessful. The trial judge denied the first motion on the ground that the deposition could not be taken prior to the expiration of twenty days from the filing of the complaint. . . . The second notice of taking was suspended and stayed by the court on the ground of Mr. Shands' poor health, June 27, two weeks before the July 10 postponement of the trial. August 1 the trial judge vacated the other three notices on the ground that the court was "in the process of trial on plaintiff's motion for Temporary Injunction, and the exercise of [the] court's discretion." This appears to us to have been a clear abuse of judicial discretion.

Counsel for Meredith filed a motion that the University produce records of all students admitted to the February 1961 term, the 1961 summer terms, and the September 1961 term for inspection July 1 to July 7. The motion, filed June 20, was not heard until July 27, because of Mr. Shands' ill health and because of the crowded court calendar. August 1 the district court ordered the records produced for inspection, but limited inspection of records to applications for undergraduate enrollment in the 1961 summer terms, and to applications to the graduate schools. This order was manifestly erroneous and was one of the causes for the poor state of the record in the hearing for the preliminary injunction.

July 10 the trial judge announced that the hearing on August 10 would be a trial on the merits. August 1 this ruling was reversed; the trial judge ruled that the August 10 hearing would be a continuation of the June 12 hearing on the preliminary injunction.

July 19 the defendants filed their answer. The answer supplemented the Registrar's letter of May 25 by giving a large number of additional reasons, many of them trivial, for the University's having refused Meredith admission. The answer emphasizes the following reasons. (1) Meredith failed or refused to submit the requisite alumni certificates. (2) Meredith "was not seeking admission to the University of Mississippi in good faith for the purpose of securing an education," considering all of the circumstances and particularly the fact that as a consequence of transferring to the University he would lose credits and G.I. benefits.

(3) Meredith's fear that his application might be denied because of his race "shocked, surprised and disappointed" the Registrar. It was so "rash" and "unjustified" that it raised grave questions as to Meredith's "ability to conduct himself as a normal person and a harmonious student on the campus of the University of Mississippi." The Registrar, for himself and the other defendants, all of whom adopted his answer, denied that "he understands and interprets the policy of the State of Mississippi as being that Negroes and whites are educated in separate institutions of higher learning."

August 10 the hearing on the motion for a preliminary injunction, which commenced and was adjourned June 12, was resumed. But on August 11, it was recessed again. Mr. Shands had to appear in another court August 14 on motions he had filed in another suit. The hearing resumed August 15 and concluded August 16.

At the end of this hearing, the trial judge gave the defendants until September 5 to file their brief, and the plaintiff ten days thereafter to file a reply brief.

The last date to register for the fall semester was September 28. The trial judge did not decide the case until December 12. He entered an order in favor of the defendants December 14, 1961. That shot the first semester of 1961-1962. The commencement of the second semester was not far off—February 6. Immediately following entry of the order, Meredith's counsel filed a notice of appeal and moved this Court for an order advancing the appeal. This Court heard the appeal January 9 and rendered its decision January 12. We affirmed the district court's denial of the motion for a preliminary injunction. We suggested that the district court proceed promptly with a full trial on the merits.

In that decision we disposed of one of the reasons the University stressed in rejecting Meredith—the requirement that he furnish alumni certificates. We held that such a requirement is a denial of equal protection of the laws in its application to Negro candidates for admission. Again we pause, this time to say that if there is any question as to the scope of that ruling, we now hold that the requirement of recommendations, whether from alumni or from citizens generally, attesting to an applicant's good moral character, or recommending an applicant for admission, is unconstitutional when, as this case demonstrates, the burden falls more heavily on the Negroes than on whites. This is not to say, of course, that good moral character is not a reasonable test for admission.

We held that on "the muddy record" before us it was "impossible to determine whether there were valid, nondiscriminatory grounds for the University's refusing Meredith's admission." We made certain observations for the guidance of the district judge presiding at the trial. We emphasized that, *"Within proper legal bounds,* the plaintiff should be afforded a fair, unfettered, and unharassed opportunity to prove his case."

The trial on the merits set for January 15, 1962, commenced January 16. At 2:00 p.m. on that date it was postponed until 3:00 p.m. January 17, to give the defendants' counsel an opportunity to confer with the defendants. At 3:00 p.m. January 17 the defendants' counsel moved for a continuance on account of Mr. Shands' illness; he was hospitalized. The two special assistants stated to the court that they were not prepared to proceed with the trial. The district court continued the case until 2:00 p.m. January 24, 1962.

Before the trial, the district court quashed that part of a subpoena requiring the Registrar to produce admission records for the February 1961 term; the Registrar was required to produce only records commencing with the first summer term. This holding, seriously handicapping plaintiff's counsel, apparently overlooked our ruling in the earlier opinion: "The limitation of evidence to that pertaining to the summer session of 1961 is clearly erroneous. It is erroneous since the policy and practice of the University in admissions were at issue."

February 5, 1962, the district judge entered an order denying all relief requested and dismissing the complaint. The same day, the plaintiff appealed to this Court and also filed a motion for a preliminary injunction pending appeal on the ground that unless Meredith were admitted to the February 1962 term, the case would become moot. This Court heard the motion February 10. A majority of the Court, Chief Judge Tuttle dissenting, denied the motion February 12. . . . Still anxious to give this case full study on an adequate record, we held that the appeal would not necessarily be moot; that Meredith could avoid the mootness by attending Jackson State College for one quarter of the school year or by being permitted to choose courses not necessarily leading to his graduation. Meredith pursued the latter course.

The net effect of all these delays was that the February 1961 term, the two summer terms of 1961, and the two regular terms of 1961-1962 slipped by before the parties litigant actually came to a showdown fight. Some of these delays, as in any litigation, were inevitable. Some are attributable to continuances of doubtful propriety and to unreasonably long delays by the trial judge. We refer, for example, to the delay between the end of the trial, August 16, and the entry of the district court's order, December 14. Many of the delays resulted from the requests of defendants. We do not question Mr. Shands' good faith or the fact of his illness, but the Attorney General's Office is well-staffed. And—there are plenty of lawyers in Mississippi ready, able, and more than willing to represent the University. We draw the inference that not a few of the continuances and the requests for time in which to write briefs were part of the defendants' delaying action designed to defeat the plaintiff by discouragingly high obstacles that would result in the case carrying through his senior year. It almost worked.

As a matter of law, the principle of "deliberate speed" has no application at the college level; time is of the essence. In an action for admission to a graduate or undergraduate school, counsel for all the litigants and trial judges too should be sensitive to the necessity for speedy justice. . . .

IV

We turn now to the reasons the University gave in its letter of May 25 for rejecting Meredith.

A. Alumni Certificates—Letters of Recommendation

1. One of the most obvious dodges for evading the admission of Negroes to "white" colleges is the requirement that an applicant furnish letters or alumni certificates. The Board established the requirement by resolution, November 18, 1954, just a few months after the Supreme Court decided Brown v. Board of Education. We mention it again at this point in the opinion because its adoption and incorporation in current Bulletins (Catalogues) of the University show affirmative action by the Board to evade desegregation. The action unquestionably was part of conscious University and State policy. It was action that must have been preceded by discussion among members of the Board.

The University's continued use of the requirement seems completely unjustifiable in view of decisions denying the use of such certificates at Louisiana State University and at the University of Georgia. Since at least 1958, . . . the Board has been on notice that the courts construe such a requirement as an unconstitutional discrimination against Negroes. If the Board has any doubt about it, that doubt should have been resolved in 1959 when a similar requisite of the University of Georgia was held to be unconstitutional. . . . We regard the continued insistence on the requirement as demonstrable evidence of a State and University policy of segregation that was applied to Meredith.

2. Although defendants' counsel deny that the alumni certificates were for discriminatory purposes or had discriminatory effects, they assert that the enabling resolution of the Board was an administrative order having the effect of a state statute. For this reason, they say that a three-judge court should have passed on the constitutionality of the certificates. (This position is, of course, inconsistent with the defendants' we-still-say-its-scissors denial of any state policy of segregation in Mississippi's colleges.) We hold that the Board resolution was an administrative order having an effect similar to a statute, and that it constituted a broad State policy and University policy. We hold, however, that its manifest unconstitutionality makes a three-judge court unnecessary. . . .

3. The evidence also shows that the requirement of alumni certificates was discriminatorily applied to Meredith. The Registrar testified that

the files of white transfer students admitted to the 1961 summer session contained letters of recommendation which did not mention good moral character. He explained that such students were permitted to register pending the receipt of all required certificates. No such latitude was extended Meredith.

B. The University's Policy Regarding Transfer Students from Non-Member Colleges of Regional Associations

February 7, 1961, just six days after the University received Meredith's application, the Board adopted the following resolution:

"[T]hat all state-supported Institutions of Higher Learning may accept transfer students from other state supported Institutions of Higher Learning, private colleges or denomination colleges only when the previous program of the transferring college is acceptable to the receiving Institution, and the program of studies completed by the student, and the quality of the student's work in said transferring college is acceptable to the receiving Institution and to the Board of Trustees."

This resolution stiffens the policy as stated in the University Bulletin, General Catalogue, Issue 1960:

"ADMISSION FOR TRANSFER STUDENTS: ADVANCED STANDING. Students may be admitted from *other approved institutions* of higher learning upon presentation of official transcripts of credits which certify honorable dismissal and eligibility for immedate readmission." (Emphasis supplied.)

The May 25 letter advised Meredith that he was denied admission because "students may not be accepted by the University from those institutions whose programs are not recognized." Translating, the Registrar said this means that Meredith could not transfer to the University because Jackson State College was not a member of the Southern Association of Colleges and Secondary Schools. It also means that the Board, which runs Jackson State too, could set up at Jackson State and other Negro colleges a program inherently incapable of ever being approved.

But this reason is no longer valid. December 16, 1961, Jackson State was admitted to membership in the Association.

The reason was never valid, and again demonstrates a conscious pattern of unlawful discrimination.

Before December 1961, as the Registrar testified, not one of the three Negro colleges was a member of the Association. They were, however, on the Association's *approved* list of Negro Colleges. At the time Meredith applied for admission, the University catalogue, as quoted, provided that transfer students might be accepted from another "approved Institution of Higher Learning." The College Accrediting Commission of the State of Mississippi . . . has approved Jackson State College.

In defending its position, the University draws a distinction between "accepting" credits and "recognizing" credits, a distinction that eludes the Court. The defendants' explanation is that "the justification for only recognition was the fact that the appellant could not transfer from Jackson State College." Any reasonable interpretation of the resolution would limit its effect to transfer students with credits only from non-approved or non-accredited colleges. It seems to us indefensible to ignore Meredith's attendance at such accredited universities as Maryland, Kansas, and Washburn on the excuse that his last college was Jackson State.

At the trial, plaintiff's counsel inspected 214 files of students denied admission to the Summer Sessions of 1961, the September Session of 1961, and the February Session of 1962. Not one was a student who had credits from both accredited and non-accredited colleges. Thus, Meredith was not in the same category with any other student *denied* admission for lack of credits. There were six instances of students denied transfer from non-accredited schools; these students, of course, had no credits to transfer. In five instances the applicant had attended only the one non-accredited school from which he requested transfer. One was in the same academic class as the plaintiff, in the sense that he had attended an accredited school, Bucknell. Unlike Meredith's transcripts, his Bucknell transcript states: "Permitted to withdraw. Academic status unsatisfactory." At the time of his application he was taking a course in English composition at an un-accredited junior college and taking a remedial reading class somewhere else. Even so, in spite of his miserable record, the Registrar advised the boy's mother that the University of Mississippi would admit him on probation if he were eligible to return to Bucknell and if he maintained a "D" average. Thus, Meredith was not treated the same as another in the same category but with an inferior record.

In short, the transfer policy was both discriminatorily applied and irrationally construed in order to bar Meredith's admission.

C. Transfer of Credits from Jackson State

May 9, 1961, the Registrar wrote Meredith a letter in which he evaluated Meredith's 90 semester credits at 48 semester hours. Six days later, just ten days before the axe fell on May 25, the Committee on Admissions adopted a policy of accepting "credits only from institutions which are members of a regional accrediting association or a recognized professional accrediting association."

Jackson State's admission as a member of the Southern Association of Colleges and Secondary Schools removes this policy as a bar to accepting Meredith's credits from that school. At the trial the Registrar testified that the policy operated to preclude acceptance of only the Jackson State credits. It is impossible to understand, therefore, why in the letter of May 25 the Registrar gave as the first reason for turning Meredith down that the University cannot *recognize* the transfer of credits from

[an] institution which . . . is not a member of the Southern Association of Colleges and Secondary Schools." On the Registrar's own evaluation, Meredith had enough credits to be transferred as a sophomore. There is no suggestion in any of the correspondence that Meredith insisted on being transferred as a junior or that the University recognize all his credits.

We draw the inference again that the assigned reason for rejecting Meredith was a trumped-up excuse without any basis except to discriminate.

Thus far, we have covered all of the specific reasons given in the May 25 letter. On the record, as of May 25, 1961, the University had no valid, non-discriminatory grounds for refusing to accept Meredith as a student.

v

A college registrar is entitled to take advantage of play in the joints in administering an office frequently requiring deliberate ambiguity and conscious confusion in order not to offend the delicate sensibilities of some college student and his parents. We recognize the necessity for such latitude and the sagacity of the final clause in the Registrar's letter of May 25, "I see no need for mentioning any other deficiencies." But the reasonable discretion permissible in an admissions policy cannot be exercised to bring about unlawful discrimination.

We take up now the ex post facto rationalization of the turndown. It may be debatable whether the Court should consider any newly originated reasons and any post-May 25 evidence, but we sit as a court of equity. Consideration of such matters cuts both ways; the plaintiff seeks to take advantage of the new status of Jackson State College. In an analogous situation, in labor cases, evidence of a discriminatory discharge or other unfair labor practice occurring after the filing of the charge upon which the complaint is based may be considered by the National Labor Relations Board and the reviewing court. . . .

### A. *The Alleged False Registration: A Frivolous Defense*

The defendants attempted to show Meredith swore falsely before the Circuit Clerk of Hinds County in making application to register as a voter, swearing that he was a citizen of Hinds County when he knew he was a citizen of Attala County. In his opinion on the merits, the district judge declined to make a finding of fact on this point "since these facts were not known to the Registrar at the time the application was rejected," and "concluded that this testimony should not be considered" in reaching his conclusions. In his opinion on the motion for a preliminary injunction the district court said that the *defendants* "brought out on cross examination that after [Meredith] entered Jackson State . . . he swore falsely that he was a citizen of Hinds County." The district court made no finding on the alleged "false swearing," although it found that Meredith "was and is now a citizen of Attala County, Mississippi."

The complaint alleges that Meredith is a resident of Hinds County. Jackson State College is in Hinds County. Meredith registered to vote in Hinds County. That is where he lived with his wife and child. J.R. McLeod, Deputy Clerk of Hinds County registered Meredith after he received complete and accurate information from Meredith with regard to his residence. He testified that Meredith was properly registered and was "qualified to vote" in Hinds County.

Section 251 of the Mississippi Constitution prohibits registration of an elector in the four months preceding any election at which he offers to vote. But "no person who, in respect to age and residence would become entitled to vote within the said four months, shall be excluded from registration on account of his want of qualification at the time of registration."

Meredith's residence in Hinds County with his wife and child began September 1960. He registered in Hinds County February 2, 1961, which he had a right to do under Section 251 of the state constitution. As McLeod testified, "he had moved into Hinds County in time to have been qualified to have voted in 1961 (sic) since he moved in prior to the general election of 1960 . . . and on that basis I registered him." He said: Meredith "had stayed there past the general election on Tuesday after the first Monday of November which put him past one general election, and then he would have lived there a year before the next ensuing general election which would be Tuesday after the first Monday in November of '61. . . . *Yes, he was qualified to vote in Hinds County.*"

There is no false statement in the registration application Meredith filled out except the date. This he inadvertently wrote "February 2, 1960" when it was in fact February 2, 1961; the Poll Tax Exemption Certificate for Service Men, which McLeod filled out for Meredith at the same time he registered is properly dated February 2, 1961. Meredith correctly gave September 30, 1960, as the date his residence began in Jackson, in Hinds County. There can be no question therefore of any deception on his part. He stated that his prior place of residence was Kosciusko. It seems clear to us that he was open and straightforward. Meredith testified:

"I told him [the deputy clerk, McLeod] that I had been in the service [in order to qualify for a Poll Tax Exemption Certificate]. I told him that I had never lived in Hinds County. [He had not previously; the application shows the date his residence in Jackson commenced.] I told him that I had always lived in Attala County. [True enough, and necessary as a predicate for the poll tax exemption] . . . I was going to Jackson State College and wanted to register and vote in [Jackson] Hinds

County, as the voting place most convenient and closest [to his residence]. . . . I explained my whole situation to the man when I went up to register to vote."

The testimony of the deputy fully supports Meredith's testimony and the correctness of the statements in the sworn affidavit.

There is confusion in some of the testimony. Mr. Shands caused some of the confusion by repeatedly referring to the Poll Tax Exemption Certificate as the registration application. (Meredith had taken his certificate out of his pocket and was holding it in his hands during the examination.) The plaintiff caused some of the confusion by polite "Yes Sir's" to some of Mr. Shands' leading questions (e.g., "You knew it was untrue"). In the printed record these "Yes Sir's" appear at first glance to be admissions of false statements. Examining the record closer, it is evident that Meredith made no admissions of any false statements; the "Yes Sir's" simply indicating Meredith was attentive and following the questions.

We hold that the contention is frivolous. We have gone into the facts in detail only because they show a determined policy of discrimination by harassment.

### B. *Meredith a Troublemaker*

The Registrar, relying on his interpretation of Meredith's character from the correspondence and from the testimony, testified that he would have to deny Meredith admission *now*. He said, Meredith "would be a very bad influence" at the University: item one, Meredith was "a man who has got a mission in life to correct all of the ills of the world." The defendants rely more importantly on excerpts from admittedly incomplete Air Force records to support their conclusion that Meredith was "a trouble maker" who has "psychological problems in connection with his race."

Taken out of context, some portions of Meredith's record lend support to the defendants' position. The most damaging bit is a psychiatry report dated April 29, 1960:

"This is a 26 year old Negro S Sgt who complains of tension, nervousness and occasional nervous stomach. Patient is extremely concerned with the 'racial problem' and his symptoms are intensified whenever there is a heightened tempo in the racial problems in the US and Africa. Patient feels he has a strong need to fight and defy authority and this he does in usually a passive procrastinating way. At times he starts a crusade to get existing rules and regulations changed. He loses his temper at times over minor incidents both at home and elsewhere. No evidence of a thinking disorder. Diagnosis: Passive aggressive reaction, chronic, moderate. Recommendations: No treatment recommended. Patient declined any medication."

It is certainly understandable that a sensitive Negro, especially one overseas, might have a nervous stomach over the racial problem. There must be a good many Negroes stateside with similar abdominal reactions. We find it significant that the psychiatrist found "no evidence of a thinking disorder," that he found Meredith's "strong need to fight and defy authority" took a "passive" form, and that no treatment was recommended. Meredith, incidentally, voluntarily went to the psychiatrist.

The defendants expressly admit in their brief that Meredith had a good record during his first enlistment. They count on a general deterioration of attitude allegedly demonstrated in his last efficiency report. This report is for the period November 3, 1959 to July 18, 1960 at San Francisco, California, although the reporting official who made out the fitness report had directly supervised Meredith only two months. The reporting official's comments should be compared with the comments in the report dated May 22, 1959. It furnishes no basis for down-grading Meredith as a psychological risk on the campus. The rating official thought that Meredith had a "negative attitude toward most of the jobs assigned him" (he was leaving the service in a couple of months); that Meredith "exercises no tact or diplomacy in dealing with persons of equal or higher rank, thus causing unnecessary friction"; that he needs improvement in his outlook on the world, more allegiance to his squadron in the Air Force, less of an "antagonistic attitude" and more of a "spirit of cooperation." But he also wrote: "Sgt. Meredith has taken advantage of many opportunities to further his own education, and has counseled and encouraged many airmen to do likewise. He has a quick mind, [is] capable of clear thinking, and is not content to merely ride with the tide". . . . He (the reporting official, a sergeant) did not recommend Meredith for promotion. But Meredith's immediate supervisor, the Adjutant, a lieutenant, and the Unit Commander, a major, disagreed. They recommended Meredith for promotion "along with other airmen of equal service and experience."

One short answer to the defendants' contention is the Good Conduct Medal. Another short answer is that Meredith's record shows just about the type of Negro who might be expected to try to crack the racial barrier at the University of Mississippi: a man with a mission and with a nervous stomach.

## C. *Bad Character Risk*

The defendants are scraping the bottom of the barrel in asserting that the University should not now admit Meredith because he is a bad character risk. They rely on (1) the frivolous charge of false swearing, previously discussed, (2) alleged misrepresentation by Meredith in obtaining letters of recommendation from Negroes who knew him in

Attala County before he entered the Service, and (3) certain trivia.

At the trial on the merits defendants' counsel introduced affidavits from four of the five Negroes who had written letters of recommendation for Meredith. These affidavits purport to show that Meredith obtained his letters by misrepresentation. The affidavits were obtained by one of the Assistant Attorney Generals of counsel in this case. He testified:

"The affiants were requested to come to the law office of Mr. John Clark Love, which they did on their voluntariness—they came of their own volition. When they arrived there, they were interviewed in the presence of the Justice of the Peace and in one instance by the Notary who was there present. They were asked various questions as to the good moral character of the plaintiff. They were asked under what conditions had the previous or the first certificates which accompanied the application—under what conditions were they asked. And they replied that he stated that he was attempting to get a job and that was the reason the certificates were asked."

Mr. Love is a man of stature in the community. He is a State Senator and a former member of the State Sovereignty Commission.

There is no evidence of coercion. But the affidavits were drawn by the defendants' attorney and were taken in the presence of persons representing, to a country Negro, the power and prestige of The Establishment of Attala County and the State of Mississippi. The statements would have carried more weight had the affiants testified as witnesses in open court protected by the safeguards our system of law extends to witnesses. The defendants give no explanation for failing to call these affiants as witnesses.

None of the affiants alleges that Meredith is a person of bad moral character. Only two of the four allege that Meredith represented that he needed the certificate to help obtain a job. Each alleges that the affiant did not know the certificate was to be used for admission to the University. Each alleges that the affiant had seen very little of Meredith since he left Kosciusko in 1949; that the affiant could not now certify to his good character nor recommend him for admission to the University of Mississippi.

An unsigned affidavit from the fifth affiant, the plaintiff's cousin, states: "At the time of the signing of this statement [the recommendation] I knew full well and was aware of the purpose for which such certificate was to be executed." This unsigned statement, unlike the executed affidavits, significantly is the only one that contains the following declaration: "I am not now nor have I ever been in any serious trouble or convicted of any crime or misdemeanor."

In sum, we consider it unreasonable to attach any substantial weight to these affidavits. They do not carry enough weight in themselves nor in connection with the evidence as a whole of Meredith's character to justify a reasonable belief that Meredith is a bad moral risk as a University student.

The other asserted "evidences" of bad moral character are trivia. The defendants contend that:

1. Meredith was "adamant [in] refus[ing] to properly get and send to the Registrar certificates from Alumni as to his good moral character"; further, "those certificates which he sent in lieu of the Alumni certificates never were valid certificates as they are absolutely silent as to the position or standing of the certifiers in the community."

2. Meredith admitted that he brought stationery with him from the Air Force. (This refers to a few sheets of surplus stationery. This question as to his honesty led to inquiries as to government property being in his possession and required the production of the serial number of a typewriter purchased after his discharge.)

3. "Appellant was not a good character risk for he refused to list Wayne University in his application to the University, when the application required that the prospective applicant list all universities and colleges attended." (Meredith attended Wayne for two weeks only.)

These are on a par with the defense, asserted in the complaint, that one of the reasons for rejecting the application was that "all letters received by [the Registrar] from plaintiff were sent registered mail return receipt requested." Or with the defense, argued even now, that his application is incomplete because "appellant has not seen fit to forward a supplemental transcript from Jackson State." This transcript was introduced into evidence and is in the record. Meredith repeatedly asked the Registrar to advise him whether there was anything further he needed to do to complete his application.

The triviality of these and other of the defendants' contentions is a proper consideration for the Court in reviewing the whole case to determine whether the University barred Meredith for good and valid reasons or in fact barred him because he was a Negro.

*Conclusion*

There are cases when discrimination is purposeless but unlawful because of its effect. In this case the essence of the complaint is purposeful discrimination against Negroes as a class. The inquiry into purpose makes it especially appropriate for the Court:

(1) To study the case as a whole, weighing all of the evidence and rational inferences in order to reach a net result;

(2) To consider the immediate facts in the light of the institution's past and present policy on segregation, as reflected not only in statutes and regulations, history and common knowledge;

(3) To measure sincerity of purpose against unreasonable delays and insubstantial reasons asserted for the institution's actions;

(4) To compare the actions taken with regard to the plaintiff with actions taken with regard to others in the same category;

(5) To pierce the veil of innocuity when a statute, regulation, or policy necessarily discriminates unlawfully or is applied unlawfully to accomplish discrimination.

The defendants fail the test. There are none so blind as those that will not see.

The defendants' answer asserts and the Registrar testified that the State of Mississippi has no policy of educating Negroes and whites in separate institutions. This is in the teeth of statutes, only a few of which need be cited for illustration. It is contrary to official state publications with which every college official in Mississippi must be familiar. It defies history and common knowledge.

Similarly, the defendants assert that there is no policy of excluding Negroes at the University. The district judge found that there was a policy of segregation *before* Brown v. Board of Education was decided in 1954. The trustees and the principal officials of the University testified that *after* 1954 there has been no change in policy with respect to the admission of Negroes. They testified that the admission of Negroes had never been discussed in any meeting of the Board or in any meeting of the administrative staff. In spite of the enormous publicity given to this case by the newspapers, some of which are in evidence, the trustees and other personal defendants said that none of the officials of the University discussed Meredith's application in an official capacity. Even the Registrar had not discussed Meredith's application with anyone except with the Dean of the College of Liberal Arts, who had merely referred Meredith's letter to the Registrar, and with the Director of Development who agreed that Meredith was planning to file suit. The hard fact to get around is that no person known to be a Negro has ever attended the University. In a similar situation involving the University of Alabama the district court made the finding, which we affirmed, that:

"There is no written policy or rule excluding prospective students from admission to the University on account of race or color. However, there is a tacit policy to that effect". . . .

The policy admittedly existed when, even under the Plessy v. Ferguson doctrine, . . . Negroes were being admitted to other state universities because the facilities ("programs" here) of the Negro colleges were not equal to the facilities of white colleges. . . . By an ironic twist, the defendants, *after* Plessy v. Ferguson has been overruled, seize upon the inferiority of the facilities—programs of Negro colleges as reason for excluding Negroes at Mississippi's white colleges and universities.

Reading the 1350 pages in the record as a whole, we find that James H. Meredith's application for transfer to the University of Mississippi was turned down solely because he was a Negro. We see no valid, non-discriminatory reason for the University's not accepting Meredith. Instead, we see a well-defined pattern of delays and frustrations, part of a Fabian policy of worrying the enemy into defeat while time worked for the defenders.

The judgment of the district court is Reversed and the case Remanded with directions that the district court issue the injunction as prayed for in the complaint, the district court to retain jurisdicion.

### Judge DeVane's Dissent: July 10, 1962

After the federal court of appeals' opinion of June 25, ordering my admission, Judge DeVane filed a dissent in which he agreed with most of the appellate court's finding, but would have sustained the district court on the University's contention that the basis of its conclusions was that I would become a "troublemaker" and that my admission to the University would be "nothing short of a catastrophe."

Considered as a brief in support of appellant's case, the decision of Judge Wisdom is a masterpiece. I agree with almost everything he has to say in the opinion about the defense advanced by appellees and I further agree that appellees scraped the "bottom of the barrel" in their efforts to keep Meredith out of the University of Mississippi. In so doing appellees weakened their case very much before this Court for on every ground save one the defenses advanced are not deserving of serious consideration by this Court.

The one defense that leads me to dissent is the fear expressed by the appellees that Meredith would be a troublemaker if permitted to enter the University of Mississippi. Judge Wisdom sets out the evidence forthrightly in his opinion dealing with this issue and reaches the conclusion that it too is not a valid defense to the efforts of appellees to keep appellant out of the University. Considering the facts as he outlines them in his opinion, I disagree with the Court's conclusion on this issue.

Judge Mize heard the case, observed appellant throughout the trial and reached the definite conclusion from appellant's testimony, his conduct and other testimony that was offered that Meredith would be a troublemaker if permitted to enter the University. Under such circumstances, the opinion of Judge Mize is entitled to more weight than any conclusion that could be reached by Court of Appeals Judges where their opinion is based upon a cold, printed record of the facts at issue. This conclusion is supported by the last sentence in Judge Wisdom's opinion on this point, when he states:

"Another short answer (to the defendants' contention) is that Meredith's record shows just about the type of Negro who might be expected to try to crack the racial barrier at the University of Mississippi: a man with a mission and with a nervous stomach."

In considering this matter, I recognize that the appellees never have, and probably never will, approve the decision of the Supreme Court of the United States in Brown, et al. v. Board of Education of Topeka, et al. . . . Nevertheless, my approach to this issue, and I am sure it was the approach of Judge Mize, is the same as my approach to many laws District Judges are called upon to enforce where the District Judge would prefer that the law was otherwise. This had never deterred me in following the mandates of Congress and the Supreme Court insofar as the laws of the United States are concerned, and I am sure that it would not deter Judge Mize in ordering the appellees to admit Meredith to the University of Mississippi, if he felt that the proof on this issue was not sufficient to support his decision to deny appellant's application for entry.

In passing upon this case, I do not consider that we have a right to ignore what the effect of this decision could be upon the citizens of Mississippi and I feel that it is the duty of our Courts to avoid where we can incidents such as the Little Rock case and I fear that the result of this decision may lead to another comparable situation, particularly for "a man with a mission and with a nervous stomach." Integration is not a question that can ever be settled by Federal Judges. It is an economic, social and religious question and in the end will be amicably settled on this basis.

In my opinion Judge Mize was correct in finding and holding that appellant bore all the characteristics of becoming a troublemaker if permitted to enter the University of Mississippi and his entry therein may be nothing short of a catastrophe.

I, therefore, dissent for the reasons stated above.

### Judge Cameron's Stay Orders

After the Fifth Circuit Court of Appeals had ruled in my favor, Mississippi turned to their own son of the Mississippi soil, Judge Ben F. Cameron of the Fifth Circuit Court, who had not participated in the hearings in the case which resulted in the court's favorable order of June 25. He issued an order on July 18, the day the Court of Appeals' mandate was sent to the District Court, staying the enforcement of the mandate until the University officials could apply to the United States Supreme Court for a writ of certiorari.

On July 27 the Court of Appeals entered another order setting aside Judge Cameron's stay of July 18. It was pointed out that defendants had not taken advantage of their right to apply for a rehearing or stay of mandate to the court which had directed the issuance of an injunction, but rather had sought relief from a judge who had not been a member of the court which heard any of plaintiff's appeals. The court held that when a mandate has been issued, a stay cannot be granted; and two of the Judges were of the opinion that the stay was improvidently granted. On the following day, however, Judge Cameron entered a second stay order reaffirming the reasoning of his first order.

On July 28, the same day as Judge Cameron's second stay, the other members of the Fifth Circuit Court of Appeals set aside that order. Three days later, Judge Cameron signed yet another order extending his order of July 28 to stay the action of the other members of the court later on that same date.

On August 4 the other members of the Fifth Circuit Court of Appeals reaffirmed their orders of July 17 and 27 and declared Judge Cameron's orders of July 28 and 31 unauthorized, erroneous, and improvident, and ordered them vacated and set aside.

Two days later, Judge Cameron again reaffirmed his earlier orders and declared the Court of Appeals' orders stayed until disposition of the case by the United States Supreme Court, provided that within thirty days a certificate must be filed with the Court of Appeals stating that a petition for certiorari and record had been perfected.

### Board of Trustees' Order: September 4, 1962

Early in September the college board met to adopt the following resolution withdrawing all powers from officials of the University of Mississippi to act in my case:

Many legal and factual events have occurred relating to and affecting the application of James Howard Meredith for admission as an undergraduate transfer student to the University of Mississippi: Pursuant to the constitutional and statutory authority vested in this Board of Trustees, all prerogatives, powers, duties, responsibilities and authority in anywise connected with or relating to action on the application of James Howard Meredith to the University of Mississippi for admission to said institution as an undergraduate transfer student, and/or the admission or non-admission of James Howard Meredith as a student at said University, under and pursuant to said application or otherwise, should be and the same is hereby withdrawn from every official of the University of Mississippi; each and all of such officials are expressly denied any prerogative, responsibility, power, duty or authority to act or refrain from acting with regard to the application and/or admittance of the said James Howard Meredith to the said University of Mississippi; and the entire power, authority, duty, responsibility and prerogative with regard to action on the application and/or admission of said James Howard Meredith should be and the same to be hereby expressly reserved exclusively unto this Board of Trustees of Institutions of Higher Learning, effective immediately upon the adoption of this resolution and continuing until definitive action on said application and/or admission to be taken by this said Board of Trustees.

### Justice Black's Action: September 10, 1962

In the meantime Justice Hugo L. Black of the United States Supreme Court was asked to vacate Cameron's various stay orders. This Justice Black did, announcing at the time that he had consulted the other members of the Supreme Court on the propriety of his act.

This is a motion asking me to vacate orders of Judge Ben F. Cameron, a Judge of the Court of Appeals for the Fifth Circuit, which purport to stay the execution and enforcement of mandates of that court. The Court of Appeals held that movant Meredith, a Negro, had been denied admission to the University of Mississippi solely because of his race. The court granted injunctive relief which has the effect of requiring the admission of Meredith to the University of Mississippi at the opening of its new academic year commencing in September 1962.

Judge Cameron, however, stayed the mandate of the Court of Appeals pending action by this Court on a petition for writ of certiorari by respondents in this motion. Later the Court of Appeals vacated the stay on the grounds (1) that Judge Cameron's action came too late, and (2) that his stay had been "improvidently granted." Judge Cameron nevertheless later issued three other stays, claiming that his first stay had rendered any further proceedings of the Court of Appeals "void and beyond the jurisdiction" of that court. The Court of Appeals has treated all of Judge Cameron's stays as ineffective and void.

The respondents, trustees and officials of the University, who were enjoined by the Court of Appeals, have filed a petition for a writ of certiorari, and the movant Meredith has waived his right to a brief in opposition to that petition. In this situation I am satisfied that the Court has jurisdiction and power under 28 U.S.C. 1651 to take such steps as are necessary to preserve the rights of the parties pending final determination of the case and that 28 U.S. 201 (f) and Rule 51 of the Rules of this Court give the same jurisdiction and power to me as a single Justice of this Court.

I agree with the Court of Appeals that the stay issued in this case can only work further delay and injury to movant while immediate enforcement of the judgment can do no appreciable harm to the University or the other respondents. I further agree with the Court of Appeals that there is very little likelihood that this Court will grant certiorari to review the judgment of the Court of Appeals, which essentially involves only factual issues. I am therefore of the opinion that all the stays issued by Judge Cameron should be and they are hereby vacated, that the judgment and mandate of the Court of Appeals should be obeyed, and that pending final action by this Court on the petition for certiorari the respondents should be and they are hereby enjoined from taking any steps to prevent enforcement of the Court of Appeals' judgment and mandate.

Although convinced that I have the power to act alone in this matter, I have submitted it to each of my Brethren, and I am authorized to state that each of them agrees that the case is properly before this Court, that I have power to act, and that under the circumstances I should exercise that power as I have done here.

### District Court's Injunction: September 13, 1962

Now there were no further legal blocks that Mississippi could throw in my path to keep me from enrolling as a student at the University of Mississippi. Consequently, the United States District Court, acting under the various Court of Appeals' mandates and Justice Black's mandate of September 10, issued an injunction on September 13 against University of Mississippi officials, ordering them to admit me to the university upon my application heretofore filed and enjoined them from excluding me from admission and continuing attendance at the university or discriminating against me in any way whatsoever because of my race.

### The Governor's Proclamation: September 13, 1962

But the state of Mississippi, under the leadership of Governor Ross Barnett and the white Citizens Council, would not let this be the end. On the very day that the District Court's injunction was issued, the Governor of Mississippi issued a proclamation directing state education and university officials to defy the court orders:

WHEREAS, the United States of America consists of fifty Sovereign States bound together basically for their common welfare; and

WHEREAS, The Constitution of the United States of America provides that each state is sovereign with respect to certain rights and powers; and

WHEREAS, pursuant to the Tenth Amendment to the Constitution of the United States, the powers not specifically delegated to the Federal Government are reserved to the several states; and

WHEREAS, the operation of the public school system is one of the powers which was not delegated to the Federal Government but which was reserved to the respective states pursuant to the terms of the Tenth Amendment; and

WHEREAS, we are now face to face with the direct usurpation of this power by the Federal Government through the illegal use of judicial decree;

NOW, THEREFORE, I, Ross R. Barnett, Governor of the Sovereign State of Mississippi, by authority vested in me, do hereby proclaim that the operation of the public schools, universities and colleges of the State of Mississippi is vested in the duly elected and appointed officials to uphold and enforce the laws duly and legally enacted by the Legislature of the State of Mississippi, regardless of this unwarranted, illegal and arbitrary usurpation of power; and to interpose the State Sovereignty and themselves between the people of the State and anybody politic seeking to usurp such power.

IN WITNESS WHEREOF, I have hereunto set my hand and caused the Great Seal of the State of Mississippi to be affixed, on this the 13th day of September, in the Year of Our Lord, One Thousand Nine Hundred and Sixty-Two.

Ross Barnett
GOVERNOR

## The United States Enters As Amicus Curiae: September 18, 1962

Mississippi had declared itself in effect no longer subject to the laws of the United States. The United States now became officially a party to my case against the state of Mississippi. On September 18 the Court of Appeals for the Fifth Circuit entered an order permitting the United States to appear as amicus curiae in the case:

It appearing from the application of the United States, filed this day, that the interest of the United States in the due administration of justice and the integrity of the processes of its courts should be represented in these proceedings.

IT IS ORDERED that the United States be designated and authorized to appear and participate as amicus curiae in all proceedings in this action before this Court and by reason of the mandates and orders of this Court of July 27, 28, 1962.

*My Day in a Mississippi Jail*

While the federal courts were dispensing justice, the Mississippi system of justice was at work, too.

Early one morning I heard a knock at my door. When I answered, I found a deputy sheriff with a warrant for my arrest. I was not dressed, and he gave me time to dress and call Medgar Evers. The Law waited on the steps. When I was ready to go, we got into the police car and drove away. He stopped some place and picked up his partner and we proceeded to the county jail. Apparently, they were instructed not to give me the usual treatment. They never said a word to me during the trip to the jail, although I knew they were capable of giving the treatment, because they were using extremely vile language in their normal talk between themselves.

We went into the jail and they presented me to the jailer. He asked me some questions and what I had in my pockets. I gave him the information that he wanted and some of the items in my possession, keeping the rest, which included some money. They never put their hands on me for any purpose, not even to search me.

This was my first and only time in a jail of any kind. I was put into a big cell with a large number of other Negroes who were charged with crimes ranging from petty thievery to murder. The one I recall most vividly was a boy who was charged with killing a white man. He asserted that he was innocent and lamented in a most touching way, "Look at me, sixteen years old and fixing to die, and I ain't never loved a woman." The day I was in jail was visitors' day. I had never known what it means to have someone to love, until I witnessed visiting day in the Hinds County Jail.

Gambling was a major pastime in the jail—cards, dice, and matching coins. One young inmate asked me so persistently to give him a "stake" that I obliged him. I didn't get in any of the gambling games, but I played several games of "Whist," a favorite among Negroes. The other major pastime was telling tales and talking about why we were in jail. I guess that during the day I must have listened to the stories of seventy-five per cent of the other prisoners.

Frankly, I never expected to stay in jail all day. I understand the delay was caused by the fact that the property bond was refused and a cash bond had to be placed. Finally, about 5:00 P.M. Attorney Jack Young came and got me out.

Jail is not my idea of the best place from which to fight a war. As a matter of fact, one sure way to remove me from this world is to put me in a Mississippi jail without just cause. I have vowed that I will never eat a meal in a Mississippi jail under these conditions. I would rather starve to death.

## Conferences in New York

Shortly after my jailing in Mississippi, Mrs. Motley asked me to come to New York to confer with them about the case. I felt rather sure, however, that the primary intention was to get me out of the state.

While in New York, I was interviewed by the *New York Post* columnist, Mr. James A. Wechsler, and the following article appeared on July 24, 1962:

### AMERICAN SAGA

By all our conventional standards, James H. Meredith, the son of a dirt farmer, should be recognized as the embodiment of the American story and saluted as young-man-of-the-year by the Junior Chamber of Commerce.

Graduated from high school in 1951, he patiently and stolidly served as a clerk-typist in the Air Force for nine years, finally accumulating sufficient funds to finance himself through the University of Mississippi and then perhaps through law school. Along the way, he met and married a girl who was working on an Air Force post in Indiana.

When he decided he had amassed adequate resources to realize his dream, there was, of course, only one trouble with the life-plan. He was a Negro, and the state of Mississippi has now for many months mobilized all its legal resources to thwart his aspiration. Three full semesters and four summer sessions have passed since he began his fight to break the educational color line in that state, but victory still eludes him.

In the July issue of *Harper's*, editor John Fischer, a journalist of distinction, calls on American Negroes to form a "First Class Citizens Council" to improve the manners and morals of their people so that whites may be finally convinced "that they have nothing to fear from close, daily association with Negroes in jobs, schools and neighborhoods." He argues that only "pockets of resistance" to equality still exist, and that the time has come for Negroes to put their own house in order.

It was perhaps Mr. Fischer's misfortune that I belatedly read his piece on the way to work on the morning of the day when I was to meet James H. Meredith. I could not avoid wishing that Fischer were present then, not because he is ignorant of the Meredith case but because the impact of a "case" can be so remarkably more poignant when it is encountered in person, and because, the phrase "pockets of resistance"—like "pockets of poverty"—has become so listless a cover for a multitude of sins. . . .

Meredith coincidentally resembles a thinner image of Martin Luther King. Like King, neither his voice nor manner exhibits any surface scars of martyrdom, nor does he, by the way, affirm any doctrinaire allegiance to King or anyone else.

But let his story speak for itself. He was the grandson of slaves; his father remains his "greatest inspiration" because he cut loose from unofficial bondage by creating with his own energy and will, which included the clearing of trees, a dirt farm of his own. It brought a limited living, but he forced his children, of whom James was the sixth of ten, to walk their four miles to school and to envisage better things. . . .

"America was not exactly what I wanted it to be—but some day I could go back and make it what it should be." Throughout those years in military exile he clung to his notion: that some day he would go back to Mississippi, and gain admission to the all-white University and later become a lawyer or political scientist in that state, so that his voice could be heard and no one could call him an outsider, or an alien agitator. . . .

Who can know how many times his hope faltered? Who can know how close he came to explosion amid the polite insults of Air Force life? One can only report that he spoke yesterday with mingled serenity and solemnity about his goal—to be an active Citizen of Mississippi, and no other place. "If I ever leave Mississippi," he said quietly, "I will be leaving the country."

He remains convinced that "the politicians" are responsible for the backward racism of the state, and that, if he gained admission to the University, he would be treated decently by faculty and students alike. He insists he has no fears about being the first to cross that line. . . .

January 1961, he applied for admission to (all-white) Mississippi University and the legal maneuvering began.

It is still going on with the NAACP's legal task force representing him. But the point that is emphasized at the NAACP is that Meredith is not the familiar "test-case." This was his fight from the beginning—a long time ago, perhaps when his father dreamed, and he dared not miss a day of school.

Meredith has won some legal victories on this long road and in the end he will probably break the final barrier, even if he must finally go to the Supreme Court. This much is clear: they are not shattering his spirit; they are fools if they believe they are. By the same token, it is an unctuous irrelevance for a Northern magazine editor to lecture Negroes on their deportment when such crude atrocities as the Meredith Case cry out for national observance. One might even say that it is the miracle of democracy that James Meredith still believes in it.

*Mike Bell's Story About the Rabbits*

When I returned from New York, it was late in the summer, the trial had been completed and the verdict had been rendered and appealed and reappealed, overruled and reinstated by every court in the federal system, including the Supreme Court of the United States. How could there be any further doubt? There were few people in the United States, and even in Mississippi, who did not have an opinion about the Meredith case. I returned to my home town. I made the usual rounds, the neighborhoods, the city square, Beale Street, and I had come to rest in the pool hall where the proprietor was an ex-schoolmate of mine during high school days.

Mike Bell was high-spirited and called for the pool games to stop and gathered all the boys around to pay tribute to a town hero. Mike told them about our schooldays and why they should be proud of me. All the boys were going completely along with him. Certainly, this enhanced my sense of grandeur and I was basking in my glory.

But one boy in the crowd just couldn't seem to sense the importance of all this talk. Boldly, he spoke up and said that he didn't understand what the whole University of Mississippi business was about. He wanted to know what my objective was, what was the goal. Young curious minds will ask questions and demand answers. However, I had seen this little fellow before a couple of times and I remembered where. My youngest sister was still in high school, and I had seen him at our house and probably had not treated him with the deference that he perhaps considered appropriate.

Nevertheless, the question had been put and I was looked to for an answer. For forty-five minutes I outlined the history of the Negro in Mississippi, pointed out all the ills of the Mississippi society, and my hopes for the future. When I had finished, my friend said, "Yes, I agree with all that, but I still don't see what you are trying to accomplish, what you expect to gain, even if you go to that school." He had placed before me a simple, basic question, and I did not have a clear, concise, and simple answer. I started out again for another thirty minutes. This time I tried to express my great wish that my efforts would somehow sweep the multitude of Negroes into unstoppable action. That I hoped my deeds would lead to Negro unity, which in turn would lead to the breaking of the Negroes' restraining bonds.

About this time Mike felt a need to rescue me and he cut in to tell the story about the rabbits. I really don't know what the story did to the boy who was putting me on the spot, but it clarified my own thinking in a way that I had never before experienced. The symbolism was magnificent. I feel utterly unqualified to relate this story, but to the best of my recollection it was as follows:

A long time ago, it used to be the sport of the great hunters to go to Africa (I don't know why he chose Africa) and hunt rabbits. Every year they would kill thousands of rabbits. One day as the hunting season was about to begin, the rabbits were sitting in the bush watching all the ships coming in and unloading the many hunters and their fine guns and well-bred dogs, coming to take their sport at hunting and tracking down and killing rabbits. Seeing all these preparations being made against them, one wise rabbit said, "The hunters have been coming to Africa for all these years and hunting us down and killing us one at a time. Now since we are going to die anyway, why should we run and be chased around first? Why don't we just all get together and march down to the sea and drown ourselves?" The rabbits all agreed. They were going to march to the sea and drown themselves rather than be shot one at a time by the hunters.

On the appointed day the wise rabbit got in front of his brothers and sisters and started the march to the sea to drown themselves. They started the march, and on their way to the sea they first ran into a herd of elephants. When the elephants—the largest animals in the world and known to stampede over all others—looked up and saw all the rabbits marching together one after the other, they scattered to the four winds in fear of this solidarity. The rabbits marched on toward their destination of death.

The next animals they met were the tigers. The tiger is known for his agility, speed, boldness, and deadliness in the face of his foe. But the tigers, seeing all the rabbits marching together, fled and hid themselves from this strange phenomenon.

Finally, the rabbits met head on with a pride of lions. Everyone knows that the lion is king of the jungle and fears no one. But when the lions saw all these rabbits following behind their leader on their way to the sea to drown themselves rather than being killed one at a time by the hunters, they scattered in panic and disappeared into the depths of the jungle. The rabbits marched on.

At last, they reached the dogs of the hunters, dogs which were trained to search out rabbits and chase them into the range of the hunters' guns. But when the dogs saw all these rabbits marching together, instead of chasing them, they turned and ran past their masters. The rabbits marched on until they were in view of the hunters. The hunters aimed their guns, but when they saw all these rabbits following their wise leader in their march to the sea to die together, the hunters threw away their guns and ran for their ships without firing a shot, never again to return.

After seeing all these strange things happen—the elephants, the tigers, the lions, the dogs, and the hunters running away in fear before the united line of the heretofore harmless and helpless rabbits—the wise rabbit turned around, held his hands high, and halted the rabbits just before they reached the sea. He said, "Man, wait a minute. We don't have to drown ourselves, all we have to do is stick together."

# 7

## The Last Days Before Admission: September 1962

SEPTEMBER had arrived, and in the United States universities begin their fall terms during this month; the registration period at the University of Mississippi was scheduled for September 19 to 24. The Meredith case had dominated public attention in the state for more than a year, and for at least six months it had had a near monopoly in the area of prime concern. It would have been hard to find a Mississippian who was not conversant with the prospects of a Negro attending the University of Mississippi. Judge Mize had betrayed his fellow white Mississippians and had complied with the order of the Fifth Circuit Court of Appeals to change his ruling against me and to issue an injunction against the state of Mississippi and the university, forbidding them to deny my admission. Ordinarily this would have seemed clear and final, but there were few, if any, who believed that this would settle the case. The major test was still to come.

### The Question of My Security

Obviously the first item of consideration at this point was my security. Without me there could be no resolution of the immediate questions in search of answers. Certainly if I were disposed of or eliminated the showdown could not occur. Over the past twenty months my personal view toward this question of security had been fairly well established. My major guideline was that no obvious

signs of security should be displayed unless and until there was absolute and concrete evidence of "a clear and present danger." It had
been my decision to stay in Mississippi and conduct my life in a
completely routine manner, whereas the policy of the NAACP
Legal Defense and Educational Fund and the Justice Department
had been to keep me out of Mississippi.

We had also differed on the manner of handling the harassments
and intimidations of the Negroes in my home town who had signed
the recommendations for me to be admitted to the University of
Mississippi. The Legal Defense Fund had wanted to make an issue
of the events and to file complaints to the Justice Department and
the Civil Rights Commission. I had vetoed this idea each time for
two reasons. The first was that I felt that the ultimate responsibility
for the security of one's life and property rested with the individual
citizen. The price of changing one's relative position in society is
essentially high, and every man is obligated to shoulder whatever
part of the burden that may fall on him, even when it may be necessarily unequal. It was my belief that harassment and intimidation
were to be expected for they are part of the price, and that these
men in my home town were obligated to defend their own interests
so long as it was humanly possible. No one should attempt to aid
them, or even had the right to help them, unless and until they specifically asked for it. The second reason was that there was nothing
that the Justice Department or Civil Rights Commission could do
which would effectively aid these men in any way that was basically
meaningful. The only result would be to publicize the situation to
the rest of the United States, and under our system of law, with its
right to trial by a local jury, this meant in effect—nothing.

*The Trick.* Frankly, I "smelled-a-rat" when I got a call in Kosciusko from Mrs. Motley in New York. She wanted to know how
quickly I could get to Memphis. It was too simple a request, "Meet
me in Memphis as quick as you can get there; I will explain everything when you get to Memphis." This city had never been mentioned in the twenty months that the case had gone on. I had been
through Memphis, perhaps as many times as I had been through any
city, but I had never stopped except for gasoline. Mrs. Motley had
given me the name of a lawyer in whose office I was to meet her. I immediately packed my old Air Force shaving kit and, supposing that
it would an overnight affair, took along one extra pair of pants and
a shirt and was away in less than a hour.

Going directly to the lawyer's office, I met Attorney A.W.

Willis, Jr., for the first time and asked him where Mrs. Motley was. He started to go through a prescribed routine, but it was against his nature. I was in a bad frame of mind and proceeded to raise a moderate amount of hell. Willis came straight out and said that the whole scheme was a trick "to get you the hell out of Mississippi." He explained that he was no party to anything and that he was simply asked to find me a place to stay and to relay a few messages. He then got on the phone and called New York and we talked. I was incensed by the whole affair.

A.W. Willis, Jr., was a man whom I liked immediately. He has a definitely new approach to the question of Negro rights. Almost totally free of the idealism that dominates the thinking of most outstanding Negroes, his approach was realistic and based on a concept of reward in proportion to power. Only an A.W. Willis could have kept me from going back to Mississippi at this point. Nevertheless, it is this issue—whether I should fight my war against the system of "White Supremacy" in Mississippi from inside or outside the state —that has aroused my greatest concern about its correctness or logic. Remaining out of Mississippi during the most crucial period is perhaps the only clear-cut instance of my accepting an arbitrary decision which had not met the test of my decision-making formula.

My first night in Memphis was spent in a rooming house. The people were really quite nice, but this was a completely new experience for me. I had always traveled in the midst of relatives and personal friends or friends of friends, and for anyone to have the audacity to make arrangements for me to stay in a common, impersonal rooming house was more than I could stand. I knew that one of my first cousins lived in Memphis, but I did not know her married name. I called my mother and learned her name but she did not know her address. I went to bed and tried to console myself but it was impossible.

After a very poor night's sleep, I got up before five o'clock in the morning and found a telephone book. My cousin's number was listed. I called and told them that I would be right out and I would talk to them when I got there. I then got my shaving kit and quietly left the rooming house. The taxi had some trouble finding the address because it was in the newest Negro housing development near the southernmost city limits of Memphis. It was a relief to see the house—a new three-bedroom brick bungalow with a nice lawn, and a new Chevrolet was in the carport. I picked up the morning paper on my way in to be greeted by a rather puzzled set of cousins. My cousin Katherine, my mother's sister's daughter, her husband Robert Terrell, and my cousin Irma Jean Battle, Katherine's younger sister, all were there to hear my story. Robert was visibly amazed at my coming to their house at such a crucial point as this. They were all public school teachers in the Memphis school system and former Mississippians.

Willis had kept me from going back to Mississippi the day before, but there can be no doubt that it was cousin Katherine and her hospitality that made it tolerable for me to sit out twelve days in Memphis. She gave me the most royal treatment. I was given the master bedroom—exclusively—in spite of my protests. Everything was done to insure my absolute comfort and contentment. By the time I called A.W.'s office to check in with him around nine o'clock, a general alarm had gone out. They thought I had gone back to Mississippi.

*Chief U.S. Marshal James P. McShane.* Willis told me to come down to the office because I was supposed to meet somebody and he couldn't tell me who it was over the phone. I went down and learned that Chief U.S. Marshal McShane was in town and wanted to have a top-top-secret meeting with me. The only thing that I knew about U.S. marshals was what I knew about Wyatt Earp and Matt Dillion, and I thought they had gone out with the Lone Ranger. I have always been one who was intrigued by secret operations but this degree of secrecy was incomprehensible to me.

McShane arrived with the Chief U.S. Marshal of Tennessee. They were both big men, but they seemed extremely apprehensive. McShane was not the McShane he was to be a few days later. He definitely is more at home in situations of danger than he is in secret negotiations with people whom he doesn't know. I tried to crack a few jokes but they didn't go over. The meeting was very short and its only result was that I had met McShane for the first time. Obviously, he did not know what his government wanted him to tell me or what he was to find out from me. The only thing that he knew for sure was that they definitely did not want anyone to know that he was talking to me. I had to promise that I would never reveal that I had attended this meeting and the arranged communications channel was entirely indirect. Willis was to contact the Tennessee Marshal by a coded message to a private number but was not to call his office and vice versa if they wanted to contact us. The case was taking on wider dimensions.

My next meeting with McShane a few days later was more informative. Apparently the federal government had decided to play an overt role in the Mississippi affair, although how extensively was not yet known. We talked about the question of my security and the fact that the state of Mississippi, as well as the vigilantes, would now be seriously considering doing away with me. My name had become sufficiently known around the country, and even outside of it, to force the federal government in its own interests to make an effort to prevent my being removed from the scene by unnatural causes.

McShane told me that the government proposed to have U.S. marshals escort me to the campus when I attempted to register. Of course, Barnett had issued his nullification doctrine on September 13, and it was clear that the state would resist. I was not necessarily opposed to this action by the federal government, but I had to be concerned not only with the present but also with the future.

*Force or Psychology.* The main question that I had to answer was whether or not my security would be best insured by the use of external and temporary force, such as the U.S. marshals, or by psychology which, of course, is real and permanent. Violence has two effective methods. The direct application of violence and the threat of violence. The actual use of violence is a very rare occurrence, even in Mississippi; it is the threat of violence that maintains the system. Furthermore, direct violence is seldom, if ever, used without the concomitant element of wide publicity, both before the event and after. Otherwise, violence is only committed by fanatics and misfits, and there is no assurance against them under almost any circumstances. I was convinced that my chances of being seriously harmed without proper warning were extremely slim.

There are great psychological advantages to resisting the threat of violence right down to the very point of actual violence. It establishes a condition of normality from which each competing side can press for a turn in its favor. For example, let us say that it is the local rule that a Negro must get off the sidewalk whenever he meets a white, or else the Negro is threatened with violence. If the Negro resists this threat and refuses to get off the sidewalk to the point where violence will actually be required to force him off the sidewalk, the controller of violence then has to face the concrete situation. The chances are very good that he will change his demand so that the Negro does not have to get off the sidewalk, but instead he must now make sure that he does not bump into the white.

I have spent many years studying the institution of lynching. In its present form, lynching is a religious ceremony, a highly ritualistic event. The ritual has to follow well-defined specifications. There has to be a commonly accepted justification that meets one or more of the traditional requirements. In Mississippi a lynching has to be tied to the virtue of a white woman. The two most unacceptable crimes for a Negro is to rape a white woman or to kill a white man. These two acts are equally guilty of threatening the virtue of the white woman. When the religious fervor is ripe, if a Negro looks at a white woman or talks back to a white man, it can be construed to be identical to raping or killing.

Since lynching is a religious ceremony, there are certain basic and essential conditions that must exist before a lynching can be finalized. This was my "ace in the hole," the necessary conditions. It would be quite impossible for a preacher to move the football fans in a stadium to feel solemn religious devotion at the beginning of a big popular game. However, if the star player was killed in a mishap during the first half of the game, the preacher could certainly move the audience to the deepest form of devotion at half time. The necessary conditions would have been provided.

What are the essentials of a lynching ceremony? There must be a common victim for the lynching community and he must be guilty in the minds of the lynchers of threatening the virtue or purity of the white woman. It is important to understand that the whole community is always involved in a lynching, even though the actual violence itself may be done or even observed by only a small group from the community. If the community is not totally involved, it would not constitute a lynching. It would just be a killing or a murder. Once the victim and the crime have been established and the necessary advertisement completed, the ritual can then begin. It is not permissible for any individual member of the lynch group to commit a personal, unjustifiable crime against the lynch victim. The lyncher must maintain his innocence. It must be understood that the lynchers are the same people that will go to work or about their business the next day and work quite amicably and in a friendly manner with other Negroes, even the close relatives of the victim. The ritual basically involves the process of provoking anger and hostility in the victim and of instilling fear. To unbalance any of these essentials would render the lynching impossible.

These may all be thoughts from the top of my head, but at the time I believed them and felt that I could react in such a manner to raise sufficient doubts as to the application of these necessary conditions, and therefore render the lynching ceremony inoperative. In the first place, there is no reasonable link between the idea of a Negro going to a white school and the threat to the virtue of the white woman. Second, with the proper use of human psychology I believe it is quite possible to frustrate a lynching ritual.

In any event, I was absolutely sure that if protection was given for one day by the federal government, it must be given for the entire period. It was on this issue that talks broke down time and time again between myself and the federal government. They had in mind making a grand display and then going back to Washington and sitting back in their "lay-back" chairs, while I finished the best way I could with what they had begun in Mississippi. If there was a choice between my going by myself and taking my chances and my going with the marshals and their leaving after the registration ceremony, I definitely would insist on going by myself. I know Mississippi white folks well enough to know that if you demonstrate to them that they are obligated to take care of you, they most assuredly will comply. I knew that once the U.S. marshals had accompanied me to the university, thereby suggesting to the whites that they were expected to take care of me and only the U.S. marshals' presence prevented it, I would be doomed the minute they withdrew.

*A Telephone Conversation with Katzenbach.* When the government and I were unable to agree on this issue, it was decided that I should talk to Assistant Attorney General Nicholas Katzenbach. The call was connected one evening at Attorney Willis's house. There was mutual understanding during the conversation, except on the issue of how long the marshals would remain in Mississippi. Each time the subject came up, he would talk a while about nothing and make no commitments. I made it unequivocally clear that this was the item of number-one importance, but I was thoroughly convinced after talking to Katzenbach that the federal government would do nothing that it was not forced to do.

This conversation made it necessary for me to give serious attention to the widespread rumor—it had even made bold headlines in the Mississippi newspapers—that a deal had been made between Barnett and Kennedy. The most popular version was that Barnett would permit me to enroll if I were escorted by the marshals; after I had registered, the marshals would withdraw from Mississippi and it would be impossible for me to stay there in their absence. Under this plan, everybody would have gained, except me and the rest of the Negroes. The federal government would have carried out its responsibility of enforcing the federal court order. Mississippi would have gained because in a matter of a few days the university would be all white, plus the fact that my short stay could have been credited to forced action by the federal government.

*To Keep Me Out of Mississippi.* The question of whether or not I would proceed to the University of Mississippi to attempt to register from inside or outside the state was not even debatable. I was to be kept out of Mississippi at all costs. Attorney Willis even suggested that, to keep me out of the state, they would detain me by force, if necessary. In any event, I always went into Mississippi from either Memphis, Tennessee, or New Orleans, Louisiana.

*The Move to Millington Naval Air Station.* After the federal government had committed itself firmly to taking action in my case, we moved to Millington Naval Air Station. I thought I was out of the military, but I found myself right in the middle of it all again, including the question of rank. Arrangements had been made for me to live in the officers quarters and eat in the officers mess, but I had been an enlisted man in the Air Force. The Commander came around to ask me a few "essential questions," as he called them, about whether I was in the reserves or in any way connected with the military. I seemed to have satisfied him with my answers and he said everything was all right. But the Navy was the last to integrate its forces, and it is doubtful that a Negro naval officer had ever been stationed at Millington. I ended up by staying in a barracks and eating in the Base Exchange cafeteria. The Shore Patrol stopped me the second time I went into the cafeteria and detained me until they got clearance from headquarters. The old military routine of "hurry up and wait" was to be a most vital part of my life for the next week or ten days.

### Mississippi Acts

Meanwhile, the state of Mississippi was busying the machinery of "White Supremacy" justice to insure that the Mississippi "way of life" would not be changed. On September 19 a state court at Jackson had granted a temporary injunction, requested by several citizens of the state:

To James Meredith, a resident of either Attala or Hinds County, Mississippi; John D. Williams, a resident of Lafayette County, Mississippi; Robert B. Ellis, a resident of Lafayette County, Mississippi; Harr

G. Carpenter, a resident of Sharkie County, Mississippi; S. R. Evans, a resident of Leflore County, Mississippi; Charles Fair, a resident of Winston County, Mississippi; Vernon S. Holmes, a resident of Pike County, Mississippi; E. Ray Izzard, a resident of Copiah County, Mississippi; J. M. Lipscomb, a resident of Noxubee County, Mississippi; Leon Lowery, a resident of Desoto County, Mississippi; Ira L. Morgan, a resident of Lafayette County, Mississippi; Tally D. Ridell, a resident of Clark County, Mississippi; M. M. Roberts, a resident of Forrest County, Mississippi; R. B. Smith, Jr., a resident of Tippah County, Mississippi; W. O. Stone, a resident of Hinds County, Mississippi; Thomas J. Tubb, a resident of Clay County, Mississippi; Robert E. Lee, a resident of Jones County, Mississippi; Warren H. Tool, a resident of Harrison County, Mississippi; Samuel Verdon, a resident of Hinds County, Mississippi; Sam H. Allen, a resident of Lee County, Mississippi; Robin Patton, a resident of Lafayette County, Mississippi; Tom Hopkins, a resident of Lauderdale County, Mississippi; Joe Bennett, a resident of Monroe County, Mississippi; Jack Stewart, a resident of Hinds County, Mississippi; Robert F. Kennedy, a non-resident of the State of Mississippi believed to be a resident of either the District of Columbia or of the State of Massachusetts; Thomas B. Etheridge, a resident of Lafayette County, Mississippi; Robert Hauberg, a resident of Hinds County, Mississippi; William T. Robertson, a resident of Lafayette County, Mississippi; Loryce E. Horton, a resident of Hinds County, Mississippi.

Until further order of this court you are enjoined, restrained and prohibited as well as the employees, agents and representatives of the Boards of Trustees of Institutions of Higher Learning; of the University of Mississippi; of the United States Department of Justice; including but not limited to, the employees, agents and representatives of the Federal Bureau of Investigation; the office of the Attorney General of the United States; all United States Marshals and Deputy United States Marshals within the State of Mississippi or who come within the State of Mississippi from doing anything or performing any act, the execution of which is intended to enroll and register the Negro, James Meredith, as a student in the University of Mississippi; or do any other thing contrary to the laws and the statutes of the State of Mississippi which would aid or abet the integration of any university, college or common school within the State of Mississippi.

The state legislature had been called into special session to deal with this issue. After a midnight session, a new law was passed aimed explicitly at me. Mississippi Senate Bill No. 1501 was enacted at the first extra session of 1962 and approved by the governor on September 20. It said that no person shall be eligible for admission to any state institution of higher learning if he has a criminal charge of moral turpitude pending against him in any Mississippi state court or federal court. The law further stated that any attempt by anyone to enroll in any of the institutions of higher learning in the state of Mississippi while a criminal proceeding is pending or who has been convicted shall be guilty of a misdemeanor and punished by a fine not exceeding three hundred dollars, or one year in the county jail, or both.

Immediately upon passage of Senate Bill No. 1501 by the Mississippi legislature, the United States as amicus curiae petitioned the U.S. District Court to enjoin its enforcement. At the same time an injunction was asked against my arrest on state charges of false-voter registration, for which I had been convicted and sentenced to a year in jail in absentia in a justice of the peace court in Jackson earlier the same day. A temporary injunction against my arrest under the false-voter registration conviction was granted, as well as against any arrest under S.B. 1501.

At 3:00 P.M. on September 20 the Board of Trustees of State Institutions of Higher Learning adopted a resolution investing Governor Ross Barnett of Mississippi with the full power, authority, right, and discretion to act upon all matters pertaining to or concerned with my admission to the University of Mississippi:

President T. J. Tubb reported that James H. Meredith had been directed to appear at the office of the Board of Trustees, 1007 Woolfolk State Office Building, Jackson, Mississippi, on Thursday, September 20, 1962, at 3:00 P.M. but that Meredith was expected to appear at the University of Mississippi.

M. M. Roberts moved that the Board invest Honorable Ross R. Barnett, the Governor of the State of Mississippi, with the full power, authority, right and discretion of this Board to act upon all matters petraining to or concerned with registration or non-registration, admission or non-admission and/or attendance or non-attendance of James H. Meredith at the University of Mississippi and that a certified copy of this Resolution together with copies of the conflicting injunctions of Honorable S. C. Mize dated September 13, 1962, and Chancellor L. B. Porter dated September 19, 1962, previously served upon the members of this Board, be furnished to the Governor in his capacity as the Chief Executive Officer of this State, the representative of this Board, and the repository of its full rights, power, authority and discretion for such course of action as the Governor shall deem legal, fit and proper in the premises.

*The First Attempt to Enroll*

It was heartening to me to learn that the governor of the state of Mississippi had recognized me to be of such stature that he himself, bolstered by his sovereignty, should be the appropriate one to deal with me; he had had himself duly appointed registrar of the University of Mississippi, effective the day that I was scheduled to register. Naturally, since the governor had made such detailed preparations for the occasion, it was fitting that due preparation should be made for my arrival.

*The Preparations.* Marshals and border patrolmen continued to arrive at Millington. Command posts were established and direct "hot lines" were installed to Washington. The Chief Marshals and military Commanders gathered for a planning session in the Base Commander's office. I was pretty sure at this point that whatever it was they talked about, it wouldn't amount to very much in terms of concrete action. The day was moving along, but no definite word had been given. The marshals and I went through a few practice sessions, acting out our roles and actions once we got to the university.

Finally in the afternoon, the word came from Washington to proceed. It was about one hundred miles to Oxford, Mississippi, from Millington Naval Air Station, and we would have to make good time in order to arrive during the registration period, which was scheduled to end at 4:00 P.M. We left in two cars. I rode with Chief Marshal McShane and a Justice Department lawyer in a car driven by a border patrolman. We stopped at Attorney Willis's house en route to pick up my shaving kit and to make a dramatic car switch designed to insure secrecy. We didn't waste any time; border patrol cars are geared for speed. After making the car switch, a Hertz Rent-A-Car began to follow us and they tailed us all the way, no matter what the speed. McShane became a little concerned, particularly since there were two Negroes in the car. He finally asked if I recognized them. I wouldn't commit myself, but I was sure that one was Larry Still, a reporter, and his photographer, E. Withers.

*The Trip to Oxford.* During the first leg of the trip to Oxford uneasiness was apparent and there was little talking. I do recall McShane's amazement at my answer to his question, "How does it feel, Jim, to see that sign?" referring to the big green "Welcome to Mississippi" sign. I told him that my feeling was always one of mixed emotions, but that to me Mississippi was the most beautiful country in the world—in natural beauty. This seemed to have disarmed the Chief U.S. Marshal for a few miles.

I thought, as we drove along the highway, how utterly ridiculous this was, what a terrible waste of time and money and energy to iron out some rough spots in our civilization. But realistically I knew that this action was necessary. I knew change was a threat to people, that they would fight it, and that this probably was the only way it could be accomplished.

Although I had traveled this old highway (U.S. 51) many times and passed the big highway patrol station at Batesville, I had never considered the prospect of stopping. This station by prior arrangement was to be the first junction between the federal forces and the powers of the state of Mississippi. It had been prearranged, I suppose, because it would be better for the United States to surrender to Mississippi than for its representatives to be captured by state troopers. Colonel T.B. Birdsong, the aging commander of the troopers, was waiting. The only delay was caused by the call that McShane made to Washington to confirm that the deal was still on.

In the meantime the two Negro reporters that had been following us pulled into a gas station across the street. There were a couple of white reporters in the highway patrol yard taking pictures of us as we sat in the car. The Negroes came over to get a shot but were asked to leave. They made a forceful protest and spoke about freedom of the press, and so forth. I don't think the highway patrol knew what they were talking about, but it would have made no difference to the troopers, because they were Negroes.

A student helper from the University of Mississippi had dutifully proven his loyalty to the federal government by stealing a set of registration forms and instruction sheets and delivering them to the Justice Department attorney, so the lawyer could make sure that I knew how to fill out the forms when I got to the university to register. Of course, the student had betrayed his own state of Mississippi by doing this, and I feel sure that if his fellow students and Mississippians had been aware of his crime, he would have paid for it. For his troubles, he only wanted permission to take a picture of Chief Marshal McShane and me.

Naturally I refused to acquaint myself with the registration forms and instruction sheets. I had registered in eight different colleges and universities in the United States and abroad for many terms and sessions, and the idea of my receiving special instructions to fill out forms that any ordinary white could do was a personal affront. Furthermore, I knew that I was not going to be registered at this show. This was Barnett's chapter in Mississippi history and he was not about to let me enter the university quietly.

Batesville to Oxford was the final leg of the trip. It was a long drive for me. For the first time in my life I had knowingly lost complete control of my fate. The caravan was formed and personally directed by Colonel Birdsong, who left no doubt in anybody's mind that Mississippi was in command. Two state trooper cars were in front, Colonel Birdsong was directly in front of our car, and a state trooper car was directly behind us; the other federal government car and more highway patrol cars followed. For a moment I almost forgot that I was not the Governor or the President. All the other traffic had to pull over and stop and let me have the road. Of course, I had been under the impression that only "important" personages received this type of special recognition. Although I was sure that this was just an act that we were going through, for the first time I had to face the definite prospect of my staying on the campus, if I were admitted and assigned a space in the dormitory.

This was my first visit to Oxford. I have traveled extensively throughout the state but Oxford is off the main route to anywhere, and I had never been there. I thought about the purpose of all this; I was full of my "Divine Responsibility." The twenty-five-mile drive from Batesville to Oxford cannot be surpassed as an area typifying the system in Mississippi. The Negro shanties along the route, with an occasional mansion to emphasize the contrast, gave me a perfect view of what I was fighting against. I was fighting for the permanent dwellers of these never-painted shacks and the little naked and half-naked children that ran around outside and played in the dirt. Certainly I was fighting against the forces that kept this status quo of extremes in existence.

Equally revealing and, as a matter of fact, the most vivid memory that I have of the trip were the signs of the Negro's efforts to improve his lot and change his status under the prevailing system and the obvious futility of the attempt. In the midst of a cluster of shanties or on the periphery you would see the savings of a lifetime wasted in a concrete-block structure. This was as far as the Negro had gotten on the modern house that was to replace his shack before his brief prosperity had run out and he had to cease work on the new home. An even more telling example was an occupied new house of modern design, sitting far up on a high hill beside the highway. If it were completed, which it will never be, it undoubtedly would be a beautiful sight. It had a completely finished look, if you approached it from the direction of Oxford. But from the other direction it was a bona fide representation of the Negro struggle. Here was found, as the outside wall, the black tar paper normally used as insulation between the interior and the outside brick. The bricks had not come, nor had landscaping been possible, and both were necessary to complete this ambitious project. Clearly, the only way for the Negro to substantially change his relative position in this society was to change the entire system. I had begun a conscious effort to change this system.

*At the University.* We drove past the new drive-in hamburger stand, the drive-in movie theater, and the drive-in motel (all white), up a steep hill, and right at the top was a big sign, even larger than the "Welcome to Mississippi" sign, which said "Welcome to Oxford, the Reforestation Capital of the World." Whatever Mississippi does, it does zealously, whether it is playing football, crowning beauty queens, keeping Negroes in their places, or planting pine trees. We drove past the Rebel Chevrolet dealer, the new bowling alley (white), and several smaller buildings and houses. The entire town was out to see history turned upside down.

When we came to the main back entrance, the state trooper guide drove on past. Naturally I could not enter the campus by the main front entrance; since the back entrance was used as much as the front entrance, it might be called a de facto main entrance, and consequently I couldn't use it either. We finally entered the campus by a small side entrance and curved through the faculty residential area until we came to the selected spot. I was to face my honorable governor in the Continuation Center. This building was connected by a ramp to another building which belonged to the Alumni Association. It had been arranged that my attempt to enroll would take place thirty minutes past the regularly scheduled registration period for that particular day.

The state of Mississippi claims that its state troopers number only a few hundred. If this is true, then they all must have been assembled in this one place. The troopers were lined up shoulder to shoulder on the right-hand side of the street across from the Continuation Center. Jammed up behind them were three or four thousand people, most of whom I assumed to be students. To the humming of the crowd we emerged from the car and walked briskly into the building.

Inside, I was immediately approached by the first representative of the huge welcoming committee. A "mean-looking peckerwood" walked up to me and said he was the sheriff. He proceeded to serve me with two or more sets of summons. I thanked him, handed the documents to the Justice Department lawyer, and that was all I ever heard about them. There was a lot of talking and shaking hands. Barnett talked about how good business was, wanted to know if the lawyer was "any kin" to someone he knew, shook hands (except mine), and invited them to "come see me" some time.

Then we settled down to the business of the day. The keepers of the honor of the state were to be our witnesses. I recognized several members of the college board among the group. They all took seats starting from the back (quite a switch). There were several empty rows of chairs between them and the front of the room where we were. The reason was obvious: if they were called to court to testify, certainly they wouldn't have heard a word. But if Barnett slipped in his diligence in upholding the Mississippi "way of life," they would have been his witnesses. At a long table were three chairs: one for Barnett as Registrar, another for his assistant, Ellis, and on the other side of the table, a chair for the honored guest. I was surprised that they would let a Negro sit with them. Ellis read a written statement making Barnett the registrar, but he refused to give the lawyer a copy, however. Then Barnett took out his long proclamation, stamped with the seal of the "Great and Sovereign State of Mississippi." I guess I was supposed to say my lines at this point, but the coordinators had failed to give me the script, so Barnett finally wanted to know if there was any further business. I got the message and addressed myself to "Mr. Registrar," looking at Ellis, but the Governor informed me that he was the Registrar, so I had to restate my intention to enroll to Registrar Barnett. He then proceeded to read his proclamation.

MISSISSIPPI

EXECUTIVE DEPARTMENT

JACKSON

TO: JAMES H. MEREDITH, APPLICANT FOR ADMISSION AS A STUDENT
  AT THE UNIVERSITY OF MISSISSIPPI:

Pursuant to the authority vested in me under the Constitution and the laws of the State of Mississippi, I, Ross R. Barnett, Governor of the State of Mississippi and for the protection of all citizens of the State of Mississippi, and all others who may be within the confines of the State of Mississippi.

Therefore, you, James H. Meredith, are hereby refused admission as a student to the University of Mississippi, and any other person or persons who, in my opinion, by such admission, would lead to a breach of the peace and be contrary to the administrative procedures and regulations of the University of Mississippi and the laws of the State of Mississippi.

Take due notice thereof and govern yourself accordingly.

> IN WITNESS WHEREOF, I have hereunto set my hand and caused the Great Seal of the State of Mississippi to be affixed on this the 20th day of September, A.D., 1962.
>
> GOVERNOR

ATTEST:

SECRETARY OF STATE

When he had finished reading it, he handed it to me. I was finally given a piece of the show, and at least I would have a souvenir to pass on to my children and their children and their children's children. The Justice Department spokesman, on stage now, attempted to protest and warned the Governor that action would be taken against him. However, he soon seemed to sense that the most logical thing to do was to get out of there. I thanked the Governor and we hastened out to our waiting car, which sped away with hordes of shouting, rock-throwing students hot on the chase. The state troopers led us on our way to the Tennessee line as fast as one could imagine. The first registration attempt was over.

### The Contempt Trials

The United States government no longer faced a mere threat, but a direct and definite challenge. And now the only way for either side to escape a showdown was to remove me physically from the arena. The courts had rendered their decision. Every citizen of the United States, including me, a Negro in Mississippi, had the right to attend any publicly supported school anywhere in the several states, and especially in the state of his residence and birth. The state of Mississippi had elected to reject this decision and to resist with every available resource, including the use of organized violence. Mississippi had purposefully and forcefully rejected my right to attend the University of Mississippi. The federal government could either capitulate or retaliate. There was no other way out as the events that were to follow proved.

The first contempt trial was held September 21, the day after Barnett's rejection. The Chancellor of the University of Mississippi, the Dean of the College of Liberal Arts, and the Registrar were charged with civil and criminal contempt, and the proceedings were heard in Mississippi before U.S. District Judge Mize. The Judge found all the officials "not guilty" and ordered their acquittal.

The case was moved to the Fifth Circuit Court of Appeals in New Orleans, where, in an unusual sitting of the court, all the justices except Ben F. Cameron of Mississippi sat to hear the case. They were Chief Judge Elbert Parr Tuttle, Judges Joseph C. Hutcheson, Jr., Richard T. Rives, Warren L. Jones, John R. Brown, John Minor Wisdom, Walter Pettus Gewin, and Griffin B. Bell. At this hearing on September 24 the university officials expressed willingness to comply with the court's order to register me. The court then ordered the board of trustees to rescind its action purporting to relieve the university officials of registration duties and to revoke the action naming the governor agent of the board in affairs pertaining to my enrollment.

But Mississippi with Barnett at the helm meant to stay a step or two in front. On that day, September 24, Governor Barnett issued a proclamation which declared that the federal government's action in the Meredith case was a "direct usurpation" of the reserved powers of the state "through the illegal use of judicial decree," and went on to assert:

Now, therefore, I, Ross R. Barnett, Governor of the State of Mississippi, by the authority vested in me under the Constitution and laws of the State of Mississippi, do hereby proclaim and direct that the arrest or attempts to arrest, or the fining or the attempts to fine, of any state official in the performance of his official duties, by any representative of the Federal Government, is illegal and such representative or representatives of said Federal Government are to be summarily arrested and jailed by reason of any such illegal acts in violation of this executive order and in violation of the laws of the State of Mississippi.

The United States government could not tolerate this defiance and at 8:30 A.M. on September 25, 1962, the Court of Appeals for the Fifth Circuit entered a temporary restraining order:

IT IS ORDERED that the State of Mississippi, Ross R. Barnett, Joe T. Patterson, T. B. Birdsong, Paul G. Alexander, William R. Lamb, J. Robert Gilfoy, J. W. Ford, William D. Rayfield, James D. Jones, Walton Smith, the class consisting of all district attorneys in Mississippi, the class consisting of the sheriffs of all counties in Mississippi, the class consisting of all chiefs of police in Mississippi, and the class consisting of all constables and town marshals in Mississippi, their agents, employees, officers, successors, and all persons in active consort or participation with them, be temporarily restrained from:

1. Arresting, attempting to arrest, prosecuting or instituting any prosecution against James Howard Meredith under any statute, ordinance, rule or regulation whatever, on account of his attending, or seeking to attend, the University of Mississippi;

2. Instituting or proceeding further in any civil action against James Howard Meredith or any other persons on account of James Howard Meredith's enrolling or seeking to enroll, or attending the University of Mississippi;

3. Injuring, harassing, threatening, or intimidating James Howard Meredith in any other way or by any other means on account of his attending or seeking to attend the University of Mississippi;

4. Interfering with or obstructing by any means or in any manner the performance of obligations or the enjoyment of rights under this Court's order of July 28, 1962, and the order of the United States District Court for the Southern District of Mississippi entered September 13, 1962, in this action, and

5. Interfering with or obstructing, by force, threat, arrest, or otherwise, any officer or agent of the United States in the performance of duties in connection with the enforcement of, and the prevention of obstruction to, the orders entered by this Court and the District Court for the Southern District of Mississippi relating to the enrollment and attendance of James Howard Meredith at the University of Mississippi; or arresting, prosecuting, or punishing such officer or agent on account of his performing or seeking to perform such duty.

IT IS FURTHER ORDERED that Paul G. Alexander and J. Robert Gilfoy be temporarily restrained from proceeding further, serving or enforcing any process or judgment, or arresting James Howard Meredith in connection with the criminal actions against him in the Justice of the Peace Court of Hinds County, Mississippi.

IT IS FURTHER ORDERED that A. L. Meador, Sr., be temporarily restrained from taking any further action or seeking to enforce any judgment entered in the case of A. L. Meador, Sr. v. James Meredith, et al.

IT IS FURTHER ORDERED that Ross R. Barnett be temporarily restrained from enforcing or seeking to enforce against James Howard Meredith any process or judgment in the case of the State of Mississippi, ex rel. Ross Barnett, Governor v. James H. Meredith.

In compliance with the Court of Appeals' order, the Board of Trustees of State Institutions of Higher Learning at noon on September 25 took action to revoke and rescind its actions of September

4 and September 20, and to instruct university officials to receive me "to actual admission to, and continued attendance thereafter" at the university without discrimination on account of race or color.

*Dillard University.* New Orleans was in many ways even more insulting and demeaning than Mississippi. I can never forget my shockingly degraded feeling when I watched the stream of streetcars and city buses in downtown New Orleans. The front of each was filled with whites and the back was packed with blacks. There could be no question about where one's "place" was in this city. I can surely understand why the streetcar was named "Desire." Such a mass public display of the "system" was less obvious in Mississippi, because there were so few cities, and fewer city buses. Negroes had to walk.

The attention of the world was focused directly on the hour-to-hour, blow-by-blow account of this struggle between state and federal power in the United States. Frankly, I had only a passing interest. I knew that, whatever the outcome, I would still be obliged to devote the remaining part of my life to fighting for the rights of my people.

Even to fight the contempt case against the state of Mississippi, we Negroes still needed a place to lodge and to eat. The Dillard University guest house had been secured for our lodgings and its dining hall was our eating place. The NAACP Legal Defense and Educational Fund had practically transferred its operations to New Orleans, certainly most of its top lawyers and staff were there. The downstairs part of the guest house had been turned into a temporary office and the upstairs was used for sleeping. Our presence on the campus was technically a secret. I suppose this was because Dillard is subsidized by the state of Louisiana.

*My Wife's Visit.* The most pleasant event of my stay in New Orleans during the contempt trials was a visit from my wife. Only two weeks before I had left my wife in Jackson to go to Memphis, and in some ways these weeks of separation had seemed much longer to us than the six years that we had been married. We had both read in the newspapers and heard on the radio and on television continuous prophecies that by the next issue or the next program I probably wouldn't be around any more. The ever-recurring theme of everyone with whom I talked—newsmen, lawyers, Justice Department people, well-wishers, and enemies—was the question of life and death.

Finally, the time had come for the train to arrive. Medgar Evers went to meet her at the station. I waited. We were sitting downstairs when they arrived. This was no place for long greetings and conversations. We left the others as if they were not there and went slowly up the stairs to the privacy of our room. There was no talk, just love. Love in a state of unspoken mutual understanding that it could be the last. This was love in its purest form.

## The Second Attempt

At the well-staged contempt trial, during which each actor played his role superbly, the governor and all the key aspirants to high office spoke their lines for the state of Mississippi, always keeping in mind the upcoming state election. The chief actors for my side were Burke Marshall, Chief of the Civil Rights Division, Chief U.S. Marshal McShane, and Jack Greenberg and Mrs. Motley of the NAACP Legal Defense Fund. The latter were by no means happy with the Justice Department for attempting to steal all of the show. Obviously they lacked confidence in my future, now in the hands of a wavering and noncommittal federal government. The judges sat through the proceedings with an air of great concentration, as if there was really something to decide.

The Board of Institutions of Higher Learning had capitulated to the Fifth Circuit Court of Appeals, revoked the appointment of Barnett as registrar of the university, and promised to "allow" me to register. The Attorney General of the United States and the Governor of Mississippi had agreed that the next attempt to register would be at the state capital; presumably it would be more convenient for Barnett to block my enrollment there. I knew that this attempt would be just another performance; the University of Mississippi is at Oxford, two hundred miles from Jackson, and no one had ever heard of a student enrolling in a university at the state capitol building. Had the governor not failed to block me, I had already decided that I would refuse to register anywhere except at the university itself and in the proper offices. But Barnett made sure that the decision was never mine.

*The Flight from New Orleans.* John Doar of the Justice Department and Marshal McShane picked me up early in the morning of September 25 at the guest house at Dillard. We switched cars a couple of times and finally arrived at New Orleans' old airport, which is seldom used now. Segregation was still the law there. Not only was I refused service at the snack bar, but I had to go down in the basement and use the toilet for "colored" employees, because the rest rooms were for "whites only." John Doar and McShane were obviously embarrassed.

Finally we boarded the plush Cessna 220, which would become our primary mode of travel for the next several days. The pilot was a topnotch flyer from Florida and a very friendly person. McShane sat beside him in the front seat and John Doar and I were in the back seats. For the next three weeks or so almost every time I appeared in public I was flanked by McShane and John Doar, two of the bravest men I have ever known. I never saw either of them weaken under any and all conditions of danger. We taxied out to the airstrip and then waited while a faked flight was being staged. To fool the newsmen, and maybe to frustrate the state of Mississippi, another plane took off at the time we were scheduled to leave. It flew around for a few minutes and returned to indicate that we had changed our minds and returned to New Orleans. Then we took off and headed for Jackson.

I had my first long talk with John Doar on this trip. He had been a successful small-town lawyer and a Republican, who had been almost totally uninvolved in the Negro situation, before he had been appointed to the Civil Rights Division by President Eisenhower. Once he had become engaged in the effort to insure the civil rights of the Negro, his dedication to this cause appeared genuine. I probed into his reasons for and his ideas concerning his involvement, because I wondered what a white man thought and how he justified devoting a major portion of his life to the battle for civil rights. Certainly no white could be drafted into such an occupation; essentially his participation must be voluntary.

I remember telling Doar that I considered such maneuvers as we were going through to be an utter waste of human manpower and intelligence. At the same time I realized their absolute necessity in the process of changing social patterns in the established societies of the world. I looked out on all sides at the natural beauty of the land of my birth, and thought again as I had for many years—what a wonderful place Mississippi could be.

All our philosophizing abruptly ceased, however, when a fleet of Mississippi National Guard planes suddenly began to circle and cut across us from every direction. At first, the pilot was a bit upset and made some unscheduled maneuvers and turns, but the Guard planes settled down at a reasonable distance from us and just kept us under observation. Evidently they had decided to obey the Geneva Convention's rules of international warfare and were not going to fire on an unarmed enemy plane. We flew on to the Jackson airport, landed on a back runway, and taxied into the National Guard area.

*At the Capital.* We had to remain in the plane while contacts were being made and security procedures were carried out. Finally we unboarded and got into one of the U.S. marshals' cars. Three or four cars and several marshals had been waiting for us. A few National Guardsmen were in the area, but either they didn't know what was going on or they deliberately stayed away. I suspect the latter was the case. We took a back road out of the airport, but the press and mobile radio units managed to stay on our trail.

At the federal building in Jackson, where we were supposed to meet the school officials for the registration ceremony, it was obvious that the show would not take place there, because there was no crowd. We went to the office of the U.S. Marshal of Mississippi, and Doar and McShane made several calls to Washington and elsewhere. Meanwhile, the word had passed around and a small crowd gathered in front of the post office. For security reasons, they decided to leave through a side entrance for the rendezvous with the governor at the state capitol building.

A large crowd had assembled at the capitol and there was no doubt that we had the right place this time. The "mean-looking" state troopers cleared a path through the hostile crowd which was shouting "Nigger, go home," and which already had many of the characteristics of a mob. We went up several floors to the meeting place.

The script went something like this. The board and university officials had told the court that they would comply with its orders and they had met to execute this agreement. However, while they were meeting, the governor and the state legislature, which had been called into special session to deal with this crisis, had come and were physically restraining them from performing their task. The governor was to block the representatives of the federal government and me from meeting with the board and university officials, theoretically ready and waiting to register me.

It was a fair plot, but one could easily determine from the mood of the crowd, the governor, and the members of the legislature that the "playing" part was over. Perhaps the people at the top might have been able to agree to further deals, but it was obvious that holding back the worked-up racial hatred of the Mississippi whites would be difficult. The situation had indeed become serious.

When we reached the room where the registration was supposed to take place and the television cameras had all been set in place, the door was squeezed open and the Governor was thrust over the threshold by the wildly shouting Mississippi state legislators. In a voice filled with emotion, he read his second proclamation and handed it to me. (The only comical thing about the whole event was Barnett's asking, "Which one is Meredith?" I was the only Negro near the Governor at that moment.)

I, Ross R. Barnett, Governor of the State of Mississippi, having heretofore by proclamation, acting under the police powers of the State of Mississippi, interposed the sovereignty of this State on Sept. 14, 1962, and in order to prevent violence and a breach of the peace, and in order to preserve the peace, dignity and tranquility of the State of Mississippi, and having previously, on Sept. 20, 1962, denied to you, James H. Meredith, admission to the University of Mississippi under such proclamation and for such reasons, do hereby finally deny you admission to the University of Mississippi.

On our quick trip back to the airport, I witnessed a contrasting scene that has remained in my memory and perhaps always will. After leaving the state office building, the first traffic light is a long block away. In the car in the lane beside us, I had noticed a white woman making what were apparently unpleasant gestures at us and shouting incomprehensible remarks. As fate would have it, the red light caught us. The woman stopped, made a last remark, and then broke down and cried with her face buried in her hands. Just as the light was about to change, Marshal McShane asked me if those were some of my friends, indicating a group of six or seven Negroes standing on the corner. I suppose they had been waving at us, but I hadn't seen them. I waved at them as we pulled away from the light. They were all common folk, my people, maids still in uniform and common laborers, but the enthusiasm, the friendliness, and above all, the pride that they displayed in contrast to the hostile and painful attitude of the whites, climaxed by the crying woman, were overwhelming. This was what I was fighting for, and I had my reward in the brief seconds that I saw my unknown friends on that corner.

To end this day, Barnett had planned to emerge from his place of victory onto the crowded streets of Jackson just as the people were getting off from work, and in this way to swell the size of his faithful crowd of loyal "white supremacists" waiting to give him his victory cheers. Unfortunately Barnett's elevator got stuck in between floors (I suspect more than the hand of God was at work here, since there are a lot of Negro manual laborers in the capitol building), and by the time they released him all of his spectators had gone away.

Later that same night the Fifth Circuit Court of Appeals issued an order to show cause why the Governor should not be cited for civil contempt for preventing me from registering at the university.

It appearing from the verified application of the United States, amicus curiae herein, that on the afternoon of this day Ross R. Barnett, having been served with a copy of the temporary restraining order referred to above and having actual knowledge of the terms of that order, deliberately prevented James H. Meredith from entering the office of the Board of Trustees in Jackson, Mississippi, at a time when James H. Meredith was seeking to appear before Robert B. Ellis in order to register as a student in the University, and that by such conduct Ross R. Barnett did willfully interfere with and obstruct James H. Meredith in the enjoyment of his rights under this Court's order of July 28, 1962 and did willfully interfere with and obstruct Robert B. Ellis in the performance of his obligations under this Court's order of July 28, 1962, all in violation of the terms of the temporary restraining order entered by the Court this day.

IT IS ORDERED that Ross R. Barnett appear personally before this Court on September 28, 1962 at 10 o'clock A.M. in the courtroom of the United States Court of Appeals for the Fifth Circuit, at 600 Camp Street, New Orleans, Louisiana, to show cause, if any he has, why he should not be held in civil contempt of the temporary restraining order entered by the Court this day.

The Marshal is directed to serve a copy of this order upon Ross R. Barnett, forthwith.

> Signed this September 25th, 1962,
> at 8:20 o'clock P.M.
> Richard Rives
> CIRCUIT JUDGE
> John Minor Wisdom
> CIRCUIT JUDGE
> Walter P. Gewin
> CIRCUIT JUDGE

## The Contempt Trials Continue

After the Jackson episode, we were back in New Orleans for more contempt trials. Once again, it was the same old routine, but there was more interest, however. All the world had seen Barnett on TV or heard him on the radio or read about him in the newspapers.

The first night back at Dillard I attended a school dance. And it was at this time that I learned that I was being guarded around the clock. A big tough-looking white fellow stopped me on my way to the dance to tell me that he was a U.S. marshal assigned to guard me and that he hoped I wouldn't mind his joining me at the dance. He assured me that he would try to make himself as inconspicuous as possible. Imagine a white cop going unnoticed at a Negro dance in the Deep South. My biggest problem was explaining him to the student officials at the door, but once that was done, everything went off smoothly.

When we arrived at the court building for the Barnett trial, there were white pickets supporting the position of Barnett and Mississippi. Even the master segregationist, Leander H. Perez, Sr., showed up and caused a brief stir when he was not permitted to enter the already full courtroom.

The most crucial issue, as far as I am personally concerned, almost never got into the record. As a matter of fact, I became a courtroom lawyer for a few minutes in order to get my plea before the judges. The question of where I would stay, if ever I were registered at the university, had been systematically avoided by all parties for different reasons. I had pressed this issue all along but had not absolutely demanded a satisfactory resolution. But my last trip into Mississippi had thoroughly convinced me that I was not going to be caught in "peckerwood territory" with my flanks open. Mississippi and the university officials avoided the question, because they knew that I could never live in the community and go back and forth to school. This was an easy way to get rid of me: let me enroll and then evade the issue of providing me quarters on campus. The University of Mississippi has less in common with the areas outside of and surrounding its campus than it has with the city of New York. They are definitely two different worlds. The federal government's objective was to get me registered and then to wash its hand of the matter as quickly as it could, if possible. The NAACP had gained its stature by winning cases, and they would not place an almost-won case in jeopardy over one side issue. I had mentioned this unsettled matter to both sides throughout the day but to no avail, and when the court started to go through the motions of closing the case, I stood up and addressed the judges on the question of housing. Mrs. Motley finished my plea, and they promised to look into the matter.

That night Judge Wisdom called me on the phone to talk about the actual conditions in Mississippi and especially about the mood of the people at the state capital. We also talked about the housing problem. The next day we went to his chambers and talked further about the intangibles of the whole situation and about the housing problem in particular. He assured me that the matter would be taken care of.

Later, I received a call from the Governor of Michigan, who told me of his plans to present the Mississippi case to the Governors' Conference that would meet soon. The whole country was involved in this crisis in one way or another, it seemed.

*McDowell's Visit.* During the student government crisis at Jackson State College, a young, ambitious history and political science major, Cleve McDowell, had managed to make himself known. He had indicated his desire to attend the University of Mississippi. With this in mind, I arranged for him to spend the weekend in New Orleans with me.

An event took place while he was with me which, I believe, was as much a shock and surprise to me as it was to him. We had heard about some affair in one of the big halls, and we went in and mingled with the people for about an hour, dancing, talking, and having a good time. Then one young lady with whom I had danced and a couple of her friends came up and asked if I wasn't James Meredith. They must have passed the word around, because a number of people started to greet us. The master of ceremonies came to the microphone and, after announcing my presence, said something about the cause that this affair was supporting and asked me to come to the stage. I was really embarrassed, but I told the people to support the good cause whatever it was, and that was as far as I got. I have never been mobbed to this extent before or after. They literally swamped me for at least forty-five minutes to an hour. Everyone there must have seen Barnett at the state office building surrounded by his supporting mob of racists; they must have thought that I would be dead soon and therefore should have all things possible. I could not guess how many women must have offered themselves to me or asked me to go home with them. I am sure that not one of them later suspected that she had done anything of the sort. It was fantastic, and one of my greatest lessons in the empathic limits of my people.

### The Third Attempt

I had heard the court pronounce itself helpless to provide further remedies or suggestions in my case and tell the United States government pointblank that it alone now had sufficient power to deal with the state of Mississippi. What would the government do? Its general rule is to do only what it must, and where change challenges status quo and status quo resists, the government usually accepts the status quo. Barnett and the state of Mississippi knew that the rules of politics were on their side. The judges had removed themselves from further direct participation, but they had not failed to take a stand. The integrity of the court was at stake, and the eight judges at New Orleans had all but told the government that it must enforce the law.

I got up early on September 26 and wrote what I called then a "statement," but what I will now acknowledge was a last will and testament. I gave the handwritten copy to Mrs. Motley with a request that in case something happened to me to release it.

In this time of crisis, I feel it appropriate for me to clarify my position as to my intention, my objectives, my hopes, and my desires.

For several months I have been involved in a struggle to gain admission to the University of Mississippi. The prime objective is, of course, to receive the educational training necessary to enable me to be a useful citizen of my own home state of Mississippi.

There are those in my state who oppose me in my efforts to obtain an education in the schools of my state. They do this because I am a Negro, and Negroes are not allowed to attend certain schools in my state. The schools that we are forbidden to attend are the only ones in the state that offer the training which I wish to receive. Consequently, those who oppose me are saying to me, we have given you what we want you to have and you can have no more. And if you want more than we have given you, then go to some other state or some other country and get your training.

What logic is it that concludes that a citizen of one state must be required to go to another state to receive the educational training that is normally and ordinarily offered and received by other citizens of that state? Further, what justification can there possibly be for one state to accept the responsibility for educating the citizens of another state when the training is offered to other citizens in the home state?

We have a dilemma. It is a fact that the Negroes of Mississippi are effectively NOT first-class citizens. I feel that every citizen should be a first-class citizen and should be allowed to develop his talents on a free, equal, and competitive basis. I think this is fair and that it infringes on the rights and privileges of no one. Certainly to be denied this opportunity is a violation of my rights as a citizen of the United States and the state of Mississippi.

The future of the United States of America, the future of the South, the future of Mississippi, and the future of the Negro rests on the decision of whether or not the Negro citizen is to be allowed to receive an education in his own state. If a state is permitted to arbitrarily deny any right that is so basic to the American way of life to any citizen, then democracy is a failure.

I dream of the day when Negroes in Mississippi can live in decency and respect and do so without fear of intimidation and bodily harm or of receiving personal embarrassment, and with an assurance of equal justice under the law.

The price of progress is indeed high, but the price of holding it back is much higher.

The same crew—the pilot, McShane, Doar, and myself—flew up to Oxford from New Orleans. This time an ever larger force of U.S. marshals met us, but there was an agreement between the federal government and the state of Mississippi that everybody would be unarmed. Can you imagine a law enforcement officer in an area where law and order have broken down without his arms? It happened at Oxford.

When we landed at the airport, there was a large welcoming committee—a whole battery of newsmen, U.S. marshals, highway patrolmen, and local antagonists. The newsmen took lots of pictures of us disembarking from the plane and asked for my predictions on the outcome of this attempt. My only comment was, "At least I am getting in plenty of flying time." I can think of no better way to explain my personal and private view of this waste of my limited time as a living being. Of course, my public view was much broader and I knew the necessity of going through at least part of these steps to bring about a major social change. The marshals, having left their guns in Memphis, were generally unhappy, if not disillusioned. The local citizens cursed, spat, and threatened with more than usual viciousness, while the highway patrolmen, apparently a well-disciplined group, escorted us through to the cars which would take us to our place of encounter.

*The Blocking by Paul Johnson.* State troopers were all over the place. They too were bound by the no-gun rule. But it was evident that their guns were not back in Jackson; they were within easy reach. Some of them could be seen handling their gunbelts, and it was hard to tell if they were putting them on or taking them off. If I know Mississippi white folks there were not many unarmed people there. They had guns on the seats, in their boots, under their belts, in their pockets, and everywhere. We were led to the roadblock about a half mile off the campus where Lieutenant Governor Paul Johnson had set up his retinue, including the properly oriented TV cameramen and radio and news reporters. The story was that Barnett had been unable to take off in his plane because of bad weather. This was strange because we did not have any bad weather to prevent our flying in, and Paul Johnson was there. I rather think there was another explanation. The election for governor was approaching, and a blocking by Paul Johnson of the federal forces that sought to invade the "Great and Sovereign State" of Mississippi and to impose a Negro on the greatest of all its institutions would certainly enhance his chances of winning the election.

There they stood, like the proverbial Russian Bear, in battle formation. Except for the Little General (Paul Johnson), they indeed looked like bears. I think the state troopers must be a sort of private club for Mississippi's famous football team members who fail to go on to the big time. The average height of the troopers must have been at least 6'2" and the average weight about 230 pounds. Even McShane, who appears to be a giant among ordinary men, seemed slight in comparison to these bullies. They lined up beside Johnson and formed a solid wall of human flesh. We got out of our cars and all of us—McShane on my right and Doar on my left with marshals flanking them on the sides—moved up to the line.

McShane went through the motions of serving court orders, injunctions, and summons on Paul Johnson. When he refused to take them, McShane touched Johnson with the papers (a legal technicality) and let them drop at his feet. Then the Marshal told the Lieutenant Governor that we wanted to proceed to the university for the purpose of registering. Johnson took out his proclamation and read it. It was the same as the one that Barnett had read and given to me, except that it had Johnson's signature and seal. He then informed us that he would not permit us to go any further.

We started to move back and forth down the line, as if we were looking for a hole to go through. The most comical part about this scene was that Johnson tried to keep up with McShane. Evidently he wanted to remain directly in front of the Marshal, but we could move more rapidly, because there were fewer of us. The sheriffs, who had been in the background, started to move up closer toward the front line. Most of the eighty-two sheriffs were reputed to have been present that day to show the solidarity of the state. Of course, the no-gun rule could not be enforced on them because they were independent of the governor's orders. A third group also moved in closer. These were apparently sheriff's deputies and university police who were supposed to hold back the students and prevent them from coming to the front line.

Faced with this provocation, McShane decided to get tough, so that the state of Mississippi would not think that it had bluffed the federal government. He moved in on Johnson with clenched fists and demanded that he stand aside; Johnson was obviously startled by this new turn of events, but the Citizens Council had its special representative, a well-known state legislator, right beside Johnson to see that he did not falter. Therefore Johnson balled up his fist at McShane long enough for the cameramen to take a picture of it. There was quite a lot of bumping and pushing. I could not pass up this golden opportunity to get in a little elbowing and shouldering. I chose the Citizens Council special representative as my target. He was beside Johnson and directly in front of me, and I realized how unbearable it would be for him to have a Negro pushing him around. I turned my left shoulder to him and gave him a couple of hard bumps and one or two sharp elbows. I didn't see this, but one of the marshals said that when the representative drew back to hit me, the marshal pulled me back and stepped between us. I had seen this marshal get in front of me, but I thought he just wanted to get in some shoving and pushing.

This little activity of mine almost caused a crisis within our ranks. They reasoned that the worst possible thing that could happen was for me to hit one of the white folks. The marshals asked me not to defend myself in the future, even if a serious fight should break out. Of course, I understood their point of view and I hoped we would never face the test, but I did not make any promises. For nine years I had been required to qualify with a carbine every six months, and for the last two years of my service I had been required to become proficient with the .45 automatic, due to a special assignment. It was inconceivable to me that I should refrain from doing what I had been taught to do, to defend myself if attacked by my greatest enemy—the Mississippi "peckerwood."

One incident never really became important, but it could well have been had I decided to bring it to light during the election campaign. McShane had asked Johnson to stand aside and let "Mr. Meredith" through; Johnson answered that he was not going to let "Mr. Meredith" through, a fatal error for any Mississippi politician to make—to call a Negro "Mister"—even accidentally.

### Contempt Convictions

The next day we were back in court in New Orleans. Both the governor and lieutenant governor were being tried for contempt of court. When the governor failed to appear or respond to the show cause order issued against him, the Fifth Circuit Court of Appeals, with eight judges sitting, on September 28 found him to be in contempt of its temporary restraining order of September 25, 1962. He was ordered to be committed to the custody of the Attorney General of the United States and to pay a fine of $10,000 per day, unless before October 2, 1962, he had shown the court that he was fully complying with the restraining order and had notified all the officers under his jurisdiction to cease interference with the orders of the courts and to cooperate in my admission to the university.

The lieutenant governor also failed to appear or respond to the show cause order issued against him, and the court, with three judges sitting (Rives, Brown, and Wisdom), on September 29 found him to be in contempt of its temporary restraining order of September 25,1962. He was ordered to pay a fine of $5,000 per day.

### Another Futile Attempt

Undoubtedly the most tension-filled attempt was the one that did not take place. After the "no-gun" episode with Paul Johnson, confusion and frustration overcame the federal forces. It was clearly evident that nothing short of pure force would budge Mississippi from its defiant position. Nevertheless, the government still searched for another solution; it did not want to resort to force. The morale of the U.S. marshals was at its lowest ebb. Most of them had left their home offices in haste and under the impression that their stay away from their families would be short. In addition, the chances of violence had multiplied with each foray into Mississippi, and the helpless, unarmed situation of the marshals was totally against their better judgment.

We were to make another try on September 27. The big question again was arms. At first, there was the "no-guns" business. The marshals were not about to buy this. Then the federal government suggested that the marshals wear their sidearms exposed but unloaded, and the bullets were to be left in Memphis. The day had passed into the afternoon, Barnett was already in Oxford and his crowd was gathering, but the people in Washington could not make up their minds. Finally, the hot line brought the word from Attorney General Robert Kennedy to make ready for the mission. This was to be the biggest force yet—about fifty men. The marshals were scared. At this time I really learned McShane's true capacity for leadership; he simply walked through the group of marshals and one could feel fear running away from his presence. They loaded the cars with tear gas and gas guns. We practiced putting on our gas masks and the caravan was made ready. The question of sidearms was never really settled. It was ordered that the guns be unloaded and the issue was dropped at that point, leaving the decision of what to do with the bullets to the individual marshals. They kept them in their hands and pockets.

I never did believe that this attempt was anything more than a bluff. I can never believe that the men responsible for the conduct of the affairs of our great nation were so naïve or unwise that they would send fifty despised men into Mississippi at "lynching time." It was late in the afternoon before we even left Memphis. I thought of the line in Handy's *St. Louis Blues,* "I hate to see that evening sun go down." It was sinking low in the west by the time we started the hundred-mile drive from Millington Naval Air Station to Oxford.

Since the communications system had proven faulty on each occasion before, there was a communications-relay plane in the air this time to act as a link between us and Washington. The caravan with the trio—McShane, Doar, and Meredith—riding in the second car sped down the new interstate highway, that had only two traffic breaks between Memphis and Batesville, at between 90 and 110 miles per hour. Except for the periodic checks of the communications system between the cars of the caravan and the plane hovering and circling above us, there was almost complete silence all the way.

*The Turn Around.* We had sped down the road for some seventy miles, when the communications plane relayed the word from the Attorney General to turn back. There was almost rejoicing at the news; the caravan came happily to a halt. The radio stations had ceased all regular programming and were devoting full time to reporting the preparations for the coming battle. Most of the news was about Barnett and his crowd which had grown to enormous proportions as darkness approached. Even though they had reconfirmed the report from the communications plane, that was not enough for McShane and Doar. The three of us in one car left the entire caravan on the highway and drove five miles to Batesville to telephone the Attorney General and confirm the order from him personally. With all the news reports describing us, we stood out like a sore thumb in Batesville. Apparently most of the true Mississippians had already gone to Oxford to take part in the battle, for the town seemed to be empty. Doar and McShane made their call and we went back to rejoin the caravan without incident.

Certainly the only logical thing to have done under these conditions was to turn back. Darkness would have fallen when we reached the place where Barnett waited for us. This is the best possible time for mob action. If the Attorney General had not given the word, I would have ordered the marshals to turn back myself. It might be thought that I did not have the power to do this. Indeed, I had the power at all times to order any negative action. Many people often forget that I was not a prisoner or a ward; I was a citizen, a free agent. It was my rights that were being forcefully denied me, and I always remained free to choose not to exercise the privileges concerned at any time. The fact that a citizen is denied certain rights and privileges does not mean that once these rights and privileges are extended to him he is required to exercise them. The greatest of all human freedoms is the freedom of choice. Consequently, at all times when the government had ordered its forces to commit a positive act in my behalf, I had the power as a citizen to order that action stopped. There were to be many occasions when I had to remind the government officials that I was a free citizen of the United States.

In any event, the showdown was averted by the wise action of the federal government. We returned to Memphis, but at a much slower speed than we had left it. We listened to the blow-by-blow account of the developing battle on the radio on our way back to Millington. The radio newsmen were not going to miss that extra money, and they kept on reporting, as a good sports announcer will do, when he makes a sorry fight sound as though the two men are tearing each other apart, and, in fact, they are hardly raising a hand. The most amusing report of all came just as we were passing the Peabody Hotel in downtown Memphis. The radio announcer boldly announced that "the caravan is now approaching the University of Mississippi."

# 8

# Two Days: September 30-October 1, 1962

THE two days—September 30 and October 1, 1962—may well go down in history as one of the supreme tests of the Union. The use of force to defy the legitimate mandates of the world's most powerful government is basically significant. Insurrection against the United States by the state of Mississippi became on these days a reality.

## The Decision To Use Force

The state of Mississippi had clearly shown its intention not only to threaten to use violence, but to use it. In the face of this direct challenge the federal government had no choice but to act to enforce its authority. President John F. Kennedy acted at the crucial moment on September 30, 1962, by issuing a proclamation and executive order:

BY THE PRESIDENT OF THE UNITED STATES OF AMERICA

A PROCLAMATION

Whereas the Governor of the State of Mississippi and certain law enforcement officers and other officials of that State, and other persons, individually and in unlawful assemblies, combinations and conspiracies, have been and are willfully opposing and obstructing the enforcement of orders entered by the United States District Court for the Southern

District of Mississippi and the United States Court of Appeals for the Fifth Circuit; and

Whereas such unlawful assemblies, combinations and conspiracies oppose and obstruct the execution of the laws of the United States, impede the course of justice under those laws and make it impracticable to enforce those laws in the State of Mississippi by the ordinary course of judicial proceedings; and

Whereas I have expressly called the attention of the Governor of Mississippi to the perilous situation that exists and to his duties in the premises, and have requested but have not received from him adequate assurances that the orders of the courts of the United States will be obeyed and that law and order will be maintained;

Now, therefore, I, John F. Kennedy, President of the United States, under and by virtue of the authority vested in me by the Constitution and laws of the United States, including Chapter 15 of Title 10 of the United States Code 1, particularly sections 332, 333 and 334 thereof, do command all persons engaged in such obstructions of justice to cease and desist therefrom and to disperse and retire peacefully forthwith.

In witness whereof, I have hereunto set my hand and caused the seal of the United States of America to be affixed.

Done at the city of Washington this 30th day of September in the year of our Lord Nineteen Hundred and Sixty-Two, and of the independence of the United States of America the One Hundred and Eighty-Seven.

JOHN F. KENNEDY

BY THE PRESIDENT:
Secretary of State.

EXECUTIVE ORDER

PROVIDING ASSISTANCE FOR THE REMOVAL OF UNLAWFUL OBSTRUCTIONS OF JUSTICE IN THE STATE OF MISSISSIPPI

Whereas on September 30, 1962, I issued proclamation No. 3497 reading in part as follows [quoted in entirety above] and

Whereas the commands contained in that proclamation have not been obeyed and obstruction of enforcement of those court orders still exists and threatens to continue:

Now, therefore, by virtue of the authority vested in me by the Constitution and laws of the United States, including Chapter 15 of Title 10, particularly sections 332, 333 and 334 thereof, and section 301 of Title 3 of the United States Code, it is hereby ordered as follows:

Section 1. The Secretary of Defense is authorized and directed to take all appropriate steps to enforce all orders of the United States District Court for the Southern District of Mississippi and the United States Court of Appeals for the Fifth Circuit and to remove all obstructions of justice in the State of Mississippi.

Section 2. In furtherance of the enforcement of the aforementioned orders of the United States District Court for the Southern District of Mississippi and the United States Court of Appeals for the Fifth Circuit, the Secretary of Defense is authorized to use such of the armed forces of the United States as he may deem necessary.

Section 3. I hereby authorize the Secretary of Defense to call into the active military service of the United States, as he may deem appropriate to carry out the purposes of this order, any or all of the units of the Army National Guard and of the Air National Guard of the State of Mississippi to serve in the active military service of the United States for an indefinite period and until relieved by appropriate orders. In carrying out the provisions of Section 1, the Secretary of Defense is authorized to use the units, and members thereof, ordered into active military service of the United States pursuant to this section.

Section 4. The Secretary of Defense is authorized to delegate to the Secretary of the Army or the Secretary of the Air Force, or both, any of the authority conferred upon him by this order.

JOHN F. KENNEDY

The White House
September 30, 1962.

## The Final Preparations

The call now went out all over the United States for U.S. marshals, border patrolmen, and federal prison guards. As political appointees in their local areas, the marshals were not fighting men, nor were all of them trained in the art of riot or mob control. The usual background for a marshal is some form of police work. Moreover, due to the unusual nature of this assignment, it was necessary for the chiefs to have training sessions at Millington Naval Air Station for the marshals.

The marshals brought back some exciting tales about their training-school experiences. One of the problems was the fact that no one could distinguish a marshal from anyone else. The newsmen took immediate advantage of this and joined their ranks. One newsman, less (or more) astute than the others, secured a horse. He somehow convinced the navy guard that he was an inspector and proceeded to the practice area where he reviewed and recorded the action of the trainees and took numerous photographs. Somebody got suspicious and apprehended the horseman. Two of the other newsmen in the ranks then began to feel uncomfortable, especially when the marshals started to look suspiciously at the cameras that they carried instead of guns. They broke out of the ranks and ran for the fence. The military might have its shortcomings but they keep good fences around their installations, and the newsmen were caught. The government was in a worse predicament after they were caught than it had been before. The two newsmen were well-known correspondents for the nation's biggest news media. What would the government do with them? It finally brought them back to the barracks and asked me if I would let them interview me. I had been carefully shielded from the press up to then. I don't know if the newsmen demanded me as an alternative or if the government offered me as a bribe.

In the meantime, the Army was moving in, in great force. The entire Naval Station had been turned into a drill field. One of the most notable things to me was that Negro officers and men were with the army units. Many of the drill sergeants were Negro non-commissioned officers.

*No More Advisers.* After the last futile attempt to enroll, it was evident that I would become more and more isolated. Finally, on September 29 the moment came when I was left on my own. There were no more advisers at this point. Of course, I could understand the position of the NAACP Legal Defense and Educational Fund, since the case was completely out of the legal field now and they were so far removed from the scene and the pertinent facts, that it would have been unwise for them to advise me to go or not to go.

*The Deal.* Adding everything up and weighing it, I am absolutely sure that my greatest uncertainty was over the talk about a deal between the federal government and the state of Mississippi. Any one thinking about this matter afterwards might fail to understand or appreciate my apprehension regarding a possible deal during this crucial period. It must always be remembered that I was a Negro in Mississippi and I was acutely aware of my history as a Negro. The Negro had existed for a long time; the whites had existed for a long time; the federal union had existed for a long time; the state of Mississippi had existed for a long time; and the question that we now faced—the extension of citizenship rights to the Negro—was not new. Certainly, there must have been deals made in the past between the federal government and Mississippi. How could I, a Negro, who had never once received my due, and who knew of not one single occasion where any of my foreparents on the Negro side had received his due, not be concerned about this prospect, especially when no official of the federal government would commit himself or his government as to the exact extent of its involvement?

*The Flight from Memphis to Oxford.* It was Sunday. Barnett had

had his greatest day of triumph the day before at the "Ole Miss" football game in Jackson, and General Walker had issued his famous call for volunteers to come to Mississippi. Activity was at a peak at Millington. We would go today. Late in the afternoon we boarded the "Ole Miss" special. Ironically, it was the first time we had changed planes. The Florida pilot had had to return home; we had a new plane and a new pilot, but the three traveling companions— McShane, Doar, and Meredith—were the same. We took off and arrived in Oxford before the final clearance was given; we had to circle the airport for some time before the word came from Washington to land.

## The First Night

When we landed, the Oxford airport was unrecognizable. There were rows of Air Force and other planes, mostly transport planes, and hundreds of marshals. The two most noticeable things were the floodlights and the tense atmosphere. We unboarded and hurried through a host of men wearing U.S. deputy marshal armbands, all of whom seemed to close in on us. We then slowly proceeded in a caravan to Baxter Hall and arrived there between dusk and darkness. The campus was completely vacated. There were no obvious signs that school was in session. The entire student body had either caught the "Barnett Special" train to Jackson or found their own means of getting to the football game. Without ceremony, we moved into Baxter Hall to spend the first night; there was not even a dorm chief present to give me the rules of the hall.

*My Rooms in Baxter Hall.* I suppose you could call it an apartment. Since they knew some government men would be staying with me, I had been assigned two bedrooms, a living room, and a bathroom. The first thing that I did was make my bed. When the trouble started, I could not see or hear very much of it. Most of the events occurred at the other end of the campus, and I did not look out the window. I think I read a newspaper and went to bed around ten o'clock. I was awakened several times in the night by the noise and shooting outside, but it was not near the hall, and I had no way of knowing what was going on. Some of the students in my dormitory banged their doors for a while and threw some bottles in the halls, but I slept pretty well all night.

I woke up about 6:30 in the morning and looked out and saw the troops. There was a slight smell of tear gas in my room, but I still did not know what had gone on during the night. I did not find out, until some marshals came and told me how many people were hurt and killed.

Some newspapermen later asked me if I thought attending the university was worth all this death and destruction. The question really annoyed me. Of course, I was sorry! I hadn't wanted this to happen. I believe it could have been prevented by responsible political leadership in Mississippi. As for the federal government, the President and the Attorney General had all the intelligence facilities at their disposal, and I believe that they handled it to the best of their knowledge and ability. I think it would have been much worse if they had waited any longer. Social change is a painful thing, but the method by which it is achieved depends upon the people at the top. Here they were totally opposed—the state against the federal government. There was bound to be trouble, and there was.

## The Registration

There was no lingering or turning back now. At eight o'clock the three of us—McShane, Doar, and Meredith—with a retinue of marshals and soldiers left Baxter Hall for the Lyceum Building to get on with the long-delayed business of my registering as a student at the University of Mississippi. The signs of strife and warfare from the night before were everywhere. But at this moment the power of the United States was supreme. Even the Mississippi National Guard had proven without a doubt that its first loyalty was to the Commander-in-Chief of the Armed Forces of the United States— the President.

The border patrol car in which we rode to the administration building was a shattered example of the violence of social change. We had used this car to make our first attempt to enroll on September 20, 1962, and then it had been a spotless, unmarred specimen. Now it was battered and smashed: bullet holes had riddled the sides; the windows were all shot out. McShane sent one of the deputies back into Baxter Hall to get a couple of Army blankets to put over the back seat so that we could sit down. The marshals had suffered also. It would have been hard to find one who did not bear some mark of the process of violent change: Bandages, bruises, and limps were the rule.

We entered through the back door of the Lyceum Building. Fortunately, I did not know that it was the back door at the time;

otherwise, I would have had to confront the question of whether this was a concession to the Mississippi "way of life." It was a dismal day. Even the newsmen were spiritless. Inside the room behind a desk sat Ellis, the Registrar. He was a lone stand-out, the only man on the scene with spirit—a spirit of defiance, even of contempt, if not hatred. Doar stated our purpose and the Registrar pointed to a group of forms to be filled out by me. I looked at them and filled out all but one—my class-schedule form. As I studied it, obviously Ellis knew what was on my mind. One course on my schedule not only was a duplicate of one with the same title which I had already completed with the grade of A, but when I got to the class, I found that the instructor was using the very same textbook. Ellis said to me, "Meredith (he is the only official at the university who did not address me with the usual title of courtesy), you may as well sign." I tried to discuss the matter with him, but it was no use. I signed and decided to take the matter up through other channels. The schedule was later changed to suit my needs.

We left the room. The press had been patient and I consented to stop and talk briefly with them. There was not too much to ask and less to say. The first question asked me was, "Now that you are finally registered, are you happy?" I could only express my true feeling that, "This is no happy occasion." Truly, this was no time for joy.

On my way out of the Lyceum Building, I encountered my first Negro. What would his reaction be? What would our relationship be? What would be our communication? He had his cleaning tools, as all Negroes on the campus must keep them visible, and under one arm was tucked a broom. As I walked past, he acted as if he had not even noticed anything unusual on the campus, but just as I passed he touched me with the handle of his broom and caught my eye. I got the message. Every Negro on the campus was on my team. Every black eye would be watching over me at the University of Mississippi. Later on, I got to know this fellow very well. He told me that he just had to let me know that they were with me all the way, and to bump me with the broom handle was the best way he could think of to communicate with me.

## The First Class

At nine I attended my first class; it was a course in Colonial American History. I was a few minutes late and was given a seat at the back of the room. The professor was lecturing on the English background, conditions in England at the time of the colonization of America, and he pretended to pay no special attention when I entered. When the U.S. marshals decided to come inside the room, however, he asked them to remain outside. This was a precedent that was followed during my entire stay at the university. I think there were about a dozen students in class. One said hello to me and the others were silent. I remember a girl—the only girl there, I think—and she was crying. But it might have been from the tear gas in the room. I was crying from it myself.

I had three classes scheduled that day. I went to two; the third did not meet because there was too much tear gas in the room.

*Return to Baxter Hall*

This day, October 1, 1962, was a turning point in my three years in Mississippi. The first phase—to breach the system of "White Supremacy"—had been accomplished; even if I only had a toehold in the door, the solid wall had been cracked.

The return up the hill to Baxter Hall, after attending the classes, also marked a turning point in my own personal struggle to contribute what I could to the fight for human freedom and dignity. I felt a sudden release of pressure that I perhaps cannot put into words. I recall that I remarked to John Doar about this feeling of relief, and he did not seem to understand at all. Perhaps this was not the time for philosophizing, since I was the only one who had gotten any rest the night before. But I had the feeling that my personal battle was over. The pressure from that inner doubt, always present in one's mind, that one's best might not be good enough, was now released. The often debated question of whether or not I would break before the system bulged no longer troubled my mind.

To me, it seemed that the ultimate outcome was relatively insignificant; whether or not I went on to graduate appeared to be a minor issue. The important thing was that I had the privilege of choice. At the same time I was aware that Negroes recognized only "Success" and "Titles," and I had bypassed the title several times, knowing full well that if I should fail in this effort, I would be soon forgotten. However, as we slowly ascended the hill toward Baxter Hall, it appeared to me that the particular steps that I had chosen to take in an effort to carry out the mandate of my Divine Responsibility had been proper and timely.

# 9

## The First Three Months: October-December 1962

---

THE tensions during the first months at the University of Mississippi can hardly be described. My own recollection of the fast-occurring events is somewhat vague. Fortunately, I wrote two magazine articles during this period which recorded some of my feelings at the time, and I shall use these to describe my activities during the first semester.

### The Statement of October 9, 1962

My first public statement one week after my enrollment has been considered one of my most controversial, since it concerned the resegregation of the army units and certain statements made by the NAACP.

Certainly no price is too high to pay for the right to enjoy full American citizenship. Yet, when it comes to forfeiting one particular right or privilege, it is quite possible to get the bad end of the bargain. Two things have occurred and are now occurring that have made my struggle most difficult.

The first concerns the military. The first two days of my stay at the University of Mississippi, the military units looked like American units. All soldiers held their positions and performed the task for which they had been trained and ordered to do. Since that time the units have been resegregated. Negroes have been purged from their positions in the ranks.

On Thursday, October 4, 1962, I brought this to the attention of the proper authorities. On Friday I was informed that the situation would be corrected and the Negroes would be put back into their places in the ranks.

On Monday, October 8, Negro soldiers were indeed seen again among the soldiers. The ones I saw, however, were on a garbage detail truck and unarmed. The white members of the detail were armed. This condition constitutes a dishonor and a disgrace to the hundreds of thousands of Negroes who wear the uniforms of our military services.

Negro soldiers were purged from the ranks 100 years ago in a somewhat similar situation, and today, in 1962, this is an intolerable act. My conscience would not allow me to go on observing this situation without, at least, letting the Negro soldiers know that I did not like their being dishonored.

The other thing is the claim of some individual or individuals in Mississippi that I was picked, selected, or chosen by them to integrate the University of Mississippi. This inflammatory claim is not only untrue, but I consider it a blot on my character and an insult to my dignity. I am not defending myself, but I consider it of utmost importance that the persons who claim to be Negro leaders should be individuals of unquestioned integrity and not individuals who will make irresponsible statements to gain personal ends.

I have good reasons to believe that this and similar accusations have resulted in stronger opposition to me by the students at the university. If it were true, I must admit that I would think their opposition would be in some ways justified. Integration or desegregation has never been my goal. Better educational opportunities for myself and my people have always been my major consideration.

I would like to thank all of the millions of Americans who have supported me and especially those thousands who have sent me letters and telegrams. Also, I thank the many persons in foreign lands who have offered their support and warm sentiments.

Further, I would like to express my thanks to the federal marshals and to the Justice Department for the fine way in which they have handled all matters concerning my entering and remaining at the university.

My feelings were so strong on the issue of dishonoring Negro soldiers that I had decided to leave the university rather than accept these conditions, and I had informed the U.S. government of this decision. In response to my statement, the Negroes were put back into their proper places. Negro soldiers wrote me expressing their appreciation of this protest; the letters came from servicemen holding every rank in the military from private to colonel. And only one letter disapproved of my statement.

Of course, the most disheartening aspect of this situation was the fact that I had to make the statement, because no one else would. I had seen to it that everyone, who should have been concerned, knew about this matter and had asked them to act. The white press, the Negro press, and the Negro leaders all closed their eyes and shunned my request. It made me wonder just how often the Negro had been sold out not only by the whites but also by his own people.

### My Thoughts on Fear and Death

During the first few weeks almost all of the focus was on the possibility of my being killed by the "White Supremacists." People have asked me if I was not terribly afraid the night we went to Oxford and thereafter. My apprehensions had been faced a long time before that. The hardest thing in human nature is to decide to act. I was doing all right in the Air Force as a noncommissioned officer when I decided to return to Mississippi. I got married in 1956 and my wife was able to work as a civil servant on the same bases where I was stationed. I had to give this up, this established way of doing things, this status and security, and try something new and unknown. The big decision was made, not at the University of Mississippi, but at that time. Once I had made that decision, things just had to happen the way they did.

A quotation from Theodore Roosevelt was perhaps more important than anything else in helping me make the critical decisions. I think I had read it in my base newspaper around 1952, and everywhere I have gone since then—every place I have lived or everywhere I have worked—I have put that clipping in front of me: "It is not the critic who counts, not the man who points out how the strong man stumbles, where the doer of deeds could have done them better. The credit belongs to the man who is actually in the arena; whose face is marred by dust and sweat and blood; who strives valiantly; who errs and comes short again and again; who knows the great enthusiasm, the great devotion, and spends himself in a worthy cause; who, at the best, knows in the end the triumph of high achievement; and who, at the worst, if he fails, at least fails while daring greatly, so that his place shall never be with those cold and timid souls who know neither victory nor defeat." At various times different parts of that quotation have been important to me, but when I made the decision to return to Mississippi to try to gain admission to the university, the part I kept remembering was the "cold and timid souls who know neither victory nor defeat." I did not want to be one of those.

As for fear of death or personal injury—and I consider this most important for everybody to understand—I had put death or the fear of getting hurt in the same category with legal objections to my entering the university, or moral objections, or objections on the grounds of custom. They were all just ways to keep me out of the university. It would not have mattered if I stumbled and fell and couldn't go to classes, if I cut my finger and could not write for a month, or if I was shot and killed—these were all just obstacles in my way. I might have done quite a bit to prevent my being killed. I did this several times. But this was because, if something happened to me, it would have been a setback for all the Negroes in Mississippi. If I lost an hour's sleep during that period, it was over some philosophical point, but not over what might happen to me personally. I was sure that if I was harmed or killed, somebody else would have taken my place. I would have hated to think that another Negro would have had to go through that ordeal, but I would have hated more to think that no one would. There were others.

I had an older brother who was scary as a boy. Back home he would not go certain places after dark or walk here or there. I always walked wherever I wanted. I walked four miles to Boy Scout meetings at night, and I always went through all the hollows and the places where you were supposed to be afraid to go. I must admit that my hair has stood up on my head at times, but I never ran. They used to say, "If you see a 'hant,' put your hand on it." Most of the time you will find it isn't there. I think it is an utter waste of time to worry about dying. It is living that matters—doing something to justify being here on God's green earth. I do what I do because I must. I have never felt I had a choice. There is an urge that I cannot explain easily—I guess that is as close as I can come to defining it.

There is something else, too, relative to my attitude toward fear, and it is hard to say right. People can misunderstand it. But it is this —generally at home I was always thought to be pretty smart. I was not particularly proud of it; it was just accepted, a more or less acknowledged fact. I was a champion in my group in Mississippi, but when I went to Florida to change high schools, I wasn't a champion at all. I had to fight to keep up; I had not been prepared. I have felt many times that, given the opportunity, I could have developed into practically anything. One of the biggest influences on my life has been this feeling that I was never able to properly develop my talents. I am sure that this has been a strong motivating force with me, as it has with many Negroes. It has caused me always to try to see myself in relation to the whole society. Too many Negroes see themselves only in relation to other Negroes, but that is not enough. We have to see ourselves in the whole society. If America isn't for everybody, it isn't America.

My ideas about life and living were perhaps the real reason why I could stand in the midst of what appeared to be an obvious danger to others and not show any signs of fear. Actually, I never felt the fear or recognized the danger as others saw it. Others might view the situation as one of life facing death; I saw it as death facing life. The Negro in Mississippi was dead because he could not live. I was fighting to live. Where there is life, there is chance. My only real fear is death.

The fear of bodily harm is another question altogether. What is it that would allow Negroes to be so viciously violent to one another and at the same time to be meek as a lamb before the white man? Why was it possible for a group of Negroes to fight, cut, and shoot each other, and one white man could come into the area and subdue them all by calling them a bunch of "no good niggers"? The answer is simple. The organized society of the South had provided immunity from the law for the feared white man. This knowledge pervaded the society. I understood that the Negro's fear of the white man was a fear that existed only in his imagination and not from a real condition. I knew that in a man-to-man encounter there were few men in the world that I could not subdue, both mentally and physically. At twelve years of age I could strike a match with a .22 rifle. I had had nine years of training in military service, and few men possessed greater potential for doing bodily harm than myself. Why then should I fear any man? My belief in my supernatural or superhuman powers was another important factor. Whether it was true or not, I had always felt that I could stop a mob with the uplift of a hand.

And finally I believe in the immortality of ideas and in the immortality of those who manifest them. Because of my "Divine Responsibility" to advance human civilization, I could not die. If one places society above self, and I do, life never ends. Everything that I do, I do because I must; and everything that I must do, I do.

### The University's Side of the Story

It is easy for those of us who were on the other side to condemn and place the blame confidently and entirely on those whom fate had placed on the opposite side. But we must always remember that the process of social change essentially involves human beings. The officials of the University of Mississippi were men of both pride and feelings.

Chancellor J.D. Williams delivered a speech on October 31, 1962, the last day of the month in which I had registered as a student, to an audience of Mississippi whites at Greenville, Mississippi. In this speech, "Another Mississippi Story," he said:

We at the University of Mississippi have had our souls tried of late. . . . Today is the last day in the month of October, 1962. I shall never, so long as I live, forget the first day of this month. The first hours of October, 1962, found me in my home in the spot that I love more than any other place in the world, the Ole Miss campus. I have had the privilege and the honor to head the University of Mississippi longer than any other chancellor or president in her 114-year-old history. For 16 years the University has been my life, but in that night of horrors I wondered whether any other chancellor had ever had cause to feel such bitterness and anguish.

The University had become a pawn in a combat between powerful political forces. With little consultation with administrative officers, without giving adequate notice, the effective control of the University was taken out of our hands. The Lyceum—which even during the Civil War had been a hospital, a place of mercy—had become a battle-post. A yelling mob filled the center of the campus. Within a hundred yards of my front door a visitor to our country [Paul Guihard, a French reporter] had been murdered, shot in the back by some faceless assassin. Nearby another corpse [Ray Gunter] had lain. The toll of wounded was rising every minute. The air was filled with the sound of shots, the bursting of tear-gas shells, the explosions of gasoline bombs, and the cursing and howling of the mob. We could only hope that the troops rushing toward Oxford would arrive soon to end the destruction and the bloodshed.

That night one might well wonder when if ever the University could return to its role as an educational institution. But when the time came for eight o'clock classes, every professor was at his post. Don't be misled by the inevitable rumors. Some faculty members were heartsick, some were angry, some were frightened; but not one shirked his duty. They met their classes and they taught their classes, that first day and every day since. . . .

I have been especially moved by the loyalty of our colored workers. We have always had particularly fine relations with our Negro staff members. They have been friends as well as workers. Students have come back to the campus in later years no more interested in revisiting their professors than seeing Bobby ——— again at the cafeteria, or Calvin ———, or Dean ———'s right-hand man, Bishop ———, or some other colored friend.

The riot was particularly terrifying for those people [the Negroes]. Those living just off the campus had seen the mob come sweeping around their houses. When they tried to come to work, they were cursed and abused by strangers. The campus was filled with armed soldiers, and most of the Negroes were turned away. Some few did get in, though; and by the time the last of the rioters were being cleared off the eastern end of the campus, colored workers were in the cafeteria preparing breakfast for the students. By the end of the week 95 per cent of our colored help was back at work, their faith and their confidence renewed.

Just as heartening as the support on the campus has been the support from off the campus. First, let me mention the Board of Trustees. It is only too easy to misinterpret the Board's actions. Believe me when I say the Board is entitled to the admiration and support of everyone who loves the University.

The Board members were caught, just as the University was, in the conflict between two powerful political forces. Nothing would have been easier than for them to save themselves from trouble by leaving the University a victim of these powerful forces, but they did just the opposite. To prevent such treatment of the University, they took upon themselves the full responsibility for the Meredith case, putting themselves in jeopardy to secure the safety of the University administration. . . .

Our students, the overwhelming majority of our students, have been loyal to the University. They . . . entrusted their future to our hands. We cannot short-change them, we cannot betray their faith, by giving them a third-rate education. Ole Miss graduates must have at least an equal chance at the starter's gate with those who graduate from our nation's best universities. It will be a betrayal of the high calling of education if we drive away from our campus those men who will not submit it to thought control, if we discourage those students who are eager to meet the challenge of new ideas, if we close off certain avenues to knowledge and make of them dead-end streets. . . .

The following day, November 1, 1962, the Chancellor spoke to the male students. I was asked not to attend the affair, but a copy of the speech was sent to me. It read in part:

I have asked for this opportunity to meet with you for the purpose of discussing what is today the University's most serious problem. That problem is the maintenance of peaceful and orderly conditions on the campus.

Over the past month, we have heard various sounds that are not part of a normal campus life—exploding tear-gas shells, gunfire, jeering and shouted obscenities, shattering of glass, and "cherry-bomb" barrages. These sounds do not have a place on a university campus. The University has a solemn obligation to you. That obligation is to see that your education is not further disrupted by that small minority of the student body which has persisted in creating disorder on the campus. The University cannot tolerate acts that impair its standing, acts of a minority that damage your reputation and jeopardize your future.

My responsibility is clear. It is to preserve the University, to maintain its accreditation, and to see that it continues to serve you as the best institution in the State. I am prepared to take whatever steps are necessary to fulfill this responsibility.

Let me be as explicit as possible about our present situation. The shooting of fireworks, the possession of fireworks, the throwing of bottles or other missiles, the possession of firearms and ammunition, the use of obscene and profane language, the committing of any act of violence or any act tending to disorder will be regarded as *serious* violations of University regulations. Swift and drastic disciplinary action, including expulsion from the University, can be expected. . . .

Later, the Chancellor had a booklet prepared to show the part played by the University in my case. It was released on November 15, 1962. The prefatory letter and the summary follow:

To the Reader:

For purposes of the record, I have directed the preparation of the following document, which I believe to be a fair and accurate record of the part played by the University of Mississippi in what has become known as the Meredith Case.

The intent of the present report is to put the successive events of the Meredith Case into proper perspective.

Our hope is that those who are sincerely interested in the welfare of the University of Mississippi, especially those other members of the academic community whose good opinion is of such vital significance to the future of the University, will study this document with thoughful attention.

J. D. Williams
Chancellor

RECAPITULATION AND COMMENTARY

*Supplementary Report on Discipline* by L. L. Love, Dean, Division of Student Personnel

This report summarizes what the University Administration, the University students, and the University faculty and staff have done to this point to control conditions which have arisen in connection with the admission of James H. Meredith to the University of Mississippi. Particular attention will be given to student discipline. For the most part, the report will be factual, though an occasional opinion, clearly labeled as such, will be expressed. . . .

## Steps Taken Prior to Meredith's Arrival

Through all of the period up to September 30 administrative officials and others were using every opportunity to discuss with students the problems of keeping the University open, avoiding violence, the meaning of the injunction issued by the District Court, and the like. All of this was done in the setting of an intensely inflammatory Mississippi press and the defiant statements of persons in high places. *But the efforts were extraordinarily successful.* Without equivocation, I say that the conduct of students until 4 p.m. September 30 was all that anyone could possibly have expected.

Prior to September 30, the University had employed extra police from neighboring cities as a precautionary measure. All of them had gone home for the week end—another indication of the total surprise to the University of Meredith's arrival on September 30.

## Sunday, September 30, Prior to 4 p.m.

As previously mentioned, the conduct of students had been superb. The Administration had every reason to believe that Meredith would arrive, accompanied by a large contingent of U.S. marshals, on October 1 or 2. The Administration planned to continue at an intensified pace the efforts, which had been so successful, to effect the orderly admission of Meredith.

I reached the Lyceum within five minutes after the marshals arrived to find them surrounding the building, shoulder-to-shoulder, armed. Mr. Clegg [Assistant to the Chancellor in charge of University Development] arrived at about the same time. (Perhaps here is the place to say that the Lyceum is the symbol of Ole Miss. Even after it became known that Meredith was in a dormitory, there was little demonstration there; the anger was directed at the marshals who surrounded the "symbol.")

Mr. Clegg and I met and talked with the half-dozen officials of the Department of Justice who were present. Our Chief of Police and the Director of the State Highway Patrol were present. The officials were supplied with everything for which they asked. They had no idea how to bring Meredith to the campus, I suggested a roundabout way and sent our Chief to guide them.

The Department of Justice officials requested a direct telephone line to the White House. I offered one line. It was not long until my entire suite of offices was taken over. This greatly hampered University operations, as that suite is the nerve center for communication on the campus, especially in a time of crisis. We opened the Dean of Women's suite, and it was not long until that was also taken over. These areas were not evacuated for more than 40 hours. The difficulties faced by our personnel were almost insurmountable. Early in the evening I managed to make a telephone call which brought five men from the Division of Student Personnel into the Lyceum. They were of great assistance, but terriby handicapped in their efforts by difficulties of communication. The frustrations of that night and day of horrors for persons trying to do a vital job are forever etched on their memories. . . .

The Outsiders

Outsiders were participating actively in the early stages of the riot. At dark there was a sudden influx of a very large number, some it later developed from as far away as Georgia and Texas. The campus was flooded with armed undesirables. The perimeters of the campus are long and heavily wooded. A novice would know that it would take at least 1,500 troops to insure that no mob invasion would occur. Adequate notice was given, for the papers were full of stories for days about the large number of persons who were going to converge on the campus from everywhere.

One illustration is significant for several reasons. A student managed to work his way into the Lyceum to tell me that General Walker was present and was a very active agitator. I reported this information immediately to every Justice Department official in the Lyceum and heard the information telephoned to the White House. I repeatedly urged the officials to take General Walker into custody—that by so doing they might break the back of the riot. I could get no response until I finally forced one. It was that they "did not have force enough." Before Deputy United States Attorney General Nicholas DeB. Katzenbach left for Washington some days later, I discussed the Walker situation with him. At that time he said they had no basis for preferring charges at the time I reported Walker's presence. Yet they did have the basis for picking up 160 "nameless" men. . . .

University Disciplinary Measures—September 30–October 1

On October 1, Mr. Katzenbach asked Doctor Haywood and me if the University would handle the discipline of the students apprehended. We agreed and we agreed to do it promptly. Although Mr. Katzenbach was asked several times for names, not until a letter dated October 10 did he submit seven names, of which one was not a student, with allegations. The six students were referred to the Student Judicial Council in the usual manner on the day the letter was received. On October 11 Mr. Katzenbach submitted three more names; the two who were students were referred on October 12. On October 15, Mr. Norbert Schlei, Assistant

Attorney General, submitted two more names. One was later withdrawn because the Justice Department had made an incorrect identification. I personally verbally placed each of these students on temporary disciplinary probation with the warning that any further misbehavior would result in immediate dismissal. All of these cases were heard as rapidly as possible by the Student Judicial Council. Its recommendations were studied by the University administrative officers and the results announced to the press on October 27.

Two very important points need to be made. The first is the fact that the Justice Department withdrew its allegations against five of the eight students with the admission that it did not have sufficient evidence to convict. Even so, these five were referred to the Student Judicial Council for violation of University regulations. The Justice Department produced witnesses against the other three. One was proven completely innocent of all allegations made by the Justice Department but was found guilty of violating a University regulation. The other two were found guilty of various offenses, none of which involved firearms or other dangerous weapons. All eight received sentences varying from disciplinary probation for the remainder of the current semester to dismissal from the University with the sentence suspended. The latter has the effect of disciplinary probation for as long as one is a student in the University. The action taken was fair and just, in my opinion. . . .

## October 12–October 28

At the request of the Army, all guns were ordered removed from the campus, though many students are avid hunters. On October 12, a "get tough" statement was issued, warning that further disorders would result in serious consequences; the first emotional crisis was over and it was time for the University to proceed with its normal functions.

In this move toward normality, a pep rally and street dance were scheduled for 6:30 on October 18. It was surrounded by many precautions to avoid a possible incident. The Justice Department had been notified. Yet, knowing that, the Department representative chose that evening to have a young secretary eat with Meredith in the Cafeteria. This was foreign to every custom these students had ever known; yet, to their eternal credit, nothing happened. . . .

## October 28 *et sequitur*

Just prior to October 29 I had approached the Justice Department with the suggestion that the rigid controls on Baxter Hall (where Meredith was quartered) and on neighboring Gerard Hall be relaxed— that the students had earned it. The Justice Department was receptive and I had every reason to believe that desirable changes would be made quickly. I had arranged to talk to the men in Baxter at 10 p.m., October 29.

But that evening fireworks, shipped to the campus in large quantities by an outside source, were set off in the entire dormitory area. I made my talk during the very worst part of the demonstration. The number of students actually participating was small, but very active. Perhaps 300 of those who were outside of their dormitories at any one time were spectators only. I found it easy to talk the spectators into returning to their dormitories, though fireworks continued to explode for most of the night. Many of the fireworks were aimed at the soldiers. There was considerable jeering.

On October 31, Army officials heard a rumor that 17 sticks of dynamite had been taken into Baxter Hall (where Meredith resides). At about the same time a soldier was slightly injured by fireworks thrown from Lester Hall. The Army asked that a thorough search of both dormitories be made. This was done immediately under the supervision of campus police. No dynamite was found. However, enough evidence was found on one man, already under suspicion, to result in his expulsion. . . .

On November 1, Chancellor Williams spoke to all male students in two groups. He used a constructive approach, but made it perfectly clear that the University was ready to part company with students who violate University regulations.

Throughout this period, as in the preceding ones, the Chief of Police and I have cooperated closely with the Federal Bureau of Investigation and with Army Intelligence. We have been particularly interested in furnishing leads which may lead to court action against groups and individuals from the outside who have been fomenting difficulties on the campus. . . .

## My Thoughts During the First Weeks

People seem always to want to know what I thought and how I felt during the first few weeks at the University of Mississippi, what was being said to me and how I reacted. I think a few excerpts from an article written at the end of the second week for the *Saturday Evening Post** can best depict my feelings and attitudes:

I have received hundreds of telegrams and thousands of letters, most of them expressions of support. One guy sent me a piece of singed rope, and another sent a poem, I guess you'd have to call it:

> *Roses are red, violets are blue;*
> *I've killed one nigger and might as well*
> *make it two.*

*Vol. 235, No. 40 (November 10, 1962), 14-17. © 1962 The Curtis Publishing Company.

But most of the letters and telegrams have supported me, and some of them have been really touching—letters from 10- and 11-year-olds who think I am right and offer me their help.

As far as my relations with the students go, I make it a practice to be courteous. I do not force myself on them, but that is not my nature anyway. Many of them—most, I would say—have been courteous, and the faculty members certainly have been. When I hear the jeers and the catcalls—"We'll get you, nigger" and all that—I do not consider it personal. I get the idea people are just having a little fun. I think it's tragic that they have to have this kind of fun about me, but many of them are children of the men who lead Mississippi today, and I would not expect them to act any other way. They have to act the way they do. I think I understand human nature enough to understand that.

It has not been all bad. Many students have spoken to me very pleasantly. They have stopped banging doors and throwing bottles into my dormitory now.

One day a fellow from my home town sat down at my table in the cafeteria. "If you're here to get an education, I'm for you," he said. "If you're here to cause trouble, I'm against you." That seemed fair enough to me.

If the decision is made to keep the marshals and troops on the campus until I complete my course, it is all right with me, but I hope that will not be necessary. I think the marshals have been superb. They have had an image of America—that the law must be obeyed, no matter what they may think of it or what anybody else may think of it—but they are certainly a distraction on the campus. The thing that grieves me most about all this is that the students are not getting the best college results because they are spending too much time looking on at these various events involving me. I did not get much studying done that first week, and I don't think anybody else did.

Personally the year will be a hardship for me. My wife will be in college in Jackson. Our son John Howard, who will be three in January, is living with my parents in Kosciusko. I expect to see them both very often, but I do not think that families should live apart. On the other hand, this is nothing new to my wife. We spent most of our courtship discussing my plan to come back to Mississippi some day, and I guess you could say her understanding that I would try to do this sometime was almost part of the marriage contract. She has been truly marvelous through all of it. I called her three nights after I entered the University, and she picked up the phone and was so calm you would have thought we had just finished a game of 500 rummy and she had won. She is a remarkable woman.

I don't think this has had any effect on my family in Kosciusko. I have talked to my father. He asks me how I am, and I ask him how he is. He knows what I mean by the question, and I know what he means by the answer. That is the way it is in our family.

Later, in an article that was published in *Look*,* I made the following comments and observations regarding my stay at the University of Mississippi. Some of my thoughts at the moment on various subjects were also included.

You always hear the white Southerners say, "Our Negroes don't want integration," they don't want this, they don't want that, and "you can't legislate morality." The fact of the matter is that no white citizen in the South knows what the Negro wants. He knows what the Negro tells him he wants, but there is no effective communication. For example, if the white man asks a Negro does he believe in sit-ins or college integration, the Negro never thinks about what the truth is. He thinks of what he can tell this man to get him off his back.

Among Negroes, you hear so much about the Uncle Toms and the Nervous Minnies and all this kind of thing. I have never met one. I have met a lot of expedient Negroes, those who do the thing that they feel they have to do at the given time, either to better their own position or to take an intermediate measure that will better their people's position. But, basically, I think we all want the same thing. There is no group of Negroes that does not have the same drives. And the only way to accomplish our goal is to use the resources of all of us.

This is rightly so. It is essential that America solve her racial problem because, in the first place, human society, civilization itself, must advance. Elimination of oppression and prejudice, of restriction on human rights and development—these are essential to the advance of civilization. If America is to hold her rightful place as leader of the world, the democratic world, we must come nearer to our ideal of human equality and justice.

The job has just begun, and everywhere you look, you see things that reflect the inequalities still existing in our society. At the university, the saddest day of every week for me is Thursday—because that is ROTC day. When I go to class that morning, the Reserve Officer Candidates have on their uniforms. In the afternoon, I often go out to watch them drill up and down the streets near my dormitory. I know that not one Negro in Mississippi has the privilege of taking part in the ROTC program. Surely, there is one Negro in our state who would make officer material. The Regular Army units guarding the campus are fully integrated, including Negro officers, but the country does not get any Negro officers from Mississippi ROTC training. It's a loss for the country in general. For the Negro, it is more than a loss, individually or financially; it affects him even down to his soul.

Personally, I have not been able to conclude that people are just concretely mean and naturally evil. I do not think that the worst segre-

* Vol. 27, No. 7 (April 19, 1963), 70–78.

gationist, even the "White Supremacist," wants to see other people suffer. He does not want to see the Negro living in a run-down shack with rain coming through the roof. The basic problem is that none of us knows how to make the transition from one way of life and one status to another. People are afraid of change.

I have spent the biggest portion of my life trying to settle on some method—some simple, effective method—of bringing about the uplift of the Negro in general and Mississippi Negroes in particular. As I see it, we have to start making long-range plans and work together for predetermined goals. The first thing we have got to do in Mississippi, if the Negro is to improve his lot, is to get Negro doctors, lawyers, businessmen, and professional men into our community. Not just teachers. Today, there are only four Negro lawyers in the whole state, and they all have offices in Jackson. Through a cooperative effort, we could in five years have a doctor and a lawyer in every major town in the state. In ten years, we could have a lawyer in every county and a doctor in every town, small as well as large. Within fifteen years, by this community system, the Negro can obtain his rights—including the right to vote—and help decide his own destiny and the destiny of his people. In twenty years, the Negro in Mississippi, working diligently, cooperatively, quietly, can lift himself up to a complete position of respect and decency.

I think that the Negro has been widely misled about the realities of the political structure of the South. It is not hopeless. We all speak of our constitutional rights. But when a Negro speaks of constitutional rights, he speaks only of the Constitution of the United States. If we took a poll of Negroes, we would be surprised to discover how few know that states have constitutions. However, the things that affect the daily lives and welfare of the people most are the provisions written into the state constitutions and statutes. This is a fact of life. I have been accused of being a states' righter because I have consistently refused to condemn or otherwise talk too unfavorably about the white Southern leadership in Mississippi. As I see it, solving our problem will call for a full effort on the part of everyone affected by it. This includes the Negro, the segregationist, the government at both state and local levels, the churches, and all other institutions. We must have more communication and coordination within the community. And of course it is of utmost importance that the Negro, the one who is actually suffering, do far more in the future than he has done in the past. I feel that, whereas the Negro certainly needs organization and planning on the national level, the real solution to our problem must come on the other levels—regional, state, and local.

The best way to start is to find some common ground for communication, and being together in an institution of learning puts you on common ground. If I just wanted to learn that two and two is four and that Columbus discovered America, I could have stayed at Jackson State and got that. Books are just one of the purposes for which an individual goes to a university. Harvard might teach you better that two and two is four, but Harvard cannot teach you better how to use two and two is four in Mississippi. If a Negro goes to New York and gets a master's degree in school administration, he will have a far greater handicap in working with a white superintendent in Mississippi than will a Negro who attends the University of Mississippi and sits in the same class with the future superintendent, even if they never speak to each other. The mere fact that they are there together gives common ground for working out the mutual problem that confronts us everywhere in our community.

*Around the Campus*

Many little comical, and sometimes annoying, incidents occurred around the campus during the first two months. For example, I had dinner one day with a professor who had eaten with me several times. After dinner, one of the students in the dining hall said to him, "Say, Doctor, who are you going to be having dinner with when your nigger friend leaves?" The professor laughed. "Well," he said, "it looks as if I'm going to have to start eating with you."

I seldom paid any attention to the yells. The thing I did notice was the language the white students used, including the women students. I have always heard it said that Negroes use bad language, but the Negro cannot match the vileness of the words many white students yelled. And the part that was most difficult for me to understand was that they did not care who was listening; they did not show any respect for their women, or any instructor or parent. This to me indicated that our state had degenerated to an extremely low level.

The students had little things they did to try to annoy me. At one point, they started to get off the sidewalk whenever I came along. I felt that this was quite a change in Mississippi, where the Negroes have always had to get off the sidewalk to let the "white folks" by. I noticed they had all kinds of bumper stickers. For instance, the symbol of Ole Miss is a kind of Rebel colonel, and they invented a new colonel with his face painted black, and with big, thick red lips. Down at the bottom of the sticker, was printed "Kennedy's new colonel."

About a month after I moved into Baxter Hall, somebody put a sign up over the water fountain in the hallway—"White Only." It wasn't long before somebody else changed a couple of letters and had it read "White Phoneys."

In one classroom, if the light was not on, I would turn it on. Some students would get up and turn the light out. Of course, no one else could see any better than I could. Around the campus, if I happened to hold a door open for the student behind me, he might stop and not come in. Or, if one of them happened to be holding a door open, he might look up and see me and just turn the door loose. Tricks such as these did not distract me any more than they did the other students, and many students told me so. If you slammed a door or threw a bottle anywhere in our dormitory, it sounded all over the building. Whether they liked it or not, we were in it together.

The marshals were wonderful fellows. The living room of my apartment in Baxter Hall was used as the headquarters for the soldiers and marshals. There were always five or six soldiers and four or five marshals present. Not that this was what I would consider an ideal college surrounding; nevertheless, it was a surrounding. Many people wrote and said that they knew that I must be very lonely. As a matter of fact, one of the hardest things for me to do was to find a way to be alone.

Every time I moved, the marshals and soldiers were reporting over their radios in code. A marshal who walked with me had a radio in his pocket hooked up to his ear like a hearing aid. The simple radio code for the soldiers was "Peanut" and a number. They had code names for me: for the marshals, I was "package"; for the Army, I was "cargo." "Hear this! Hear this! Peanut Six, this is Peanut Two proceeding from building 80 [cafeteria] to building 46 [Baxter Hall] with cargo."

*Strategies and Maneuvers*

Undoubtedly December was a month of strategies and maneuvers. No matter what the qualifying circumstances were, I was physically present on the campus of the University of Mississippi and I had been there for two months. The primary goal of the opposition could no longer be to prevent me, or any Negro, from entering the school. The objective now was to get me out. The question was how.

It must be remembered that the opposition was dominated by the white Citizens Council, which had taken great pains to try to build an image of respectability, both inside and outside the state. Consequently, its leaders held the reins on the roughnecks and the direct-action violent boys. A serious split had now developed in the Citizens Council due mainly to the handling of the University of Mississippi case during the final days before my admission. A group more prone to the use of the time-tested methods of intimidations, harassments, and direct violence had broken away from the respectable element.

My greatest concern was for the protection of my family; in my own case there was little danger of physical harm. I was constantly assured by the government people around me that I was more heavily guarded than the President of the United States. The Mississippi press even checked the record and determined to its biased satisfaction that I was the best-guarded individual in history. Also, the press corps had a completely free run of the campus and kept their cameras, mikes, and pens ever ready and watching for any hostile move. I knew that the opposition would probably turn its attention to my family, since it was virtually impossible to get at me.

### The Need for a Rest: The Christmas Holiday

After two months in the University of Mississippi and nearly two and a half years in the state of Mississippi fighting the system of "White Supremacy," my family and I were in need of a rest. I had planned to go to Monterrey during the summer to study Spanish at one of the Mexican universities, but I had to cancel the program because of the court case. I now made plans to spend the Christmas holidays in Mexico. But when I revealed these plans to those having an interest in the case, there was solid opposition. They thought it would look as if I had lost faith in America if I visited another country. This appeared to me to be illogical reasoning.

Another crisis arose during the early part of December. It was widely rumored that I was unable to study because the students kept up too much noise in the dormitory. I was amazed at the ease with which everyone could so readily believe that a cherry-bomb explosion would only disturb me while the other students went normally about their business. Nevertheless, my friends, all over, believed that my academic days were limited and offered every form of assistance, especially those in the NAACP Legal Defense Fund. In spite of my efforts to assure Greenberg and Mrs. Motley that there was no problem, they still made arrangements for me to be tutored at one of the Ivy League schools. There was also the long-standing conspiracy between the Justice Department and the NAACP to keep me out of Mississippi when I was not on campus. This still remained one of the most vital aspects of the whole case.

*The Christmas Holidays Begin.* The first night of the Christmas recess I spent in Jackson. I had agreed, as a concession, to go to New England. It was another one of the few times that I made an arbitrary decision, failing to apply my decision-making formula. My wife, as always, did not express any opposition to my actions. But there were friends who begged and pleaded to the point of tears that I not only stay in Jackson for Christmas but also insisted that I had done enough and should not return to the university after the holidays. The question of leaving Mississippi under duress weighed heavily on my mind.

The next morning I went to New York where I was met by Mrs. Motley. She was visibly shaken by the sustained pressure of the ordeal. From the beginning, she and her family had been emotionally involved in all of the proceedings. Certainly without her personal interest the case would never have come this far. At the airport she indicated the personal burden she would have to bear if anything were to happen to me or my family.

*The New Haven Fiasco.* We rented a car from one of the rent-a-car agencies and drove from New York to New Haven. Mrs. Motley is from New Haven and her mother and family are still there. I had been to her home before for a brief visit but the circumstances were different now. This trip was a rather solemn one. I do remember discussing Mrs. Motley's future; I was concerned about her health. It seemed clear to me that she could not endure too many more of these southern cases, and I warned her not to try to keep up this pace. I am sure that she too was beginning to ponder this question. She expressed a keen distaste at the prospect of becoming a judge and sitting around for thirty years or more; she preferred a more active career. In any event, she had been constantly in the field in Mississippi, Alabama, Georgia, South Carolina, Louisiana, and other places since the late forties, and fifteen years of this type of duty is enough for any man, and certainly for a woman.

Since it was late when we arrived in New Haven, we made only a quick visit to her family and went on to the final destination—Yale University. Frankly, I disliked the whole idea so much and Yale seemed so out of place for me at the time that I honestly do not remember a single descriptive feature of the university. We went to the home of a Law Professor who was more or less to be my host at Yale. He had the key to the apartment in which I was to stay during the holidays. The apartment was clean, well furnished, and comfortable, but to me it was cold and empty. Nothing that I was fighting for was there—my people, my family, my friends, freedom of choice, warmth, love, closeness. I was all alone and unhappy. What is life without living?

The next morning I went out to get a haircut, but mainly I just wanted to find some Negroes. I had a choice of three small barber shops within the block where I stopped, and I chose the one that was newly painted and had the brightest lights. There were three chairs and two persons ahead of me, so I got a shoeshine while I waited and listened to the conversations. Ironically, my picture was on the front page of the newspaper that morning; I don't remember now what the story was. Somebody picked up the paper and started talking about the "Ole Miss" situation. Then they started a conversation about me—what kind of a fellow I was. I had discovered that I could go anywhere in the country without being recognized because of my size and complexion. Most people thought that I was large and very dark. I am neither.

When my turn came, I drew the only lady barber in the shop. She asked me how I wanted my hair cut. After looking me over, she inquired, "Your face looks familiar, where are you from?" I said, "Mississippi." She jokingly asked me if I knew James Meredith. I answered, yes. She laughed and went on to finish the haircut. When I paid her, she said, "You know, I still think I have seen you somewhere before." I left. It was part of the program that I should not let my identity become known while I was in New Haven. This was a paradoxical situation. The very people for whom I was fighting and who would have opened their hearts to me, I was expected to stay away from.

My host was a transitional Jew. The family was Jewish, but they didn't practice all of the traditional rites and ceremonies. My presence may have made them more self-conscious, for they decided that they should really celebrate the Jewish holiday properly. Actually, as they explained it, there was no need to be profoundly Jewish in an all-Jewish neighborhood, such as they came from in New York City. The wife asserted that she had never known any persons well other than Jews prior to her college days. Only after they came to Yale where Jews were few did they bcome acutely aware of their heritage. Two families got together for the celebration and threw me in for novelty. It was an interesting experience but I felt terribly out of place.

The next day was tutoring day, and the schedule had been carefully arranged. Frankly, I considered this idea of my being tutored in order to compete with a bunch of Mississippi students the height of insult. Furthermore, if I could barely stomach a southern cracker as my teacher, certainly I couldn't take a superior-minded New Englander. Nevertheless, they came. The first was a French expert. She was foreign-born with a very mixed nationality. Her first language was French, but she had lived most of her life in the United States. We were supposed to have a two-hour session, but after thirty minutes she decided that maybe we shouldn't try too much the first day. We had a brief talk about the matter and mutually agreed that this type of learning process was not for me. She left.

The American Colonial History man was next. I had already completed all academic requirements for a Bachelor of Arts degree with honors in history and my major concentration was American history; now because I had decided to go to the University of Mississippi, I was being insulted with an elementary course in American history. I asked him to leave his notes and I would look over them. He appeared offended and left.

A session in mathematics was scheduled for the afternoon. The instructor didn't show up at the appointed time. Several hours later the wife of my host came over to the apartment. The tutors had been by to see her. We talked about many things. I was very impressed by her straightforwardness and lack of pretentiousness, characteristics not always found in many of the white Americans who call themselves liberals. She returned to a point which she had raised two or three times before and I had persistently overlooked it. She couldn't understand how the Negro could put up with what he has to in the United States and not explode. By "explode" she meant resorting to direct action, and not of the nonviolent kind. She kept pushing me for an answer but I evaded it. The question strikes deep at the heart of the Negro question; I had my answer but only time could reveal it.

The unfamiliar surroundings were closing in on me and squeezing me to death. Even the weather demanded a decision. It had started to snow heavily and a big storm was forecast. As soon as she left the apartment, I began making long distance calls. First I called Jackson, but my wife had left for Chicago. I called Kosciusko and talked to my mother and father. There had been some harassment but, as always, my father accepted all responsibility for their welfare. I called Chicago but my wife had not yet arrived; I left word for her to wait in Chicago until she heard from me again. I called the train station, because I didn't want to drive in this weather. No trains were available. When I called the airlines in New York, I was lucky to get a seat on the morning flight to Chicago, if I could get to New York. I then called Dick Gregory in Chicago and talked to his wife; I asked her to have Dick meet me at the airport there. Finally, I called my host and told him that I was leaving.

My host did not try to dissuade me, even though the streets of New Haven were covered with ice. He got in his car and led me to the turnpike. It was snow-covered and icy but, fortunately, traffic continued to flow. I didn't waste any time, and when I turned off at 125th Street, it was midnight. I thought about Mrs. Motley, and I had to choose whether to go straight to her house or to stop in Harlem. Harlem was closer.

By 12:15 I was at the hat-check rack in Small's Paradise. The hat-check boy looked up and said, "James Meredith!" He had never seen me before. We shook hands and I whispered to him that I was supposed to be incognito. He took me over to the head waiter and whispered something to him. The head waiter ushered me in, gave me a choice seat by the dance floor, and wouldn't take any money. Everybody was jolly and the place was swinging.

The band took an intermission around two o'clock, and someone invited me to go along with them to a society club's annual dance. It was lavishly staged; I had never seen anything like it before. There were two or three bands and everything was free. This was the first time in months that I had been able to relax in peace. It was great to be among my people after the University of Mississippi and Yale.

*Rendezvous in Chicago.* I arrived at O'Hare Airport in Chicago the next morning. Gregory was late, but by the time I got my bags, he had come. Dick was silent, a rare accomplishment for him, and I assumed that he was tired. He took me to the house of my wife's aunt, where my wife was waiting. Everybody was solemn and quiet. Someone had shot out the windows of the house the day before and they showed me the evidence. I tried to shrug it off and be cheerful. They all looked sick. Dick suggested that we go somewhere and he and I left. As we headed south on Lake Shore Drive, I decided to turn on the radio. The news announcer was just finishing the story about the shotgunning of Meredith's family. I started to ask Gregory what the man was talking about. Almost at the point of tears, he explained why he hadn't told me about the incident; he had had to let me find out the hard way, because he didn't have the heart to tell me. Everyone had been afraid to break the news to me.

As soon as we got to a phone, I called Kosciusko, and my sister answered. When I asked her what was going on, she said, "Some so-and-so tried to kill me, but I jumped behind the refrigerator." She reported that Cap had pretended that it didn't bother him, but she thought he was a little upset. I talked to him and he said that everything was all right. "We ain't worried," he added. The local police had offered to stand guard near the house, but he had turned them down, because that would just give the shooters a better chance. We all knew that the law was involved in the shooting, anyway.

There was no question now but that I must return to Mississippi immediately. I knew those "peckerwoods," and the only way that I could draw their attention from my folks was to focus their evil designs on me. I got on the phone again. I talked to the NAACP Legal Defense Fund lawyers. They wanted only to dissuade me from returning to Mississippi. I talked to the Justice Department and they were not ready to do anything. The spokesman said that they could not assist my family in any way, nor could they offer me any protection during the vacation period. This was all right with me. It simply meant that I would have to provide my own protection for myself and my family. I made reservations on the next flight to Jackson.

My primary concern now was how to keep the "White Supremacists" from striking at my family again before I got back to Mississippi. The only channel open to me was to let them know that I was coming back. Immediately I decided to call my first unrequested press conference. When I asked Dick where to hold it, he arranged for it in his downtown Chicago office.

### The Return to Mississippi

My return to Mississippi on Christmas Eve in 1962 is a turning point in my struggle against the evils of "White Supremacy." At the most crucial times in the fight I had always had to attack the system in Mississippi by raiding it from Tennessee or Louisiana and retreating after each confrontation. It was now a battle that would definitely be staged from within. This was as I had wanted it all along. What was the logic, what did it prove, for a Negro to go to a previously all-white school in Mississippi and not be able to live in the state?

*The Negro Marshals.* The federal government had had second thoughts about the prospects of a Negro protecting himself in Mississippi. At the last minute they issued an emergency call to two of America's top Negro U.S. marshals—one was Luke Moore, the Chief Marshal of the District of Columbia—and they were given thirty minutes to clear up pressing business and get packed. They had to drive at a speed of over a hundred miles an hour to catch the jet, already being held for them. They were still too late. I had taken up residence among my people long before the Negro marshals arrived in Mississippi.

Where would we stay? The door was always open at Robert Smith's house. The Smiths are a truly great and unreservedly good family, always doing more than everybody else and forever shunning any credit for their efforts. The one serious question concerned security. The main guest room was in the front; it had a huge picture window and a double bed. The other guest room had twin beds, and since the marshals thought that it would be too unsafe for me to sleep in the main guest room, they suggested that I share the other room with one of the marshals. Of course, this left us with an unsolvable problem—my wife. My wife and I slept in the main guest room.

The unprecedented aspect of the Negro U.S. marshals being in Mississippi was that they had guns and the authority to use them. Negro soldiers had been withdrawn from the University of Mississippi the day after the riot because Southern Congressmen had objected to Negroes bearing arms against whites in the South. This is a cardinal sin. Wherever there are Negro policemen in the South, it is the law, written or unwritten, that the Negro officer's authority does not extend to whites. But here were Negroes with unrestricted authority and guns to back it up.

I could never describe in words the Negroes' pride in the marshals. Certainly the Mississippi Negroes held me in high esteem in December 1962 and they showed it in every possible way, but the Negro U.S. marshals were the greater attraction. Negroes would drive a hundred miles and admit that they had just wanted to get a look at a "colored" marshal. You would see people bumping into or brushing against the marshals just to feel their guns. The girls loved to get a chance to dance with the marshals, so they could see or feel "that gun."

The Negro marshals who came to Mississippi were superior examples. They were a credit not only to the Negro race, but also to the United States. Their conduct was, at all times and in every way, above reproach. They looked the part of lawmen—six feet tall and weighing 180 pounds. On the other hand, they were true Negroes, conscious of their role, and they made a grand display. I remember that one of them loved to rear back in his chair and unbutton his coat, intentionally letting it fall open just enough for the spectators to see his gun—if they strained a little bit.

*To Be with My People.* During the twenty months that had elapsed between the time that I applied for admission to the university and the time that I was forced in, I had spent many hours among my people; often it had meant getting up late at night and visiting their places of recreation or going out early in the morning to watch the women on their way to slave in some white woman's kitchen. My frequent contact with the hardships of my people had given me the will to continue. During this Christmas season my greatest desire, perhaps indeed my absolute need, was to be with my people.

There is one thing that Mississippians—Negro and white—have in common with the rest of the world: they celebrate the Christmas holidays. Of course, they do it separately. The biggest event of the year in Jackson was the annual dance of the leading Negro social club, The Sophisticated Laverettes. I was being honored with their annual award. Most of the town's Negro elite were out and much too sophisticated for anything except a Negro social affair. Stealing the show with her dress and charm was the young pretty wife of the retired principal of the oldest Negro high school in Jackson, and in her own right the biggest Negro businesswoman in Mississippi. All of my old Jackson State College group were there along with all of my favorite dancing partners. The dancing trophy went to Sam Bailey, the insurance man. Sam is at least fifty years old and can out-dance his seventeen-year-old daughter. He can do every dance in the book; whenever there was an impromptu dance performance you could expect to find Sam Bailey in the center with some young girl. The older girls just couldn't take it.

The marshals were swamped and apparently enjoyed it. We had gotten to know each other very well by now, and they had gotten to know my people and were not too apprehensive, nevertheless, one of them was always by my side. About an hour after midnight one of the marshals was dancing and the other was sitting beside me at a table. Someone got his attention and he leaned over to listen to what the person was trying to say. This gave me the opportunity to move off in the other direction and head for the door; I got out of the building without anyone seeing me. The marshals thought I was dancing.

Once outside, I was stuck. Even though I had had no plan when I got up, I had to keep going now that I was free in Mississippi for the first time in months. I felt in my coat pocket, luckily I hadn't left my car keys in my overcoat pocket. I got in my car and headed for Stevens Rose Room some ten miles away. When I got there, Joe Dyson and his band were playing some good dance music. This was a different kind of crowd. Stevens was the place where everybody went—all classes and types. But it was dominated by the Younger Modern Set. The college crowd was at ease here, even with all of the lights on.

This was the first time that I had been in Stevens since I had gone to the University of Mississippi. When I walked in, the place almost turned out. And I will never forget the reaction of Big Daddy. The first time I had gone to Stevens some twelve years before, Big Daddy, who was a bouncer then, threw me out because I wasn't old enough. Now that he was older, he had taken an easier job as a waiter, and there was no longer any need at Stevens Rose Room for strong-arm men. Every time that I had gone to Stevens I had seen Big Daddy and often talked to him. When he saw me, he rushed up, grabbed my hand, and squeezed it hard with his big, still powerful, hand. He said, "You son of a gun, I didn't know that was you tryin' to get in them white folks' school." He grabbed me around both shoulders, hugged me hard, and exclaimed, "You showed 'em, boy, damn right, you showed 'em." He may not have been able to control his emotions and he may not have been able to express himself in the best English, but what he said meant a lot to me. This was what I was fighting for: The pride of my people.

Meanwhile, the marshals had discovered that I had disappeared, and no one could give them an account of my movements. They took off for the Continental Room, which was in the opposite direction and eight or nine miles from the place to which I had gone. By the time they had reversed their course and arrived at Stevens, I had already left for my favorite spot. Mr. P's was "rocking and juking." The place was packed and Elmo was "working out" (playing real good). The boys had come in from the sawmills still in their dirty overalls, and some of the maids still wore their soiled white uniforms. The white folks had kept them late but they were not going to miss their fun. Then there was Miss Fox, home from Chicago, looking good, smelling sweet, and talking loud. I slid back in a corner and watched. This crowd liked their music loud, long, sexy, and fast. In the middle of the winter, their clothes would be "wringing wet" with sweat. After being mistreated all day, all week, all month, all year, and all of their lives by the white man and the system, without this or some other outlet, they would "just lay down and die." The average income among this group was certainly less than fifteen dollars a week. It was these people that I felt obligated to raise from this blind pit of helplessness. It was for them that I would give my life. The marshals by now had spotted my car parked outside.

*Negro Marshals in My Home Town.* For the first few days after I returned to Mississippi, I deliberately stayed out of Kosciusko. My folks had come down to Jackson on Christmas Day, however, and we had spent the day together at Robert Smith's house. After it had been clearly established that I was back in Mississippi in person to face the opposition, I went to Kosciusko to see my people. It was a quiet visit. We went to my father's house and had a big country dinner. The marshals loved to talk to my father, who was a great talker. After dinner we went down to Beale Street where I could see my friends; they all wanted to meet and shake hands with the "colored" marshals. We didn't stay long, just long enough for everybody in town to know we were there. The law kept us under close surveillance, but they said nothing. I am sure that the federal government had sent some of the white marshals ahead of us to seek the cooperation of the local police.

We went back to the house to say good-bye and to take a last look at the buckshot holes in my father's house. They had really meant business with those shotgun blasts. The holes were from an inch to an inch and a half in diameter. Any one of those slugs could have killed a human being. To protect my family and property I would not hesitate to kill the culprit who would commit such an act of violence. Men who would do such a thing as those who tried to kill my family do not deserve the right to live in a civilized society.

*James Baldwin in Jackson.* Baldwin had called from New York and said that he wanted to come to Mississippi to see me. I met him at the Jackson airport. I imagine this was his first visit to Mississippi. Naturally, he would stay with the Smiths. All the beds were taken up, but the sofa made quite a comfortable bed. It was New Year's Day, 1963.

We had been invited to a New Year's Day (hog jowl and black-eyed peas) party at Mary Bell's house. James Baldwin and the marshals were my guests. We ate until we couldn't eat any more, because Negroes don't run out of food in Mississippi, especially black-eyed peas and cornbread on New Year's Day. After eating and relaxing, they started playing some good music and we started to dance. The best that I can say about Baldwin's dancing is that he is game. He was a strange sight doing the New York twist at a Mississippi house party.

That night we went to a big James Brown Dance at the College Park Auditorium—a very misleading name, because it is a city auditorium, the only one of its kind built for "Negroes Only." It is a huge place, the largest in the city, and it was full of Mississippi Negroes. We found seats up high so that we could get a good view of everything.

James Baldwin is a searcher. One can almost forget that he is around. He just watches and observes and asks probing questions from time to time. He never professes to know the answers to the questions of the world. He has a sharp mind and a keen sense of feeling.

*A Math Tutor at Jackson State College.* Shortly after I returned to Mississippi, a professor of mathematics at Jackson State College came over and offered his help. Everybody wanted to do his part in the fight against the system of "White Supremacy" in Mississippi. The faculty at my old alma mater had always supported my wife and me in every reasonable way. But the professor was pushing Mississippi pretty hard with his offer, and I could not refuse him.

I went over to his office three or four times, while the marshals sat outside in the car and drew quite a bit of attention on campus. He was a topnotch teacher and even if I had been in trouble with my math, I couldn't have failed after three review lessons with him.

Ironically, now I couldn't pass this course with my purpose in mind, because I felt that it would have been a grave injustice to the Negro students who would follow me if I accepted any kind of outside help. We had a long talk about this, and I don't believe that he ever really understood. I am sure that he never agreed with me. But I had to keep faith with my purpose. I could not prostitute my Divine Responsibility.

# 10

*

## The Decision: January 1963

JANUARY 1963 was my month of decision, at least as far as my public life is concerned. The decisions that I had to make were concerned primarily with the question of my Divine Responsibility and how best and most effectively to carry it out. My mission was clear. I had to devote my life to the cause of directing civilization toward a destiny of humaneness. My immediate objective was to break the system of "White Supremacy," which appeared to me to be detrimental to my purpose. My goal was total victory. Temporary or partial victory and relative advancement had no place in my thinking. I was prepared to retreat from every battle if by so doing it would improve my chances of winning the war. Most great wars have been lost because the generals, blinded by the glories of temporary victories, were advancing when they should have been retreating. I could not jeopardize the prospects of establishing a new order in Mississippi by compromising with evil in order to allow America to say to the world that we have a Negro in the University of Mississippi.

### The Issues

*The Ordeal of the First Semester.* People were always saying to me, "You are in the University of Mississippi, and that's the important thing." But so many unusual and unique circumstances were a part of my stay there that I seriously doubted that I was in a true sense a student of the university. I was inclined to go along with the die-hard segregationists on this point. Just having a Negro in residence did not mean that the university had been integrated. Most of the time, I was perhaps the most segregated Negro in the world.

No student should have to be subjected to the sort of ordeal I had to undergo during the first semester. Though no price is too high to pay for liberation, I am convinced that you can pay a price for one piece of freedom that is greater than the benefits you get. We all have to decide how best to utilize our time, our energy.

I had reason to believe that the longer I continued at the university under such abnormal conditions, the more I would benefit the advocates of "White Supremacy." The conditions tended to make me a superhuman or nonhuman individual. I was afraid that, if I had to continue that way, it would become a standard for the Negro. If he couldn't endure the hardships that I did and make it, then he might not seem deserving. Negroes who would otherwise have been ready to seek training in the best educational institutions would be discouraged from the effort. Many tended to place unrealistic hopes in the prospect of my successful attendance, thereby escaping their own responsibility to do all that they individually could do, wherever they were, to bring freedom to us all. At the same time, the moderate whites in Mississippi let the emotional minority browbeat them into neglecting their responsibility, which was to work seriously to correct the situation.

Certainly, I must acknowledge, I had not expected the tensions to continue so long. As one who had grown up in Mississippi, I knew, of course, that the university represented the image of segregation and discrimination. But I had really thought that Mississippi, almost surrounded by token integration in Tennessee, Arkansas, and Louisiana, would act with reason, particularly after the example of the University of Georgia. Here was just a step, really a small step, toward getting into a position to solve our problem. When I entered the university, the political leadership of our state was, in my opinion, most responsible for what had gone on in Mississippi. They had the strongest hand. Where they have led, the people have nearly always followed. That these leaders chose to make a showdown fight over integration at the college level seemed to me to be completely illogical.

*Freedom of Association.* With the state government taking the position that it did, the students had no choice but to act as they did. I talked with many, and they almost convinced me that most of them really believed that their position was right. To maintain their pride and back up their families who were the leaders of the state, they had to support the stand taken by the state of Mississippi.

Through it all, the most intolerable thing was the campaign of ostracizing me. It did not harm me directly. If anyone does not want to associate with me, I am sure that the feeling is at least mutual. I don't think anyone should be forced to enter into association with anyone else unless they choose to do so. However, the ostracizers also assumed the right to see that no one else associated with me. If a white student sat down and drank a cup of coffee with me or walked with me across the campus, he was subjected to unhampered intimidation and harassment. I had been denied my privileges all along, but these whites had not been. Now they had lost a simple freedom. This was a setback for the Negro, because any time there is a move backward, the person already down suffers more. This campaign, which apparently had been permitted by the university officials, really resulted in a reduction of everybody's rights.

On the surface, of course, the most unusual thing on campus was the presence of the soldiers and the marshals. They drew a good deal of attention. Most people seemed to overlook the breakdown of law and order that had brought them to the campus. Their continued presence was to me the complete manifestation that the normal enforcement of law and order was still broken down.

*The Negro Problem v. My Grades.* There was extensive speculation about my grades. This was a fictitious issue from the beginning; the real question, as I saw it, was the Negro problem. The opposition wanted to divert the attention of the world from this fundamental question and to focus it on the frivolous issue of the ending of the present semester. At no time was there a possibility that I would not be eligible to return for the second semester and every responsible person knew this. The administration had sent a letter to all of my instructors telling them not to discuss my academic standing with anyone. Furthermore, it was virtually impossible for anyone to fail to qualify for readmission after the first term under the regulations at the University of Mississippi. I could have failed five of six courses and still have been eligible for readmission.

What then was the objective of this stress upon the idea of my failing? First, we must always remember, and many of us too often forget, that the Negro in America is fighting a bitter and clever enemy. So much praise is usually given to the Negro and his friends that we overlook his foes. The opposition was completely coordinated and oriented. They always looked at both sides of the coin—the winning side and the losing side, and focused their attention on coming out the best they could, no matter which way the coin fell. The opposition had much to gain by drawing attention to me as an individual. My name was well known and if they could break me as an individual it would be so much the better, but, failing in this, they could make my experience an impossible standard and thus discourage other Negroes.

Focusing on grades was a naturally emotional gimmick in the United States, where ninety-eight per cent of the population has had the experience of sweating out grades themselves. School in America and grades at the end of the terms are almost synonymous. The real key was the semester. Time and civilization move on forever, endlessly, but semesters always end. An answer to this secondary question of "pass or fail" would serve to satisfy the demand for an answer to the basic question of Negro citizenship rights. I could not stand by consciously and let the Negro be tricked by this scheme.

*The Right To Fail.* The first step in countering this move by the opposition was to attack the age-old idea that the Negro was duty bound to succeed whenever he was given an opportunity and that he was not entitled to equality of opportunity, which included the possibility of failing, in the first place. It appeared to me that "the right to fail in a publicly supported institution was just as important as the right to pass." This statement was quoted and debated widely in the United States. The general feeling seemed to be that the Negro did not have this basic right, although the whites were granted it. I can never accept a double standard. There is no right or privilege that I would concede solely to the white American, not even for a minute.

*The Right of Access.* I felt a great responsibility not to let my cause be sold out on such a trivial matter. It was an established fact that I was more than able to compete under any ordinary circumstances. Therefore, whatever grades I made would prove nothing about my ability, or the Negro's ability. This question was answered long ago, I wouldn't waste my time proving it. The real question was whether Negroes including Negroes in Mississippi, were to obtain the best education that their states offered. This was the basic issue—the right of access.

My great purpose is to make way for the average Negro. Negro progress up to now has been on the basis of selection. Great efforts have always been made to obtain for the superior Negro the right to do certain things. This is a position I have always been cautious about. It's very dangerous. But if we make way for the average, the above-average will always find his place. If getting a degree from the University of Mississippi were all I ever did with my life, I would have done very little.

Throughout the first semester, I received about two hundred letters a day. Most of the people who wrote, particularly the Negroes, said that they had great admiration for me. They were praying and hoping that I would make it. Their basic attitude alarmed me. The letter that disturbed me most came from students at Alabama State College, a Negro school. The major message conveyed in this letter was that they had committed themselves to God and to me, to prove to the world that Negroes are somebody. The letter was alarming, because they had relieved themselves of all responsibility. They thought there was nothing more that they had to do. I feel that every young Negro must make a personal contribution toward the accomplishment of his freedom. You can't confine the struggle for human freedom and dignity to one place or to one man. To free the right arm and cut off the left arm is not progress.

*The Safety of My Family.* I had told my friends that they could pat me on the back and tell me how great I was, they could put all the adjectives they wanted on my name—all this still made me no less human. Another problem, and a basically human one, I had to resolve was whether my staying at the university was worth the intimidation and harassment that my family had to endure. My father was seventy-one years old, had worked hard, lived a good life, paid all his debts, never was in trouble, was a good citizen— but he could not sleep in peace because of the danger of someone attacking him violently. He had not gone to the University of Mississippi, or done any of the other things that the opposition might have been fighting. Yet they fired into his house with shotguns. Our system of law allowed such a thing to happen with impunity, and it is tragic.

The most realistic understanding of what my family and I were going through came in letters from people in foreign countries. But the letters from people in this country, especially from Negroes, often did not even acknowledge that I had any right to be concerned about the welfare of my family. For a long time not one in a hundred seemed to understand at all. This pointed out to me the unrealistic hopes that the Negroes hold about the future. In their failure to conceive of all the costs, both physical and mental, they showed that they were failing to realize the real price that they would themselves some day have to pay if they were to do their part. They were still looking for a miracle to save them.

*An Alarming Incident.* Then, on a Sunday just after New Year's, I had an experience that convinced me that, unless something was done, the advantages we might win might be less than those we would lose. An old gentleman who had been the first Negro to visit me at the university called to ask if I would go with him to a funeral in Oxford. A lot of people there wanted to meet me. After the funeral, all the people—from the relatives of the deceased down to the Boy Scout who had been directing traffic—came and shook hands with me. Several insisted that I stop by the house. Afterwards, I decided to visit one of my ex-classmates from Jackson State College, now a high school teacher in Oxford. The old gentleman and I went up to the teacher's door. His wife answered, but she would not let us in. So we went back to the house of the sister of the lady who had been buried that day. You know how Negroes are at a funeral. They had every kind of food laid out; the only thing expected is that you get a plate. So I did. And just then my former classmate came in.

He said he wanted to see me for a minute privately, and I asked him to wait just until I finished eating. He seemed somewhat apprehensive, but when I asked if he was in a hurry, he said, "No, no, not particularly." We went back to an empty room. For the first time in my life, someone invited me not to visit him. He asked that I not come to see him again. What was so shocking to me was the reason that he didn't want me to visit him: He said he'd been informed by his principal in the local Negro high school that any teacher who had anything to do with me would lose his job. He begged me for understanding and mercy. He even gave me another reason for not wanting to associate with me. He was afraid that his father-in-law would lose his job. His father-in-law was a street cleaner in Oxford, probably not making more than twenty-five dollars a week. Here was a man who not only would give up his rights and privileges and liberty, but would give up his soul. And for what?

The real tragedy was that this individual was a social science teacher in a high school. The thought kept running through my mind, what could he teach? I don't think children in any nation should be instructed by people who have to sell their own souls. They have really given up more than they have to offer. There is a certain minimum of self-respect and self-direction that one must maintain in order to be a man. Once he loses that, he is lost for all useful purposes.

*The Best Use of My Time and Energy.* The only thing in the world that I fear is death. Because of this fear, I am forever conscious of the prospects of wasting my time. The question of the best use of my time and energy presses me the hardest. What route do I take that leads closest to my desired goal? Many things caused me to wonder if continuing at the University of Mississippi under the prevailing circumstances was making the best use of my time. Certainly attending the university was no goal in itself to me. The objective was to replace the system of "White Supremacy," and there were many alternative ways in which to seek to achieve this goal.

### The Statement of January 7, 1963

Meanwhile, the campus situation was getting nastier and nastier. The campus branch of the Citizens Council and Ku Klux Klan had used the Christmas period to formulate and coordinate their efforts to restore the university to its former order. The time had come to act.

Every aspect of my decision-making apparatus had been satisfied. I arose early in the morning and wrote a short statement for the press. I called my wife to inform her that I was about to make a statement so that she would know what it was all about when she heard it over the radio. She was still with the Smiths, because her school had not resumed classes. Robert's curiosity was too much for him, and he couldn't stay off the extension. This was understandable because the Mississippi news media had kept me in the forefront to further their conspiracy to distort the issues in the minds of the public. I told Robert what I planned to do and why. We said good-bye and hung up. Five minutes later my phone rang. It was Robert. He was afraid that the public would not understand the position I was taking. I read my statement to him; he understood and agreed.

It was now six o'clock in the morning. I sat down at my portable typewriter and made copies of the statement. I shaved and went through my morning routine. At seven I called one of my classmates, who had been enrolled as a student in one of my classes by a leading newspaper syndicate to keep tabs on me, and told him that I would be releasing a statement at eight o'clock at my dormitory.

At the time I really didn't know that he was a full-time employee of this syndicate, but I knew he was an informer to somebody. In the first place, he was the only person in my class that ever talked to me. One day just before Christmas recess he had stopped me and said that he was writing a general survey story of the campus and thought that he should get my views on a few things. Later I saw some information in one of the South's leading newspapers that came from "Close Sources," and I knew who the close source had to be. He had given me his name and telephone number and had stressed the point that he could be reached at all times even when he was out. A strange set-up for a student. I had two telephones in my room but I couldn't be reached when I was out, except through the marshals or through the Army.

At ten minutes before eight my phone rang. It was Robert Smith. He had gone to work and opened his store, but he was still troubled by the events that were soon to take place. We went through the statement again, and here Robert L.T. Smith, Jr., proved his genius. He said that my statement was too cut and dried: "You have to give them something to work at." He suggested the insertion of one word, "unless." I had said that I had decided not to enroll for the second term—period. I added another clause, "conditions are made more conducive to learning," and the statement was ready.

It was almost eight, but I had to retype the statement before I could give it to the waiting newsmen, some of whom had arrived as early as 7:15. By 8:10 when I had finished typing, a crowd of newsmen were waiting for me. The marshals were getting apprehensive. I handed out the copies that I had typed, and there were not enough to go around. One wire service reporter had had a student in my dormitory get a long distance line for him and had kept it open for over an hour. There were many questions from the group but I answered none.

For some time I have considered my course of action for the future. There are many factors, many issues, many aspects, and equally as many consequences.

I have decided not to register for classes during the second semester at the University of Mississippi unless very definite and positive changes are made to make my situation more conducive to learning. This decision is based on a consideration of all the elements pertinent to the "Mississippi Crisis" at its deepest meaning and of all the aspects of my personal relationship in it, with it, and to it.

It should be noted that I have not made a decision to discontinue my efforts to receive educational training at the University of Mississippi. Rather, my decision is not to attend the University next semester under the present circumstances.

We are engaged in a war, a bitter war for the "equality of opportunity" for our citizens. The enemy is determined, resourceful, and unprincipled. There are no rules of war for which he has respect. Some standard must be set. Some pattern must be established so that those who are fighting for equality of opportunity and those who are fighting for the right to oppress can clash in the struggle without disaster falling upon either group. Presently, there is too much doubt and uncertainty regarding the procedure to be followed in settling our problems. No major issues have been decided legally or officially, illegally or unofficially.

When I combine the political and educational reality with my personal possibilities and probabilities, the results lead me to the foregoing decision.

As to what I will do, I am not prepared to say at this time, since I am still studying two or three alternatives. However, I plan to remain in Mississippi.

I think that I should also add that I will have nothing further to say about this matter until after the end of this semester, at which time I will be free to answer any questions and acknowledge any request.

*The Immediate Reaction.* The reaction was immediate and widespread. The first was, of course, on the campus. The campus opposition smelled the sweet glory of victory and intended to make sure that the "unless" never occurred. Crowds followed me everywhere. All the normal reactions expected of educated white Mississippians were resorted to—rock throwing, cursing, chanting, stomping, and beating on tables with knives, forks, spoons, trays, and fists.

Some conditions did begin to change favorably. Before, I had never noticed the campus police around where I was. But when I left my first class after making my statement, the campus police were there. Of course, it is very important that the welfare and protection of the student be in the hands of the local police. We have no national police force, and the federal government is limited in its actual power over the daily lives of the people. It can act only in the event of an extreme crisis, such as the riot at the University of Mississippi, and even then its action is of a very doubtful and uncertain nature. That is the structure of our governmental system. It was still clear to me, however, that the university administration and the federal government were seeking only to lessen the tension, not to change or correct the conditions in any basic way. And just like putting salve on a wound when the blood has been poisoned, they were treating the symptom, rather than the cause.

The Negro reaction was of prime importance to me, since it would provide the answer for me. I shall never forget the very first indication of the Negro's feeling which came while I was in a morning class. When I returned to my room, I found a telegram. I opened it with great apprehension; the contents I felt would have a tremendous effect on me. It was a one-sentence message that said in effect: you fought your fight and we are with you whatever you decide to do—Signed, Sammy Davis, Jr. I remembered that I had met Sammy on Thanksgiving night a few weeks before. Dick Gregory had taken my wife and me to see him perform at a big new club, the Villa Venice, in a town north of Chicago, and after the performance we had gone to his dressing room. Very emotionally, Davis told us of the agony that he had felt during his performance because he had wanted to honor my presence but that he had been requested not to do so for security reasons. I had thought then that he was just putting on another show. Out of the many, many thousands of letters, telegrams, and calls, it seemed ironic that the very first came from a performer who, it would be assumed, would be asleep in the early morning.

The reports that I might not stay produced a most heartening change in the mail that came to me. The president of the student body in a Negro school in Texas wrote a letter signed by a large number of students. They hoped that I would find my way clear to remain at the University of Mississippi, but this was now only a minor consideration. The main point was that they realized their own obligation to move forward and were prepared to work hard for their aims, regardless of what happened in Mississippi. This was what I had long looked for, and the same general trend soon began to appear in a strong majority of the letters from Negroes, especially from those under thirty-five. I had many Negroes tell me that they had become so involved in my decision that they could not sleep at night. One of my good friends put it this way: Every Negro in America was in college.

The changed attitude gave me the most satisfaction. So often in the past, when a Negro encountered something he disliked, he could suppress it in his mind. It was worse than forgetting; what he disliked just was not a reality to him. But now the Negro was unable to suppress his awareness of his situation. An old man, a gentleman eighty-five or ninety years old, once told me that anything you keep thinking about you are bound to do something about. Humanly and physically, the individual is not able to think about this matter, to keep on thinking about it, and not do anything about it.

Certainly Negroes were not yet one hundred per cent together. I would say that only about three fifths of those who communicated with me after my statement were thinking in what I considered to be sensible terms. Maybe the other two fifths were still looking for God, the government, or the world to give them whatever they thought they wanted. But a definite majority indicated that they not only recognized their situation, but felt a real need to do something about it. No longer would they merely look across the street to see how another Negro was doing in order to judge how well they were doing. They now looked at America in all of its aspects to see what America has to offer. And they are convinced that America has more to offer than what they are receiving. They know that it is up to them—not God or some "selected" individual—to do their part to bring about the changes necessary. Every Negro is active, at least in his mind, and very conscious of his desires. If we are going to have equal opportunity, we have got to have it for everyone.

The majority of white Americans reacted vigorously to this statement. As usual, most of the mail came from white Americans and it was 99.9 per cent favorable. Most of them, however, were not ready to grant equality to the Negro. Yet there were many who felt that Mississippi was pushing its case too far.

The federal government now issued a long overdue attack against the administration of the University of Mississippi, and the Attorney General dispatched Katzenbach to the university.

*Other Reactions: Pro and Con.* On January 18, 1963, Hugh Clegg, assistant to the chancellor and director of development at the University of Mississippi, announced that the university was reprinting Paul Flowers' "Greenhouse" columns which had appeared in the *Commercial Appeal,* January 14 and 15. The first column read as follows:

> If I were a Negro, even the most militant, rankling in my heart over slavery and its tragic aftermath, eager to enjoy every civil right in the Constitution, and determined that my grandchildren should have opportunity unrestricted, I believe I would be bitter against James Meredith.
>
> If I aspired, as a Negro, to pass from "second class citizenship" into participation on a par with every other freeborn American, I would

consider James H. Meredith a traitor to his group. I would tag him as one who, by arrogance, monumental indiscretion, and a genius for alienating men of good will; that he has made the path that much rockier for Negroes who in years to come will ask only to demonstrate that they have ability and determination to disprove the theory of superior-inferior races.

Months ago, in those dismal hours when James Meredith was admitted to the University of Mississippi at bayonet point, while irresponsible politicians on state and national levels were devoting all their energies to rouse the rabble, there were silent multitudes who believed that James Meredith was a sincere seeker after education.

His unenviable position, caught between Federal stupidity and state demagoguery, inspired considerable sympathy among men of good will, and they wished him success in his admittedly difficult, and unpleasant, undertaking.

As a self-appointed "martyr to a cause," a cause defensible under the Constitution and endorsed by the Supreme Court of the United States, James Meredith knew that he was embarking on a stormy sea, and it comes with bad grace for him to complain against tempests he surely must have known would rage about him.

If James Meredith, even under harrowing circumstances of admittance and enrollment at the points of bayonets and amid the stench of tear gas, had been willing to do his best at his self-appointed task . . . if he had been willing to hold his peace when ill-considered words could only aggravate the turmoil . . . he might have proved what he professed to want to prove.

But, it was not to be so. First, talking out of turn, he denounced the Army of the United States for its methods of selecting troops sent to Oxford to protect him . . . troops deployed to implement his enjoyment of a constitutional right.

He had the fundamental right as an American citizen to speak out. But as a student of the university which, by implication, he pledged to embrace as his Alma Mater, he had no right to embarrass the institution and its administration, men of fidelity and devotion to honor who were ready and willing to treat him as they would treat any student.

When James Meredith uttered those words against the Army, he forfeited a bond of sympathy that had assumed impressive proportions. He invited the die-hard opposition to bracket with him all other Negroes who ask for equality of opportunity.

Followed then interviews and press conferences, for national and international consumption, with inflammatory scripts prepared by the National Association for the Advancement of Colored People, each incident calculated to precipitate more strife rather than to establish peaceably the right of an American citizen to use facilities his own tax dollars helped provide and maintain.

Then came the final straw, James Meredith's denunciation of Chancellor J. D. Williams, the administration and faculty of the university . . . reckless and unfounded charges of harassment and persecution; a weak and cowardly effort to shift responsibility for his academic failure to other shoulders, even as a petulant schoolboy blames "that mean old teacher" for his shortcomings and failing marks on a report card.

If any individuals and groups touched by this sorry episode can come out with clean hands, they are Chancellor Williams, his administrative staff, and the faculty.

Politicians in Washington and Jackson have aggravated the mess; student minorities have brought shame on their Alma Mater; troublemakers who never even saw a Miss America or the triumphant Ole Miss football team except on television, have provided free fuel to feed the fires of "Hate Mississippi—Hate the South" bigots; but Chancellor Williams and his colleagues have comported themselves with dignity and grace, and human decency throughout.

By his own behavior James Meredith, especially in his wild tirade against the university administration, has thrown up an iron curtain against those of his own people who in future years will come in all sincerity to prove themselves as citizens. James Meredith has damaged their cause beyond calculation, whether by indiscretion or through malice.

He has not hastened an era of one-level citizenship in areas where the idea still is unpalatable. Indeed, by his reckless, irresponsible talk and behavior, he may have set back, at least for a generation, realization of his people's dream.

Thus, if I were a Negro, I believe I would be bitter against James Meredith, for ignoble failure and treason to the nobler ideals of a cause.

Dr. James W. Silver, a professor at the university, who later would write *Mississippi: The Closed Society*, answered Flowers' comments, January 18, 1963:

Mr. Paul Flowers
The Commercial Appeal
Memphis, Tennessee

Dear Paul:

Upon seeing your announcement that an official of the University of Mississippi is reprinting your columns of January 14 and 15, I read them once again, and once again I failed to discover the "overload of grief, compassion and charity" you claim for yourself. Instead, I find bitterness, rancour and, what is worse, ignorance.

Your resounding words are at fault, it seems to me, for the following reasons:

(1) You equate "Federal stupidity and state demagoguery" ("irresponsible politicians on state and national levels") which is nothing less than an intellectually sloppy performance indicating your unwillingness to face the facts. The agents of the Federal government made some mistakes in carrying out their responsibilities; the record of persistent, deliberate, and fundamental irresponsibility on the state level, by contrast, drew headlines and editorials in the Commercial Appeal when it came to one of its critical peaks last September 30.

(2) Your denunciation of James Meredith's criticism of the U.S. Army conveniently neglects his simultaneous blast at the NAACP. To have included the latter would have blunted your charge that Meredith is merely a tool of the NAACP.

(3) As for Meredith having invited "the die-hard opposition to bracket with him all other Negroes who ask for equality of opportunity," it seems clear that a man with a mission would consider this an honor, and would be indifferent to the wishes of the die-hard opposition.

(4) Instead of the "inflammatory scripts prepared by the NAACP, each incident calculated to precipitate more strife," there is overwhelming evidence that Meredith makes his own plans, usually without script. Furthermore, if you have been able to penetrate his mind to the point of explaining his motivation, you have done something well beyond the capacity of those who are associated with him. Mr. Meredith is a very complicated human being; above all, an individualist.

(5) You write Meredith's "reckless and unfounded charges of harassment and persecution; a weak and cowardly effort to shift responsibility from his academic failure. . . ." This implies, at the present moment, an unwarranted omniscience on your part (regarding his "academic failure"), and is evidence of a colossal misunderstanding of the man's character—commensurate only with your shallow insight into his harassment.

(6) It would be difficult for you to specify Meredith's "wild tirades against the University administration." His words have been mild compared with the criticisms of the faculty members in the AAUP [American Association of University Professors]. On the contrary, Meredith has been almost unfailing in his favorable comments on the university—administration, faculty and student body.

It seems to me that when you write of Meredith's "ignoble failure and treason to the nobler ideals of a cause," you convict yourself of the very faults you attribute to a man obviously beyond your comprehension. I say this with no malice because I believe that Meredith is beyond the understanding of all of us. Nor do I think his fellow Negroes have reason to be bitter toward him.

Your columns, however well-intentioned and filled with honest, righteous indignation, tend to place you among the "silent multitudes," those pious souls who have kept quiet throughout the storm, waiting patiently with a restless anger to pounce on the first (or the second) false step of a much beleaguered and maligned individual.

Written, I hope, with some compassion and charity.

Yours,

James W. Silver

Bob Considine made the following comments in his syndicated column:

### THE SOUTH'S CHIVALRY

No one with any understanding of James Meredith's ordeal could reasonably censure him if he were to decide, as he said he may, that he will skip the next semester at the University of Mississippi. He will do so, he declared, "unless positive changes are made to make my situation more conducive to learning." Only the University itself, and especially its student body, can make such changes.

Ever since he enrolled at Ole Miss, Meredith's life has been in peril, threatened by hotheads on and off the campus; United States marshals have had to go with him constantly and some 300 soldiers have been kept nearby in case of disorder. Shots have been fired into the home of his father. A palpable atmosphere of hostility toward him has been omnipresent even when the violence has been contained and the taunts silenced. To say that this situation has not been conducive to learning sets something of a new record for understatement.

At the same time, however, there was justification for Attorney General Kennedy's gentle expression of hope that "in making a final decision on this, Mr. Meredith will consider that he chose to go to the University of Mississippi and the energies and hopes of his fellow citizens have been involved in his admission and continued attendance." Two lives were lost and a great many bodily injuries were suffered in the rioting that accompanied his enrollment at the University.

Moreover, Meredith has become a symbol in a vital sense, a symbol of Negro hopes for equality of opportunity, a symbol of the power of the United States to insure that opportunity. If Meredith is driven from the University of Mississippi, as Autherine Lucy was driven from the University of Alabama, racists will conclude that violence affords an infallible formula for keeping the Negro submerged. And they can be expected to resort to it again when new efforts are made to shatter segregation.

If Governor Ross Barnett triumphs at Ole Miss and succeeds in keeping the imprint of his bigotry on that institution, James Meredith will not be the sole loser. The University will lose; Mississippi will lose; the American people will lose.

The Legal Defense Fund was very anxious that I should decide to return for the second semester, and that is stating their position mildly. But there was no pushing. I am sure that they all understood. I know Mrs. Motley and Greenberg did.

### The Last Day of the First Semester

The last day of the first semester was observed by the students at the university as if it were the last day of days. Apparently, they were sure that their threats, curses, bricks, and bottles; dining-hall demonstrations, and the works, had proven for all time that Mississippi white folks would remain supreme forever.

The Big Send-off is an event to be remembered. It was a nice springlike day—clear and sunny as only it can be in Mississippi during this season. Each time I went to class the students would line the streets on both sides. Such repeated displays were not for the most glorified hero, only a fallen victim could be accorded this sustained deference. Television cameras, radio recorders, flashes from the photographers' bulbs, queries from the press reporters—all were as abundant as Mississippi rednecks. My procession must have been quite a sight to witness—the marshal and soldiers, all the rest, and me.

The last day was also an examination day. I had four final exams. The question of my being eligible for readmission to the next term had already been resolved by the two exams taken the day before. I was positive that I had turned in an A paper in my political science course and at least a B or better paper in my history course; just these two courses, even if I had received the lowest possible grades in the other courses, would have given me more than enough points for readmission. But this was an important examination day, and I knew it well. The prospects of my graduating in the shortest possible time were in the balance on this last day of the first semester. Mississippi has one of the toughest systems in the country for raising your grade-point level once it falls below par. (That is, it had, but the system has now been changed.) Therefore, I needed to maintain my average if I wanted to graduate in six months.

Actually, I was pretty sure of the grades I was going to receive, and as a matter of fact each grade was identical to what I had expected. Only one grade during my whole stay at the university was not what I thought it would be. This was a second semester course in Southern History. The professor had given me a B+ on the midterm examination and had written me a note saying that I could easily make an A in the course, if I would give more body to my answers, which he was sure that I knew. I thought that I had done better on the final examination, but he still gave me a B for the course. This could have resulted from the term papers that we had to submit. I used my interpretation of Southern History quite freely and it was known to be at odds with many of the traditional concepts. And there is always the possibility that a large number of other students did much better, too, and naturally he couldn't give everyone an A.

The last day was also one for consultations. Some few members of the faculty, led by Dr. James W. Silver, had taken a very great interest in the recent events at the university. I had promised Dr. Silver that I would stop by his office and see him before I left the campus. It was after five before I had finished my last examination and arrived at his office. He was most concerned about whether or not I would return for the second semester. I was not prepared to answer that question then, because all the pertinent data were not yet available to me, and certainly not properly evaluated.

It is hard for me to understand, however, why everyone was always so willing to conclude a negative from a simple question of doubt. Actually, I had never said or done anything that could be construed as a positive indication of withdrawal from the university. I had even left most of my belongings in my dormitory room, just like all the rest of the students. Most newsmen, U.S. marshals, federal government officials, university officials, and most of my friends knew this, and I repeatedly reminded them of it. It was never a question of whether or not I would return to the university but, rather, would it be necessary for me to decide to leave the school and not to continue my studies there under the prevailing circumstances. It must be remembered that the primary object of my taking the stand that I did was to focus attention on the important issues and not to let the opposition succeed in making petty issues the dominant public concern.

*Leaving the Campus.* When I finally got back to my dormitory and started to load up the old blue Cadillac, which had already suffered all manner of abuse from our mutual enemies, it was getting quite late. I carried out some of the many thousands of letters that I had received from the many people who were concerned. I wanted to take these to the secretaries that were working on my mail, in order to save the expense of postage. There were so many letters that even now, three years later, all of them have not been opened. But I have vowed to read every letter if it takes ten years.

I had to carry all the items by myself, while thousands of students and spectators looked on, and the area looked like an outdoor stage or athletic event with all the television and photographers' flood-lights. Normally, the marshals would have helped me, but they were under orders to keep hands off, I guess because the South could have made bad publicity for the government, picturing it as using mar-shals for my stewards.

The boys had really fixed my car. God only knows what they had not done to it, but when the mechanic took the engine apart several weeks later, he found a pound or more of sugar still undis-solved. When I tried to start the car, I ran the battery down, and my old Negro friend came from out of nowhere to my rescue. He got a young Negro with a jump cable, but his battery was not the same voltage as mine, and we could not use his car. One of the newsmen offered his car, and we tried for a long time to get it started from his battery, but to no avail.

My Negro friends then went to get a mechanic. Meanwhile, the campus police, anxious to get me off the campus as quickly as pos-sible because the crowd was really growing as night fell, were giving every assistance; one even rolled up his sleeves and got under the hood to try his skill at getting the engine going; he failed also. Finally, the mechanic arrived. He was a middle-aged white man who didn't seem to be a bit disturbed by all the commotion or by whose car he was working on. He worked for nearly an hour and decided that he could not fix it there; it would have to be taken to his shop just off the campus.

The campus police anxiously suggested that, since it was all downhill, if we got the car in the street and gave it a push, it would roll on its own. In any event, I would be off campus and they could care less after that.

I got behind the wheel and the marshals formed their caravan two cars in front and the rest behind. Two worried campus police, two brave Negroes, a Justice Department lawyer, and one or two news-men—all gave me a running push down the hill. Just to see what would happen, I put the car in low gear and turned on the ignition; the engine started just like that.

We headed for Memphis. As far as one could see, and farther, cars trailed behind me; there were several cars of marshals, newsmen, and soldiers, but the rest were mostly students, I imagine. There are no stops for the first eighty miles after you leave Oxford, but when we arrived at the first traffic light, it was red. The old Cadillac stopped dead. The marshals behind me pushed the car to the closest service station. A young fellow came out and, giving me very courteous service, was about to hook up the electric battery charge when another fellow came out, cursing and raising hell, and ordered me off his property. Apparently someone had told him who I was.

The marshals were still concerned because they had been directed to escort me to Memphis and there turn me loose on my own. Although we were now in Tennessee, the Memphis city limits were still a few blocks away. They got behind me again and pushed me off toward Memphis. After a couple of blocks, I got the car started again, and drove to a Negro service station that I knew and asked them to see what they could do.

The marshals left me at this point. The newsmen stayed around, however. I called my lawyer, whom I had come to see, and he came to get me. After our conference, we went to meet another man whom we were supposed to see. By midnight we were back at the station to see about the car. They had not been able to do anything with it. I vowed that the next time I went to bed it would be in Mississippi. They didn't think the car would make it, but they got it started, filled it up with gas, and I took off on the two-hundred-and-twenty-five-mile drive to Jackson. It was just past midnight.

*Arrival in Jackson at 4:00 A.M.* I headed toward Jackson all alone. I was tired, I had had a long and busy day, but the big problems were to keep the car engine running and myself awake. Neither was an easy task. There were times when I just had to stop and get out and wake myself up. I would pull over by the side of the road, put two or three big books on the accelerator pedal to keep the motor racing, walk around in the cold air for a few minutes, and be on my way again. The road kept getting behind me.

About fifty miles from Jackson at three o'clock in the morning in the heavy swamp bottoms of the dirty Big Black River near Pickens, the old Cadillac developed new symptoms. I had owned this car for five years and the red oil-pressure light on the dash had always been dead, now it was very much alive and glowing brightly. I kept on going.

After another ten miles the engine was knocking badly and keeping up a terrible noise. I had to slow down to a crawl. Finally I reached Canton, the last big town before you get to Jackson. I had planned not to stop at any places along the way, because I had been in the news on an hourly basis for the past three weeks without a break. Everybody in Mississippi was involved in my case in one way or another, and I was not in the mood to foster any changes in my relationship with my fellow Mississippians at this particular time, especially with the poor white crackers who would be hanging around the gas stations.

There was no choice; I had to stop. I started looking the gas stations over carefully, searching for one with a Negro attendant. I spotted one, and pulled in to the pump. The Negro came over to serve me. He recognized me right away, but, after speaking, went on as if nothing was happening. I told him to put two quarts of cheap oil in and he did. About that time one of the white attendants came over and grabbed the gas pump and asked, how much? I didn't say anything, just pointed to the Negro, who told the white boy that he "had everything." The white fellow went away. When the Negro finished, I paid him and went away with his best wishes.

I moved on toward Jackson. The noise had lessened some and the oil-pressure light had dimmed a bit, but it never completely went out. By the time I reached Jackson the crisis point had again arisen, but I could care less now, because if I had a sanctuary anywhere in the world I had it here. Ironically, the old Cadillac stopped for good as I made the last turn across the railroad tracks, heading toward my new place of residence. I was about a half block from my house and it was downhill, so I threw the car out of gear and let it roll down to a stop at the entrance to our parking lot. It was two or three months before anyone ever got the old car started again.

It was just after four o'clock in the morning. As I turned off my lights and started to get out of the car, four or five cars approached me from two directions. I didn't know who they were or what was going on. The first car stopped behind me and two white men got out and started toward my car. I remained in the car. Before they reached it, another car had pulled up in front and two Negroes jumped out and ran toward me. They stopped the white men. I still didn't have any idea who they were. There was some loud talking and I recognized the loudest voice. It was Dick Gregory ordering the whites to leave with the help of his emergency pistol. With him was Medgar Evers, who didn't need his pistol; Robert Smith, Jr., and Sam Bailey were close behind in another car. They had been waiting for me to return. Two of the other cars stopped close by but the men didn't get out. I recognized the cars; they were

U.S. marshals. The two white men that Gregory had chased off were two local newsmen who had also been waiting for me.

My wife had just moved into Jackson's newest and most modern Negro apartment building, owned by Robert Smith, Jr.; I had not been there before. We went upstairs to greet my wife. The boys wanted to talk about the future. So we left and went over to Robert Smith's house to talk—Medgar, Dick, Robert, and myself. We talked the rest of the night about the question of whether or not I should return to the university. Actually, they did most of the talking; I just listened. About daybreak Medgar, acting as spokesman for all three, stated their opinion that "if at all possible I should go back" and asked me for an up-to-the-minute view of the prospects. I reminded them that I had never left the university, that my belongings were still there, and the final decision would rest with the people of the United States, but mainly with the Negro. They still interpreted this basically as a negative reply; but, on the other hand, they all seemed very pleased with my position.

## The Feelings of My People

The Mississippi Negro has suffered as much at the hands of other Negroes in the past fifty years as he has at the hands of the whites. He has always been ridiculed for his illiteracy and backwardness, for coming from the state with the worst record in every kind of human mistreatment, as though he was responsible for his chance of birth. He suffered in the colleges and universities, in the cities of the North, in the armed services. Wherever he might go, if there was a bottom, he was in it ideologically. I have never talked to a Mississippi Negro in one of the professions, who did not tell me of his suffering in school because he was from his state. Too many times I have visited my friends in Chicago, Detroit, St. Louis, or wherever, and have them call me off to the side and instruct me not to say anything about Mississippi, because they didn't want "their friends" to know they came from there. In the armed forces the case against the Mississippi Negro was so great and so fundamental that the "Bar Girls" in the Negro section of town near the world's largest air base in Tachikawa, Japan, associated the word "Mississippi" with any very dark or illiterate or riotous Negro G.I. These girls had for all practical purposes grown up with Negro G.I.'s and had never been influenced by white soldiers. The stereotyping of the Mississippi Negro is almost complete.

The feelings of my people in Mississippi were as strongly for me in January 1963, as perhaps they could be. It was not only that I was defying white folks, but equally important to them I was redeeming their chance of birth in the state. It may seem strange, but it was this point that thousands of Mississippi-born Negroes were most grateful about. Hundreds of Negroes in the North, many of whom had left years before, wrote me that they had always denied being from Mississippi but were now broadcasting it far and wide. Many youngsters wrote to tell me that their grandparents were from Mississippi.

In Mississippi the understanding of my people was different from those elsewhere. I cannot recall a single Mississippi Negro telling me that I had an obligation to go back to the University of Mississippi, and this had been the urgent advice of many of the others. I credit this to the complete empathy that Mississippi Negroes had with me. The peak of this feeling was reached during the last ten days of January. Most of them acted toward me as if they really felt themselves to be me. It was a strange experience, but a very necessary one for me, I believe, because it was for them that I existed, and without this indication of their closeness to me, I would not have had a purpose or any reason to continue. They knew the depth of the struggle that we were involved in with a real and determined enemy.

Jackson State College, which I shall always consider my school, was in the middle of the second quarter. I had never lost sight of the fact that one of my prime motives for attempting to gain admission to the University of Mississippi had been to force the state to put more money and support into the Negro schools, if for no other purpose than to keep Negroes out of the white schools. I have no doubt that one of the main reasons I received the cooperation and support from the administration of Jackson State College that I did was because I had made it a point to remind them of this motive. I knew very well that the only way to really help the Negro in Mississippi educationally for the next few generations was to improve the Negro schools; I have consistently believed that if every white school in the state were, in fact, open to the Negro, there would not be a dozen Negroes in Mississippi who would attend them. Of their own free will they would prefer the Negro school. But the choice should always be theirs to make. Customs and laws should not keep them from enjoying the privileges of full citizenship.

My wife was a senior in Jackson State College and our apartment was just a few steps from the campus. I spent most of my time with my old friends in the regular places, but most often at the College Inn. It was just like College Inns all over the world, I suppose; records on the jukebox, pinball machines, hamburgers and hot dogs, light lunches, and dancing in the back room. Whenever I went there, the feeling was so strong that I usually had to dance with at least two girls, before the record had finished. Some of them would just hold me and cry. Most of the time there was not much talking, just understanding.

The Elk's Rest was my favorite spot for meeting my friends and relaxing. It was the only place in town where every day of the year you could find something going on and somebody around, or they would soon show up. The feeling was strong at the Elk's Club, too, but the regulars were pretty close to normal. On the weekends when the place was filled with the every-now-and-then patrons, it was different. After a few rounds of drinks, everybody would insist that I join them. And as soon as one group started expressing its feelings, the whole place would get in the mood. Most of these people I knew either casually or well, and they were experiencing feelings that they were unused to. Some fellow, not satisfied with shaking my hand twenty times, had to give me a big, hard hug; he then got his wife and asked me to kiss her. She was shy and he had to push her up close enough. Then I was hugged by most of the men in the place and had to kiss most of the women. Of course, I never did mind shaking anybody's hand, or being hugged by any woman, or even kissing pretty women, but I had to condition myself to being hugged by men and to kissing ugly women.

*My Wife and My Family.* In January, my wife and my family were the same in their attitude toward me as they had been during the entire ordeal. Their position on my decisions was always neutral, and their support in carrying out a decision was always complete. My family was my strength. I had known for a long time that any doubt or reluctance on their part would automatically mean the end as far as further action was concerned. There was no weakening in my family, absolutely none, and it was as plain as sunshine. My wife never once failed to be the least excited person during the most trying of all periods. All my folks had a very deep understanding of life and living. Flowing blood and hot breath was not the essence of true living for any of them. There were greater realities that they were conscious of. Only a family of stature can sustain the pressures of change without faltering.

*The Visitors.* I had many visitors during this period of decision.

They came from all walks of life and for all kinds of purposes. The first one was a well-known newsman from one of the Jackson daily papers. He wanted to check the authenticity of an Allen-Scott report in their syndicated column that I had signed a contract for a book and that Attorney General Robert Kennedy was angry about it and working behind the scenes to stop it.

Another visitor was a Negro preacher from California. He was the pastor of the largest Negro Baptist church in that state and came to offer me "a home in California," in the event I should decide not to go back to the university. It was a grand gesture on his part because he had slipped into Mississippi to see me. His wife was not well and would probably have "died of worry," if she had known her husband was in Mississippi. He had told her he was going to Hot Springs, Arkansas.

Jack Greenberg also came down to talk with me. He never mentioned directly what he came to talk about, but I was pretty sure what his interest was. I indicated to him very strongly that I would probably go back. Of course, I couldn't say for sure, because I can never make decisions in advance; I can only make a decision as to how the decision will be made. He apparently still was not convinced that I was going back when he left to fly back to New York.

A.W. Willis came down from Memphis the day before I was to make my final decision. He walked in and asked if I had got my call from President Kennedy yet. I said, "No, what call?" He just laughed. He was referring to some scheme that he was involved in with a professor at the University of Mississippi and one of President Kennedy's White House advisers; the President was more or less to order me to go back, if I decided otherwise. I think Willis was one of the few persons that really believed that I was going back. He returned to Memphis that same day.

James Baldwin, who had left a few weeks earlier, was back with his fur-lined leather jacket. This time he had his photographer along to take pictures. Baldwin was emotionally involved on this trip. He did a story for *Life* Magazine and in it he wrote that "James Meredith is the most noble individual that I have ever known." I regarded this as one of the greatest tributes ever paid to me.

*Advice from Friends.* Although I tried to examine and weigh all the issues, conditions, circumstances, and consequences objectively, there can be no doubt that the evaluations and advice of the old Jackson State College In Group influenced me a great deal. I had written to several of them shortly after the statement of January 7, explaining to them the situation as I saw it and asking their opinions and advice. The old group was scattered now, after graduating from Jackson State. The answers came from Oklahoma and Iowa where some were doing graduate studies; James Allen, Jr., who was now a high school teacher in Chicago, sent a complete evaluative survey of our efforts since August 1960. The most useful of all was a twelve-page letter from Ruby Lee Magee, the only female member of the In Group, the first woman and second student ever to win a Woodrow Wilson Fellowship at Jackson State College. She was now doing graduate work in political science at Harvard (Radcliffe) University. Her letter, which I received three days before the decision was reached and announced, must speak for itself.

1/22/63

Dear Jay,
    Your letter was received with much rejoicing mingled with not a little bit of serious contemplation, in fact I have (between exams) spent the week trying to think of something constructive to write. The fact is there is no easy or sure answer and any proposal must be made with utmost precaution. It is understood that, as always, ultimately the decision will be yours and will be accepted as the best course to, as you say, aid the cause. . . .
    So far Northerners realize that you are independent and self-propelled. Southern whites have tried to put over the idea that you are conceited and act on selfish interests. Up until your last press conference this view had not been accepted, but now some Northerners are beginning to question your motives. This is quite silly on their part and shows a complete lack of understanding of the situation. . . . The nation is waiting for your decision about next semester (I saw you loading your things in your car to leave on T.V., and so did millions of other Americans tonight). This will be your biggest audience—and possibly the most interested—so make the most of it. It is the highest card in the deck.
    At this point, I believe, the most important thing is to stay at Ole Miss. I realize that this is easy to say, but nevertheless I must. If you leave now, the students and other Mississippians will think they have won the right to continue their hideous brand of oppression. This must not happen at all costs and I know the cost to you is almost too heavy to ask but I am convinced you can and will find a way.
    For the first time on January 7th the Ole Miss students were able to get an indirect reaction out of you (indirect because your statement was primarily directed at the federal government). Before then, they (the students) had hurled insults and harassed in vain. You stayed cool and unaffected. This is probably why they became worse, because they thought they were finally getting results. Four of the students were on

T.V. shortly after you, and were overjoyed at the idea of their having made you consider leaving. To them this was complete vindication of their actions....

I have been trying to imagine what action or actions would be open to you if you decide to return. So far I can think of very little, I know you are playing politics and if you return this must continue but the method is highly important. Robert Kennedy is about the only one in Washington who is really interested and his interest is not too deep. The only answer, at this point, seems to be to find a way to force him (and the Justice Department) to force Chancellor Williams to expel some students. This is the only thing that will put an end to the heckling. He was on T.V. tonight and asserted that only 25 students were involved in the riots! This is an open lie—and hopefully it may have some effect on the accrediting association and might induce them (out of disgust, if nothing else) to remove the school's accreditation. This would hurt a lot of Mississippians and might calm them down somewhat.

Ideally, I would like to see President Kennedy or his personal representative make an affirmative statement based on the moral grounds involved in this situation. So far he hasn't opened his mouth about your situation (except for his 15-minute compromise speech on the night of the riots)—and I believe this is a big drawback. The time for this was before the riots—when Barnett went on T.V. on Thursday night (in September) and announced his proposed course of action. This case was identical to the Little Rock Case (Cooper v. Aaron) and if Jack or Bobby had brought this forcefully before the people it might have helped prevent Barnett's leading the people to believe they had a chance to defy the national government.

The second time for a strong affirmative statement by the President or some member of government could be the week after you have gone back—if you decide to return for the second semester. They probably won't do it, but the idea has merit.

The only other possible solution would be to get more Negro students at Ole Miss as soon as possible, preferably next semester. I have not heard anything further about the two students who were supposedly applying. I know this is a lot to ask of anybody but it is even more to ask you to go it alone because you are a centralized target for the students and they foolishly believe that if they get rid of you (make you leave) all their problems will be over. But if there were more Negro students they would be forced to face facts and spread their hate and ignorance over a wider area, thereby ruining its effectiveness....

Everyone realizes that you are under great pressure and we all know that you must find some way to let off some of the built-up frustration. This is all well and good, but the "ultimate goal must always take precedence over everything else." That is what you told us for two years, remember: It still holds. The nation has the image of a very determined, hard-fighting young man aiming at a goal that only he can reach, in this instance. The problem of the moment is to prevent the creation of a void which might not be filled in the immediate future. That would be the greatest tragedy. At the moment you are the only one who can prevent it. . . .

In summary, at this point the most important thing seems to be getting more Negro students into Ole Miss, preferably next semester, but next year at the latest. Second, some students need to be expelled and other severely disciplined. Third, loss of accreditation might shock a few Mississippians enough to get some positive results. Fourth, the President should make a forceful statement to the American people and especially to Mississippians. Just asking you to continue isn't enough, the federal government must give you every type of support and give full backing to court actions.

I talked to Bill Higgs on the phone tonight. He seems to be genuinely worried, but I still have faith and confidence that you will be able to continue even under increased pressures.

Sincerely,
Ruby

## The Day of Decision

Greenberg had sent Tom Dent, the public relations man for the Legal Defense Fund to Jackson, "just in case he was needed." It was also well known that I had great respect for Tom Dent and that he might have a favorable influence on me. He stayed with us the few days that he was there.

I had weighed carefully all the considerations that were before me. It had been a most trying decision-making process. Looking back it is easy to convince myself that there was never any real question— that everything always pointed toward the decision that I finally made. However, I am not so sure that the decision was that clear at all. Perhaps I could have just as easily decided not to return. Frankly, I saw absolutely nothing that I had to gain personally by going back. I had already been accepted long before by one of the best law schools in the country and had an open agreement to enter one of the leading graduate schools, if ever the Mississippi crisis went against me. The goal that I had my mind and heart fixed on was breaking the system of "White Supremacy." The major question that I had to answer was how best to accomplish this aim. Going to the University of Mississippi was just one of the possible alternatives.

Tom was worried when I went to bed the last night before the day of decision and had not prepared a statement. Early in the morning on January 30 I got up and drafted a short statement; Tom then took it to have copies made to give to the newsmen.

The walk to the Masonic Temple, two blocks away, was a solemn one; I went alone. Many spoke to me, but there was no talking. I don't know how many people were there waiting, five hundred to a thousand, I would guess. Without a doubt this was the largest news conference in my life. Every media and area was represented, local, state, national, and foreign—the world was involved.

A very unfortunate incident occurred before these newsmen and this huge group of my closest friends and supporters. The microphones had been set up on a small stage and behind the table where I was to sit someone had put a huge "NAACP" sign on the wall, an extremely inappropriate thing to do. This was a nonpartisan occasion and I stood for all my people, no matter what their loyalties or enthusiasms. I had the sign removed, but I invited Medgar Evers to sit beside me during the press conference, although I knew full well that the Southern press would say that he was there to tell me what to say. They did. Medgar Evers was not just a representative of the NAACP, he was a devoted worker for the Negro. There are few men that I would put in his class.

The news conference got under way, and I read my statement which said in part: "After listening to all arguments, evaluations, and positions and weighing all this against my personal possibilities and circumstances, I have concluded that the 'Negro' should not return to the University of Mississippi. The prospects for him are too unpromising. [A white radio newsman from Jackson applauded.] However, I have decided that I, J.H. Meredith, will register for the second semester at the University of Mississippi."

After it was over, most of the Negroes come up to shake my hand. Even the Mississippi Negro schoolteachers came out in open support.

# 11

## The Second Semester: February-May 1963

THE decision had been made; now it was time to return to the university to register for the second semester. The question of whether or not I would return had become by far the biggest issue of my stay at the school, and too much importance had been placed upon my returning. The assumption that it is more significant for a Negro to go to a school than for him to be free to choose whether he will attend or not attend is one that I can never accept.

*The Return Trip*

All in all, more security measures were taken for my second enrollment than for the first. The U.S. marshals, as usual, were escorting me. There were just more of them than normal. We drove from Jackson to Oxford with a fleet of helicopters and light Army planes flying circular and zigzag cover for us all the way along the two-hundred-mile trip. Soldiers were posted along the road in the countryside around Oxford. I shall never forget one scene: A young fully armed soldier was dutifully standing his post while an old man amused himself by talking to the young serviceman who seemed to be really enjoying the tongue lashing that the old Mississippian was giving him. I thought how easily the soldier could have been the grandson of the old man. As we approached Oxford, the number of soldiers increased. They were stationed in every strategic location, on the roofs of tall buildings, at gasoline stations, and so forth. There were jeep patrols, troop trucks, and staff cars all over the place.

To back up the marshals and soldiers, or to add to the danger that they faced, there were Chief Tatum and the campus police, which had been recently enlarged by sheriffs and their deputies. Chief Tatum was all right, but I would rather face a lynch mob any day than some of the members of the campus police force or any of the sheriffs' deputies.

### My Meeting with Chancellor Williams

After I returned for the second semester and registration was completed, the Chancellor requested that I come to see him. I had not seen him during the first semester. When I arrived in his office, it was filled with television equipment. I waited for a few minutes while the Chancellor finished his interview, and because of the television equipment in his office, we met in the conference room. The Chancellor is a pleasant man. I will always remember the first time I saw him at the first hearing in Meridian. Just as our party was about to enter the elevator, the defendants and lawyers for the University of Mississippi were getting off the elevator. The Chancellor was the only one of the group to act in any way as if we were human. He nodded slightly as he passed.

He gave me a hearty handshake and asked me to take a seat. We talked for several minutes. He was quite candid regarding the difficulty of his position and the many pressures that were being applied to him by the different interest groups in Mississippi. I explained to the Chancellor that I had done everything possible to make his position and that of the other officials of the university as normal as possible. I had always been very careful to place the major part of the blame where it should be with Governor Barnett and other state officials.

The Chancellor then turned to the unpleasant aspects of our meeting. He told me of the great displeasure that he had experienced during the break between the first and second semester. He had gone to Chicago for a meeting and, while walking in the downtown area on Wednesday, he had seen on the top of one of the tallest buildings the news flashes of the day. It gave the time, temperature, and "Meredith to announce decision on Friday." I doubt that the Chancellor was experiencing as much discomfort in pondering the prospects of my making a decision as I was in going through the agony of making it. I expressed the hope that the Negro would soon receive his due and we would never again have to make news by just wanting to enjoy the rights and privileges of being a citizen of the United States.

He then made his only request of me. The Chancellor asked me to state publicly that my only purpose in attending the University of Mississippi was "to get an education." Of course, I had to tell the Chancellor frankly that I could never honor this request. Any Negro that went through all of the trouble required to attend the University of Mississippi and only wanted to get an education would have to be crazy. My purpose was to break the system of "White Supremacy," and going to the university was just one of the many steps.

As a final gesture, Chancellor Williams gave me copies of two speeches that he had delivered regarding my enrollment and a booklet that he had had prepared entitled "The University of Mississippi and The Meredith Case." The Chancellor felt that some accounts of the Meredith case did not reflect a fair picture of the university, and his efforts were designed to give a better picture.

### A Typical Trip to Jackson

During my stay at the University of Mississippi, I spent only two weekends on the campus (and to my knowledge that was one weekend more than any other student there). I went to Jackson to see my wife as often as possible.

Often I drove my own car, but the marshals preferred that I ride in theirs, I suppose, for security reasons. Mississippi, however, started to accuse the federal government of using taxpayers' money to transport me around. The irony of being chauffeured in Mississippi by a white driver made it quite easy to recognize me along the highway. The Washington office sent several directives to the effect that I couldn't ride in the cars, but it could never make them stick. It was just not feasible for the marshals to offer maximum protection without close contact. And if there was anything in the world that the U.S. marshals didn't want to do, it was to stay on the campus of the University of Mississippi if they didn't absolutely have to. In many ways their life was made more uncomfortable than my own. By Tuesday of each week they began to make sure that I had made plans to leave the campus on Friday, and if I didn't feel like driving my car, they would not let this stop us from leaving the campus.

One of the memorable aspects of the trips to Jackson was the opportunity it gave me to drive through the countryside and feel the closeness of the purpose for which I lived. Everywhere I looked, I saw people for whom I was fighting and the lives of drudgery that they were forced to live—the rundown shacks for homes, no toilets, no water, no lights; the little dirty Negro children and their over-burdened mothers and spiritually broken fathers. I also saw an un-developed Mississippi aside from its social pattern. One of the greater problems is something to share. One half of nothing is no better than one tenth of nothing. My hope in Mississippi is to build as well as to assure equal benefits from what is produced.

Kosciusko, my home town, was on the route to Jackson. I usu-ally stopped there to see my folks and say hello.

*A Typical Class Day*

I would usually awaken around five-thirty or a quarter to six to the click of the steel-plated heels of the soldier walking his post in the hallway from one end of my apartment to the other. I shaved and put on the sweet-smelling after-shave lotion that one of my many friends had given me for Christmas. At seven I would walk out the only way open, through the living room (the marshals' head-quarters). All the other doors had been blocked. The team of mar-shals for the day would join me, and I would head down the long flight of steps outside the dorm toward the sidewalk. When I reached the second step one of my watchers would yell, "Hey, Nig-ger! There's that Nigger!" I had been at the university ten months before I ever descended the fifteen or twenty steps without someone calling me nigger. They must have kept their eyes on those steps twenty-four hours a day. As I walked the two blocks down the hill to the cafeteria, I could hear the routine window-to-window com-ments. I think I would have been very disturbed, if not thoroughly frightened, if I had walked the whole distance without anybody saying anything. I would have known that they were up to some-thing very drastic.

At the dining hall I would meet my cursing "friend," Senator George. I have never met old George under any circumstances with-out his calling me some bad name; even when I could not hear, I could see the words form on his mumbling lips. George had plenty of competition, of course. The Negro cooks and help always had a warm greeting for me and knew exactly how I preferred my food. I got scrambled egg and crisp bacon and a big glass of grape juice. It was my busiest day, so I picked up a box of raisin bran on the side.

Since the class in History of the New South was at eight o'clock and I always liked to be the first one in the room, I usually went from the cafeteria by the back door to the Graduate Building where the class was held and read *The Mississippian* (university newspaper). The professor, an old-line Mississippi aristocrat, is the only instructor that I have ever had in any school with whom I have never had a conversation of any kind. Once, we met head on in a narrow corridor and he spoke. Also, he wrote a note on my midterm exam paper, saying that I could raise my B+ to an A on the final if I gave more substance to my answers. This was ironic because the moderates on campus felt that he just might fail me in his course, since he was a known conservative.

On my way to the course in the Legislative Process in the Political Science Building I would stop by the post office and pick up my mail. The post office was probably the only place where there was unsupervised contact with other students at the school. It was usually crowded. Every now and then one of the boys would stick his foot out in a gesture to trip me. Often I would kick back at a couple of them. Most of the students crowded in to their boxes, even if I were in the narrow corridor where the individual boxes were. A few, especially girls, would never come in while I was there; they just waited out in the hall and sneered.

This class was taught by my adviser and the head of the department. A fine man of high character and a native Mississippian, he went the full official and formal limit and no further. Personally, I would expect no more. He was the only professor on the first day that I attended classes to read to the students the letter from the university directing the school to comply with the court order. I vividly remember his shaken look on that day; he had been deeply grieved by the events that had taken place in his state.

After the political science class, I would stop by the library to read for a little while in the reserved books reading room. There was less friction in the library. I cannot recall any rudeness or indifferent treatment from the library staff or from any of the students working there. Some students, of course, always left the room when I came in, but I am a firm believer in individual freedom of action. There were numerous occasions when the library had to be vacated because of "bomb scares." At one point, I stopped going to the library because I hated to see the other students suffering so much inconvenience.

The worst event of all, and the most dishonorable, was having my reading glasses stolen. I usually went upstairs to the commercial room to do my studying. On this day the room was full. I went to the washroom and left my books and reading glasses on the table. When I returned, the glasses were gone. The campus police were called and everyone was questioned, but naturally no one had seen a thing. A few days later, one of the witnesses couldn't live with his conscience any longer and came over to tell me who did it. He also confessed to the marshals on condition that it would go no further. He would not testify in public. I guess I could understand his predicament.

By noon I always liked to be in a good position in the "chow" line. This was the biggest meal. From habit, or principle, I always went to the right side of the dining hall. For some reason more students usually went through my line. Very often the other line would be much shorter, yet they would wait in the much longer line on the right. Of course, I don't know why this was so, but I used to tell the marshals it was because the best food was always on my side. The Negroes cooked the food and brought it to the line, but it was served by whites. The Negroes knew that if the white servers got a chance they would give me some bad pieces of food; therefore, the Negroes made certain that every bit of food that was put on my line was the best.

It was always a heartbreaking sight to see the young Negro boys and girls who should have been in junior high or high school wiping the tables and carrying the trays for white students.

In the afternoon I would go to the Peabody Building for a math class. It was made up primarily of freshmen students and had a personality of its own. The instructor of the algebra class was a retired Navy Captain and a native Mississippian, but I never had any reason to believe that he would not be perfectly fair to me as a student in his class.

At three o'clock I had a two-hour biology laboratory class. We spent two hours peeking through microscopes at green leaves and frog blood. I had less interest in this than I had in Barnett's genealogical history, but it was required because the general science course I took at Jackson State College did not have any equivalent at the University of Mississippi.

After biology lab, I stopped by the library to read for a while and wait until time to eat supper. Five minutes before the dining hall was due to open, I left the library in order to get an early place in the cafeteria line. When I got in the line on the right as usual, a bumpy-faced antagonist of mine got in the other line opposite me. He was absolutely the foulest-mouthed individual that I have ever met, and that is saying a lot, considering the run-of-the-mill student at the University of Mississippi. As always, for the first few moments, he kept up a barrage of the nastiest curse words ever heard, calling me every manner of sons of a bitch, mother f—s, coconut-headed coons, baboons, and bastards. I would interrupt, "Now, Boy, you know you don't mean all of that, do you? You know you like me. Why can't we just be friends?" He answered, "Yeah, yeah. Let's be friends, Nigger. By the way, are you going to Jackson this weekend?" "Yes, I plan to go," I said. "Well, I'm goin' to ——, you ever go down on Farish Street [the main Negro street in Jackson]? Look, I'll meet you down on the low end of Farish Street, I got me a couple of nigger bitches down there. Man! Them whores sure got some good ones. Yeah! Come on down on the low end of Farish. . . . I'll turn you on to one of my nigger bitches." About this time the lines opened up, and I went to the right and he went to the left, still yakking.

### Visits Off Campus

My most regular visit off campus was to the barber shop in the heart of the Negro community. The barber was a very hard-working and progressive Negro, especially by Oxford standards. He had worked for over twenty years at the University of Mississippi, beginning there at the age of nine or ten. He lost his job shortly after the war, because he wanted his salary raised to ten dollars a week and, most of all, because he was "getting uppity." He related his experiences to me many times and considered the greatest thing that ever happened to him was his getting fired from the university. He had a wife and family and could not even provide them with food and shelter, let alone buy the land to build a home.

The real tragedy is that the average salary paid to the Negro workers at the university is still not more than ten dollars a week, years after he was fired for wanting a raise. Certainly the average Negro worker at the University of Mississippi today does not get paid enough to provide for the bare necessities of living. They make much less than the same workers at the Negro institutions in the state, because the university is firmly committed to "White Supremacy."

My barber had a tough life the first years after he was fired from the university. A barber-training program had been set up to train Negro ex-servicemen under the G.I. Bill, but since he had not been in the army, he was not eligible for the free training. It was a real struggle for his wife and him to dig up the two dollars each week for his fee; often it just could not be paid. In the end he passed the barber's state board examination and got his license.

He pointed out that now he had his own home, his own barber shop, a car, and was able to go on vacation now and then. He had sent his children through college and was thus able to give them a good start in life. He reported sadly that his old co-workers who had stayed on at the University of Mississippi had not even a roof that would keep the water from running through.

The marshals and I made the trip to his place many times. We would drive off campus, turn at the airport road, drive down past the Negro high school, and then turn right onto the dirt street flanked by unpainted sardine-shaped "shot-gun" structures that served as the homes of most of the Negroes in Oxford. There were just blank stares from the Negroes while we were driving down the paved streets of the "white folks." But from the moment we made that turn things changed. Little children ran along, shouting and waving. The old women sitting out in the yards and the worrying mothers standing in the doorways waved and spoke as I passed. Unfailingly, a crowd of old men and teen-agers would begin to grow in the barber shop. It seemed that all of the women would suddenly remember to come for a cold drink or a pack of cigarettes from the vending machines that the barber had in his shop. The marshals, with their radios going full blast, reporting back to their headquarters and to the Army command, could always expect a lively group of inquisitive observers.

*The Country People.* This note came from a friend.

April 29th 1963

Mr. James H. Meredith
My dear Mr. Meredith,
This is to say I am sorry. Not able to contact you by phone. MP's either Marshals.

Sincere & Well Wishes
Roger Thompson.

The fact that Mr. Thompson was unable to reach me through the military police or the marshals may not have been coincidental.

Roger Thompson had become a rather familiar face to the soldiers and the marshals; he was about sixty-five and lived near Oxford. He had worked around the university off and on most of his life. He was the first Negro to visit me on the campus and had made it his special mission to see that I was not lonely in spite of the many, many threats that were directed to him by the local system of "White Supremacy." The marshals dreaded his visits because I usually drove him the six miles to his home down those narrow, dark, back-country roads. His visits were almost always at night.

During the course of the year he took me all over the Oxford countryside, and I met almost every Negro family within ten miles of Oxford. Some were apprehensive, of course, but I had to literally break myself away in order to leave most of the country people.

*Dinner with Friends.* My first dinner invitation came from Ray and Sarah Kerciu. A teacher in the art department at the university, he had become well known for his true-to-life paintings of the scenes of the riots and other events connected with the Mississippi incident. I had not met Mr. Kercui before, although I had seen his wife several times. She was a secretary in one of the departments and had joined me two or three times in the cafeteria to have her morning coffee. We arrived at their flat in grand style—the campus police, the military, and, as always, the U.S. marshals and a Justice Department representative. There was no one in Oxford and few people in Mississippi who did not know that I was dining out with "white folks." I enjoyed the evening.

The next invitation came from a professor who lived in the town. He was a quiet man and devoutly religious; he belonged to one of those small firebrand denominations. I guess it was his religious devotion that gave him the courage to take this step. He had a very lovely family, one of the most charming that I have ever met. My retinue was about the same as before, except the campus police were relieved by the city police for this event.

The repercussions of this visit were great. Unlike the Kercius who had no children, the professor had four, ranging from about seven to thirteen years old. The oldest boy had to give up his Boy Scout activities which he loved so much, as a result of the dinner invitation. The most cruel act was directed at the youngest girl. As in most schools across the United States, the school children in Mississippi often exchange Christmas gifts. Every child's name is placed in a hat and each one draws a name. The name drawn is to be kept a secret, but is often revealed. The day before the holidays begin all gifts are placed under the Christmas tree. The little girls and boys find their Christmas presents and open them for all the others to see. The professor's daughter opened her package and found a black doll with a card attached that read, "NIGGER LOVER."

This was too much for the professor, and he was one of the many faculty members who looked for another job. He got his new job but there was another problem. He had been at the University of Mississippi for a long time, and since he had planned to make Mississippi his home, he owned the house in which he lived. He could not find a buyer for his home now that he was labeled. The problem was solved, however, when the rumor spread that he was planning to sell his house to me so I could bring my family to live with me in Oxford. The house was located in one of Oxford's most exclusive areas, and he not only got a buyer, but he also got his price.

These invitations were appreciated, all the more so when one really understands the nature of the truly segregated society in Mississippi. For me personally, however, the first invitation that I received to have dinner with a Negro family in Oxford was the high point of my stay in Oxford. This letter was dated January 26, 1963, nineteen days after my statement that I might not return for the second semester, four days after I had actually left the campus at the end of the first semester, seven days before I announced that I would return to the university, and ten days before I actually returned. Later, when I asked them about this, they assured me that: "We wotten worr'd. We know'd you wuz comin' back."

Oxford, Miss.
January 26, 1963

Dear Mr. Meredith.

My husband and I would appreciate your presence in our home. Please accept invitation at your convenience. We would like for you to have dinner with us. If you accept let us hear from you.

Yours truly,
Mr. and Mrs. ——

When I returned to the university to begin the second term, many thousands of letters from all over the world were waiting for me, and I could not possibly read most of them at that time. My usual practice was to go through the mail and pick out all the letters posted in Mississippi. My first impression was that this letter was a prank. The very address was suspicious; University Avenue is the most important street in Oxford and is the main entrance to the university.

I knew that no Negroes lived on this street between the downtown area and the university, unless they were in the servant quarters behind the big houses. I had received several letters from Mississippi whites who were trying to use the language of the Mississippi Negro, and these were easily detected, but this letter was too genuine to be one of those. The next time I went off campus I checked the house number and found that the address was on the other side of town, and one look at the house left no doubt that the occupants were indeed Negroes. I went back to the campus and answered their letter.

I stayed on campus one weekend especially to have dinner with them. We arrived about 12:30—myself with the marshals watching me, the local police watching the marshals, the soldiers watching the local police, and the Oxford rednecks watching the soldiers. Mrs. ——, a big two-hundred-pound woman of fifty-five, welcomed me; Mr. ——, a five-foot-five inches, one-hundred-fifteen-pound man of sixty-eight, invited me to "Make yourself at home! Sic as it is."

Their four-room house, very modest to say the least, was a tribute to the management skills of this couple who had never made enough money in one year to require the filing of an income tax form. The highest they had ever climbed up the labor ladder was to chop a little corn in the summer, pick a little cotton in the fall, cook and clean for the white folks, and do a little gardening.

They were completely relaxed and cared little about what the "white folks" thought about their having me for dinner. Mrs. —— had invited several people to come for dinner that Sunday, but she hadn't told any of them that I was coming. Of course, once the local authorities were notified, as they always were by the marshals, the whole town knew. All but two showed up on time for dinner. Mrs. —— really talked about the "scary" ones who didn't come. Later in the afternoon they stopped by for a fleeting moment, to give some excuse that she would not accept. (I suspect that she had sent word to them expressing her feelings.)

We had a first-class Negro southern-style dinner of hard fried chicken, chicken and dumplings, boiled chicken and baked duck, roast beef and fried lamb chops, barbequed ribs, sugar-cured ham, pickled pigs' feet, and meat (Negroes in Mississippi call pork, meat) accompanied by lettuce and tomatoes, black-eyed peas and pot liquor, turnip greens and candied yams, cabbage and collard greens, butter beans and English peas; with corn bread, hot biscuits and butter, and white bread (loaf bread); iced tea, lemonade, Kool-ade, cold water; a coconut cake, an apple pie, a sweet potato pie (my favorite), and also canned peaches and pears with ice cream. It was a good meal.

After eating all this food, we settled in the living room to talk. I remember Mr. —— telling how he had rejoiced to see the white rioters being marched along the street in front of his house, after being captured by the soldiers during the riot on September 30. He loved to recall the look on the faces of the "peckerwoods" with their hands folded across the top of their heads.

Mrs. ——, a jovial and outgoing person, could not let her husband monopolize the stage for very long. She told of her exploits with the white folks for whom she had worked and how many times she had told them to go to hell and walked off the job. She said she used to listen to them ranting and raving sometimes half a day, and she would act just like she didn't know they were in the world and go about her business as she was accustomed to do. They usually would give up and let her alone, but if they persisted until her "nerves run out," then she would ask: "Miss Mary! Is you talkin' to me? Well! I jest left." They always came back to beg her to return, because she was a good cook.

Then she got on the subject of Negro churches. I had attended the Oxford high-Baptist Church a few weeks before, and she said that she had joined that church several years before when she moved from the country into town. She had withdrawn her membership, however, because "them Negroes tried to be too biggity." She went back to her Baptist Church in the country every preaching day (once a month), where they "still had religion." She told how she liked to hear that good singing and praying, and preaching and shouting. Over at the church in town the people's "lips were so tight" that they couldn't even say "Amen."

## A Few Games of Golf

Ironically, I had learned to play golf at the age of fourteen or fifteen. For some typical Mississippi reason the Kosciusko Golf Course had adopted a rule at the outset which barred the use of white caddies. Even the use of a player's own son was discouraged. As a result, the forty cents for nine holes and seventy-five cents for eighteen holes was reserved for the Negro boys of the area. The caddies were permitted to play on the course on Sunday mornings as long as no white players were using the course.

The University of Mississippi has a good, rugged golf course. I had planned to use the golf course as my major recreation on the campus, but during the first semester I simply did not have the time. Dr. Jim Silver, remembering his promise to do something to make life more wholesome for me at the university during the second semester, asked me to play a game of golf with Dr. Russell Barrett and him. I had planned to go off campus, but I told him that I would come by his office after lunch if I didn't. I don't know if I really had a choice, because the security arrangements had been made for me to play golf. As soon as I returned from lunch and lay down for a short rest, the chief marshal came in to inquire if I had forgotten about my golf game. The Army command and the campus police wanted to know the exact program.

I put on my crepe-soled shoes, since I didn't have my golf equipment with me. Silver was waiting for me at his office. We walked the block to the clubhouse to meet Barrett and pay our green fees. The club manager was expecting me, of course, and was as friendly as one could imagine. I bought a couple of used balls, some tees, and a season's ticket, entitling me to unlimited play on the course for the complete school year. Barrett did not show up for some reason that I have never known. One of the university chaplains did join us for the round. I had never seen or heard of him before, nor have I seen or heard of him since. He was a very congenial person and I enjoyed playing with him.

The course was crowded with players, although it was very windy and cold. This could have been because it was Valentine's Day, but a part of the large crowd can definitely be credited to my being on the course. The campus police were out in full force. Eisenhower probably never had as many Secret Service men guarding his golf games as I had United States marshals watching me play my first game at the University of Mississippi. The Army was also out in force, including two helicopters which circled the field of play constantly.

The very first drive I hit sent a contingent of soldiers scurrying for safety in the graveyard of the Confederate soldiers killed a hundred years before. The ball was lost in the cemetery and I never found it. While looking for my ball, I noticed that there were no headstones, monuments, or other normal signs of a cemetery. I inquired about this strange appearance, and the story goes that a work detail of Negroes was ordered to clean up the graveyard and that was exactly what they did, without exceptions.

We moved slowly over the hilly course: the marshals tense and apprehensive, the chaplain appeared to be wondering how in the world he had ever got himself into this mess, and Silver's great question seemed to be whether he would live long enough to get out of it. I was really out of practice, since I had not played regularly for two years or more, but I was warming up as the game progressed.

When we reached the number 3 green, which is close to the road and directly in front of the veterans' apartments, there was a large crowd of spectators. The campus police and soldiers kept them across the street, but they didn't keep them from shouting and making remarks. My game suddenly improved. I was about one hundred and fifty yards out on what appeared to be my third shot (actually it was my fourth because I had completely missed one shot on the other side of the hill), with everybody watching the Negro play golf. Even some additional jeeps and trucks of soldiers appeared, many of them probably were off duty and just wanted to see. The main Army camp was very close to this hole. I swung and had no idea where the ball was going, but it headed straight for the flag and landed on the front edge of the green, stopping dead about twenty-five or thirty feet from the pin. Everything got quiet. The others approached the green and we readied for the putt. I hadn't come within two feet of the hole all day with a putt, and in addition I was using Silver's putter. I approached the ball, lined the putt up with professional-like care, gave it a hard tap, and watched. To my great surprise it went straight toward the hole, stopping only a half inch away. We waited a couple of minutes to see if it would drop, but it didn't. The hecklers were lost for words.

The number 4 tee was just as much in view of our audience. I teed up my ball for the demonstration shot. My first drive had gone into the cemetery, another had gone into the woods, one had dribbled off the tee in front of me, none had gone down the fairway all day. I used my old, but never understood by anyone, long-ball-hitting form from the days when I could hit a ball two hundred and fifty yards in the air, although I was only five feet and six inches tall and weighed one hundred and twenty pounds. It was a fast, long back-swing and a swift, hard downswing that resulted in both my feet rising off the ground. After reading a few golf books, I think it is a mystery that I ever hit the ball in the first place. Anyhow, I swung and it was straight down the middle and with a strong wind directly behind it; it turned out to be the longest ball that I ever hit on the

University of Mississippi golf course. I never came within fifty feet of the distance again on the same hole, and I saw few drives that ever went farther during the many rounds that I was to play later.

It took us more than two and a half hours to play seven holes. Silver appeared quite relieved and jumped at my suggestion that we go home at this time. I think he had had second thoughts about endeavoring to change Mississippi's social patterns in such an openly exposed arena. I played with Silver maybe two more times, but the initiative was all mine.

I didn't play again for over a month, but after I started to play in the spring, I played fairly regularly. The security measures varied slightly from game to game. The second time they used only one helicopter for air cover. And the first time they decided not to use the helicopter, the most fantastic security precautions were taken. Soldiers on foot completely surrounded the golf course. A most unusual scene to witness. But this was a fantastic period in human civilization. What was at issue? What was at stake? Whom were the soldiers guarding? What were they on guard against? Every answer that personalizes must be incomplete. The very life and existence of Western and Christian civilization was at stake. It is still at stake.

The man who became my regular playing partner seemed the most inappropriate possible. As far as I know, he had never lifted his voice in defense or defiance of anything. He was nervous and fearful. All he did was perform his duties as head of his department during the school year and spend every summer in a villa in France. Dr. —— just turned up one day and we played golf. Unlike the other vanguards at the university, such as Jim Silver, Russell Barrett, Wofford Smith, and the military commander Colonel ——, who played with me occasionally to fulfill some sort of obligation that they felt they had, the professor played with me because he liked the game. We didn't fight any wars, we just played golf.

There were many side incidents to my golfing experiences at the university. It was not unusual for my ball to disappear from the fairway when there were other players in the area. Occasionally, someone would hit a ball into our midst. The first time that I drove my own car to the clubhouse all four tires were flat when I returned. The club manager said, "I thought I heard a funny noise outside." It happened on three subsequent occasions. Strangely, they never cut the tires, but just removed the valve stem. A couple of fraternity houses overlooked the golf course, and the "selective" boys always kept up a barrage of shouts and curses. I am sure that they must have been responsible for the flat tires as well.

### The Students

People are always asking me the unthought-out question: Did any of the students ever make a gesture of friendship toward you? What do people think Mississippians are? They are human, too. Everywhere I have ever been I have had friends and friendship. The University of Mississippi was no exception. One might get the impression that I am defending the Mississippi whites by taking this position. But let me make it clear that my purpose is not to defend Mississippi, rather, it is to place all Americans in the same basic category with the Mississippians. It is only in this perspective that we can ever begin to comprehend the nature of the racial and social problems facing the United States today.

There was never a moment at the University of Mississippi that I did not have more friends than I could accommodate. Friendship is always expressed in relative terms. There are no exclusive acts, words, or deeds than can be used to judge the quantity any more than the quality of friendliness. A straight face when everyone else is sneering may be worth more than a pat on the back when everyone else is cheering.

The students showed their position in many ways, or perhaps I should say they showed it in practically every way. There were many, many students who visited my room in the evenings until the Rebel Underground started taking names and publishing the list. Whenever a student got up and moved as I sat down in the dining hall, other students would always fill the table around me, even though there were empty tables nearby. The classes, except the first- and second-year courses that I had to take, were generally congenial. Some students were talkative and friendly in each of my regular classes. Many spoke on the streets and sidewalks and probably more than they would normally. The second week that I was on the campus a pretty little freshman girl came up to me in the Student Union as I turned away from my mailbox and, with hundreds of dumbfounded rednecks looking on, said in the truest southern tones, "I am —— —— and I c–o–m–e from ar–kan–sas and I just wanted to tel–l y–o–u how proud we are to have you he–r–e." I was completely surprised, almost shocked.

*Student Letters.* I received many letters from students at the University of Mississippi. All that were signed were wholly favorable. They came intermittently throughout my entire stay at the school. A few examples will probably be the best introduction to their writers. This one is from a Mississippian whom I never met.

October 23, 1962

Dear Mr. Meredith,

Perhaps it is presumptuous of me to write to you like this but after all we are now both students of the UM.

Of course, I don't expect you to remember, but I spoke to you the last time I saw you on the way to the language lab. I guess you must have changed courses or lab periods now.

I have been busy with my studies since things have almost returned to normal on the campus. I haven't taken time to look for you and I seldom see you now unless it is in the cafeteria. I tried to telephone you Sunday night but the operator said that they had changed your number. I guess that some people have been giving you some insulting remarks by way of telephone.

I would appreciate your autograph or your letter if it isn't too much trouble. After all you are quite famous or infamous depending on one's point of view.

I wonder what courses you are taking. I am a premed student in the school of liberal arts. I transferred from Jones County Junior College in Ellisville, Mississippi, and this is my first year here too, even though I am a junior. Will see you around campus I hope.

Yours truly,
J.T. ——

The following letter is from one of my French literature classmates.

21 November 1962

Dear Mr. Meredith,

Some of your friends would like to have autographed copies of your article and your picture [in the *Saturday Evening Post*] which are enclosed.

I would like one to me personally and there is a line from Musset's "Lanuit de Mai" (pg. 120, line 148), "Rien ne nous rend sigr et gu'une grande douleur," which I would appreciate your including, or a substitute if you feel that too pretentious.

Please sign both the article and the photo.

I sincerely wish you good luck.

Charles ——

This letter which came near the end of the second semester is from a student whom I perhaps never saw at all during the entire year. Certainly, I wouldn't have known it if I had seen her.

May 6, 1963

Dear Mr. Meredith,

I would like to express my respect and admiration of your courage in doing a necessary but extremely difficult job—acquiring equal opportunities for Negroes in Mississippi. I know that I could never have stood up under the pressures you have been subjected to. Negroes should have equal job opportunities, equal educational opportunities, and equal rights under the law. To deny all men equal opportunities violates basic Christion and democratic beliefs that have made our country great, I feel. I have been troubled because I disagree with the majority of the students' views here, yet I am unwilling to take a stand that would lose me all my friends here.

But this summer I am going to be attending the University of Idaho summer school in Moscow, Idaho. I know I'll be asked lots of questions concerning you, the riots, student reactions, etc. And I wondered if there was anything special you would like to have conveyed to the students I meet up in Idaho? Anything you said would have much more influence than something I said as a personal view, I'm sure.

Best wishes to you and your family.

Sincerely,
Donna ——

The following letter is not from a student but from a university chaplain (Episcopal), a man who had exerted as much or more personal energy to effect a change in the attitude of the students as any one I know. The gift was a Bible.

August 11, 1963

Dear Mr. Meredith:

I had so hoped to be here to attend your graduation next Sunday. It has been a long, hard year for you, and I wanted to see the fruits of your travail. However, I must be in Washington all this week with church leaders to help influence the Civil Rights Legislation. We are to confer with administrators and legislators. I hope it will do some good. I am then going to New York to stay from the 25th to September 3rd except for the March on the 28th to Washington.

Please let me know how to keep in touch with you.

I was distressed to learn of your wife's illness. She has been much in our prayers.

Please accept the graduation gift as a sign of my esteem.

Yours faithfully,
Wofford Smith

It is important to note that my opponents at the University of Mississippi did not write me and that no well-grounded "White Supremacist" would ever write a Negro a letter of protest. He would never accord me or any other Negro such recognition: The management of the affairs of an inferior people is to him the exclusive responsibility of the superior race. Consequently, if a "White Supremacist" wanted to tell a Negro anything he would write to the "proper" white person, such as the Chancellor of the university, the Governor of the state, the Federal Judges, the Attorney General, or the President of the United States.

Only one identifiable white person in the South wrote a letter attacking me personally. She was Mrs. Gaillot, the excommunicated Catholic who sought to have the Pope dethroned. This letter was encouraging in many ways because it showed a weakening in the fortress of "White Supremacy." If such people gain the leadership of the system of "White Supremacy," it would be only a question of time before we could triumph victoriously over the system. It is not the radicals, ultra-reactionaries, and violence-prone whites that I am worried about. It is the calculating traditionalists, like the Russells of Georgia, the Eastlands and Coxes of Mississippi, the Longs of Louisiana, the McClellans of Arkansas, the Wallaces of Alabama, allied with certain religious and educational leaders of the South and North, that I am afraid of. Anyway, Mrs. Gaillot's letter speaks for itself.

New Orleans, La.
May 3, 1963

James Meredith
c/o University of Mississippi
University, Mississippi

The New Orleans States Item of this date stated "you know of nothing you have done to offend anyone."

I feel justified in telling you what you have done. You are the reason my son's registration was cancelled for the Fall Semester. You have "coveted your neighbor's goods." You have forced your way in this all white school.

You will never be accepted socially or equally by God's White Holy people who obey Him.

You asked if the Negro's opportunities should be limited to just a few areas. Indeed, they should. You can thank Satan for your being in America, because legally in God's law you belong in the continent of Africa on His property. Do you doubt that all the earth belongs to God? God said "Thou shalt not enter into the league with them (Negroes), nor with their Gods (Satan). Let them not dwell in their land. . . ." (Exod. 23 32). America in the beginning was given to the white men.

When will you learn that God said, "Every beast loveth it's like, so also every man that is nearest to himself. All flesh shall consort with the like to himself, and every man shall associate himself to his like. . . ." (Ecc us. 13 19).

The Ole Miss, God obeying students know that you are not of their like. In all honesty, if the President, the Attorney General, the Supreme Court, Pope John and Bishop Cody agree they are "like to itself" with you and your race, then help yourselves.

If you have any fear of Jesus Christ in you, then go back to your own people, and teach them that God loves them, and wants them, if, they obey Him and His Laws.

/s/ Mrs. B. J. Gaillot, Jr.

C.C. U.P.I.
    A.P.
    THE MISSISSIPPIAN
    SHREVEPORT JOURNAL
    STATES ITEM

*A Lecture Series Affair.* Unquestionably, the most profound and memorable expression of friendliness occurred at one of the Lecture Series sponsored by the university. This was slated to be the biggest affair of the year because the subject was "Communism." Of course, it was taken for granted that any lecturer approved by the ultra-right wing of Anti-Communists would speak on this topic. Since the turnout was expected to be so great that the usual place for lectures on campus would not be large enough, it had been decided to hold this lecture in the high school (white) auditorium which was just off the campus.

I arrived at the auditorium a little early and most of the seats were still empty. The marshals had already begun the practice of trying to be inconspicuous at these affairs. Since only a special clientele attended, most of the faces were familiar to the campus police and university authorities; strangers were easily recognized. The marshals took seats in front and back of me, but not on the same row. I sat in the middle row of seats in the center of the auditorium. The seats started to fill up in front and in back of me and to the sides, but no one sat in any of the six seats on either side of me on the same row. I guess by now all of the good-willers had made their gestures, because they took seats elsewhere. Some of the liberals even came to me later to apologize in a way for the abandonment.

Finally, one of the Navy Four Termers, who was also a political science classmate, came in with his wife. They hesitated for a moment, then cautiously took the two end seats, still leaving four seats between us which were never filled. The auditorium was full by now, and just as the chairman started to introduce the speaker, four students started down the aisle—two girls in front followed by two boys. They turned and entered my row. There were six vacant seats. The girl leading passed the first four seats and kept on walking. The chairman stalled his introduction, because no one looked at the stage at that moment. She took her seat next to me and the others next to her. I knew the two girls from a class I had with them. The other girl had spoken to me once or twice in the classroom, but the one that sat next to me had never spoken to me, although she may have nodded a greeting or smiled slightly when I passed her seat in class. She was one of the "Campus Beauties," who are selected each year, and to top it off she was from the heart of the Balck Belt in the Mississippi Delta. Even more remarkable, she was from the home town of James Eastland, our Senator from Mississippi.

When she was settled in her seat and before the audience stopped looking, she leaned over and whispered in my ear, "You know this took nerve, don't you!" I heard her clearly but it didn't register for some reason or other. I asked her what she had said, and she repeated it exactly, "You know this took nerve, don't you!" Nothing else was spoken that evening, and she never said another word to me although I saw her every day in class. It is impossible for me to capture the depth of feeling involved in her emotions. There is no question but that it was deep and profound.

## Visits by Friends and Relatives

I had many visitors during the second semester at the university. The ones I remember best were the visits by my father, my wife, one of my older sisters and her children, and my youngest sister. Each time we had dinner in the dining hall without any apparent trouble. I had taken them for a tour all around the campus. A professor who knew when they were coming for a visit had invited me to bring them by his house on the campus. I went by his house twice but it was locked up and the blinds were all closed. The professor had got cold feet and had taken his family off the campus.

About a month earlier James Allen, Jr., had visited me. He was the first Negro to join me for dinner at the dining hall on campus. He came to visit on March 23, which was also the day the spring football game was played. The game drew many visitors to the campus, and there was quite a commotion when we entered the cafeteria. The managers were rushing around like chickens with their heads cut off. All the Negro workers appeared from the kitchens and storerooms to get a cautious view of the scene. They gave me their signs of approval. The campus police acted as if they wanted to do something, but didn't know what. Several legislators and some members of the board of trustees were in the crowded cafeteria at the time. No official action was taken. The rednecks, however, beat on the tables with knives, forks, and plates, made all kinds of threats, and shouted obscenities, but they did not try anything more direct. We finished our meal and went back to Baxter Hall.

Another visitor was my cousin James C. Meredith, a Captain in the Air Force. He came and stayed three or four days with me on the campus, and he was the only one to spend the night in my apartment. His visit really upset the military command. They first asked him not to wear his uniform. Then they asked him to stay at the military camp. He understood the problems the Army faced, especially if something had happened to him, and tried in every way to cooperate, so long as it did not interfere with his visit with me.

While on the campus, he used my Volkswagen, and unaccustomed to driving one, he had some difficulty at first in getting it started. The marshals thought his conduct was superb when a large crowd of students, shouting insults at him, gathered around the car. When it started, he simply nodded and smiled politely at them.

## Meet the Press

To close the second semester and my first year's study at the University of Mississippi, I was privileged to be the guest of the radio and television program, MEET THE PRESS, on May 26, 1963. There were some sixteen million television viewers, which included President John F. Kennedy (when the program ended, the White House was on the telephone to congratulate me for "a fine performance"). In addition, there were millions of radio listeners both in America and around the world. Some parts of this thirty-minute interview follow:

MR. BROOKS: This is Ned Brooks, inviting you to MEET THE PRESS. Our guest today is James H. Meredith, the first Negro student ever knowingly admitted to a white university in Mississippi. His enrollment precipitated one of the nation's most serious domestic crises since the Civil War.

We will start the questions now with Lawrence E. Spivak, permanent member of the MEET THE PRESS panel.

MR. SPIVAK: Mr. Meredith, I am sure you expected difficulties when you enrolled at the University of Mississippi, but did you expect that the going was going to be as rough as it finally turned out to be?

. . . . . . . . . . . . . . . . . . . . . . . . .

MR. MEREDITH: From time to time, immediately preceding each event, it was quite evident to me that it would be as bad at is was.

MR. SPIVAK: Would you have enrolled if you had known in advance how much difficulty you were going to have?

MR. MEREDITH: Certainly. The point is not the difficulty. The most important point is that I feel that all citizens should be entitled to education that is offered by their states, and certainly this was the objective.

MR. SPIVAK: Now that you have finished your first year, what do you think you have accomplished there?

MR. MEREDITH: I have gone to school for a year, but I'd say the most important thing that has been accomplished by this whole endeavor has been to make this country and the world aware of the seriousness of the problem that exists in this country—the racial problem.

MR. SPIVAK: There have been conflicting reports on what you hoped to accomplish when you first enrolled. Are your hopes of what you would accomplish fulfilled? Have you accomplished everything that you hoped to accomplish, thus far?

MR. MEREDITH: Certainly I hope to see the day when all citizens, including Negroes, enjoy all of the benefits that this country has to offer. Certainly this is not the fact. But realistically, many things, I think, have been pointed up, and now it is up to the country and the people, to do something about it.

MR. SPIVAK: You wrote an article for "Look" earlier this year, and in it you said this, "I am convinced that you can pay a price for one piece of freedom that is greater than the benefits you get." There were two men killed at Oxford, hundreds were hurt, and the country has spent millions of dollars. Do you personally think it has been worth the cost?

MR. MEREDITH: I think it is very bad that men had to be hurt, and killed, but I think that the Negro, including me, certainly had nothing to do with anyone's getting killed.

MR. SPIVAK: No. I understand that, of course.

MR. MEREDITH: And change is always a very difficult thing. Certainly we should expect this to be rough, just as all changes.

MR. SPIVAK: You yourself at one time feared and many people say that they think your admission to the university under the circumstances has helped the advocates of white supremacy, rather than the other way around. What is your conclusion on that?

MR. MEREDITH: I certainly hope this is not the case. I still have great faith that this idea of white supremacy is going to lose its effect in this country, and I hope that anything I have done hasn't helped it. This hasn't been my aim.

MR. SPIVAK: One other question: I believe you applied for admission to the university shortly after President Kennedy was inaugurated. Was there any connection between the date of your application and the new Administration coming in?

MR. MEREDITH: Yes. I considered the election of the current President as being very important to the Negro and the problem, because the election of 1960 was the first time that the civil rights issue had been a major issue with both parties, and of course the Democrats had the stronger civil rights platform, and I felt that either the Administration would have to take great steps to correct this problem, or the consequences wouldn't be good.

MR. SPIVAK: Were you promised any support by the Administration in advance of your application?

MR. MEREDITH: Not before, but shortly after, when they found out about it. They showed concern all the way through.

MR. SPIVAK: Were you suggesting a minute ago that had the Republicans been elected, you might not have applied?

MR. MEREDITH: I think you can draw that conclusion.

. . . . . . . . . . . . . . . . . . . . . . . . .

MR. MEREDITH: I thought it was very important. I have felt for a long time that it was becoming essential for this country to eliminate the segregation laws and the discrimination laws from the official records or from the legal standpoint, because of the world situation. I think the Cold War situation—certainly the emergence of Africa has a great effect on this. I felt that it was essential that something be done, and I felt that the Democrats took the strongest stand and therefore would do more.

MR. MEREDITH: But hadn't you already had evidence that General Eisenhower had taken a long step in desegregating the Armed Forces and had also sent troops into Little Rock—so that you had reason, I would think, to believe that the Republicans would do as much, hadn't you?

MR. MEREDITH: I don't think so. Of course, I am a supporter of no particular party. I don't mean to imply that, but I felt at the time that we had a better chance with the Democrats.

MR. SITTON [The *New York Times*]: Mr. Meredith, President Kennedy is being urged to send troops to the University of Alabama before its scheduled desegregation next June. . . . Do you think he should send troops to the University of Alabama in view of the governor's pledge of defiance there?

MR. MEREDITH: I think that the Negro is entitled to go to that school, and if it is felt that this is necessary to insure their admission, I certainly think it should be done.

. . . . . . . . . . . . . . . . . . . . . .

MR. SITTON: Have you seen the President or the Attorney General, or do you plan to see them during your stay in Washington?

MR. MEREDITH: No, I have not seen them. I do not plan to.

MR. VAN DER LINDEN [*Nashville Banner*]: Mr. Meredith, apparently the President and his brother, the Attorney General, are being warned that the Negro demonstrations and riots in Birmingham and other Southern cities are likely to spread into the North unless something is done very soon about job discrimination and, in effect, segregation in schools because of housing.

The Attorney General met Friday with a group of Negroes in New York City..., and that has been reported in the newspapers as the scene of quite a violent argument in which the Negroes said the Attorney General was not doing enough to cope with this problem; there had to be some radical action in the North. Do you agree with that?

MR. MEREDITH: Basically I think enough is not being done.

MR. VAN DER LINDEN: What should they do?

MR. MEREDITH: In the first place, they should pass legislation that would give some real authority. This hasn't been done in the past at all.

MR. VAN DER LINDEN: What can be done by Executive Order? Can the President do more, say, in integrating housing or in getting more jobs?

MR. MEREDITH: I think that the basic need is for real strong legislation, and as I understand the Kennedys' policy, it has been to use the Executive Order in more administrative—

MR. VAN DER LINDEN: Do you think they will have to pass a real tough bill now—for admission to the restaurants as well as to the schools?

MR. MEREDITH: That would be to cover the area of civil rights and equal opportunity in jobs and housing and so forth.

MR. VAN DER LINDEN: You want the Kennedys both to put their personal pressure behind that drive?

MR. MEREDITH: I think the whole country should put its energy behind it.

MR. KAPLOW [NBC News]: Mr. Meredith, have you been in contact with the two Negroes who are planning to enroll at Alabama in the next couple of weeks?

MR. MEREDITH: No, I have not.

. . . . . . . . . . . . . . . . . . . . . .

MR. KAPLOW: If you did [talk to them], what advice would you give them?

MR. MEREDITH: I think that most Negroes are prepared for whatever is to come, and I don't think there is any particular advice that they need.

MR. KAPLOW: They are going into a situation that is apparently similar to your entrance to Ole Miss. Didn't you learn a few things which you feel might help them in going into what might probably be a difficult situation?

MR. MEREDITH: I don't think I learned anything new. You see, we have been living under this basic situation all of our lives, so every Negro is, I think, prepared to accept whatever is to come.

MR. KAPLOW: Have you detected any change in attitude to you or treatment of you at Ole Miss in the nine months you have been there?

MR. MEREDITH: It has changed from time to time. I would not say necessarily that it has become better. The students are still not free to associate with me or to take a position that they would want to, if they wanted to take one different from what is the normally accepted position.

MR. KAPLOW: Have you been able to tell whether there is anything appreciable that has happened to change the attitude in any way? A number of professors, I understand, have resigned or are planning to resign and presumably—

MR. MEREDITH: This is a good indication to me that there is not much that has really been done, because I know many are dissatisfied that there has not been any real effort made really to correct the situation.

MR. KAPLOW: Do you feel it is as bad, practically, as when you went in?

MR. MEREDITH: I think it is, and I think it will continue to be so long as this issue between the state and the federal government is unsolved.

. . . . . . . . . . . . . . . . . . . . . . . .

MR. SPIVAK: Would you recommend that other Negroes apply for admission to Mississippi in view of the experience you have had there?

MR. MEREDITH: I think that Negroes everywhere, including Mississippi, should be entitled to the education and training that is offered by the states if they want it and are qualified for it.

MR. SPIVAK: Do you think there is any possibility that other Negroes will be able to go to the University of Mississippi immediately after you leave, or while you are there, without soldiers and without marshals?

MR. MEREDITH: I don't think so. I would feel rather sure that they couldn't unless and until these issues are solved. . . .

MR. SPIVAK: Then really nothing has changed, despite your rough year?

MR. MEREDITH: Basically, I would say.

MR. SPIVAK: One of the reasons you yourself said you were going to the University of Mississippi was because you wanted to get an education. How much of an education were you able to get there this year?

MR. MEREDITH: I will tell you, I have learned an awful lot. I have learned a lot both in the classroom and perhaps more out of the classroom.

. . . . . . . . . . . . . . . . . . . . . . . .

MR. SITTON: Mr. Meredith, you have been quoted in the past as having said there is no one organization in the South or in the nation addressing itself to all of the Negro's programs. It this a criticism of the NAACP?

MR. MEREDITH: I don't have any particular criticism of any organization. But I think that there are some areas that are in serious need of attention.

MR. SITTON: Could you be more specific?

MR. MEREDITH: Yes, particularly in actually getting opportunities for the Negro, actually getting him prepared. For instance, in Chicago there are a number of medical schools, but there are fewer Negroes going to medical school now than there were in 1955. As a matter of fact, I understand that there are only twelve in the medical schools. I read in the paper when I was through there that there was only one more doctor in the city of Chicago than there was in 1938—one more Negro doctor. And this is, I feel, because of the lack of opportunity for the Negro to prepare himself for training. This is the area that I am most concerned with.

MR. VAN DER LINDEN: Mr. Meredith, I would like to read you, in brief, a news item which says, "The registration records in Hinds County— that is, Jackson, Mississippi—show that Meredith obtained a license tag for a Landeau style Thunderbird purchased from a dealer in Gary, Indiana, at a price of $4,495, and Meredith apparently left the car in Jackson for his wife's use." It says here that you confirmed that you had this new car. Could you tell us if that is a fact?

MR. MEREDITH: That is a fact, and my wife is getting the second thing she said she wanted when she married me. That is a college degree, and she will get that tomorrow.

MR. VAN DER LINDEN: Will you tell us how you managed to finance this on a college student's income?

MR. MEREDITH: I didn't know I had a college student's income.

MR. VAN DER LINDEN: Could you tell us what your income is from, I mean, is it from the newspapers, magazines, or what?

MR. MEREDITH: I have written two magazine articles, and I was paid for those articles.

MR. VAN DER LINDEN: I would say that your year at Oxford has been rather profitable. I judge you are starting a campaign now for a million dollar Meredith fund.

MR. MEREDITH: That is an education fund.

· · · · · · · · · · · · · · · · · · · · · · · ·

MR. VAN DER LINDEN: Could you tell us what that money will be used for?

MR. MEREDITH: Yes, it will be used basically for two purposes, to grant scholarships and loans to college students, but I am also equally or more concerned with high school students, finding high school students, say, at the ninth grade level and helping them to prepare themselves for college work. Most of our students have to work or they have to help support the family, and consequently, they don't get a chance to prepare themselves. All the time I have people tell me that they have scholarships, but they can't find any one to take them. No one is qualified, and this I would like to do something about.

. . . . . . . . . . . . . . . . . . . . . . . . .

MR. KAPLOW: Mr. Meredith, this money for the car, I don't understand. Was that money obtained from the sale of these articles, from the writing of these articles?

MR. MEREDITH: I would like to say that when I entered the University of Mississippi I had two cars, three farms and a lot of other things, and personally I don't consider it anyone's business where I get my money. I don't see where that has any relevance.

MR. KAPLOW: Mr. Meredith, you said a little while ago, basically nothing has changed at Ole Miss, but you learned a lot, both in and out of the classroom. I would like to know what you learned out of the classroom. I assume when you say "in," you mean the regular curriculum and study and so on?

MR. MEREDITH: Yes, I learned a great deal more about the depth of this problem. For instance, you always hear so much talk about the rednecks or poor whites being the real problem. The real problem is the power structure. The real problem is the system of law and the legal structure. This and the political system, this is the real problem in Mississippi.

MR. SPIVAK: Mr. Meredith, in the "Saturday Evening Post" article which you wrote, you said, "If I can't live in Mississippi, I very definitely intend to leave the country." Are you planning to settle in Mississippi when you get through with your schooling?

MR. MEREDITH: I, at this time, certainly do, but actually that statement had another meaning, and that meaning was that I should have the right to live there, as any other citizen, if I so choose. This is the thing that is important to me.

MR. SPIVAK: In your interview with the Washington Post yesterday, I believe it was—it appeared in today's paper—you suggested that you thought that Mississippi in 20 years would be a show place. Do you think that changes are going to come that fast in Mississippi?

MR. MEREDITH: I think so. Mississippi led the nation in creating this serious problem we have and putting the Negro in his place, so they call it, and it has the largest percentage of Negroes, the problem is most pressing, and I think it will be solved.

MR. SPIVAK: There is one question I'd like to ask you; I couldn't quite understand what you said about it at the time. When you decided to return to the university to begin another semester you made this statement: "I have concluded that the Negro should not return to the University of Mississippi. The prospects for him are too unpromising." But you also said, "I have decided that I, J. H. Meredith, will register for the second semester at the University of Mississippi." Would you explain what you meant by that?

MR. MEREDITH: Yes, it didn't do me much good. Every time I see my name now, it is "Negro James Meredith." But of course the meaning is that we should come to the point where an individual is not judged by his race. Before, in the first semester, it was extremely important that I was a Negro there, and I think the day should come when I should be a student there.

MR. KAPLOW: Mr. Meredith, what effect do you think your experience had on the overall desegregation issue?

MR. MEREDITH: It has proven one thing, that the 1954 Supreme Court decision was not completely adequate. It has to be reinforced.

MR. VAN DER LINDEN: Mr. Meredith, at the New York meeting I recently mentioned, James Baldwin, the author, says the Attorney General was asked to have his brother, the President, personally escort the two Negro applicants into the University of Alabama, and the report from Baldwin is that Bobby Kennedy just laughed. Do you think that is a funny idea, or is it a good idea?

MR. MEREDITH: I don't think this would be the proper thing for a President of the United States to do.

MB. SITTON: Mr. Meredith, in the past you have expressed an interest in politics. Do you plan to run for office when you complete your studies there at Ole Miss?

MR. MEREDITH: Where?

MR. SITTON: In Mississippi.

MR. MEREDITH: I don't think I could win. No one is registered to vote. I don't think it would do me much good to run.

MR. SITTON: How long do you think it will be before a Negro can run with a chance of success in Mississippi?

MR. MEREDITH: Unless there is some stronger action taken, it will be a long time.

# 12

\*

## Spring and Summer: June-August 1963

---

THE beginning of the first summer term found us back in court again before Judge Mize. The question to be decided was whether or not the University of Mississippi would have to provide accommodations for my family on campus. Clearly I was entitled to one of the many apartments available, but Mississippi wasn't giving an inch in any direction. The odds were heavily stacked against me on this issue, and even the Army commander had called to inform me that his headquarters had advised him that the Army could not protect my wife and child if they were to join me on the campus of the university.

The university just simply lost my request for housing. In early April I had checked on the status of my housing application:

April 11, 1963

OFFICE OF THE REGISTRAR
UNIVERSITY OF MISSISSIPPI
UNIVERSITY, MISSISSIPPI

Dear Sir:

I have applied for admission to both terms of the 1963 Summer School. Before the start of the 1962-63 school year I made a $25.00 deposit and a request for an apartment appropriate for my wife and one three-year-old child beginning with the first term of the 1963 Summer School. However, on April 10, 1963, I checked with the Director of Student

Housing and was informed that he had no request for an apartment from me and suggested that I write your office to check on its status.

Please advise. Thank you.

Sincerely,
J H MEREDITH

*The Compromise*

In court in early June the state of Mississippi pursued its usual evasive tactics, calculated to delay a decision, with the knowledge that time was its greatest ally. Judge Mize, in a little courtroom reminiscence during a recess period, expressed some of his personal feelings off the record. He couldn't understand why I had to push so hard. After recounting the history of my case, he said that he felt that I had "done all right and had gone a long way." He thought that I should be willing to concede something to Mississippi and its "White Supremacy" way of life. In a private sense, Judge Mize had always been a better person than I would normally have expected a white in Mississippi to be. He always shook hands whenever he met us and used appropriate courtesy titles. I thanked the Judge for his advice and expressed regret at having to meet him at this level and in an atmosphere of battle.

The Judge had set another case to be heard on the same day, because the same lawyers were arguing both cases. This was the Cleve McDowell case. McDowell had applied for and had been admitted to the Law School at the University of Mississippi, but the state of Mississippi would not permit his enrollment without an order from the federal court. A compromise was in order. The state or the court could have easily stalled to prevent his enrollment during the summer. However, it was thought that the summer was the best time for him to start, because the main part of the student body would be away and there was less chance of trouble. Here was a chance for all parties except me to come out looking good, and the result for me was that I would simply still be looking.

The Judge therefore ruled that McDowell should be enrolled, and no ruling was made in my case which meant that it would die with the passing of time. The Mississippi lawyers and the Attorney General were happy because they could not be accused of losing everything for their state; the NAACP Legal Defense Fund was happy because they had won an integration case at the graduate level of the University of Mississippi almost without a fight. All in all, the compromise was logical for the moment.

## A Roommate at the University of Mississippi

For some reason, or for the lack of a reason, McDowell was given the extra bed in my room. He had registered the day before I returned to the campus. They were very generous to McDowell and me in allocating us space. We were not only assigned to a dormitory by ourselves, but no other students were assigned to our end of the campus. It looked as if they were giving the Negro his half of the campus now, all we had to do in the future was to occupy it.

Cleve McDowell was a son of the Mississippi soil. He was from Drew, in the heart of the Black Belt; his father was a poor farmer. McDowell had been among the first group of highly capable Negro students picked from high schools around the state and put through a special program designed to "spoon feed" them through college in order to qualify them for further training after their undergraduate work was completed. McDowell had graduated from Jackson State College in three years with honors.

I had taken a keen interest in McDowell because of his obvious potential and acknowledged ambition. I was forever conscious of the possibility of my treading a dead-end path at the University of Mississippi, and I wanted to do everything possible to see that this did not happen.

The most urgent problem facing McDowell during the two terms that we were roommates was the question of his safety. Was he to be protected by the marshals and the soldiers, and if so, to what extent? I discussed the matter at length with John Doar of the Civil Rights Division and Chief U.S. Marshal Luke Moore. It was clear that the U.S. government did not want or plan to keep guards at the University of Mississippi after I left. I certainly agreed with the argument that the state and local authorities should protect the life and property of the citizens of their areas, but as long as these authorities refused to accept this responsibility, then it was the responsibility of the federal government.

I could understand McDowell's frustrations. When it became clear that he was not protected to the same extent that I was, McDowell requested permission to carry a gun. His petition was stimulated primarily by the harassments and intimidations that he suffered whenever he left the campus on weekends. One day during the second semester McDowell asked permission to use my phone to call Washington to talk to Chief U.S. Marshal McShane. I heard him talking at length about the gun on the phone. The young man wanted to live.*

## A Visit to Camp Meredith

*The Mississippian* (the campus newspaper) had tagged the post where the main body of soldiers was permanently stationed as "Camp Meredith." Colonel Lynch (how the names can creep in) was the last commander of the troops at Oxford. He was a fine soldier. Although I had met all the commanders and even played golf with one, I knew Colonel Lynch better and had more contact with him than with any of the others. He always came to inform me of any major changes in policy.

One day he invited me to come down to the camp, have dinner with him, and tour the area. The Colonel took me around the headquarters building. I saw the control board on which they had kept me pinpointed; they had always known my exact whereabouts during the entire period that I had been at the university. An identical board was in the Pentagon in Washington. He showed me the "hot lines" to the Attorney General's office and to the Pentagon. After pointing out all the nonclassified aspects of the headquarters, the Colonel turned me over to a Captain, who showed me around the grounds. The buildings at the site were as permanent as temporary can be. Officially, the camp was nonpermanent, and nothing was supposed to be tied to the ground. It is fantastic what the Army can do with sandbags and rope. Everything was spic and span and whitewashed. Even the toilet facilities were very modern. After showing

* As it turned out, McDowell was not given protection. He was subsequently expelled from the University of Mississippi shortly after the beginning of the fall semester in September 1963. Ironically, he was expelled for carrying a gun. He had been assigned a room in one of the men's dormitories. No other students were given rooms on his floor, and he was completely exposed to students and outsiders alike, because access to the building was free and open. Due to this fact and as a result of other harassments, McDowell had obtained a gun, just in case.

I suppose everything would have been all right if he had paid closer attention to the time. As I got the story from McDowell, he ordinarily kept the gun in his car. Once when he was late for class he had to park in a no-parking zone, and he was afraid to leave the gun in the car in case the police might search the car if they stopped to give him a parking ticket. So he stuck the gun in his coat pocket (typical Mississippi style) and hurried up the steps to his law class. In his haste, he stumbled and the gun fell out of his pocket. A couple of late classmates witnessed this misfortune and called the sheriff. The sheriff was dutifully awaiting McDowell's descent down the law school steps for the last time at the University of Mississippi.

me the physical plant, the Captain turned me over to a Negro Company Commander. He took me inside the barracks and introduced me to some of the troops. His Sergeant was also a Negro. The First Lieutenant showed me a new type of gun that had been issued to his men after they were assigned to duty at the University of Mississippi.

We joined the Colonel in the dining hall for dinner. The food was very good and plentiful. However, the most memorable thing about the meal was the attitude of the officers and soldiers toward me and their mission. They were extremely warm and friendly. As a veteran of nine years of military life, I can understand a soldier's displeasure with almost any assignment, certainly I could have understood a soldier's being unhappy with this mission, but there was no evidence of dissatisfaction. The Colonal bade me good-bye with the remark that the Army had just wanted me to see what precautions were being taken to insure that every citizen of the United States enjoyed his rights.

### The Death of Medgar Evers: June 12, 1963

The death of my friend Medgar Evers has had a most profound effect upon me both publicly and privately. Since I had been considered the most likely victim, it took time to absorb the reality of his death. A few minutes after he was shot, my wife and Robert Smith, Jr., telephoned the news to me from Jackson, even before it was known that he was dead. I went back to bed but I could not sleep. I didn't go to breakfast that morning because I had no desire to eat. The newsmen came to me after my first class and asked for a statement. I had nothing to say. They pressed me for a statement and I promised that I would prepare one.

Another vital consideration was the Army. I had already been advised that the Army was pulling out that very same day. I had been approached by the government and by the university, and asked not to criticize the withdrawal of the troops. On the other hand, some very important people at the university called on me to exert every effort to keep the soldiers on the campus. I felt it my duty to seek McDowell's opinion on this issue, because it was he who would be on the spot after I was gone. He thought that the troops should stay as long as the question of his safety was not settled. I gave great weight to McDowell's opinion in deciding what course I would take.

By mid-morning on the day that Medgar Evers was killed, I released a two-part statement on his death and the removal of the soldiers from the campus of the University of Mississippi. Many considered this statement to be the most bitter that I had ever made.

Early this morning, one of America's leading young men, Mr. Medgar Evers, was shot in the back under the cover of darkness, and killed. Without warning and without cause, he was murdered. A Negro's life is not worth the air it requires to keep it alive in Mississippi.

Medgar Evers was one of my best and most beloved friends. He served his county with the pledge of his life during World War II. For the next eighteen years he devoted his life to making America truly the land of the Free. We must not fail him now. We must continue to march toward his life's goal.

This system under which we live in Mississippi, and throughout the South, must be changed at any cost. Nothing is provided under this system for the Negro that is worth having. We can, we must, and we will change this system. The system of laws in this state must be changed. If I were charged with the responsibility of finding Medgar Evers' killer, I would look first and last among the ranks of the law officers of this state. The chances are at least 100 to 1 that the killer is to be found there.

I want to point out that if you hear anyone placing the blame on some insignificant person, extremist, or radical individual, he is just trying to deceive you and the public. The blame clearly rests with the governors of the Southern states and their defiant and provocative actions; it rests with the blind courts and prejudiced juries—it is known both by blacks and whites that no white man will be punished for any crime against a Negro, especially if it is in one of the controversial areas. Look at what happened to the guilty parties in the University of Mississippi riots. Nothing!

Second, and most important, the federal government has clearly demonstrated that it will be of no real help. All of this behind-the-scenes trickery is adding nothing but encouragement to the lawlessness of the White Supremacists. Governors Barnett of Mississippi and Wallace of Alabama have proven without a doubt that a white man can do anything he wishes to a Negro and go unhampered. If the federal government had taken a firm stand in Mississippi and Alabama, Medgar Evers would be alive today.

I, James H. Meredith, call for a general boycott of "everything possible" by "all" Negroes within the boundaries of the state of Mississippi. I want this noncooperation by Negroes with the system of "White Supremacy" to last until the system is changed.

Further, it is a basic human right and the guaranteed right and privilege of every American citizen, that a person be entitled to the protection of his life and property. Since it is an established fact that the Negro in Mississippi is not provided this protection generally by either the state government or by the federal government, it is imperative that Negroes unite together and protect themselves. I say to the Negroes that you should not unite for purposes of aggression. On the other hand, I say to you that we are obligated to unite to protect our persons and our property, and our loved ones.

May God bless this land with peace. But if we must die for what is right, then let us go like Medgar Evers in "Honor." Remember the words of Patrick Henry, "Give me liberty, or give me death."

Concerning the University of Mississippi situation, I seriously question the timing of the removal of troops from the campus for obvious political purposes. I certainly agree that troops should not be necessary to insure the safety of any citizen in this or any democratic nation. However, there is a serious federal-state conflict existing at the present time. The state of Mississippi recognizes no responsibility to protect or safeguard the lives or property of certain individuals—I was one of them—who are, according to Mississippi, in violation of its laws even though the federal laws maintain that these individuals are entitled to all these privileges, plus more. My belief is that the federal government has the responsibility to protect the lives and property of its citizens when the individual states fail to carry out their responsibilities. What is the point of keeping troops two miles away from the source of potential trouble? If they are needed at all, they are needed on the spot.

I should add that I believe the real heart of the problem is the lack of clear and effective legislation. Whereas the government may or may not be operating at its limits, nevertheless, if it did all that was possible under the present laws, it would still not be enough.


*The Aftereffects of Evers' Death.* The death of Medgar Evers caused more pain among the Negroes of Mississippi, especially in Jackson, than any event during my lifetime. Many persons broke down physically in the weeks that followed his death. I had long felt that too much burden was being placed on the shoulders of the Mississippi Negro in the total struggle for Negro freedom. I also had very serious doubts about the feasibility of the methods and tactics being used. I had talked to Evers many times and at length about these matters and I knew that he had serious reservations also. But he was a man who was dedicated to the cause of human freedom and he was a supporter of his organization. He supported it as eagerly when he differed with it as he did when he agreed with it.

The Negro had to move toward more realistic goals, especially the Mississippi Negro. I felt it my duty to prevent anyone from using him and to do all I could to prevent a needless and purposeless disaster. Many people from far and near were doing their best to agitate the Negroes into violent retaliation. The day after Evers was killed a white boy was shot while driving past one of the busiest Negro corners in Jackson. I worked hard to contact the right persons to keep my people in a sound state of mind. After working throughout the night, we decided to call on the older leadership of the Jackson community to plead for calm. Early in the morning we got the Reverend R.L.T. Smith, Sr., out of bed to apprise him of the developing situation and asked him to call a meeting of the leaders. He did this and they issued a public statement asking for calm and orderliness.

Nevertheless, I still viewed the tense situation in Jackson with grave apprehensions. Consequently, the day before the funeral, I issued a statement which called for self-restraint and offered an alternative to violence.

Two weeks ago I made my first public speech. I said then that we stood near the peak; today, if my judgment does not fail me, we stand at the crest of a clearly defined area in our struggle for equality of opportunity. I further stated that I did not feel heroic as many credit me, but that I did feel "responsible." Responsible to do all I can to liberate my people.

At this crucial moment, following the death of one of my best friends, one of America's greatest fighters for freedom and most trustworthy leaders, as well as the person perhaps most responsible for my admission to the University of Mississippi, I felt obligated to take my stand, to take the steps that my best judgment leads me to believe will most advance our cause.

First, I want to make it clear that I speak as an individual, as a scholar, as a student of history, politics, and social change. I do not pose as a leader of any group or school of thought, save those who coincidentally agree with me, nor do I pose as a spokesman for my race. But I speak as a citizen of Mississippi, the United States, and the world.

After carefully analyzing the total racial picture, I have concluded that we should begin a massive nationwide "passive resistance movement." This should begin with a "general strike." By strike I mean to refrain from doing any work for a specific period of time for the purpose of solitude or prayer. One hour should be observed to commence simultaneously with the memorial services for the death of Medgar Evers. It should be followed by a boycott, general or selective, or both, by all Negroes against the perpetuators of "White Supremacy" wherever they are to be found, North or South, East or West.

Why do I draw these conclusions and make these recommendations? The Negro is at his highest point relative to a "good-will" attitude by all concerned with the racial problem in this country. I believe the greatest need at the present time is for strong civil rights legislation. Equally important is the need to expose the legislators to the world. The only way to do this effectively is to step from the limelight and let it focus on the halls of the United States Congress. And at the same time let it focus on the legislatures of the fifty individual states, and the city councils of our many cities.

My greatest fear at the moment, as it has been for a long time, is the fear of the eruption of major racial violence. Don't misunderstand me, I do not fear death, because I am already dead. I only fear that I will not someday live. It has been apparent to me, however, that James Baldwin was very close to the truth when he quoted the biblical text, "No more water, fire next time." The Negro is not yet prepared for the fire. Certainly, we do not want to go to war and try to win our freedom, as President Kennedy said, "in the streets," before we give our legislators a last chance.

Further, this period of passive resistance will give the Negro a chance to prepare himself for the next phase. As a student of social change, I see clearly that we will not win this fight unless the Negro combines his resources and becomes more efficient. I see a definite need for a meeting of all Negro leaders and interest groups within six months for the purpose of coordination and to decide the direction of our movement, lest we defeat ourselves.

Our women and children must be pulled from the ranks of the streets. They must be removed from the possibility of public violence. Wherever violence is possible, it is the responsibility of the male to man that position. This does not mean that the women will not have just as important a role as ever. There is plenty for them to do in a passive resistance movement. What do you think would happen if all maids stayed home for one week? The whole economy would stop moving.

So, my brothers and sisters, I feel it my duty to say to you that we should immediately start a campaign of passive resistance to last for a period of at least six months, better still a year, and I feel it would be most effective if it lasted for eighteen months. This process alone will perhaps bring our enemy to his knees, and surely it will give our legislators a chance either to redress our grievances or to prove to the world that they will not. Second, and equally important, it will give us a chance to establish machinery that will be able to effectively deal with the situation if the government and legislatures fail to meet their responsibilities. We must make every effort to keep down incidents that will draw the limelight away from the Congress and the Government. Let us put them on the spot before the judgment of the world and God.

*The Funeral: June 15, 1963.* Millions in the United States joined to honor the memory of Medgar Evers. Thousands came from every section of our nation to be with the Evers family on this their saddest day. The family in its hour of crisis showed its character; it stood as a living symbol of courageous strength.

The public aspects of the funeral were under the management of the NAACP National Office, since as a Field Secretary of that organization, he had been a national officer. No doubt my greatest disappointment regarding the public aspects of the affair was that there was no place for me at the funeral.

Many comments were made that questioned the appropriateness of some of the speeches of eulogy. I will not pass judgment on them because I can clearly understand how one can lose himself in his feelings over such tragic events as Medgar Evers' death. At one point the audience became noticeably restless with the management of the funeral. The master of ceremonies was honoring the presence of dignitaries but had overlooked Martin Luther King, Jr., obviously not by accident, and the people continued to call his name. The master of ceremonies then held a quick conference on the stage and it was decided to acknowledge King's presence.

After the funeral, a procession was formed to march the two miles to the funeral home in the heart of downtown Jackson.

*The Rear Guard Turns on the City.* Those elements bent on creating incidents that would lead to a useless flow of Negro blood had not given up their evil designs. The Negro leaders of Jackson had made a solemn agreement with the city authorities that there would be no public demonstration connected with the funeral of Medgar Evers. Whether or not this was a wise agreement does not concern me in this instance. The important thing is that there was an agreement. All agreements should be honored or changed if they cannot be kept. The question of the integrity and effectiveness of leadership is vital when an agreement either will not or cannot be honored. Leadership cannot be a one-way affair. Either leadership extends in every direction and pervades throughout or it is not leadership. It cannot be positive or negative; it must be both at the same time.

The strife specialists succeeded in maneuvering a large segment of the rear guard, turned it around, and marched on the city. This move was inexcusable. They did not get far before they were met by the police who formed a solid human wall, three-men deep and fully armed. I shall never forget this scene of folly. These disenchanted and misled Negroes, throwing Coke bottles pointblank into the ranks of inhuman white thugs passing as law officers, charged the heavily armed policemen who had drawn their weapons. At the least, the battle should have come from a position of cover. A clear distinction must be made between bravery and foolhardiness.

*John Doar Acts.* There is probably nothing more ineffective than a leaderless mass. The Negro leaders made vain attempts to disperse the crowd but were themselves set upon. At this point, John Doar of the Justice Department, perhaps the white man with whom I had spent more time than any other, stepped between the police guns and the Negro rocks and restored order in an act of bravery and judgment seldom matched in human history. The personal courage of John Doar deserves great tribute. But the incident represented the total failure of the Negro leadership.

Perhaps the biggest irony of all regarding the death of Medgar Evers was made known to me when the accused slayer was arrested; he had supposedly had an earlier mission to kill me at the university. This had been reported to the F.B.I. and an investigation of the allegation had been made before Evers was killed.

Medgar Evers' position was immediately filled by his brother Charles. I wrote to him to express my satisfaction at his accepting this very great responsibility and my confidence in his judgment and ability.

### Negro Students at the University of Alabama

The summer moved on. The biggest events in the civil rights struggle were now taking place in Alabama where James Hood and Vivian Malone were enrolled during the summer over the defiant opposition of Governor George Wallace. I was most impressed by the courage and character of the two students, especially with Miss Malone. Her picture appeared on the cover of a national magazine and I wrote to commend her for her efforts.

### The NAACP Convention in Chicago

The fifty-fourth annual convention of the NAACP in Chicago was probably the stormiest in its history. The events of 1962 and

1963 clearly pointed to a crisis in the Negro's struggle for civil rights. The question of the proper method to use in the fight was causing great stress and strain both within the different groups and among them. Within the NAACP were strong forces who held differing views on the question of tactics. Those who believed in the legal and more restrained type of protest demonstration opposed those who advocated the so-called nonviolent direct-action-type demonstration which was calculated either to end favorably or in civil disorder. The shock of Medgar Evers' death, just three weeks before, still plagued the conscience of the nation. All of this made itself apparent throughout the convention.

The sessions were stormy, delegations were walking out, and the youth were marching on the board as it met. The day before I was to speak, Mayor Richard J. Daley of Chicago was booed off the platform and not allowed to speak. No clear reason for this was apparent. On the same day, the Reverend J.H. Jackson, president of the National Baptist Convention, the largest Negro organization in the world, met the same fate as Mayor Daley. Although Reverend Jackson persisted, he was not allowed to deliver his speech. Again, no reasonable explanation or justification could be found for this treatment of a sincere and dedicated Negro leader. Discontent was in the air.

*My Chicago Speech.* I had only expected to make a few remarks at the Youth Freedom Fund banquet to which I had been invited. A few days before I was to speak, however, I received a letter from the NAACP National Office requesting a copy of the text of the speech that I would deliver on July 5 at the Morrison Hotel in Chicago. I called them to talk about the situation, and they insisted on a speech. In order to comply with their request, I wrote it out by hand and typed it myself, just in time to give a copy to McDowell, who personally delivered it to the NAACP officials in Chicago.

After completing my final examinations on July 5, I left the campus immediately for Memphis to catch a flight that would get me to Chicago one hour before I was to speak. When I arrived, only my wife and James Allen, Jr., met me. I thought it was rather unusual not to be met by anyone from the youth group. Arriving at the banquet hall just a few minutes before I was supposed to speak, I expected to be greeted by some officials there, but no one did. I was led onto the platform to my seat on the left side of the dais. It appeared very odd to me that not one of the seats on my side was occupied. When I was introduced to the presiding officer and offered my hand, he refused to shake it. And when the man who introduced me to the audience spoke only a one-sentence statement, saying that he had no introduction, there was no further doubt in my mind that something unpleasant was going on.

As I arose to give my speech, only about one third of the audience arose in courtesy. The others just sat there in dead silence, not even clapping. Some of those sitting were people that I knew. This was not a very pleasant situation, but these were our youth and they can be forgiven for any act that they commit, as far as I am concerned. It was widely reported that they booed me and interfered with the normal delivery of my speech. I can say categorically that these reports are absolutely untrue. As a matter of fact, by the time I was half way through the speech most of the audience had begun to respond. And at one point near the end, the entire audience was warmly responsive. Certainly my speech was given the most complete coverage and review of any that I have made.

(Appropriate greetings and recognitions.)
Thank you, NAACP National Youth Work Committee, for inviting me to be your guest speaker for this 1963 NAACP National Convention Youth Freedom Banquet. It is my hope now that I can prove to the youth council, college chapter delegates from 48 of our states and to the regular delegates from 49 states that I am worthy of your selection.

When I first talked to Dr. Morsell about this affair, I agreed only to attend, but not to speak. I had an unquestionably sound excuse. I was in summer school and carrying the heaviest load that I had ever carried before in any school, trying to complete my requirements for graduation by the end of the summer. All this is quite true, but there was one outstanding reason that I did not give then that I shall acknowledge now. The letter inviting me to be the guest speaker also stated that the theme of the convention was "Emancipation's Unfinished Business." I had made a private vow a long time ago that I would not participate in any event celebrating the Emancipation Proclamation. Of all the things that have occurred affecting the Negro in the United States, I consider the issuance of the Emancipation Proclamation to be the most detrimental and far-reaching in its effects.

I want to quote to you in full the meaning given in Webster's Dictionary, the foremost authority in the use of the English language, for Emancipation Proclamation: "A Proclamation issued by President Lincoln in September, 1862, effective January 1, 1863, freeing the slaves in all territory not under Union control." In a modern context this would be about equivalent to the President of the Republic of

China (Taiwan) issuing a document freeing all the peasants on the Chinese mainland.

The only thing the Proclamation really did was to give the Union an excuse for not freeing the Negro once they had conquered the South and actually had the power to free and reestablish the Negro. To my knowledge, the American Negro slaves are the only group of human beings ever granted freedom without some provisions being made for their reestablishment and continued livelihood. Instead of resettlement for the Negro, when the Civil War ended, four and a half million Negroes were left unattached, with nothing, no land, and nowhere to go except back to their former slave masters. Consequently, a human social system was created worse than any form of slavery. At least in slavery everyone had a place. The freed Negro had no place. If you don't believe me, just ask yourself frankly, "Where is my place?" Oh, I know you are going to say, "It is right along with all other Americans." But is it? No! Okay, that's all I am going to say on that subject. I am not going to try to prove anything here tonight. I have no theme, no point to make, and as a matter of fact, I don't even have a subject. My purpose here tonight is to provoke.

I want to provoke you into removing the greatest dissatisfaction that I have with the whole movement to eliminate the racial problem in this country. My greatest dissatisfaction today is with the very low quality of leadership present among our young Negroes and the childish nature of their activities. Students all around the world are waking up. Now is your turn.

So let us move on along our road of provocation. Have you heard the song, "Only Believe"? "All things are possible, if you only believe." Many times I have listened to my people sing this song. Last Sunday I heard it again. Only believe. But this time it had a new meaning for me. Because on that day I was to hear a small-time preacher, in a small church, in a small town in Mississippi, tell his congregation, consisting mostly of young children, that he would rather see his blood flowing in the streets than to stop his activities aimed at uplifting the young people and making a better life for them. Yes, he had been visited earlier by the white power structure and warned that either he would change his ways or else "something bad" would happen to him. "Only believe, all things are possible, if you only believe."

In twenty years Mississippi is going to be the Negro show place of the world and the United States of America is going to be truly the land of the free and the home of the brave. This is not going to be so merely because I say that it will be so. It will be so because, and only because, you accept the challenge before you. Not only is it a challenge to you ... here tonight, it is an opportunity for you to serve the cause of the advancement of mankind. Yes, and above all else, it is an obligation that you must meet.

Regretfully, I must admit that I am most sadly struck by the ineffectiveness of our Negro youth leaders. It must be acknowledged, however, that this is due largely to the interference in and intrusion on youth activities by "so-called" adult youth leaders, who seek to conduct and direct student activities instead of playing their proper role of advising and supervising these activities. As a matter of fact, I am firmly convinced that our youth of today are fully capable of plotting their own destinies and I intend to do my best to see that their unwitting adult progress blockers are pushed aside so that they can move forward.

The two great shortcomings of our youth are discipline and knowledge. There is that quality about knowledge that makes for discipline, and that quality about discipline that makes for effectiveness. I can't help but recall the Tokyo demonstrations. Three years ago the President of the United States planned a trip to Japan. The student government associations wanted to prevent the President's visit and, by doing this, to weaken the ruling Japanese government and cause it to be replaced. They called out over a million student demonstrators. I was in downtown Tokyo on that day and saw with my own eyes the largest demonstration the world had ever seen. And as far as the eye could see, I saw complete order and discipline. Every student had a leader; every leader knew who his followers were and every follower knew who his leader was. There was something magical about this order and discipline. The bystanders and onlookers did not pile in and make a mob. No, they were captivated by a frame of mind the like of which I had never seen before, nor afterwards. And the students were successful. Not only did the Prime Minister have to ask President Eisenhower not to visit the country, but he had to give up his position.

All societies grant to their student populations some special privileges and immunities. Students somehow have a right to engage in unusual and experimental activities not condoned for any other segment of the population, and consequently when nonstudent elements join their groups, the students themselves lose their special privileges.

Now, let us turn to one of the biggest fallacies hindering the progress of the Negro. It is the idea that age necessarily brings with it knowledge and wisdom. I can think of many instances where the parents work their skin to the bone to send Billy and Sue through school to learn the latest methods of efficient living, and Billy and Sue finish school and let Mamma and Papa continue to live the rest of their lives without the benefit of the new methods of hygiene or the techniques of economizing, simply because they are older than "we" are and "we can't tell them anything."

Further, there is not much to this business about maturing judgment either. We all know that George Washington led colonial forces in the French and Indian War at a very early age. At twenty-five, Alexander the Great had conquered the world; at the same age Booker T. Washington had founded Tuskegee Institute; at thirty, Napoleon was master of all of Europe; at the same age the President's brother is in the United States Senate.

You know the Negro youth has that "yeah, maybe, but not me" attitude. Anyone of you out there could be the owner or manager of a large department store, president of a corporation, or even mayor of the city of Chicago. "Only believe, all things are possible, if you only believe." But let us not kid ourselves, we not only have to believe, we've got to know something, too.

For the first time since I've been at the University of Mississippi, I am going to voluntarily speak on the subject of money. You all have heard of my wife's new Thunderbird, haven't you? Well, I did a little checking around and I found that millions of new cars are sold every year in this country, and I've looked high and low and I have not found a single soul that I felt deserves one of these new cars more than my wife, who has stuck with me throughout my entire ordeal.

Maybe I should emphasize the importance of what I am about to say for the next few minutes. It may sound as though I'm bragging or it may just seem so simple that you will take it lightly. Negroes have a tendency to think that everything that is significant must be very complicated. The most efficient and effective way of doing things is usually, if not always, the simplest. I can readily say that I have never done anything in my life that was hard for me to do, and I can definitely assure you that I do not intend to start now.

I learned my management techniques from the best teacher of them all, my father. He was the first in my family to ever own a piece of land. He is a man that never earned enough money in a year's time to require the filing of an income tax form. Yet he is the same man to whom all members of the community turned when in need, always to be helped.

Back in 1958, long before many of you ever heard of the University of Mississippi, my rating officer in the Air Force wrote in his evaluation report that "Sergeant Meredith is the most financially responsible individual I have ever known." That same year, at the age of twenty-five, I completed my seventh year of military service. My pay was then $180 a month, the highest that I had ever received, yet, up to that time I had bought and paid for two cars and one truck, two farms and the house in which I was living. Literally, I could account for at least nine out of every ten dollars that I had ever made.

Do you think I am bragging? Well, I am not. I am teaching and in ten years I want every Negro in America to be bragging because he has a home, clothes, a car, and money in the bank. And if you think that I have been talking simple, just wait until you hear the system used to economize.

Let us start with the little money first. Hair oil: a small bottle costs 50¢, a large bottle with ten times the amount, $2.50; savings, $2.00.

Cigarettes: I don't smoke, so I save the whole amount, but let's get to you. One pack 35¢, one carton $2.75; savings 75¢. Count this up for a year's time and you have a pretty good amount of money. Clothing: the last suit I bought was a nice summer suit for $23.50 from one of "them cheap stores" that my broke high-class Negro friends would not be caught in. This same suit, including the color, was purchased by one of my friends from the exclusive men's shop with the credit charge plate on sale for $49.95. The two suits were cut from the same cloth, sewed on the same machine, and distributed by the same wholesale agency. There are few items on which I could not make a similar comparison.

For the Negro, the area in which the really big savings opportunities exist and in which the greatest inefficiency is found is in buying automobiles and furniture. I can say without any doubts in my mind that for each $1,000 spent by the average Negro buyer, I could save a minimum of $300. How do you do it? First, since very few Negroes can pay cash for items in this category, you have to establish a good credit rating. This is a must, especially for the man, and should be done at least by age twenty-one. The first time you get a job, open a bank account. If you cannot save more than one dollar a week, put that dollar in every week. What you are really trying to do is impress the banker. Because one day when you are going to want a loan, the bank is the best possible source of loans for a poor man. When you apply for a loan, the first thing the banker will do is check your savings record to see how regular you are.

Next, in building a good credit rating, buy something on credit, even if you have the cash to pay immediately. For example, your parents give you $50 to buy a suit. Buy the suit on a ninety-day-option plan. You buy on credit with an agreement that, if you pay the balance in ninety days, there will be no interest charge. You pay $20 down, put the remaining $30 in the bank, draw it out $10 each month, and make your payments to your creditor on time. At the end of a ninety-day period you will have a credit rating of "A", plus the reputation and prestige of doing business with a bank. You will then have a file with the credit bureau, your credit reference can be checked, and you can get credit anywhere in the United States. And all this did not cost you one dime. I should add that it is better to have at least three credit references.

Second, in buying big items bargaining and making the best deal is important. Always make the seller bid for your business. For example, you want to buy a new refrigerator. Go and talk to all the dealers, let them process the papers and make checks on your credit rating. Let them know clearly that you are going to buy from the seller with the best deal. After they check your record and find it good, I guarantee you that the prices will begin to fall. My ground rule is that "I never buy when I'm shopping." If it costs $100 or more, I bargain for at least two weeks; if it's $500 or more, I bargain for at least four weeks; if it's

$1,000 or more, I stop bargaining and start negotiating, which must last for at least six weeks or longer.

Brothers and sisters, this might sound childish to you. I hope not. I have never been more serious in my life. The procedures, methods, and techniques that I have described to you are not dreams or fancy ideas. These have all been tried by me and worked. I think they will work for you. Life is simple, not complicated.

(Joke about the Arab and the 17 camels.)

Now, we move to the question of the day. How to best accomplish our objective—full citizenship. I feel a duty to my country and a responsibility to my people to express my position on this vital subject. I intend to criticize no person or no group, instead I simply want to tell you how I think I can best use my energy to accomplish our goal. I think the greatest result will be realized by using my energy to advance the Negro community in the political and economic areas. My chief weapon will be educational development and training for the great mass of our Negro population.

What about the great controversial issue of a march on Washington, D.C.? My basic position is that I support any action on the part of an oppressed group to indicate its dissatisfaction or to secure redress of its grievances. Concerning the proposed march on Washington, I will say that in my opinion the march would not be in the best interests of our cause. I want it clearly understood that I have not opposed the march, instead I have expressed an individual opinion. Further, I think that this issue is primarily a political one and that the advice of the Negro politicians should be sought and their recommendations should be given due consideration. By Negro politicians, I mean the five Negro Representatives in the United States Congress, the Negro legislators in the various states, and the Negroes in high government positions, plus the leading Negro politicians both in and out of power—Republicans and Democrats.

No matter how many times the Barnetts and the Wallaces may claim that the federal government is usurping the powers of the states and centralizing it in Washington, the fact still remains that the United States has a federal government and not a unitary government. The members of Congress do not represent Washington; they represent the individual states of the Union and the individual Congressional districts within the states. "The truth shall make us free."

In conclusion, I want to say to you here tonight that I do believe. Above all things, I do believe that this world can be made into a better place in which to live. I do believe that the Negro has a destiny to be the leading spark in saving this world and advancing the cause of human civilization. Further, I am confident that we will develop the racial pride, community pride, and family pride necessary to accomplish our mission. From this year forward, let us judge our peers. Let us draw a line on our heritage in 1963 and mark it with pride. In my eyes, the most illegitimate of the illegitimate Negroes deserves the right to recognition equal to the bluest of the blue of the black bluebloods.

Thank you, NAACP youths. The future belongs to young America.


*The Speech of Rebuttal.* Immediately after I finished my speech, a clergyman came to take me to the adult session to make some remarks. I later discovered that one of the officials of the Youth Banquet delivered a rebuttal speech that had been prepared in advance. This seemed to me to have been a breach of ethics. The most serious aspect was the fact that none of the allegations which the speaker was rebutting was actually in my speech. And polls were supposedly taken of the reaction of the audience to my speech, and they showed an overwhelming disapproval. At the time I did not know about these developments, of course. When I returned to the hall many people began to apologize to me for the conduct of the group and the newsmen asked all kinds of questions.

When I began to really get the picture of what had taken place, I was deeply hurt. There was no rest or peace during the night. Early the next morning someone knocked at my door. It was a young lady who identified herself as the president of a youth chapter in Tennessee. She had taken part in the plots and was very disturbed by her conduct. In tears, she told me all about how my name had been deliberately misspelled on the signs announcing my speech; how they had planned to embarrass me by not standing or clapping and how much it had hurt her to sit in her seat and play her role when she wanted so badly to express her real feelings; she told me how the polls had been predistributed to key people to insure that the results would be prompt and as desired. I must admit that I was very impressed with the ability of the youth to carry out such a scheme. If such efficiency is maintained in their fight against the evils of inequality, then we will surely win. The young lady also told me of the adult (National Officers of the NAACP) participation in this plot. This was confirmed by others who were present at the time. I was very unhappy to learn that the nation's top Negro leaders would go to this extent to eliminate someone with whom they differed.

I left that big-shot hotel and went down to the South Side of Chicago to find my people. That evening I was scheduled to appear on a television program but I had no desire to do so. Instead, I went to Gary, Indiana, to a Jimmy Reed Dance. Jimmy Reed is one of the greatest musicians of our time. He may never reach the greatest heights during his day, but history will record his song stories of the problems, hopes, fears, joys, and troubles of the Negro people, especially in their historic move from the rural areas of the South into the big cities of the North. Once again, I had to go back to the great mass of the common people of my race to gain the strength I needed to continue my fight against the evils of the system of "White Supremacy."

After I returned to the University of Mississippi and registered for my last term, I wrote to the president and to the chairman of the board of the NAACP regarding this matter:

July 17, 1963

Mr. Arthur B. Spingarn, President
NATIONAL ASSOCIATION FOR THE ADVANCEMENT OF COLORED PEOPLE
NEW YORK, NEW YORK

Dear Sir:

It is with much regret that I write this letter to you. However, you are the individual that I felt might be able to prevent further conflict. After weighing all data before me, and talking with many persons at every stage, I am firmly convinced that I was seriously wronged on July 5, 1963, in Chicago.

Most of the nation believes that I was upset over being criticized. I was disturbed upon discovering a well-planned plot calculated to discredit me before the eyes of the nation and my people. The events that occurred on Friday night were organized from start to finish. I hope I never have to, but I can prove it beyond doubt. Further, it was not engineered solely by the youth.

I believe that you will find that all the alleged major crimes committed by me against my people are, in fact, fabrications. Nowhere in anything that I have said or written—which is all a matter of public record—will you find anything to sustain them. In addition, even if it were so of the speech in Chicago, the speech was in the hands of the NAACP well in advance, yet no member of the NAACP, youth or adult, expressed any disagreement to me prior to delivery. Instead, they deliberately set me up to dishonor me after inviting me to be their guest speaker. This sort of behavior, I feel, is unbecoming to an organization of the stature of the NAACP.

I was not sure that you and the Board were apprised of the nature of this event.

Thank you.

Sincerely yours,
J H MEREDITH

cc Bishop Stephen Gill Spottswood

*The Campaign for Governor in Mississippi*

The campaign for governor had picked up momentum as the summer grew hotter. The Democratic primary election, which is in fact the election itself in Mississippi, was set for the first week in August. The real contest in the election was between Barnett's Lieutenant Governor, Paul B. Johnson, and former Governor James P. Coleman. The contest followed the usual Mississippi pattern of name-calling and emotionalism. There is no issue in state politics save the racial issue. The question is not which of the two candidates is a racist and which is not, but, rather, which one is the most dedicated racist.

Coleman was regarded as a kind of Mississippi moderate because he had let President Kennedy sleep in the notorious Bilbo's bed while on a one-night visit to the state as a Senator during Coleman's term as governor, and because he would talk to the Negroes while they were being framed in the background. Paul Johnson's best qualifications were the fact that he had run for governor several times before and lost and that he had stood in for Barnett once at the University of Mississippi to block my enrollment.

Both men ran on their records as arch-segregationists. Johnson's main campaign gimmick was a picture of himself standing in front of McShane and me with his fist balled up. The caption below read, "Paul stood up for you!" This picture was pasted on billboards all around the state.

Coleman talked constantly about his keeping "White Supremacy" reigning supreme during his four years in office (1956-60). He bragged about how Clennon King had been handled in 1957 at the University of Mississippi by his being committed to the insane asylum; how in 1959 Clyde Kennard had been handled: he was framed and sentenced to a term in the Mississippi penitentiary. Coleman repeated over and over to his audience that "I know how to handle niggers."

One of the professors at the university, a firm supporter of and diligent worker for Coleman, asserted bluntly to me that, if Coleman had been governor when I was trying to enter the University of Mississippi, I would have been killed before I would have been permitted to enroll. I listened to Coleman's speeches and read carefully his statements, and I am convinced that he would have been the most dangerous enemy that the Negro could ever have in the governor's mansion.

There were those who championed the cause of Coleman's election. I was approached by two groups in his behalf. The first one was connected with the university and wanted me to make some statement that would hurt Johnson's campaign. The other was the federal government which was working to help Coleman get elected. Even the removal of the troops from the University of Mississippi had been timed to affect the election.

The candidates were coming to Oxford to stage big rallies for their campaigns. I stayed carefully away from Johnson's rally, but announced that I would attend Coleman's rally. For the only time during our long association the federal government then asked me not to commit a specific act. It requested that I not go to Coleman's rally because it would hurt his chances of winning.

On the day of the rally I waited until Coleman had started to speak before I left the campus. I drove around the town square where the rally was being held. For just a moment I stopped in the center of the street where parking spaces were marked off and then drove back to the campus. I was not gone from my room more than ten minutes but this visit to Coleman's rally became a major issue throughout the remainder of the campaign. Affidavits were obtained from the officials at Oxford and published, counter-affidavits were obtained and published, and charges were leveled by the different parties as to whether or not I attended the rally. Coleman lost the election.

## The Last Days at the University

One week before I was scheduled to graduate from the University of Mississippi I made the following statements in an interview which probably will express my feelings at the time better than I can recall them now.

Graduation Set     August 18

IT'S FAIRLY QUIET NOW, BUT JAMES MEREDITH
STILL HAS GUARDS AT OLE MISS

But in Meredith's view, the events of the past 12 months aren't that neatly packaged.

"This year didn't begin a year ago and it won't end next week," Meredith told an interviewer. "My people have been denied all their lives. To me, this year has been no different than any other—only to you and others."

Reflecting on his ordeal, the first Negro ever to be graduated from the University of Mississippi says, "It appears doubtful what has been accomplished."

He came to the University, he says, with two objectives. "One was to carry out the American ideal that all citizens are entitled to an equal chance for an education. There have been certain gains here, of course.

"The second, more important, objective was to replace the system based on the idea of white supremacy. I'm not at all confident we have made any real progress here.

"Ten minutes ago I walked out of my classroom. There was a federal marshal waiting in the hall. I walked outside—and there was another federal marshal.

"All this," he said, "is really an acknowledgment of white supremacy. Every citizen is entitled to equal protection of the laws—all laws. There are state, county, and campus policemen here, but none are protecting me. In order to receive my education I must get protection from some other source—federal marshals."

Asked if he felt he had at least made gains in that direction, Meredith said, "You can't make gains. There's no in-between; either a citizen has equal protection or he doesn't. If a man is innocent but unfairly sentenced to 100 years in jail, you can't say it would represent a gain if he had been unfairly sentenced to only 10 years."

The last day of classes at the University of Mississippi I wore the same clothes that I had worn the day I enrolled—dark suit, white shirt, red necktie, and black shoes. There was one notable difference. I put on (upside down) one of the NEVER, NEVER buttons that Barnett had made so popular on the campus and many students had worn during the first few weeks after I enrolled.

I am a Mississippian in all respects, even the bad ones.

# 13

*

## The Graduation and Exit: August 18, 1963

PERHAPS the most remarkable achievement of my three years in Mississippi fighting the system of "White Supremacy" is that I survived. Mississippi is well known for many things, but it is best known for its record of eliminating those who threaten the continued existence of "White Supremacy." The use of raw, demonstative violence has become a religion to the whites; its ceremonial and ritualistic aspects are a vital part of the Mississippi way of life. The very existence of the white society requires periodic doses of this violent religious lunacy; without sacrificial violence to bind it together, the white world would fall completely apart. Knowing this, my squadron commander, a white Mississippian of the aristocratic class, could assure me in 1955 with precise frankness that the Mississippi whites were prepared to kill all the Negroes and half the whites in order to preserve "White Supremacy." Mississippi and Mississippians have not changed.

### Three Years in Mississippi: An Assessment

My goal in Mississippi had been to break the system of "White Supremacy" at any cost; I have a "Divine Responsibility" to accomplish this mission. The crucial question had been how to work toward this end. At a very early age I had established the three *theoretical* interim goals to be achieved on the way to my final destiny. I stress "theoretical" because to me these goals were always merely a

323

focal point. I never considered the accomplishment of any one of them as being necessarily essential to the attainment of my ultimate purpose. At the same time, I never considered the accomplishment of one or all of them as in any way being tantamount to total success. The three goals were to become an "unadjectived" man; to run for governor of Mississippi and get all of the Negroes' votes; and to get a degree from the University of Mississippi. These were to be accomplished in reverse order.

After three years in Mississippi, what did the record show for the three theoretical aims? I had earned a degree from the University of Mississippi. It had been impossible to achieve this goal without seriously disrupting and undermining the system of "White Supremacy." Although the system had not been broken by my receiving a degree from the university, it had surely been disrupted.

On the point of running for governor and receiving all the Negroes' votes, the Negro has no effective vote in Mississippi. Therefore it would be folly to bid for their votes when they have none. There are over a half-million Negros of voting age in Mississippi, yet less than six per cent are allowed to vote. Before the second goal can be attempted, we will have to secure the right to vote for the Negro in Mississippi. Nevertheless, by accomplishing the first goal, I attained the unique position of holding the power to defeat any candidate who sought to become governor of the state. This was not a positive power to elect, rather, it was a negative power to defeat by manipulation of certain powers that I possessed.

The question of becoming a man is even further removed. There is no doubt that at the end of my three years in Mississippi more stress had been placed on my being a Negro man than ever before in my life. In spite of the fact that I as an individual had attained immortality for at least as long as the term "Negro" has meaning, it was very clear that the aim of reaching a stage where a Negro is judged simply by the standards of humanity without regard to race was indeed still a long way in the future.

## The Graduation

*The Caravan to Oxford.* Many of my friends and relatives had been looking forward to my graduation day. Mrs. Kenny Smith, the wife of Robert L.T. Smith, Jr., had vowed many times that she was going to "that graduation if it is the last thing in the world that I ever do." I didn't really think that she would go, because she seldom went anywhere except to work and to church, but she stuck by her pledge and came. There were so many Negroes going that we formed an unplanned caravan which, of course, included the U.S. marshals. (The force of marshals had been increased to three or four times its normal size.)

Following two cars of marshals, I led the caravan in my wife's well-publicized Thunderbird. My wife and son and also the Smiths were riding with me. We drove to Kosciusko where we stopped at my parents' home and ate the dinner which my mother had proudly prepared. The caravan was joined here by several cars of relatives and home-town friends. Some of them had come from thousands of miles away to attend my graduation.

In addition to the general excitement of the two-hundred-mile trip, the atmosphere was filled with the consciousness of possible trouble. From Kosciusko, we drove north on the Natchez Trace Parkway, a federal government project, where the facilities are not officially segregated. Just before we turned off the parkway onto a Mississippi highway, we stopped at a gas station to use the rest rooms because they were not segregated.

Shortly after we turned off the parkway, the Mississippi state troopers, who were covering the caravan in large numbers, began maneuvering in and out of the line of cars. The marshals tightened the caravan ranks and increased the speed. One of the troopers suddenly sped along past the caravan and tried to maneuver his car in between mine and the marshals'. By closing up behind him, a marshal, along with the one immediately ahead of me, managed to prevent the trooper from getting in front of me. He then raced off ahead of us and parked in an intersection. They didn't bother us any more after that.

*The March to the Grove.* The student captain of my group was the newly elected vice president of the student body. He had won the election on an anti-Meredith campaign. He was also a political science major and we had had classes together each term. I don't know if he ever spoke to me, although he was a very articulate individual. But he just didn't recognize my existence or that such things as Negroes could have human or equal rights. He had the responsibility of seeing that everyone was in his proper place in the line. He didn't call my name very many times, and when he did, he did it categorically.

Surprisingly, there was no opposition to being my marching mate. My marching partner in the first line-up was a young lady, and I heard some of the other graduates asking her how she was so lucky to get all of that "free publicity," assuming that she would be in the papers and on television with me. She appeared disappointed when a student came in late and the line-up had to be changed. No unpleasant remarks were made by the students, so that I could hear them.

On our march to the Grove we passed through the Lyceum Building where the U.S. government had set up its headquarters on September 30, 1962, the day I came to the campus. As I passed, I took special notice of the bullet holes that were still there, a consequence of the fighting between the state of Mississippi and the federal government of the United States. I had looked at these bullet holes many times.

We marched on past the statue of the Confederate soldier, the symbol of the blood that had been shed one hundred years ago in defense of the system of "White Supremacy." It was at the foot of this statue that General Walker had spoken to the crowd on the night of the revolt of the state of Mississippi.

We ended our march in the Grove, where the graduation exercises were being held in the open air. This was near the Circle where most of the riot had taken place on Setember 30. To one who knows the realities of life in Mississippi, the most striking thing about the Grove was the Negroes scattered throughout the audience. They were there in large numbers. Frankly, I was very surprised to see so many Negroes, but very pleased indeed.

*The Ceremony*. After taking my place among the graduates, I looked out at the curious and staring audience. Cameras were clicking in every direction. There in the audience was my seventy-two-year-old father with my three-year-old son. Throughout his life he had given his all in an effort to make Mississippi and the world free for his children and his children's children. He had lived to see the day that he had always longed for but had never really expected to see. Sitting on his knee was my son, not yet aware of the existence of the system of "White Supremacy" that would seek in every possible way to render him less than human. He seemed quite amused by the events. My gratification came from the hope that my son might be a future Governor or President.

The ceremony was routine. The speeches were rather mild, only one speaker referred to the controversial issues. He mentioned something about the encroachment upon Mississippi's prerogatives by the federal government. The Chancellor handed the diplomas to the graduates as their names were called and they passed across the stage.

When my name was called, the Chancellor handed me my diploma, shook my hand, and made some remark of congratulations. The marshals alerted themselves and the cameras recorded the event. On my walk, I noticed two familiar faces. One was my old Negro friend from Oxford, who had been so faithful in his support of me even when so much pressure was being applied to him. He kept his distance, standing about fifty yards away at the corner of a building. He had to live here after I was gone. The other was that of James Allen, Jr., the only black face among the many marshals, news reporters, and cameramen standing very near the stage. His boldness had placed him in a position to get the closest of all photographs taken of the Chancellor handing me my diploma.

After the ceremony, we marched briefly back to the campus to discard our caps and gowns. Just as I stepped outside the building two young boys rushed up to me; one of them grabbed my hand, gave it a very hard squeeze, and said, "I just wanted to congratulate you!" The two boys identified themselves as the grandsons of Mrs. ——, an English teacher at the University of Mississippi.

I walked that familiar path from the center of the campus to my rooms for the last time. I had passed word to many of the Negroes to come by Baxter Hall after the ceremony to see the place where I had spent my nights at the university. The marshals were there to end their mission in Mississippi. We had seen a lot of days together. They gathered up the last of their shotguns and tear gas and made ready to leave the campus, hopefully for the last time. The Negroes left and headed back to their homes, while I headed unwillingly in the opposite direction with the U.S. marshals.

## The Exit

I had agreed to leave Mississippi temporarily after my graduation from the university. Many people felt that it was for the best to allow a sort of resettling period. It was always against my will but, as a security measure, I was always either coming from or going to some point outside of Mississippi, while I was at the university.

On September 30, 1962, I had flown into the university airport with the U.S. marshals from Tennessee. That day two men were killed and several hundred were wounded in the fighting between the United States and Mississippi. The next day I was enrolled as a student. This was the first time in the history of the state that a

Negro had ever been enrolled in a school which Mississippi had reserved for its privileged whites.

On August 18, 1963, I drove out of Mississippi with the U.S. marshals to Tennessee, after receiving a degree from the University of Mississippi. A serious question kept plaguing my mind: Did this constitute the privilege of attending the school of my choice?

We drove at top speed down the four-lane highway that led to Memphis. But this still was not fast enough for my friend and great freedom fighter, Robert L.T. Smith, Jr., who rode with me. Everyone was silent. Finally, looking at the marshals' cars in front and in back of us, Robert asked, "J, was it like this all of the time?" Without waiting for a reply, he continued, "Man, I don't see how you stood it! I just don't see how you could take it!"

At last we arrived at my cousin Katherine's house in Memphis. She and her husband had attended the graduation exercises but had not stopped at Baxter Hall; they were waiting for us when we arrived. It was at her house that the marshals had begun their watch over me in September 1962. I suppose it was fitting that they should bid me their last good-bye at the same spot. The marshals must have been relieved. They had been as good an example of the American ideal as probably could be found. They were men dedicated to the idea of human equality and freedom for all.

My father and mother had come to Memphis with us to bid us farewell. After a while my father got me away from the crowd for a private talk. He wanted to express his satisfaction at having lived to see this day. As he evaluated the University of Mississippi ordeal and the graduation exercises, he told me his surprising conclusion about the Mississippi whites: "These people can be decent." He had watched the whites at the graduation ceremony. He knew these people, he had lived with them all his life. For seventy-two years he had seen the "meanness" and contempt in their look. Now he had witnessed a fading in this "meanness." That all-pervading hatred which accompanied every contact between the whites and blacks in Mississippi, at least for one day, had been missing from their faces. "These people can be decent."

My exit from Mississippi on August 18, 1963, marked the end of my three years in that state; it marked the end of this particular stage of my struggle to break the system of "White Supremacy" and to carry out my "Divine Responsibility."

It was the end of a long day!